ELECTORAL CORRUPTION IN BANGLADESH

To those
who are corruption-free,
and who intend to remain corruption-free

Electoral Corruption in Bangladesh

MUHAMMAD YEAHIA AKHTER
University of Chittagong
Chittagong, Bangladesh

LONDON AND NEW YORK

First published 2001 by Ashgate Publishing

Reissued 2018 by Routledge
2 Park Square, Milton Park, Abingdon, Oxon OX14 4RN
711 Third Avenue, New York, NY 10017, USA

Routledge is an imprint of the Taylor & Francis Group, an informa business

Copyright © Muhammad Yeahia Akhter 2001

All rights reserved. No part of this book may be reprinted or reproduced or utilised in any form or by any electronic, mechanical, or other means, now known or hereafter invented, including photocopying and recording, or in any information storage or retrieval system, without permission in writing from the publishers.

Notice:
Product or corporate names may be trademarks or registered trademarks, and are used only for identification and explanation without intent to infringe.

Publisher's Note
The publisher has gone to great lengths to ensure the quality of this reprint but points out that some imperfections in the original copies may be apparent.

Disclaimer
The publisher has made every effort to trace copyright holders and welcomes correspondence from those they have been unable to contact.

A Library of Congress record exists under LC control number: 00111544

ISBN 13: 978-1-138-70684-2 (hbk)
ISBN 13: 978-1-138-70685-9 (pbk)
ISBN 13: 978-1-315-20159-7 (ebk)

Contents

List of Tables vi
Acknowledgements viii
Abbreviations x

1   Elections and Electoral Corruption: An Introduction   1

2   Political Change and Developments in Bangladesh   43

3   Problems of Democratisation Before Independence (1947-1970)   94

4   Military Rule, Elections and Civilianisation   118

5   Electoral Politics and Corruption Under Civilian Rule   143

6   Caretaker Governments and the Myth of Free Elections   178

7   Conclusion   216

Appendices 231
Bibliography 261
Index 280

List of Tables

3.1	Elections and Types of Voting in Ayub Khan Era	98
3.2	The Results of Pakistan National Assembly Election, 1970-1971	108
3.3	The Results of Pakistan Provincial Assembly Elections, 1970-1971	109
3.4	The Degree of Corruption in Elections Under Military Rule in Pakistan	110
4.1	Party Nominations in 1979 Parliamentary Election	124
4.2	Results of 1979 Parliamentary Election	126
4.3	Results of the 1986 Parliamentary Election	131
4.4	March 1988 Parliamentary Election Results	135
4.5	The Degree of Corruption in Elections Under Military Rule in Bangladesh	136
5.1	Referendum Results	153
5.2	Candidates in City Corporation Elections, 1994	154
5.3	Partisan Affiliation of Mayors and Commissioners	158
5.4	The Degree of Corruption in Elections Under Civilian Rule in Bangladesh	169
6.1	Defects on the Electoral Roll (Dhaka Electoral Constituency 10, Ward No. 65, Baily Road)	180
6.2	Defects on the Electoral Roll (Madaripur Electoral Constituency 3, Ward No. 3, Ghatmajhi Union)	180
6.3	Number of Candidates by Political Parties/Independents	183
6.4	Programme Time Allocation of Total Telecast Hours (9 February - 1 March)	186
6.5	Time Distribution of TV Programmes on Election (9 February - 1 March)	187
6.6	Results of 1991 Parliamentary Elections	189
6.7	Time Allocated for the Coverage of Party Activities in the Main Bengali News (in percentage)	200
6.8	Allotted Space for Political Parties in the Four Major Newspapers (inches)	201
6.9	Placement of News Items and Photographs of Hasina and Khaleda in Four Major Newspapers (22 May-10 June, 1996)	202

6.10	The Turnout in Different National Elections in Bangladesh (1973-1996)	203
6.11	Results of Pre-Election Survey Conducted by Newspapers (Number of Seats)	204
6.12	The Degree of Corruption in Elections Under Caretaker Governments in Bangladesh	208

Acknowledgements

This book has originated from my Ph.D. dissertation *Elections and Electoral Corruption in Bangladesh: Civilian, Military and Non-partisan Regimes in Perspective* submitted to the University of Sydney, Australia, in 1999. I am indebted to Dr. G. R. Curnow (University of Sydney) and Dr. Habib Zafarullah (University of New England) for their sincere supervisory assistance. Australian government granted me scholarship and the University of Chittagong sanctioned study leave to enable me to pursue this research. I am grateful to them. Professor Lawrence Ziring (Western Michigan University), Professor Muhammad A. Hakim (University of Chittagong) and Dr. Dennis Wright (University of New England) have read this study and made useful suggestions, which have been incorporated in this work. I am thankful to them. Dr. Ahmed Shafiqul Huque of City University of Hong Kong has encouraged me to publish this study. I would like to record my regards to him.

Professor Nizam Ahmed and Professor Mahfuzul H. Chaudhury of University of Chittagong were further sources of encouragement. During my field research, Sheikh Kamrul Alam made available valuable material for the study and my former students S. M. Morshed and Sanaullah Noori provided election reports and other important documents. My cousin Sheikh Farhad Nur mailed weekly magazines that helped me analyse contemporary Bangladeshi electoral politics. District administration and election office at Magura deserve special mention for their cooperation during my data collection trip. The Commonwealth Secretariat (London), the National Democratic Institute (Washington) and the Fair Election Monitoring Alliance (Dhaka) deserve thanks for sending me their reports on several elections, as does Dr. Aminul Haque of the Coordinating Council for Human Rights in Bangladesh (CCHRB) for providing its reports on a number of elections. I would also like to record my appreciation to the staff at various libraries, namely Fisher Library, University of Sydney; Dana Poter Arts Library, University of Waterloo; Khulna Public Library; Chittagong University Library and Seminar Library of the Department of Political Science, Chittagong University. The assistance of my colleagues at the University of Chittagong is acknowledged while my brother, sisters and other relatives also helped me in various ways. I am grateful to Ashgate Publishing Limited for agreeing to publish this work.

Finally, my special thanks go to my wife Nurjahan Begum and to my two daughters Deeni Fatiha and Karishma Fatiha who patiently tolerated my continuous absence from home during drafting of the study.

Muhammad Yeahia Akhter
Department of Political Science
University of Chittagong
Bangladesh

Abbreviations

AL	Bangladesh *Awami* League
AL-MC	Bangladesh *Awami* League-Mizan Chaudhury
AL-MU	Bangladesh *Awami* League-Malek Ukil
APSU	All Party Students Unity
BD	Basic Democracy
BKSAL	Bangladesh *Krishak Sramik Awami* League
BML	Bangladesh Muslim League
BNP	Bangladesh Nationalist Party
BTV	Bangladesh Television
BUP	Bangladesh *Unnayan Parisad*
CC	City Corporation
CCHRB	Coordinating Council for Human Rights in Bangladesh
CEC	Chief Election Commissioner
CHT	Chittagong Hill Tracts
CML	Conventionalist Muslim League
CMLA	Chief Martial Law Administrator
COAS	Chief of Army Staff
COP	Combined Opposition Party
CPB	Communist Party of Bangladesh
DC	Deputy Commissioner
DDC	District Development Coordinator
DUCSU	Dhaka University Central Students Union
EC	Election Commission
FBCCI	Federation of Bangladesh Chambers of Commerce and Industry
ICAC	Independent Commission Against Corruption
IDL (R)	Islamic Democratic League-Rahim
INC	Indian National Congress
JAGODAL	*Jatiyatabadi Ganotantrik Dal*
JCD	*Jatiya Chattra Dal*
JI	*Jamaat-e-Islami* Bangladesh
JP	*Jatiya* Party
JRB	*Jatiya Rakkhi Bahini*
JSD	*Jatiya Samajtantrik Dal*

JUI	*Jamiat-e-Ulema-e-Islam*
LDF	Left Democratic Front
LFO	Legal Framework Order
MEC	Members of Electoral College
ML	Muslim League
MP	Member of Parliament
NA	National Assembly
NAP (B)	National *Awami* Party (Bhashani)
NAP (M)	National *Awami* Party (Muzaffar)
NCG	Non-party Caretaker Government
NDF	National Democratic Front
NDP	National Democratic Party
NGO	Non-government Organisation
NPT	National Press Trust
NWFP	North West Frontier Province
OC	Officer in Charge (of a police station)
PA	Provincial Assembly
PCJSS	*Parbattya Chattagram Jana Sanghati Samity*
PM	Prime Minister
PML	Pakistan Muslim League
PO	Presiding Officer
PPP	Pakistan People's Party
SAARC	South Asian Association for Regional Co-operation
SAC	Students' Action Committee
SDO	Sub-Divisional Officer
SKOP	*Sramik Karmachari Oikkya Parisad*
SP	Superintendent of Police
SPA	Special Powers Act
TDC	*Thana* Development Committee
TNO	*Thana Nirbahi* Officer
UF	United Front

1 Elections and Electoral Corruption: An Introduction

Introduction

Democracy – to a lesser or greater extent – is the most widely applied system for running a state in the contemporary world. To some it is a form of government, to others, a way of social life.[1] It entitles citizens to participate freely in the political decision making processes that affect their individual and collective lives. It makes government responsible to the will of the majority without being oblivious to the interests of the minority. It is representative in character and stresses equality of all citizens before law.[2] Political participation is the bedrock of democracy.

The application of democracy across nations, however, is not uniform. Rulers, either democratically elected or in possession of power through extra-democratic means, interpret the notion in their idiosyncratic ways. The political culture of a country determines the way democracy is practised. The degree of democratic freedom, the nature of political institutions and processes, and public's perception vary due to the differences in socio-cultural norms and customs, value systems, people's political awareness, and the stage of a country's economic progress. In developing countries, democracy does not operate according to the postulates of Western political thought. The process of democratisation there faces unforeseen stumbling blocks, dilemmas and paradoxes caused by poverty, low levels of literacy and education, social and political violence, absence of political awareness, lack of tolerance, mutual respect and trust, malfunctioning of legislative and party systems, unsound governance, and electoral malfeasance. Several Third World countries have experienced long periods of military rule that retarded the growth of effective political institutions, militarised the administration and corrupted the political system.

The countries where military intervention has occurred have, with notable exceptions, low levels of economic productivity and high degrees of social cleavage. Bienen has described it in terms of 'political gaps between rulers and ruled, economic gaps between classes, and social and cultural gaps between linguistics, racial, or ethnic groups...'.[3] The causes and nature of military takeovers vary from country to country and situation to situation, although some common causes may be identified. Chronic political instability or failure of democratic politics, economic difficulties, and social fragmentation lead to legitimacy loss for civilian regimes. The military may also intervene when its professional or corporate interests are threatened.[4] Corporate interests include adequate budgetary support, institutional autonomy and exclusiveness, protection against encroachments from rival institutions and the survival and viability of the military as a social institution.[5] Widespread political and administrative corruption or other sorts of national crises like external threats to sovereignty may also goad the military to capture political power. To do so it does not need the unanimity of the armed forces, rather a company or a battalion may be sufficient.[6]

The number of military takeovers in the Third World has gradually and consistently increased over the decades. Twelve percent of all independent states of the world were under military rule in 1961. The percentage rose to 19 in 1966, to 27 in 1973, and to 29 by 1974. By 1974, 56 percent of Third World states had experienced military rule at least once.[7] In the last two decades, however, a number of such states reverted to elected civilian government.

The military juntas adopt several strategies after seizure of power to consolidate their position and civilianise their rule.[8] These strategies vary in different countries although they reveal several common characteristics. Initially, the military elites eschew a long-term interest in politics; rather they claim that their takeover of a political authority is a temporary measure apparently to save the nation from a crisis or rid the society of social and economic problems like corruption, degeneration of law and order and widespread economic woes. They seek the co-operation of the people to solve such problems and urge them to participate in development programmes they initiate. Coup leaders declare their intentions to arrange free and fair elections and to hand over power to the elected authority. They promise to return to the barracks once their mission is accomplished but very rarely do so. They procrastinate over arranging general elections and seek other alternative means to obtain legitimacy for their rule. They use the state machinery for realising their political goals that include the launching of a political platform or a party and attempt to woo prominent political personalities and leaders from other parties. They undertake some policies in the economic, administrative and local spheres and try to publicise the changes they are purported to bring about. They exercise excessive censorship of the state-run media, especially radio and television and launch mass mobilisation schemes to publicise their policies with the objective of broadening their support base at all levels of society. In their bid to entrench their position, they invoke the support of the civil bureaucracy and the higher military echelons by furthering their interests. They weaken the political opposition by fragmenting political parties and very carefully use religion to appeal to the devout.

East and Southeast Asia, South Korea, Myanmar, Thailand and Indonesia represent military rule and the process of its civilianisation. Thailand and Myanmar afford an 'additional and unusual opportunity' for examining the effects of military training on political ethics, behaviour and values, as its military and civilian bureaucracies come from the same socio-economic groups. The situation is similar in the two South Asian states -- Pakistan and Bangladesh -- where the military rulers have civilianised their rule through stage-managed elections and influenced the democratic political culture by splitting opposition political parties and militarising political and administrative organisations. The armed forces usually play the key role in central decision making and exert considerable political influence. They claim to be the custodians of state sovereignty and the primary defenders of any external or internal attack against the government. Yet, military regimes in their bid to obtain legitimacy for their rule have to rely on the electoral exercise in whatever form, whether corrupt or otherwise. While it is simply a legitimising and consolidating tool for a military regime, free and fair elections can contribute towards transforming an illiberal civilian regime to one that might approximate features of a liberal democracy.

Democracy and Elections

Elections are one of the basic pillars of democracy and central to the process of democratic political participation. Nowadays they have emerged as a 'ritual of choice' all over the democratic world. Elections serve as the basic mechanism for both selecting and replacing ruling elites and for providing a regular and systematic succession in government. Elections help to determine how a country is governed and at the same time select who will exercise that power. They are the principal mechanism by which citizens hold governments accountable, both retrospectively for their policies and more generally for the manner in which they govern.[9] Elections reinforce party activities and intensify political awareness of the people. They educate voters, provide the foundations for representation and grant legitimacy to government.[10] A political system can display its degree of democracy through its electoral operations. The role of elections in democratic procedure varies across nations and depends upon a number of preconditions such as level of literacy, freedom of expression, and tolerance and mutual respect in politics.

Democratic systems of government are historically relatively recent, although Greek society with its electoral system based on consensus was an exception. Where democracy was unknown, rulers either enthroned themselves by hereditary succession and in some cases by force, conquest, and the like, or were selected by elites and influential members of the society. However, the democratic process of selecting rulers based on the verdict of the majority gradually emerged in many parts of the world. The importance of elections is nowadays recognised by almost every nation state; even one-party and totalitarian regimes often resort to some form of electioneering to secure legitimacy for their rule.

Political parties and elections are symbiotically related. Elections are meaningless without the participation of parties; on the other hand, parties become torpid without periodic elections. Present parties with the opportunity of placing their policies before the electorate through elections facilitate a closer relationship between them and citizens. During elections parties strive to be perceived as 'genuinely' committing themselves to the service of the people and party leaders energise themselves in focusing the campaigns on public issues and problems. Elections help originate intense competition between parties which work hard to win the support of voters. They are one of the major mechanism that help parties to measure their strength and support and to establish links with society.[11]

Elections contribute to political development by providing legitimacy and political stability to a regime. They are a powerful agent of political socialisation. Political culture, which deeply influences political development, both shapes and is shaped by the way parties and the electorate perceive and approach elections. Elections can help minimise crises and problems of development. Wider political participation, the foundation of political development, becomes conspicuous during elections. All categories of adult citizens, including men and women, the rich and the poor, the enlightened and the illiterate, the employed and the jobless, and the law-abiding and the delinquent, get the opportunity to have their say in the formation of a government through elections.

Elections in the Western liberal democracies acquired a sophisticated form in the contemporary world after passing through a long evolutionary period of reform and experimentation. Elections in early times were organised in a restricted domain. Suffrage was limited to the tax-payer, the property-holder, or one who practised a particular religious faith. Women were denied the right to exercise their franchise. Voting in many countries was indirect, the whole body of qualified voters elected an intermediate body of electors who in turn elected officials or representatives. Later, this was replaced by direct elections and the secret ballot system, and by the mid 20th century most western democracies had in place universal adult suffrage. The electoral rights of women were recognised and the voting age was lowered to increase the size of the electorate. Over time, these western democracies established elections as a strong political institution that served to make their polities reasonably representative.[12]

Third World Electoral Culture and Practice

Many Third World countries adopted or adapted Western electoral systems as constitutional requirements for changing governments or for securing a fresh mandate for ruling regimes. However, the character of elections and the electoral culture in these countries vary from those in the West. There are various reasons for this. Chronic poverty and illiteracy of the majority of voters make them dependent on their patrons who influence their choice.[13] Patronage and patron-client relationships become more effective and evident during an election.[14] In South Asian countries, it is not only active in rural areas but also similarly operative in modern organisations like political parties and bureaucracies.[15] The strength of this relationship ensures that client voters may have to vote for a candidate not of their liking. They vote for the candidate chosen by their patron mainly because they live under their political and economic shelter. Political instability and lack of mutual respect and fair competition among political parties lead to violence in elections. Bureaucratic partisanship and the ruling party's influence on the election machinery impair the integrity of the electoral system. The state-controlled media may be a hindrance to electoral transparency and can aid the ruling party in furthering its political purposes.

Although elections are considered as one of the core institutions in what we think of as democratic politics, their misuse in the Third World, in particular, is not uncommon. Elections produce different outcomes in different systems of government. Leaders of all kinds, from a military dictator to a civilian autocrat, recognise the power and importance of elections in obtaining legitimacy to govern. Elections that are held under conditions of restricted freedom, limited participation, or severely constrained choice invariably raise basic questions of democratic legitimacy. Military or some civilian leaders willing to run the country through undemocratic means, especially in the Third World, use elections as a tool for their continuation in power. These leaders make major efforts to manipulate elections.[16] The use of elections as a tool for political legitimation and consolidation by military juntas can have profound implications for political development. Even military rulers, if they desire, can facilitate democratisation by either civilianising their own regimes or creating a favourable political environment for gradual military withdrawal and smoothly transferring power to civilian politicians through elections. Military rulers can civilianise their regimes by either associating themselves with existing political parties or floating their own. Both can happen before or after the military's withdrawal from politics or simultaneously.

However, in spite of all shortcomings and inconsistencies of an electoral system, elections can decide important matters in any polity. Only elections establish that legitimate political power flows from below.[17] If one argues that elections are 'essential for democracy', it indicates the significance of free and fair elections devoid of irregularities and malpractices. Electoral malfeasance not only negates the voting right of the people but also hamper the effort to institutionalise democracy.

Free and fair elections are indeed rare in many Third World countries. The conditions of such elections are: the right to vote by the entire adult population; regularity of elections within constitutionally stipulated timeframes; free opportunity to form parties and to nominate candidates; open contestation for legislative seats; campaigns free from intimidation and violence; secret balloting without influence; and honest counting and reporting of election results.[18] In free elections, each voter has the equal chance to make a choice of their preferred representative(s) and express his/her opinion and sentiments. If this freedom is restricted, the credibility of elections is undermined. It is essential to have an independent judiciary, honest competent and non-partisan administration, democratic competition and mutual respect among the parties and politically educated voters to ensure free and fair elections. Freedom of the media, and literacy and economic solvency of the voters are some other prerequisites for free and fair elections. Elections under military juntas, civilian autocrats or one party dictators are unlikely to be free or fair although claims to the contrary may be made by their organisers. Intimidation, physical coercion, bribery, extortion, and social and political patronage are some of the ways to influence the outcome of elections in many Third World countries.[19]

Corruption is one of the main impediments in institutionalising free and fair elections in any form of polity. The practice of democracy in both developed and developing countries falters because of the absence of integrity in the electoral process. Governments, of all varieties, claiming to be democratic have exhibited a tendency to manipulate elections in various ways to cling to power. Electoral malpractices can take on such a dimension that they can become the main source of friction between the ruling and opposition parties. Electoral corruption is therefore a crucial issue, especially in developing countries and merits special attention for a comprehensive understanding of elections and electoral culture as components of the broader issues of political culture and political development.

The Many Faces of Corruption

Corruption has existed since the beginning of society; indeed it is now a global phenomenon, chronic in some countries, acute in others, while in a small number it appears to be in remission – even if temporarily. It not only exists in poverty-stricken and technologically backward countries, but also in advanced democracies. The degree, style, and consequences of corruption, of course, vary from country to country. So what is corruption, and what does it entail?

Defining Corruption: the Perennial Debate

Defining corruption is a hazardous undertaking. A number of investigators have attempted to define corruption in their studies, but only a few of them have dealt with the definitional issue as a separate research topic. Existing definitions are diverse and reflect the nature and scope of a scholar's study and his/her disciplinary background and personal standpoints.[20] Definitions presented by economists differ from those of political scientists. For instance, Ackerman, an economist, has emphasised the market mechanism and its impact on the voting process and the decision-making system in large organisations in her definition of corruption.[21] On the other hand, '...deviation from formal duty', 'favouritism' (Nye), '...illegitimate use of public power for private benefit' (Nas *et al.*), 'violation of responsibility' (Rogow and Lasswell), 'perversion of power' (Brasz), '...illegal or unethical use of governmental authority as a result of considerations of personal or political gain' (Benson), '...the exchange of money or other material goods for preferential treatment by public officials' (Gardiner and Lyman), '...improper or selfish exercise of power and influence attached to a public office' (Monterio) and '...illegal use of organisational power for personal gain' (Sherman), are some of the dimensions covered in the definitions constructed by political scientists.[22]

Another reason why researchers have not agreed upon a universal definition is because of the complex and multi-dimensional nature of corruption. The style, mechanism and undercurrents of corruption vary from society to society and organisation to organisation. Moreover, attitudes and values of the public rooted in culture influence the nature and degree of corruption. What has been termed 'corruption' in one study, is often presented as 'just politics' or 'indiscretion' in others.[23] Even definitions in wide use, such as those of by Rogow and Lasswell and Nye, are not above criticism.[24]

Despite the difficulty of providing a definition that will cover every corrupt activity of different societies and regions of the globe, there are some characteristics common to most of the widely used definitions of corruption. Abuse of power is one such characteristic; it has been described as 'deviation from the normal duties of a public role' by Nye and 'violation of responsibility' by Rogow and Lasswell. Abuse of power is a vague term and it is difficult to determine its boundary. Who is the authority to identify the abuse? If it is based on law, different explanations of abuse will be found in different societies. There is no such law that is unanimously accepted across nations. If it is based on public opinion, the same problem will remain and different publics will reason in their own way. A related point is that the formation of a particular country's public opinion is influenced by its culture. Explanation of abuse by South Asian and South East Asian publics may not be the same. In a similar vein, a clear distinction between the public opinion of North America and of the Middle East can be assumed. Even those living in the same country but belonging to different communities, social or economic classes, may analyse 'abuse' in different fashions. As Peters and Welsh state: '...studies of public opinion have differences, which may exist between the public and political elites in their assessment of appropriate standards of public conduct'.[25]

Avoiding the traditional approach to the definition of corruption, Lowi and Heidenheimer have used 'size' and 'colour' respectively to categorise different types of corruption. Lowi has divided corruption into big 'C' and little 'c'. Big 'C' or big corruption, in his analysis, is more pernicious than the little 'c' and it puts the whole society or state itself at risk.[26] Little 'c', on the other hand, does not hamper the whole society. Similarly, Heidenheimer categorises corruption by colouring it white, grey, and black. The degree of corruption identified by a particular colour is determined 'by the interaction between the judgement of a particular act by the public and political elites or public officials...'.[27]

Another group of scholars including Heidenheimer, Scott and Huntington belong to a school of thought that analyses corruption in a different way. This school, which considers the emergence of corruption as a common characteristic of developing countries, presents the modernisation thesis of corruption.[28] According to this thesis, corruption occurs and spreads widely in the transitional phase of a country's modernisation; thus in advanced and developed countries there should be less corruption. This proposition should be qualified because of the wide presence of corruption in the developed countries as well. The evidence from media reports, judicial procedures, official investigations, interviews, etc. depicts widespread corruption there. Among others, Pinto-Duschinsky bitterly criticises the modernisation thesis by giving evidence of 'rampant' corruption in ten American states and 'important recent outbreaks of corruption' in nine others.[29] Other developed countries like Britain, France, Canada, and Australia are also not immune from corruption. Experiments with the preventive mechanisms of corruption and establishing institutions for controlling it point to the non-ignorable rate of corruption in these countries. Two other causes of exposure of corruption in these countries might be that corruption has received more publicity in recent times through the media's use of freedom of information legislation, and the consequent concern of governments to eradicate or at least minimise the problem.

In the 1950s and 1960s, when a reasonable number of studies appeared on corruption, much space was devoted to the definitional dilemma and some authors wrote on this sole issue.[30] This trend did not continue for long especially after Watergate when corruption became a popular topic of research, and social scientists, in general, adopted the view that 'everybody knows what corruption is – which enables them to go beyond the question of definition'.[31] In 1978 for example, five well-known academics, among others, published books on corruption, which devoted meagre space to the definition of corruption,[32] although recently some academics again are warming to this issue. In the 1990s for example, a few writers discussed the definitional problem of political corruption, perhaps suggesting that there is still need to define what it is we are researching.[33]

A careful survey of most of the definitions of corruption highlights the politics-and administration-centred nature of corruption that may limit its boundaries. The extent of corruption, however, is much wider and it should not be restricted to politics and administration. The nature of corruption in society as a whole should be recognised in the definitions of corruption, as it can widely influence the degree of politico-administrative corruption. The definitional limitation may be supported when the focus of research is within the public sector, but in this study corruption will be considered widely instead of limiting it to politics and bureaucracy and defined as a group or individual's behavior, which deviates from legally and socially accepted role expectations for personal gain.

Political/Administrative Corruption

Le Vine defines political corruption as the 'unsanctioned, unscheduled use of public political resources and/or goods for private, that is non public ends'.[34] This definition according to Le Vine 'rests on three assumptions: that there is a distinction between political and non-political corruption; that there is a distinction between political corruption and 'corruption of process'; and that corruption is a social process...'.[35] Benson has defined political corruption in the footsteps of Bayley[36] as 'a general term covering all illegal and unethical use of governmental authority as a result of considerations of personal or political gain...'.[37] This definition does not limit political corruption only to bribery or monetary transactions, rather it extends the boundary of political corruption to all unethical actions on the part of politicians and public officials.

The nature of political corruption is such that it does not generally allow an individual to practise it alone. Corrupt officials or politicians often form a network and share the benefits. These networks of political corruption may not include individuals solely from a particular area of administration or society, but involve opportunists from different segments of society and, in that sense, the content of political corruption is wider than the government. Politically corrupt individuals thus may have a foothold on different social strata.

Political corruption is not a recent phenomenon. Political corruption in ancient Greek society was related mainly to its rulers. The Greek political philosopher Plato provided unusual advice to the rulers in his *Republic* to lead their lives without having family or private property.[38] His intention was to keep the rulers honest and corruption-free. The discussion on bribery in his *Laws* may also be mentioned here, where he emphasised the exercise of responsibility by the national officials without accepting gifts from the public.[39] It is also of interest to survey briefly selected aspects of political and administrative history in a number of countries to indicate the ubiquity of corruption, albeit in varying degrees.

The distinguished political scientist, James Bryce called corruption a disgraceful characteristic of Europe and America.[40] Indeed, in most western European countries, behind every political scandal there is the presence of organised corruption.[41] Indeed, it is a 'central and urgent' problem in contemporary American society.[42] Political corruption in America has a long history, although social scientists of America began to work vigorously on political corruption only after Watergate. The title of a book by Victor Laski, *It Did Not Start With Watergate* supports this fact.[43] The Yazoo land fraud of 1795,[44] involved politicians, former cabinet members, editors, and even the vice president of the country accepting bribes from a bank in 1833,[45] and the corruption of Railroad Legislation by a group of Iowa politicians in 1860[46] are only two outstanding examples of 18th and 19th century political corruption in America. Quoting from Odegard, Monterio has described American society as conducive to corruption.

> There is a general cultural milieu which has made corruption and racketeering an integral part of American society. Corruption is in a sense a product of the way of life of an acquisitive society where 'money talks', where that which 'works' is justified, and where people are judged by what they have rather than what they are...But even more important is the fact that they have created a society in which pecuniary values are dominant. In such a society prestige is measured in terms of wealth. Successful grafters and corruptors become respected, and a million dollars cover a multitude of sins.[47]

Scott points to high-level political corruption in early Stuart England.[48] The 17th century was a period of widespread corruption and the sale of offices was then common throughout the whole of Europe. Office selling in France was even more prevalent than England where a separate agency handled the transaction.[49] The office of the state was considered as the personal property of the crown. The crown also occasionally sold titles, the symbols of status that were considered power at that time.[50] A similar situation prevailed in other European countries in early times.

The Australian situation is not totally different. The establishment of a Hong Kong style Independent Commission Against Corruption (ICAC) in New South Wales highlights the concern about corruption in Australia. High-level corruption in Japan, economically the most developed country in Asia, is intertwined with the nation's political history. The country's Public Prosecutor's Offices indicted 99 public officials on charges of receiving bribes in 1993. Nine of the 15 prime ministers in Japan who held office between 1955 and 1993 were involved in corruption scandals.[51] Half of the Japanese members of parliament obtained their seats through illegal financing.[52] According to a Meiji University professor, the political will to control corruption has not been strong in Japan, although people have recently begun to show anger at the corrupt political-administrative elites.[53] The system of *dango* (bid-rigging) and *shito fumekin* (unexplained expending) in Japan reveal the extent of bribery in politics and administration of Japan.[54]

Corruption was rampant in the former communist countries.[55] In the USSR, it was 'integral to Soviet life as vodka and kasha...',[56] although

Soviet scholars in the 1960s and 1970s commonly believed that corruption was much more prevalent in capitalist societies. Published literature portrayed a different picture of widespread corruption in the former USSR. According to Staats,

> the national, regional and local press of the USSR contains myriad accounts of bribery, falsification of reports, party-state complicity in concealing corruption, misuse of public office and state funds, and patronage and nepotism in personal appointments.[57]

The tradition of political corruption in developing countries has long flourished and has been widely acknowledged in the literature. Each Asian country has its own tradition. In ancient China, a special type of allowance, 'yang-lien' was given to public officials to keep them corruption-free. Such an allowance, of course, did not eradicate corruption in ancient Chinese administration. The publication of 619 corruption-related reports by the *People's Daily* of China in 18 months reveals the high rate of corruption in Chinese society.[58] In East Asian countries government services have become more expensive as citizens are forced to pay bribes for everything from business licences to surgical operations. The importance of widely practised *guanxi* (connections) in East Asian business dealings highlights rampant corruption.[59] An executive of a foreign construction company in Taiwan says: '...What bothers us is that almost nothing can be done legally'.[60] In Taiwan, 2,100 government officials and business executives were charged with vote-buying, fraud, bid-rigging or related offences from 1993 to 1995. The *hung bao* culture (giving money in red envelopes) is very common in Taiwan. Thai politics and administration are also corrupt. In a survey, conducted in 1976, 'teamwork corruption' was identified in the Thai bureaucracy.[61] In the colonial politics and administration of Indonesia and the Philippines corruption was common; nor did independence lessen its ubiquity. Public officials in the post-independence period were given more opportunity to be corrupt when the bureaucracies were expanded and strengthened to meet the development needs of these states. Corruption expanded in all spheres of Indonesian society during the rule of President Sukarno, when it was judged as one of the major problems of Indonesian society by 50 percent of the respondents of a survey conducted by *Tempo*, an Indonesian weekly.[62] It was likewise a major problem in the Philippines in the 1950s when President Gratia compared corruption with incurable cancer, but his successors Mecapegal and Marcos utterly failed to deal with the problem.

The speeches of opposition members in the Malaysian parliament are often critical of corruption. The statement of Tan Chee Khoon, a former opposition leader is relevant here:

> there is corruption in high places, especially amongst politicians. A number of Alliance politicians at all levels of representative government have amassed lands, houses, bank balances, businesses, etc., during their term of office ... almost everyday I receive letters alleging corruption.[63]

Similarly, Muslim rulers of Middle Eastern states have also been known to practise political corruption. An eminent Muslim political philosopher, Abdur Rahman Ibne Khaldun, pointed to the luxurious life of the rulers as the main cause of political corruption.[64] In the present day, oil-rich Middle East is engulfed by corruption.[65]

Corruption, both in Latin American and African countries, has been growing at alarming proportions.[66] Nigeria has been ranked as the most corrupt country by Transparency International, a Berlin-based independent anti-corruption organisation. The situation in Kenya, Zimbabwe, and Ghana is similar where massive corruption is present at every level of society and administration.[67] The statement of one former official of Ghana may be quoted here. He said, '...we Ghanaians are so accustomed to bribing our officials, and they to stealing our rate-moneys, that it would be considered odd if we didn't bribe and they didn't steal'.[68]

The South Asian nations are considered a haven for political and administrative corruption and the phenomenon is as old as organised society in this region. In the third century B. C., the Indian sage Kautylla was able to identify forty different kinds of embezzlement of funds and urged his ruler to run all his ministers through an obstacle course of temptation.[69] Chandra Gupta, the Brahmin (upper cast) king of India, also detected forty ways of misusing public funds by officials about 2300 years ago.[70] In the Mughal period public officials resorted to illegal practices to boost their private purses.[71] The common people could not even see the emperor or his representative/high officials without giving gifts according to their ability. The administration of the British East India Company sheltered corruption. Its main target was to make financial profit. Its corrupt actions have been portrayed in contemporary history and literature.[72] The company's officials used their ruling influence in extorting gifts from native princes and others to amass fortunes.[73] Later, the standard of their service was developed through adopting strictness in recruitment and training. A drama (*Nil Darpan*) by Dinbandhu Mitra, for example, depicts how cruelly the officials of East India Company tyrannised the farmers of Bengal to cultivate the indigo plant that they would buy at a low price and then export to Europe at exorbitant prices. They also created artificial food crises for commercial benefit that caused death of millions.[74]

The disease, however, did not disappear after the British had left the subcontinent. In more recent times, front-page corruption stories indicted one-third of India's cabinet for corruption which resulted in the electoral decimation of the ruling Congress Party.[75] According to one study, approximately 50 percent of legally reportable income goes untaxed,[76] whereas another report estimates 68 percent of those who file their taxes through Certified Public Accountants admit to having paid bribes.[77]

Corruption has been identified as the main issue in Pakistani politics. The statement by a caretaker prime minister depicts the ubiquity of corruption in Pakistani society. He said, '…the entire nation is corrupt and even if somebody is clean, he helps in the corruption'.[78] A member of Bangladesh parliament cites the case of the education ministry which charges ten percent for having funds allocated to educational institutions.[79] It is a hard job to locate a file in some of the government offices (especially in general administration, police, customs, taxation etc.) in India, Pakistan or Bangladesh without bribing the appropriate clerks/officers. A study of Bangladesh public administration notes the prevalence of corruption in both political and bureaucratic structures.[80] Two recent surveys discovered raging corruption in the police, education, revenue-earning departments and even the judiciary.[81]

A world-wide increase in the recognition of the problem of corruption since the 1970s has caused concern among both social scientists and ruling elites in different countries, some of whom have attempted to control this problem. This concern has been reflected in the writings and publications on corruption, the establishment of institutions for controlling corruption, and the adoption of preventive measures.

Electoral Corruption

Electoral corruption, is one major branch of political corruption. It readily thrives in a society where the degree of political and administrative morality is low. It is one of the main impediments to institutionalising free and fair elections in any form of polity. The necessity of a transparent electoral system is one of the most important prerequisites for present-day democratic practice in both developed and developing countries. Electoral corruption in the Asian states negatively influences the consolidation of democracy. Governments, either military or civilian, claiming to be democratic manipulate elections to cling to power. Electoral malpractices are the main source of misunderstanding between the ruling and opposition parties in many Third World states and have often led to political crises.

Electoral corruption, however, is not a Third World phenomenon alone. It poses problems for democracy in many developed nations. Elections in America, Europe and Australia, although relatively fairer than in Asia and Africa, also reveal a history of corruption. Bribery, gifts and fraudulent practices have been normal features during elections. Intimidation and selling of votes were common in elections of western states before the introduction of the secret ballot system. Elections in 18th century England or 19th century America or in colonial states showed 'gross inaccuracies, irregularities and slipshod practices...'. Australian elections even in the 20th century are not free of irregularities. Dummy voting both in state and federal elections in East Sydney and multiple voting and impersonation in by-elections in Queensland highlight Australian electoral corruption.[82] Gradually, in Western countries, the electoral system gained fairness through the introduction of methodical voter registration, detailed regulations relating to electioneering, and the application of strict procedures during polling. The process has also been strengthened by introducing a voter identity card system and through increased public awareness and voter education in many countries.

The study of electoral corruption is especially significant as political leaders in a democratic setting come to power through elections. If the rulers themselves come to power through unfair means, it is unlikely they will control corruption in politics and society. A corrupted electoral system thus contributes to the rate of corruption in other areas of society. If rulers come to power through fair elections they may be more willing to take a strong stand against corruption in their countries.

Defining Electoral Corruption

Defining electoral corruption is as problematic as defining corruption in general. Writers on the subject, in most cases, have carefully avoided the issue. The existing literature on electoral corruption encourages a new researcher to do likewise. Seton-Watson elaborately discussed all major issues of early electoral corruption of Hungary,[83] but fell short of defining it. Richley has edited a valuable book on American elections,[84] which, among other things, deals with corruption in American elections. However, neither the contributors nor even the editor himself define electoral corruption. Sabato probably thought that everybody knew what campaign corruption was and avoided defining it although Goldberg defined 'electoral fraud' in detail.[85]

Heidenheimer in his valuable collection, *Political Corruption: Readings in Comparative Analysis*, does not define electoral corruption but describes the problems of attempting to do so. His analysis shows that electoral corruption is easy to ignore but more difficult to study than other persistent patterns of political corruption, '...because corrupt elections can, by definition, occur only as isolated instances every two, four or five years'.[86] It is a complicated area of study because electoral campaign techniques and other pre-election occurrences 'have usually drawn much less scholarly attention than have voting results'[87] and post-election events.

Two years after the publication of Heidenheimer's book, Scott's *Comparative Political Corruption* appeared with one chapter on electoral corruption. Though the author discussed the definitional problem and offered a general working definition of corruption, he carefully avoided defining electoral corruption specifically. In 1978, another useful work titled, *Political Corruption in America*, added to the corruption literature.[88] The authors included one chapter on corruption in American elections where the major issues discussed were administration of elections, conduct of campaigns, and election finance. But they refrained from defining electoral corruption or even presenting a working definition of American electoral corruption. *The Elimination of Corrupt Practices in British Elections 1868-1911* by Cornelius O'Leary, focused on major issues of electoral corruption, like bribery, treating, undue influence, violence, physical intimidation etc., but did not define it in general terms.

Researchers covering elections in Asian countries have also neglected the area of electoral corruption despite its strong links with the institutionalisation of democracy. A number of articles on political corruption, while including corruption in elections, have not defined the topic. Authors commenting on South Asian elections also have failed to define electoral corruption despite highlighting its importance.[89] Contributors on other regions of Asia have similar shortcomings. They mention fraud, forgery and irregularities but do not define electoral corruption.[90]

Thus it is apparent that the existing literature on elections does not present a coherent definition of electoral corruption. Perhaps scholars have been hesitant to define it, being put off by frequent changes of prevailing electoral laws, different styles of electoral malpractices in different party and legislative settings, and differences in the explanation of electoral corruption in different socio-political situations. What is surprising is that researchers have not provided even a working definition of electoral corruption.

In this study we shall attempt to provide such a definition, while not claiming that it will be appropriate in the context of societal and regional differences, as electoral laws, culture and norms differ sharply between different systems and societies. However, it is hoped that the following definition will help in analysing the electoral climate in many Asian and African countries, namely, that *electoral corruption is the transgression of the principles, embodied in a country's constitution (whether written or not) and laws, which govern free and fair elections in a non-intimidating environment, where those either standing for elective positions, electioneering for political parties, exercising their franchise, or supervising the process, indulge in unethical practices that may subvert the genuine outcome of the electoral process.* The breaches would include intentional preparation of inaccurate electoral rolls, bribery or vote buying, extortion or threatening voters, resorting to violence to create panic and fear among voters, perverting the course of free polling (falsification of voter identity, ballot-box snatching, false or proxy voting), exploiting the religious sentiment of the people which in many cases includes underhand donations to religious institutions, influencing the electoral machinery, using the bureaucracy, the military, law-enforcing agencies and the state-owned media for partisan purposes, and manipulating the outcome of elections.

Electoral Systems and Electoral Corruption

It is difficult to identify some electoral systems as more corrupt than others. The electoral system is one of the variables that influences the degree of electoral corruption, but there are other variables as well which have implications for electoral integrity. The income of voters, literacy rate, political awareness, activities and organisations of political parties, for instance, also bear upon corrupt actions.

Major studies of electoral systems have not been able to establish a relationship between the electoral system and electoral corruption. A number of widely cited articles and books failed to find any one electoral system superior to others for institutionalising electoral integrity and transparency.[91] Some focus on issues of representation, delimitation of electoral boundaries, and other cultural, socio-economic and political barriers that affect elections[92] but do not establish any relationship between electoral systems and electoral corruption. This is evident in the work of Crewe and Denver.[93] Another study also supports this finding although the authors discuss electoral systems and democracy, secret and open voting, the traditional dimension of elections and some other major issues concerned with electoral systems.[94]

An electoral system which is good for a particular country may not be equally suitable for another country. A particular electoral system generally develops in keeping with its society, culture, public awareness and experimentations and reforms in different spheres. It is not desirable or wise to impose an electoral system on a particular society or country from a different setting before preparing the ground to absorb it. It is important for initiators of new electoral systems to carefully consider the pre-conditions demanded by the polity for its smooth functioning and consider long-term ramifications and impact before making any change. The way the developed countries improved their electoral systems could provide useful lessons for Third World countries. Why the electoral situation in many of these countries is still steeped in corruption similar to 18th century Britain or 19th century America is a matter of investigation, although some Asian countries have improved their electoral systems.

Varieties of Electoral Corruption

Like political corruption, electoral corruption has a long historical tradition. It had its genesis in Great Britain with other countries like the United States and Canada following the tradition.[95] Fraudulent election practices, vote buying, and dishonesty of the election officials were very common in 19th century America, but only a few writings of late 19th and 20th centuries investigated this corruption. George in 1880, Harris in 1929, and Fredman in 1968 have discussed different dimensions of the early American variety. In the 1844 elections in New York city, the turnout was declared to be 135 percent. This was described by an observer as 'the dead filled in for the sick, and the city's dogs and cats must have been imbued with irresistible civic spirit, too...'.[96] In fact, elections in all parts of America were corrupt with vote buying and excessive campaign expenditures being the prominent elements. The most crooked manifestations of corruption were not found in the major urban centres but in the older agricultural communities.[97] One investigator's critical outlook toward electoral corruption was summarised as:

> indifference, fraud, corruption and violence have marked the operation of our electoral system. Nor has this condition existed sporadically or in a few particular localities. It has been a more or less permanent condition in all parts of the country.[98]

By the middle decades of the nineteenth century, another researcher reported, '...it was obvious to many Americans that the manipulation of the ballot had made voting a meaningless procedure'.[99]

As mentioned before, the nature and forms of electoral corruption vary from country to country, though there are some forms which are common to every region of the globe. Rigging, the most widespread in elections, may include: *ghost voting* (a person may impersonate a voter --living or deceased --and cast his/her vote), *multiple voting* (one person casting votes several times, *coerced voting* (an election official placing a mark on the ballot paper to identify the voter and instructing him/her to vote for a particular candidate), *bribed voting* (money and gifts offered to voters in return for their support for specific candidates or parties); and *surrogate voting* (a person representing sick and/or elderly people or absentee voters, and not necessarily voting in accordance with the wishes of the absent voters).[100] Hijacking of ballot boxes during and after polling by supporters of candidates deemed to be losing or defeated, forced stuffing of ballot boxes with unused voting papers by polling agents and supporters of candidates, snatching of identity cards from voters reckoned to be supportive of rival candidates are also some other forms of rigging. Registration of under-aged people as voters by bribing or intimidating election officials is a form of pre-election manipulation of the electoral process.[101] Post-polling corruption is attributed to tampering with informal votes or modification of results to the benefit of a particular candidate.[102] These may be done at the order of the cohorts of particular parties, often in the absence of representatives of rival parties who are invariably forced to leave polling centres.

Use of money (both legal and illegal) is an important issue in elections everywhere. Party leaders and contesting candidates collect money from businesspeople and use it in the different stages of the campaign in the hope of electoral victory. The businesspeople, on the other hand, invest their money in elections for future financial benefits. Money is used not only in buying votes; it also plays a vital role in the process of nomination.[103] The irresistible power of money in elections has been documented by Winter. He argues: '...money is only one factor influencing elections and that its impact is not on balance, either decisive or harmful'.[104] The major parties in South Asian elections nominate newly emerging capitalists in return for their substantial donations to party campaign funds. There may also be competent candidates who are reluctant to bid for money and fight the electoral battle with nominal funds in the midst of keen competition.[105] However, monetary transaction between candidates and economic elites, even though hampering the independence of elected representatives, is not considered as corruption in most of the developed countries.[106]

In the early years of the 20th century votes were sold like groceries in New York city. One study outlines the nature of selling and purchasing of votes and their price. Needless to say, in most of the countries women had no voting rights in those years and all male voters did not sell their votes; some had the integrity to resist the temptation of money. As another analysis shows, 70 to 72 percent voters were honest. But, as their votes were divided between the two contesting parties, the party which could arrange to capture the majority of the remaining 30 percent of venal votes could win the election. The price of the votes was one dollar for a Negro vote, one and a half dollars for a 'Dago', and two dollars for an American vote. A survey has portrayed the vote-selling ratio of the Irish, Negro, French, Canadian and other nationals.[107]

In late 18th and early 19th centuries, in some boroughs of Great Britain where bribery was widely practised in elections, a new broker emerged as 'borough monger'. These borough mongers would organise the voters of different blocks and sell them to the candidates in the style of the leader of day labourers through a process of strong bargaining.[108] This style of selling votes occurred also in a few South Asian states during the 1970s and 1980s when the electoral machine became extensively corrupt and voting a farce under either military or civilian autocratic rule. The leaders of hooligan groups sold votes of different electorates to different candidates in exchange for money.[109]

Wealthy parties may gain an advantage through their resources without direct bribery to voters. For example, one investigator found that motor vehicles were used in British elections to bring voters from their home to polling booths.[110] In the Lebanese elections of the 1950s, taxi fares rose considerably because of competition between contesting parties for hiring taxis for electioneering. The investigation also revealed how a candidate in Singapore employed 'women of doubtful virtue' to ride in election cars to allure men voters to the polls.[111]

The electoral system of some South Asian countries is highly defective. The Election Commissions (EC) in these countries fix a ceiling on the electoral expenditure for the candidates, but it usually is violated in every election in this region. These countries have not been able to create a mechanism to punish candidates who exceed this ceiling. Many examples may be mentioned in this regard. For example, Joyprakash Narayan, one of the prominent Indian politicians of the 1970s, who declared a holy war against corruption in Bihar, asked the then prime minister Indira Gandhi whether her opponent Nandini Satpathi had spent three million rupees in the electoral campaign in Orissa. He wanted to know how she could arrange such a big fund, given that according to the Indian law, a candidate in the *Lok Sabha* (lower house of parliament) elections was barred from expending more than 35,000 Indian rupees at that time. The examples of abiding by this law were very rare in Indian elections.[112]

T. N. Sessan, the Chief Election Commissioner of India, has admitted the defects of the Indian electoral system, especially the aspect of expending excessive money in electoral campaigns. In 1994, he publicly stated: '...In India elections were made out of caste, criminality and corruption... money power takes anyone to the seat of power and authority'. The exercise of money power, muscle power, media power and ministerial power has posed severe threats to the Indian electoral system.[113] Elections are generally fought on the strength of black money where the use of physical coercion seems to have acquired an unofficial legitimacy.[114] During elections in India the politicians collect substantial donations from businesspeople for use in their electoral campaign. One author focused on this form of corruption practised by the ruling parties of West Bengal, UP, Bihar and other states;[115] also explored was a widely practised style of changing the colour of money from black to white by politicians.[116] This trend of collecting money from the businesspeople by politicians is also popular in Japanese politics. The dependency of the Japanese Liberal Democratic Party and Socialist Party on different business groups may be mentioned here. In the 1960s and in 1970s these two political parties collected a huge amount of money by adopting this technique.[117]

Major parties in South Asian countries claim to be democratic despite their internal undemocratic mechanisms, especially the nomination process. The parties do not follow any pre-selection process in electoral constituencies to select candidates and in many cases nominate new entrants instead of long-time members of the party in exchange for a large donation to the campaign fund. This undemocratic practice in nomination frustrates dedicated party leaders and creates internal conflict within the party hierarchy. Nominating retired civil-military bureaucrats and industrialists has become a common feature during elections in South Asian states, which also negatively influences the democratic process within a party.

Patronage and patron-client relationships become more effective and evident before an election and during campaigns, especially in the developing countries.[118] The strength of this relationship, viewed as enduring by anthropologists, ensures that client voters may have to vote for a candidate whom they do not like. The patron-client relationship is strongly active in South Asian countries, not only in the rural areas but also in modern organisations like political parties and bureaucracies.[119] Clients cannot avoid voting for the candidate chosen by their patrons as they live under their political and economic shelter.

The rate of illegal exchange between candidates and voters is related to the competitiveness of an election. The winning candidates are obliged to engage in corruption after coming to power; their activities and decisions cannot neglect the interests of their financiers in the elections. In many cases the ruling party candidates illegally use public money, transport and other facilities in their electoral campaign. The Indian Chief Election Commissioner, for example, postponed the Uttar Pradesh by-election in mid 1994 after he received complaints that Chief Minister Yadav had used an official helicopter for campaigning.[120]

Offering bribes to the voters during an election is not a new custom. The case of bribing by cash is found in both developed and developing countries, though in some countries it is widely practised where per capita income and the level of political maturity are low. Besides money, electoral bribes may take other forms including making unrealistic promises by the candidates and party leaders. Even allowing for the hyperbole of campaigns electoral deception is familiar in many Asian countries where making and breaking promises are frequent. In a few South Asian countries, for example, electoral bribes start with tea, pan (betel-leaf),[121] biri (indigenous form of tobacco smoking largely adopted by the poor people because of its low price), cigarettes, lunch, sharee (the dress most widely used by women), *lungi* (a skirt like cloth widely used by males), *borkha* (a yashmak), a sheet of iron roofing, share cropping facilities, providing assistance in litigation, big donations to religious institutions and socio-cultural organisations, renovating religious institutions, repairing a broken pool, sinking tube-wells, giving cash to poor voters, etc.[122] The present-day electoral bribes of South Asian countries have a very close similarity with the 19th century electoral bribes of Great Britain which have been described by Scott:

> For many voters in large boroughs, the franchise was considered an important financial asset. Payments for votes took a variety of forms. Among the most common were free drinks, meals and entertainment, merchandise certificates redeemable through local merchants, the hiring of large number of non-working committeemen, contributing to church and charitable groups, direct cash bribes, and finally the traditional distribution of head money after the election by the winning candidate.[123]

Electoral bribes by candidates and their workers are not only offered to voters but also to government officials who conduct the voting. One writer surveying a local government election in Bangladesh noticed, both among the candidates and workers, a competitive attitude the night before the election in offering hospitality and providing good food and shelter to presiding and polling officers who came to conduct the election scheduled for the following day.[124] An election-day entertainment shopping list of a local government election candidate identifies various bribery items given to voters and electoral officers: 1,600 packs of *biri* with other things for the voters, 50 packs of medium quality and 25 packs of good quality cigarettes for polling and presiding officers.[125]

Electoral symbols have an important role in elections in South Asian countries where the ECs issue such symbols to contesting parties. The high percentage of illiterate voters know the parties by their symbols. Some rural families support a particular symbol over generations and recognise only the symbols instead of candidates during elections. Electoral campaigns, competition and decoration shape surrounding symbols and it acquire prominence in slogans, posters and graffiti. *Nauka* (boat), *dhaner sheesh* (sheaf of rice), *langal* (plough) and the *daripalla* (scales) are symbols of four major political parties in Bangladesh, the Bangladesh *Awami* League (AL), the Bangladesh Nationalist Party (BNP), the *Jatiya* Party (JP) and the *Jammat-e-Islami* Bangladesh (JI) respectively (for a detail list of party symbols see appendix B). During voting, wearing badges containing a rival party's symbol by party activists to misguide ignorant voters is a common practice in South Asian elections. Women activists in India, Pakistan and Bangladesh are found pretending to be the supporters of their rivals by attaching their symbols to their chests to influence unaware illiterate female voters with misleading information especially in the rural areas.

In South Asian countries candidates or parties do not follow the rules set by the electoral institutions regarding election expenses. To make the campaign honest and balanced, a ceiling of electoral expenses for candidates is stipulated, but most of them do not abide by the rules. They spend many times more than the maximum specified sum. The electoral institutions in South Asian countries have still not been successful in building up a strong monitoring system to cover campaign expenses during elections and have often been tardy in disciplining violators of electoral rules.

Non-Partisan Caretaker Governments

In some countries, a solution to the problems of electoral corruption has taken the form of the 'non-partisan caretaker government' (NCG). This type of interim government operates during regime transition.[126] Shain and Linz identified the following four major models of interim governments.

1. revolutionary provisional governments, which emerge after the fall of the *ancien 're'gime* in internal revolution or a coup d'etat, or as a result of a war followed by external conquest and the ousting of the home regime;
2. power-sharing interim governments, in which an incumbent authoritarian government and the democratic opposition share executive power temporarily before elections;
3. incumbent caretaker governments, in which members of the outgoing elite manage the transition until the transfer of power to a democratically elected government, or alternatively, to another non-democratic regime; and
4. international interim governments, in which the international community, through the aegis of the United Nations, directs and monitors the process of democratic change.[127]

NCGs have two basic characteristics; first, the temporal nature of the government and secondly, their limited functions. Generally it remains in power only for a short period to organise and conduct elections. On many occasions, to avoid misunderstanding between the government and opposition, NCGs are formed and empowered only to conduct free and fair elections and not to make any major policy decisions. In parliamentary democracies, NCGs deal only with routine affairs and the most urgent business. They are often called managing or administrative governments.[128] After conducting the elections, NCGs hand over power to the elected authority and then disband.

Studying Elections and Electoral Corruption in Bangladesh

Elections have always been a popular topic of research but systematic electoral studies began in the United States only in the 1940s. This continued in the following two decades and many ground-breaking works were published. However, most were on elections in the Western liberal democracies and only a few examined Third World countries most of which were written by European scholars. Third World social scientists and psephologists have only recently entered the field of analysing elections, especially to understand issues relating to democratisation and governance. Elections today are studied not only by academics and political analysts, but also by civil society organisations, the international donor community and Western governments. The concept of election monitoring has become popular in many Asian countries since 1980s. Many international organisations and non-governmental organisations (NGO) are keeping a watch on the electoral process. For example, the Commonwealth Secretariat (London) and National Democratic Institute (Washington) are monitoring many elections in Third World countries and publishing extensive reports on them.[129]

Published academic work on elections can be classified into five categories. In the first category are election-specific studies.[130] They are either analyses of particular elections or comparative examination of a number of elections in a single country.[131] The second category contains comparative studies that take either an international or a regional perspective.[132] The third accommodates studies on electoral systems.[133] The fourth represents chapters highlighting different aspects of elections in both text and reference books on political science.[134] The final category consists of election reports conducted by international election observer groups, NGOs, parliamentary teams and freelance researchers. These might lack the academic rigour of the first four categories of studies but their significance in understanding elections and electoral issues should not be under rated.

Before discussing specific studies of Bangladeshi elections, however, a chronological summary of those held from 1954 until 1996 is of help. Bangladesh was a part of greater India before 1947 and was under British colonial rule for almost 200 years (1757-1947). From 1947 to 1971 when it achieved independence after a bloody civil war, it was one of the five provinces of Pakistan. During Pakistani rule, it experienced one provincial and one national referendum, and one presidential, two local and three national assembly elections. Since independence, there have been twenty-two elections in Bangladesh: seven parliamentary, three presidential, three referenda and nine local government and several by-elections.[135] Thirteen of these twenty-two elections were held under the military (five local, three referenda, two presidential, and three parliamentary elections) and the remaining nine (four local, one presidential and four parliamentary elections) occurred under civilian governments. Two of these nine elections (the fifth and the seventh parliamentary elections) were held under non-party caretaker governments. After each of these elections, there were allegations of rigging by the defeated political parties.

In South Asia, election studies in India have been undertaken by both overseas and indigenous researchers. Elections in other countries in this region were of less interest to academics until the 1970s. The 1954 provincial assembly election in East Pakistan (now Bangladesh) received scant attention although the elections held in the 1960s have been studied by a number of investigators. Local government or basic democracy (BD) elections in Pakistan were covered by academics in their respective studies.[136] These highlighted how the BD system misled voters in establishing their choice and displayed a high level of corruption in those elections by regime supporters. One analyst showed how easily the ruling Muslim League (ML) won the first two assembly elections under the BD system.[137] He also covered the campaign and ruling party's techniques to suppress the opposition. The electoral fairness of the 1970 general elections has been thoroughly covered by several electoral analysts.[138] They characterised this election as transparent and labelled it as the 'first general election' in Pakistan.[139] However, most Pakistani studies are election-specific and published only as journal articles.[140] These studies portray the preparation, campaign, candidates, election results, causes of success and failure of the parties, allegation of electoral rigging by the losing parties and impact of the elections on the politics of the country.

The number of parliamentary elections increased in Bangladesh after the first military takeover because of the legitimacy crisis of the military rulers who frequently attempted to legalise their rule through elections. The first parliamentary election of 1973 failed to arouse interest among both the voters and academics who were able to prognosticate the one-sided victory of the ruling party, the AL. One study highlighted the nature of partisanship by surveying two constituencies.[141] Another examined electioneering and portrayed the absolute commitment and dedication of ruling party candidates who, with the help of their activists, resorted to win almost every seat[142] while other investigators illustrated their rigging activities to inflate their popularity in their constituencies.[143]

Several academics conducted research on the second parliamentary election during the first military rule. They examined how the Bangladesh Nationalist Party (BNP), a new party sponsored by the military ruler, won an absolute majority. Their articles stressed the military ruler's hard work, vigorous campaign and simple appeal to the voters to ensure success.[144] They also pointed to the re-emergence of both the AL and the rightist parties as significant political forces.[145] Another study considered BNP's massive victory as a reflection of the people's confidence in the leadership of its founder.[146]

The third and the fourth parliamentary elections held under the second military regime were investigated by a number of researchers. One paper illustrates how the military General attempted to legitimise his rule through these elections,[147] while another article claimed that these elections failed to legitimise his party's rule and intensified anti-regime movement.[148]

The sixth parliamentary election held under the first democratically-elected civilian regime was boycotted by the major opposition parties. It thus failed to attract academic attention, although a few election observers and NGOs monitored the election. However, one study investigated the election in detail and critically examined the Thirteenth Amendment of the constitution enacted by the sixth parliament.[149] It criticised those sections of the amendment that gave the president supervisory powers over the caretaker administration, and argued that such power would transform the NCG into a caretaker presidential government which would cause barriers in implementing a true representative democratic order in the country.

The fifth and the seventh parliamentary elections held under non-party caretaker government have been adequately covered by scholars.[150] These studies almost uniformly acknowledged the free and fair nature of the election. They praised the role of the NCG, the bureaucracy and the media as impartial, and argued that they restored the confidence of the people in elections. Another study criticised the caretaker government system in arranging the elections.[151] It examined the arguments and counter-arguments for an NCG and highlighted the pre-conditions for transparent elections. An NCG, the study argued, would not be able to ensure a fair election within a short span of time because of the depth and multi-dimensionality of corruption in society. It stressed the necessity of fulfilling the basic conditions of fair elections instead of arranging an election through NCG or strengthening the EC.

Both the fifth and the seventh parliamentary elections were covered critically by another study.[152] It focused in detail on the voter participation, NCG's role in controlling corruption, campaign, performance of the media, partisan role of the bureaucracy and some other electoral irregularities. The paper recognised the partisan influence over the NCG and did not see it as a permanent solution to democratic consolidation. The seventh parliamentary election attracted election observers in large numbers. Two edited volumes, although not academically rigorous, severely criticised this election.[153] Most of the articles included in these volumes focused on the partisan role of the bureaucracy, NGOs, and the media, the influence of black money and other electoral malpractices. These studies do not agree with the findings of several election reports published by international organisations and NGOs that termed the election as free and fair.

Three presidential elections were held in 1978, 1981 and in 1986 but only the 1978 election was studied by academics while the other two were covered insignificantly.[154] One study published the votes secured by the two major parties in different districts[155] while two other studies thoroughly investigated the election.[156]

Only a few by-elections held under different regimes have been comprehensively examined by scholars. The Mirpur and Magura by-elections during the second BNP regime (1991-96) created keen contests as well as controversies.[157] The investigators highlighted the electioneering and critically examined the irregularities of these elections. The study on the Mirpur election shows how the result was declared even before the vote count was complete, while the other study demonstrates the dark sides of the Magura campaign – intimidation, violence and other malpractices.

The two referenda organised by the military regimes did not draw critical scrutiny because of their relative insignificance. The one-sided campaign and the dominant role of the regime supporters ensured easy wins for the military rulers. However, one study briefly covered both the referenda.[158] It critically examined the unequal electioneering and showed how military rulers used this risk-free technique to legitimise their rule.

One electoral analyst thoroughly examined the first City Corporation election held in 1994.[159] His article covered all electioneering, analysed the results of the election and reviewed the causes of success and failure of the major contesting parties. Academics took little interest in studying other local elections. However, a number of them investigated different aspects of these elections. One study analysed the nature of village politics during an election, covering campaign techniques, the nature of patronage, styles of influencing the voters and other aspects of electioneering.[160] The influence of songs in the campaign of local government elections has been the focus of another study.[161] The same author in a separate work investigated the trend of land politics during local government elections.[162] Violence, the attitudes of the rural leaders, and the nature of village politics are topics canvassed in three other articles.[163]

This brief survey of election studies in Bangladesh confirms that no major work has been done on electoral corruption. Some studies have concentrated on other aspects of politics like democratisation, working of parliament, political events, etc. but none of these has touched on electoral corruption, recognised by academics, the civil society and Western donors as one of the most critical national problems. Most of the election studies describe the nature of electioneering but lack detailed background and analysis of these elections. None of the academics or election monitoring teams has undertaken any comprehensive study specifically on electoral corruption. Academics who researched elections treated corruption only casually rather than providing a detailed analysis of the problem. An extended study on all the elections held in Bangladesh, especially on their negative aspects, such as corruption, would to some extent fill the existing vacuum in corruption research.

In general terms, what have been the findings of those studies of elections in Bangladesh? Open violation of electoral expense rules and questionable use of government functionaries and facilities were common after almost every parliamentary and presidential election.[164] The country was under military and quasi-military rule from August 1975 to December 1990 although coups, counter-coups, and changes to the constitution continuously occurred. There were dissimilarities in the nature of elections held under the military and civilian governments. The former imposed several restrictions on the electoral process that facilitated the civilianisation of military rule. Civilian politics, on the other hand, though inhibited by similar restrictions, was not entirely bereft of electoral malfeasance. Mistrust between the elected ruling party and opposition parties and other socio-political instabilities in Bangladesh were generated mainly from election-based events and misunderstandings. Allegations of election rigging by losing parties and candidates became a common ritual in the country. In many instances, this precipitated political crisis and violence. This had a negative influence on democratic consolidation, governance and social and economic development. The opposition parties neither trusted nor co-operated with the ruling party. In the post-authoritarian milieu, the two civilian governments failed to establish a constructive relationship between ruling and opposition parties both inside and outside parliament. Frequent walkouts and cross-purpose debates in parliament, street agitation, strikes and counter-strikes became common. The *en masse* resignation of the opposition in 1995 created a long political impasse and threatened the existence of the hard-earned democracy in the country.

Indeed, the continuous hostile relationship between the ruling and opposing sides has become a common feature in Bangladeshi political culture. The nature of electoral competition and campaigns has also taken a different shape. Frequent violation of the code of conduct, the partisan role of the election machinery and the bureaucracy, electoral violence, and the use of money and muscle power give Bangladeshi elections a character different from elections where parliamentary democracy has been institutionalised. The rhetoric that 'fair polls would be impossible under this government' became a common chant before the 1996 elections and the clamour was for constitutionalising the NCG. That has been achieved but the political climate remains charged and the focus remains on elections.

The main purpose of this study is to focus on the nature of elections and electoral corruption in Bangladesh, both before and after independence from Pakistan in 1971. It will attempt to thoroughly investigate the various aspects of electoral corruption under military, civilian and NCG rule and compare the role of these governments in planning, organising and overseeing elections. The study will also portray how electoral corruption has affected the process of democratisation in Bangladesh.

In general terms the study contributes to our knowledge about elections and electoral corruption, its nature under military, civilian and NCG rule, and its various control mechanisms in South Asian countries. The focus on the electoral corruption in Bangladesh may encourage researchers of other South Asian countries to investigate electoral corruption in more detail in their own countries, thus contributing to comparative research on this topic. Both ruling elites and EC officials of different countries may benefit from this study and could use it in some way to improve their own electoral systems, while during political crises, specially those that stem from electoral problems the study could contribute to solving them by providing a source of information. General readers, on becoming familiar with the peculiarities and complexities of electoral corruption, may initiate some preventive measures to offset unethical behaviour. The study has the potential to increase public awareness regarding electoral pathology. As Bangladesh is presently involved in establishing electoral transparency by having elections conducted by NCGs, the study could provide some guidance to politicians in consolidating democracy.

Notes

[1] Laski, H. J. (1931), 'Democracy', in E. R. A. Seligman (ed.), *Encyclopedia of the Social Sciences*, vol. 5, Macmillan, New York, pp. 76-85.
[2] See, Neal, F. W. (1954), 'Democracy', in J. Gould and W. L. Kolb (eds), *A Dictionary of the Social Sciences*, Tavistock Publications, London, pp. 187-88.
[3] Bienen, H. (ed.) (1968), *The Military Interventions: Case Studies In Political Development*, Russel Sage Foundation, New York, p. XIV.
[4] Janowitz, M. (1977), *Military Institution and Coercion in the Developing Nations*, The University of Chicago Press, Chicago; Nordglinger, E. A. (1977), *Soldiers in Politics: Military and Governments*, Prentice-Hall, Inc., Englewood Cliffs, New Jersey; Welch, Jr., C. E. and Smith, A. K. (1974), *Military Role and Rule: Perspectives on Civil-Military Relations*, Duxbury Press, North Scituate.
[5] Nordglinger, *Soldiers in Politics: Military and Governments, op. cit.*, pp. 65-78.

[6] For a study of the mechanics of a coup, see, Luttwak, E. (1969), *Coup d'Etat*, Penguin, Harmondsworth, quoted in, G. Kennedy (ed.) (1974), *The Military in the Third World*, Gerald Duckworth, London, p. 24.

[7] Maniruzzaman, T. (1987), *Military Withdrawal From Politics*, Ballinger Publishing, Cambridge, p. 17. In the early 1990s a book was published on corruption in Bangladesh. See, Akhter, M. Y. (1991), *Search for the Nature of Corruption: Bangladesh*, Nibedan Publications Limited, Dhaka.

[8] For related information, see, Harries-Jenkins, G. and Doorn, J. V. (1976), *The Military and the Problem of Legitimacy*, Sage Publications, London.

[9] See, LeDuce, L., Niemi, R. G. and Norris, P. (eds) (1997), *Comparing Democracies: Elections and Voting in Global Perspective*, Sage Publications, London, pp. 361-62; Seligman, (ed.), *Encyclopedia of the Social Sciences*, op. cit., pp. 450-56; See, L. LeDuce, R. G. Niemi, and P. Norris (eds), *Comparing Democracies: Elections and Voting in Global Perspective*, op. cit; pp. 361-62.

[10] Harrop, M. and Miller, W. L. (1987), *Elections and Voters: A Comparative Introduction*, Macmillan Education, London, pp. 245-65.

[11] For related information, see, Palmer, N. D. (1975), *Elections and Political Development: The South Asian Experience*, C. Hurst, London, pp. 16-17.

[12] For detail on the struggle of the western women for gaining voting right, see, Marilley, S. M. (1996), *Women Suffrage and the Origins of Liberal Feminism in the United States, 1820 – 1920*, Harvard University Press, Cambridge; Hume, L. P. (1982), *The National Union of Women's Suffrage Societies 1897 – 1914*, published by the author, USA; Lees, K. (1995), *Votes for Women: The Australian Story*, Allen and Unwin, St. Leonards, NSW.

[13] Smith, B. C. (1996), *Understanding Third World Politics*, Indiana University Press, Bloomington, p. 216.

[14] Weingrod, A. (1968), 'Patrons, Patronage and Political Parties', *Comparative Studies in Society and History*, vol. X, July, p. 380.

[15] Akhter, M. Y. (1989), 'Patron-client Relations in Bangladesh Organization', *Administrative Change*, vol. XVII, no. 1, pp. 28-41.

[16] For relevant information, see, Etzioni-Halevy, E. (1979), *Political Manipulation and Administrative Power*, Routledge and Kegan Paul, London, pp. 18-34.

[17] For related information, see, Satori, G. (1967), *Democratic Theory*, Praeger, New York.

[18] Butler, D., Penniman, H. R. and Ranney, A. (eds) (1981), *Democracy at the Polls: A Comparative Study of Competitive National Elections*, The American Enterprise Institute for Public Policy Research, Washington, D.C., p. 3.

[19] For related information see, Mackenzie, W. J. M. (1958), *Free Elections: An Elementary Textbook*, George Allen and Unwin, London, p. 159.

[20] See, Mohan, S. C. (1987), 'The Control of Corruption in Singapore', PhD thesis, University of London, p. 24.

[21] Rose-Ackerman, S. (1978), *Corruption: A Study in Political Economy*, Academic Press, New York, Introduction Chapter, pp. 1-10.

[22] Nye, J. S. (1967), 'Corruption and Political Development: A Cost-Benefit Analysis', *American Political Science Review*, vol. 61, no. 2, p. 419; Nas, T. F., Price, C. and Weber, C. T. (1986), 'A Policy-Oriented Theory of Corruption', *American Political Science Review*, vol. 80, no. 1, p. 108; Rogow, A. A. and Lasswel, H. D. (1970), 'The Definitions of Corruption', in A. J. Heidenheimer (ed.), *Political Corruption: Readings in Comparative Analysis*, Holt, Rinehart and Winston, Inc., New Jersey, p.54; Brasz, H. A. (1970), 'The Sociology of Corruption', in Heidenheimer (ed.),

Political Corruption: Readings in Comparative Analysis, ibid., p. 41; Monterio, J. B. (1966), *Corruption: Control of Maladministration*, P. C. Manaktala and Sons, Bombay, p. 16; Benson, G. (1978), *Political Corruption in America*, Lexington Books, Lexington, M.A., p. XIII; Gardiner, J. and Lyman, T. (1978), *Decisions For Sale, Corruption and Reform in Land-Use and Building Regulations*, Praeger, New York p. 5; Sherman, L. (1978), *Scandal and Reform: Controlling Police Corruption*, University of California Press, Berkeley, p. 130; Scott, J. C. (1972), *Comparative Political Corruption*, Prentice-Hall, Inc., Englewood Cliffs, New Jersey, p.3.

[23] See for relevant information, Peters, J. G. and Welch, S. (1978), 'Political Corruption in America: A Search for Definitions and a Theory, or If Political Corruption is the Main Stream of American Politics Why is It Not the Main Stream of American Politics Research?', *American Political Science Review*, vol. 72, no. 3, p. 974.

[24] A. A. Rogow and H. D. Lasswell define corruption as 'a corrupt act violates responsibility toward at least one system of public or civic order and is in fact incompatible with (destructive of) any such system. A system of public or civic order exalts common interest over especial interest; violation of the common interest for especial advantages are corrupt...'. This definition has been criticised by Peter DeLeon. See for detail,. Rogow, A. A. and Lasswell, H. D. (1963), *Power, Corruption and Rectitude*, Prentice-Hall, Englewood Cliffs, New Jersey, quoted in DeLeon, P. (1993), *Thinking About Political Corruption*, M.F. Sharpe, New York p.24; J. S. Nye defines corruption as 'behaviour which deviates from the normal duties of a public role because of private-regarding (family, close private clique), pecuniary or status gain, or violates rules against the exercise of certain types of private regarding influence. This includes such behaviour as bribery (use of reward to pervert the judgement of a person in a position of trust), nepotism (bestowal of patronage by reasons of ascriptive relationship rather than merit); and misappropriation (illegal appropriation of public resources for private regarding use)...'. See, Nye, J. S. (1967), 'Corruption and Political Development: A Cost-Benefit Analysis', *American Political Science Review*, vol. 61, no. 2, p. 419. M. Johnston, and J. A. Gardiner have criticised this definition. See, Johnston, M. (1986), 'The Political Consequences of Corruption: A Reassessment', *Comparative Politics*, vol. 18, no. 4, p. 460; Gardiner, J. A. (1993), 'Defining Corruption,' *Corruption and Reform*, vol. 7, no.2, pp. 111-24.

[25] Peters, J. G. and Welch, S., 'Political Corruption in America: A Search For Definitions and a Theory, or If Political Corruption is the Main Stream of American Politics Why is It Not the Main Stream of American Politics Research?', *op. cit.*, p. 975.

[26] Lowi, T. J. (1981), 'The Intelligent Person's Guide to Political Corruption', *Public Affairs*, series 81, bulletin no. 82, p.2.

[27] Peters, J. G. and Welch, S., 'Political Corruption in America: A Search For Definitions and a Theory, or If Political Corruption is the Main Stream of American Politics Why is It Not the Main Stream of American Politics Research?', *op. cit.*, p. 975.

[28] For a discussion on modernisation thesis, see, Deysine, A. (1980), 'Political Corruption: A Review of the Literature', *European Journal of Political Research*, vol. 8, no. 4, pp. 449-50.

[29] See, Pinto-Duschinsky, M. (1976), 'The Survival of Political Corruption in Advanced Democracies', a paper presented in The International Political Science Association, World Congress, Edinburgh.

[30] For example, see, Rogow, A. A. and Lasswell, H. D. (1963), 'The Definition of Corruption', in Rogow, A. A. and Lasswell, H. D., *Power, Corruption and Rectitude, op. cit.*, pp. 132-34; Klaveren, J. V. (1970), 'The Concept of Corruption', published first in 1957, and later reprinted in Heidenheimer (ed.), *Political Corruption: Readings in Comparative Analysis, op. cit.*, pp. 38-40; Brasz, H. A. (1963), 'Some Notes on the Sociology of Corruption', *Sociologica Neerlandica*, vol. 1, no. 2, pp. 111-17; Leys, C. (1965), 'What is the Problem About Corruption'? *Journal of Modern African Studies*, vol. 3, no. 2, pp. 215-44; Brook, R. C. (1970), 'The Nature of Political Corruption', in Heidenheimer (ed.), *Political Corruption:Readings in Comparative Analysis, op. cit.*, pp.56-61.

[31] Deysine, 'Political Corruption: A Review of the Literature', *European Journal of Political Research, op. cit.*, p. 448.

[32] These four books and its five authors are: Rose-Ackerman, S., *The Economics of Corruption: An Essay in Political Economy, op. cit.*; Benson, G. C. S. (1978), *Political Corruption in America*, Lexington Books, Lexington, M. A.; Gardiner, J. and Lyman, T. (1978), *Decisions For Sale, Corruption and Reform in Land-Use and Building Regulations*, Preager, New York; Sherman, L. (1978), *Scandal and Reform: Controlling Police Corruption*, University of California Press, Berkeley.

[33] For example, see, DeLeon, *Thinking About Political Corruption, op. cit.*; Tanner, S. J. (1995), 'Defining 'Political Corruption' in Light of Metherell Inquiry', *Legislative Studies*, vol. 10, no. 1, pp. 48-58; Johnston, M. (1996), 'The Search for Definitions: The Vitality of Politics and the Issue of Corruption', *International Social Science Journal*, vol. XLVIII, no. 3, pp. 321-36.

[34] Le Vine, V. T. (1975), *Political Corruption: The Ghana Case*, Hoover Institution Press, California, p.2.

[35] *Ibid.*, p. 2.

[36] D. H. Bayley has defined corruption as 'misuse of authority as a result of considerations of personal gain, which need not to be monetary...'. See, Bayley, D. H. (1970), 'The Effects of Corruption', in Heidenheimer (ed.), *Political Corruption: Readings in Comparative Analysis, op. cit.*, section 53.

[37] Benson, *Political Corruption in America, op. cit.*, p. xiii, introduction.

[38] See, Plato, *The Republic* (translated by Paul Shorey) (1930), William Heinemann, London.

[39] Plato, *The Laws* (translated by Trevor J. Saunders) (1970), Hazell Watson and Viney, London, pp.187-244.

[40] Bryce, J. (1921), *Modern Democracies*, Vol. II, Macmillan, New York, p. 54.

[41] Nelken, D. and Levi, M. (1996), 'The Corruption of Politics and The Politics of Corruption: An Overview', *Journal of Law And Society*, vol. 23, no. 1, pp 1-17.

[42] See the writings by S. Rose-Ackerman, G. Benson, J. Gardiner, T. Lyman, and L. Sherman. For detail, see, Deysine, 'Political Corruption: A Review of the Literature', *European Journal of Political Research, op. cit.*, pp. 448-50.

[43] Laski, V. (1977), *It Did Not Start With Watergate*, Dial Press, New York.

[44] The Yazoo Land Fraud of 1795 highlights on the interplay between money and political decision making. For detail, see, Magrath, C. P. (1966), *Yazoo: Law and Politics in the New Republic*, Brown University Press, Providence, R. I., p. 40.

[45] For example, senator Webster wrote a letter to Nicholes Briddle, the President of the second United State's bank and asked for money when the renewal of the charter of the bank came before Congress in 1833. He wrote, '...I believe that my relation has not been renewed or refreshed as usual. If it be wished that my relation to the bank

should be continued, it may be well to send me the usual retainer'. Quoted in, Hurst, J. W. (1980), *The Growth of American Law*, Little Brown, Boston, p. 367.

[46] For detail, see, Berg, L. L. and Schmidhauser, J. R. (1976), *Corruption in the American Political System*, General Learning Press, Morristown, New Jersey, pp.18-19.

[47] Quoted in, Monterio, *Corruption: Control of Maladministration, op. cit.*, pp. 22-33.

[48] Scott, *Comparative Political Corruption, op. cit.*, pp. 36-55.

[49] *Ibid.*, p. 46.

[50] For related information, see, Scott, *Comparative Political Corruption, op. cit.*, pp. 37-45.

[51] Nelken, D. and Levi, M. (eds) (1996), *The Corruption of Politics and the Politics of Corruption*, Blackwell Publishers, Oxford, p. 2.

[52] *Ibid.* p. 2.

[53] Okano of Meiji University says: '...in the past three years people have begun to show a genuine anger at the behaviour of individual corrupt politicians and local government bureaucrats. But we have only got to where Britain was in the 18th century when it comes to actually cleaning up the system'. See, Baum, J., Hoon, S. J. and Smith, C. (1995), 'Grease that Sticks', *Far Eastern Economic Review*, March 23, p. 55.

[54] A spokesman for one of Japan's top three construction companies told the *Yomiuri Shimbun* newspaper, '...we used to allocate as much as 3 billion yen per year for *shito fumekin'*. For similar terms of bribes across the world see, appendix A.

[55] For corruption in the former communist countries and China, see, Staatts, S. J. (1972), 'Corruption in the Soviet System', *Problems of Communism*, vol. 21, no. 1, pp. 40-47; Schwartz, C. A. (1979), 'Corruption and Political Development in the U.S.S.R', *Comparative Politics*, vol. 11, no. 4, pp. 425-43; Liu, A. P. L. (1983), 'The Politics of Corruption in the People's Republic of China', *American Political Science Review*, vol. 77, no. 3, pp. 602-23; Kiser, E. and Tong, X. (1992), 'Determinants of the Amount and Type of Corruption and State Fiscal Bureaucracies: An Analysis of Late Imperial China', *Comparative Political Studies*, vol. 25, no. 3, pp. 301-31; Ostergaard, C. S. (1986), 'Explaining China's Recent Political Corruption', *Corruption and Reform*, vol. 1, no. 3, pp. 209-33; Root, H. (1996), 'Corruption in China: Has It Become Systemic?', *Asian Survey*, vol. XXXVI, no. 8, pp. 741-57; Harris, P. (1986), 'Socialist Graft: The Soviet Union and the People's Republic of China – A Preliminary Survey', *Corruption and Reform*, vol. 1, no. 1, pp. 13-32; Lee, P. N. (1990), 'Bureaucratic Corruption During the Deng Xiaoping Era', *Corruption and Reform*, vol. 5, no. 1, pp. 29-47; Findlay, M. and Chor-Wing, T. C. (1989), 'Sugar Coated Bullets: Corruption and the New Economic Order in China', *Contemporary Crises*, vol. 13, pp. 145-61; Klugman, J. (1986), 'The Psychology of Soviet Corruption, Indiscipline, and Resistance to Reform', *Political Psychology*, vol. 4, pp. 67-82; Lau, C. and Lee, R. P. L. (1981) 'Bureaucratic Corruption and Political Instability in Nineteenth Century China', in P. L. Lee (ed.), *Corruption and Control in Hong Kong*, The Chinese University Press, Hong Kong; Sands, B. N. (1990), 'Decentralising an Economy: The Role of Bureaucratic Corruption in China's Economic Reforms', *Public Choice*, vol. 65, pp. 85-91; Smis, K. M. (1982), *USSR – The Corrupt Society*, Simon and Schuster, New York; Sun, Y. (1991), 'The Chinese Protests of 1989: The Issue of Corruption', *Asian Survey*, vol. 31, pp. 762-83; Xie, B. (1988), 'The Functions of the Chinese Procuratorial Organ in the Combat Against Corruption', *Asian Journal of Public Administration*, vol. 10, pp. 71-79; Yang, M. M. (1991), 'The Gift Economy and State Power in China',

Contemporary Studies in Society and History, vol. 31, pp. 25-54; Yeh, M. (1987), 'Modernisation and Corruption in Mainland China', *Issues and Studies*, vol. 23, pp. 11-27; Gong, T. (1994), *The Politics of Corruption in Contemporary China: An Analysis of Policy Outcomes*, Praeger Publishers, Westport; Johnston M. and Hao, Y. (1995), 'China's Surge of Corruption', *Journal of Democracy*, vol. 6, no. 4, pp. 80-94.

[56] Noorani, A. G. (1974), *Minister's Misconduct*, Vikas Publishing House, Delhi, p.1.

[57] Staats, 'Corruption in the Soviet System', *Problems of Communism*, op. cit., quoted in, Noorani, *Minister's Misconduct*, op. cit., p. 1.

[58] These 619 corruption-related reports were published in the *People's Daily* between July 1988 to December 1989. See for detail, Gong, *The Politics of Corruption in Contemporary China: An Analysis of Policy Outcomes*, op. cit., p. 138.

[59] For further information about *guanxi*, see, Root, 'Corruption in China: Has It Become Systemic?' *Asian Survey*, op. cit., pp. 741-57.

[60] Baum, Hoon, and Smith, 'Grease that Sticks', op. cit., p. 54.

[61] Cited in Akhter, M. Y., *Search for the Nature of Corruption: Bangladesh*, op. cit., p. 54.

[62] Cited in Akhter, M. Y. (1991), 'Controlling Administrative Corruption: Some Suggestion' (in Bengali), *Proshashan Shamikkha*, vol. 4, no.1, pp. 56-86.

[63] Indorf, H. H. (1969), 'Party System Adaptation to Political Development in Malaysia during the First Decade of Independence 1957-1967', PhD Thesis, New York University, pp. 469-70, quoted in Marican, Y. M. (1979), 'Combating Corruption: The Malaysian Experience', *Asian Survey*, vol. XIX, no. 6, p. 598.

[64] Alatas, S. H. (1980), *The Sociology of Corruption: The Nature, Function, Causes and Prevention of Corruption*, Times Books, Singapore, p. 77.

[65] For example, see, Gillespie, K. and Okvuhlik, G. (1988), 'Cleaning Up Corruption in the Middle East', *The Middle East Journal*, vol. 42. no. 1, pp. 59-82.

[66] For corruption in Latin American countries, see, Correa, H. (1985), 'A Comparative Study of Bureaucratic Corruption in Latin America and the U.S.A', *Socio-Economic Planning Sciences*, vol. 19, no. 1, pp. 65-79; Whitehead, L. (1983), 'On Presidential Graft: The Latin American Evidence', in M. Clarke (ed.), *Corruption: Causes, Consequences and Control*, Frances Printer Publishers, London, pp. 146-62; and for corruption in African countries, see, M. U. Ekpo (ed.) (1979), *Bureaucratic Corruption in Sub-Saharan Africa: Toward A Search for Causes and Consequences*, University Press of America, Inc., Washington; Vine, *Political Corruption: The Ghana Case*, op. cit.; Brownsberger, W. N. (1983), 'Development and Governmental Corruption – Materialism and Political Fragmentation in Nigeria', *Journal of Modern African Studies*, vol. 21, no. 2, pp. 215-33; Szeftel, M. (1982), 'Political Graft and the Spoils System in Zambia – the State as a Resource in Itself', *Review of African Political Economy*, no. 24, May–August, pp.4-21.

[67] For further information on African corruption, see, Gould, D. J. and Mukendi, T. B. (1989), 'Bureaucratic Corruption in Africa: Causes, Consequences and Remedies', *International Journal of Public Administration*, vol. 12, no. 3, pp.27-57; Harsch, E. (1993), 'Accumulators and Democrats: Challenging State Corruption in Africa', *Journal of Modern African Studies*, vol. 31, no. 1, pp. 31-48; Mbaku, J. M. (1994), 'Bureaucratic Corruption and Policy Reform in Africa', *Journal of Social, Political and Economic Studies*, vol. 19, no. 2, pp. 149-75; Werlin, H. H. (1973), 'The Consequences of Corruption: The Ghanaian Experiences', *Political Science Quarterly*, vol. 88, no. 1, pp. 71-85; Mbaku, J. M. (1996), 'Bureaucratic Corruption in Africa: The Futility of Cleanups', *Cato Journal*, vol. 16, no. 1, pp. 99-118. For

related information see, Machipisa, L. (1997), 'Growing Lobby Against Zim State Corruption', *Guardian*, 17 July.
[68] Vine, *Political Corruption: The Ghana Case, op. cit*; p. 12.
[69] See, Mohan, 'The Control of Corruption in Singapore', *op. cit.*, p. 21.
[70] Cited in Tilman, R. O. (1979), 'Emergence of Black-Market Bureaucracy: Administration, Development, and Corruption in the New States', in Ekpo (ed.), *Bureaucratic Corruption in Sub-Saharan Africa: Toward a Search for Causes and Consequences, op. cit*; p. 352. The article has also appeared in *Public Administration Review*, vol. 28, no. 5, 1986, pp. 437-46. For more information on Indian political corruption, see, Dwivedi, S. N. and Bhargava, G. S. (1967), *Political Corruption in India*, Popular Book Service, New Delhi; Pandhy, K. S. et al. (1987), *Corruption in Politics*, Discovery, New Delhi; Pandhy, K. S. and .Muni, R. K. (1987), *Corruption in Indian Politics – A Case Study of an Indian State*, Discovery, New Delhi; S. Bhan (ed.) (1995), *Criminalization of Politics*, Shipra Publications, Delhi.
[71] See, Aeorongjeb, *Masiri-E-Alamgiri*, p. 83, in Chandra, S. (1978), *Parties and Politics in Mughal Darbar, 1707-1740* (in Bengali), K. P. Bagchi, Calcutta, p. 24.
[72] Misra, B. B. (1954), *The Central Administration of the East India Company 1773 – 1834*, Manchester University Press, Manchester, pp. 379-402.
[73] *Ibid.*, p. 381.
[74] R. P. Datta wrote, '...Lord Clive took 2.5 million pounds when returned from India although he came almost empty-handed'. See, Muhammad, A. (1988), 'Poverty and Underdevelopment in Bangladesh: Historical Perspective' (in Bengali), *Proshashan Shamikkha*, vol. 2, no. 1, pp.50-53.
[75] Leiken, R. S. (1996-1997), 'Controlling the Global Corruption Epidemic', *Foreign Policy*, no. 105, Winter, pp. 55-73.
[76] See, Chandra, P. and Wilde, L. (1992), 'Corruption in Tax Administration', *Journal of Public Economics*, vol. 49, no. 3, pp. 333-49.
[77] Cited in Banerjee, A. (1996), 'Can Anything Be Done About Corruption?', in, M. G. Quibria and J. M. Dowling (eds), *Current Issues in Economic Development: An Asian Perspective*, Asian Development Bank, Hong Kong, pp. 107-31.
[78] Rashid, A. (1996), 'Delayed Action: President Leghari Bumbles Political Clean-up', *Far Eastern Economic Review*, 19 December, p. 28.
[79] The MP was Major (Retd.) Bazlul Huda of Freedom Party. A few other MPs also alleged that the ministers were taking a percentage for allocating funds in areas especially those represented by opposition members. See, *The Daily Ittefaq*, 18 January, 1990.
[80] Zafarullah, H. (1987), 'Public Administration in the First Decade of Bangladesh', *Asian Survey*, vol. 27, no. 4, April, pp.468, 474-75.
[81] *The Daily Star*, 13 August, 1997; Transparency International (1997), *Survey on Corruption in Bangladesh*, Transparency International, Bangladesh Chapter, Dhaka.
[82] McGrath, A. (1996), *The Frauding of Votes*, Tower House Publications, Sydney, pp. 75-86, 99-112. For further sources on Australian electoral corruption, see, C. Copeman and A. Mcgrath OAM (eds) (1997), *Corrupt Elections: Ballot Rigging in Australia*, Tower House Publications, Sydney. Also see, McGrath, A. (1998), 'For Many, Its One Man, A Dozen Votes', *The Sydney Morning Herald*, 2 October; Hughes, C. A. (1998), 'The Illusive Phenomenon of Fraudulent Voting Practices: A Review Article', *Australian Journal of Politics and History*, vol. 44, no. 3, pp. 471-91.
[83] Seton-Watson, R. W. (1911), *Corruption and Reform In Hungary: A Study of Electoral Practice*, Constable, London.

[84] Richley, A. J. (1987), *Elections: American Style*, Brookings Institution, Washington D.C.
[85] According to R. Goldberg, election fraud or vote fraud 'may be defined as an activity that has the effect or intent of subverting the rights of voters to cast ballots free of intimidation or improper influence and to have their votes accurately counted without dilution by illegal ballots...'. Election fraud according to him, '...takes four main forms: vote buying, fraudulent registration (often to facilitate multiple voting by 'repeaters'), fraudulent use of absence ballots, and falsification of election counts. For detail, see, Richley, *Elections: American Style, op. cit.*, p. 180.
[86] Heidenheimer (ed.), *Political Corruption: Readings in Comparative Analysis, op. cit.*, p. 361.
[87] *Ibid.*, p. 361.
[88] Benson, *Political Corruption in America, op.cit.*
[89] Gehlot, N.S. (1991), 'Elections and Role of Money Power In India', *Indian Journal of Public Administration*, vol. 37, no. 3, pp. 437-47; Reddi, A. E. and Ram, S. D. (1991), 'Administering Clean and Fair Elections In India', *Indian Journal of Public Administration*, vol. 37, no. 3, pp. 311-23; Syed, A. H. (1991), 'The Pakistan People's Party and The Punjab: National Assembly Elections 1988 and 1990', *Asian Survey*, vol. XXXI, no. VII, pp. 581-97; Weinbaum, M. G. (1977), 'The March 1977 Elections in Pakistan: Where Everyone Lost', *Asian Survey*, vol. XVII, no. VII, pp. 599-618; Ziring, L. (1993), 'The Second Stage in Pakistani Politics: The 1993 Elections', *Asian Survey*, vol. XXXIII, no. XII, pp. 1175-85; Baxter, C. and Rashiduzzaman, M. (1991), 'Bangladesh Votes: 1978 and 1979', *Asian Survey*, vol. XXXII, no. II, pp. 485-500; Hakim, M. A. (1991), 'The1991 Parliamentary Elections in Bangladesh: A Review', *Politics, Administration and Change*, no. 17, July-December, pp.24-38; Quadir, F. (1991), 'National Parliamentary Elections 1991: A Review', *The Journal for Human Development*, vol. 3, no. 4, pp. 49-62.
[90] For related discussion, see, McGrath, *The Frauding of Votes, op. cit.*, p. 34-36.
[91] Lijphart, A. 'Advances in the Comparative Study of Electoral Systems', *World Politics*, vol. 36, no. 4, pp. 24-36; — 'The Field of Electoral Systems Research: A Critical Survey', *Electoral Studies*, vol. 4, no. 1, pp. 3-14; Taagepera R. and Shugart, M. S. (1989), *Seats and Votes: The Effects and Determinants of Electoral Systems*, Yale University Press, New Haven and London.
[92] Rule, W. and Zimmerman, J. M. (eds) (1994), *Electoral Systems in Comparative Perspective: Their Impact on Women and Minorities*, Greenwood Press, Westport, Connecticut, London.
[93] Crewe, I. and Denver, D. (eds) (1985), *Electoral Change in Western Democracies: Patterns and Sources of Electoral Volatility*, Croom Helm, London, Sydney.
[94] Reeve, A. and Ware, A. (1992), *Electoral Systems: A Comparative and Theoretical Introduction*, Routledge, London, New York.
[95] For related information, see, Heidenheimer (ed.), *Political Corruption: Readings in Comparative Analysis, op. cit.*, p. 361.
[96] Felknor, B. L. (1992), *Political Mischief: Smear, Sabotage, and Reform in U.S. Elections*, Praeger, New York, pp. 155-82; also cited in Sabato, L. J. and Simpson, G. R. (1996), *Dirty Little Secrets: The Persistence of Corruption in American Politics*, Times Books, New York, p. 276.
[97] George, H. (1883), 'Money in Elections', *North American Review*, CCCXVI, March, pp. 201-202.
[98] Harris, Joseph P. (1929), *Registration of Voters in the United States*, Brooking Institution, Washington, p. 2.

[99] Fredman, L. E. (1968), *The Australian Ballot: The Story of An American Reform*, Michigan University Press, East Lansing; also quoted in Allen, H. W. and Allen, K. W. (1981), 'Vote Fraud and Data Validity', in J. M. Clubb, W. H. Flanigan and N. H. Zingale (eds), *Analyzing Electoral History: A Guide to the Study of American Voter Behaviour*, Sage Publications, Beverly Hills, London, pp. 153-93.

[100] Zafarullah, H. and Akhter, M. Y. (1998), 'Military Rule, Civilianization and Electoral Corruption: Pakistan and Bangladesh in Perspective', accepted for publication in *Asian Studies Review*, March, 2001.

[101] Etzione-Halevy, *Political Manipulation and Administrative Power, op. cit.*, pp. 18-34.

[102] Richley, *Elections: American Style, op. cit.*, p. 180.

[103] Polsby N. W. and Wildarsky, A. B. (1968), *Presidential Elections: Strategies of American Electoral Politics*, 2nd ed., Charles Scribner's Sons, New York, p. 39; Gomez, E. T. (1996), 'Electoral Funding of General, State and Party Elections in Malaysia', *Journal of Contemporary Asia*, vol. 26, no. 1, pp. 81-99.

[104] Winter Jr., R. W. (1974), *Watergate and the Law: Political Campaigns and Presidential Power*, American Enterprise Institute for Public Policy Research, Washington D.C., p.10.

[105] Berg and his associates have included relevant discussions on the role of money in election in their book *Corruption in American Political System*. A few more recent studies on the influence of money on elections include: Welch, W. P. (1976), 'The Effectiveness of Expenditures in State Legislative Races', *American Politics Quarterly*, vol. 36, pp. 336-56; —— (1981), 'Money and Votes: A Simultaneous Equation Model', *Public Choice*, vol. 36, pp. 209-34; Thomas, S. J. (1989), 'Do Incumbent Campaign Expenditure Matters?', *Journal of Politics*, vol. 51, pp. 965-76; Sorauf, F. J. (1988), *Money in American Elections*, Scott, Foregman, Glenview IL; Jackson, B. (1988), *Honest Graft: Big Money and the American Political Process*, Kopf, New York; Gierzynski A. and Breaux, D. (1991), 'Money and Votes in State Legislative Elections', *Legislative Studies Quarterly*, vol. 16, no. 2, pp. 203-17; Treisman, D. (1998), 'The Role and Power of Money in Russia's Transitional Elections', *Comparative Politics*, vol. 31, no. 1, pp. 1-22.

[106] For detail on the influence of money on elections see, Mackenzie, *Free Elections: An Elementary Textbook, op .cit.*, pp. 53-58.

[107] McCook, J. J. (1982), 'The Alarming Proportion of Venal Voters', *The Forum*, 14 September, pp. 1-13.

[108] Scott, *Comparative Political Corruption, op. cit.*, p. 100.

[109] Hakim, M. A. (1993), *Bangladesh Politics: The Shahabuddin* Interregnum, University Press Limited, Dhaka, pp. 10-34; A. Matin (ed.) (1986), *Ershad's Election Fraud*, Radical Asia Publications, London; Weinbaum, 'The March 1977 Elections in Pakistan: Where Everyone Lost', *op. cit*; pp. 599-618; Syed, 'The Pakistan People's Party and the Punjab: National Assembly Elections 1988 and 1990', *op. cit*; pp.581-97.

[110] Mackenzie, *Free Elections: An Elementary Textbook, op. cit.*, pp. 153-58.

[111] *Ibid.*, p. 157.

[112] Hariharan, A. (1974), 'India, A Common Goal: Get-Rich-Quick', *Far Eastern Economic Review*, vol. 85, no. 35, p. 25.

[113] Gehlot, 'Elections and Role of Money Power In India', *op. cit.*, p. 437.

[114] For related information, see, Roy, J. G. (1991), 'Electoral Violence and Role of Law and Order Administration', *Indian Journal of Public Administration*, vol. 37, no. 3, pp.

383-91; Reddi, A. E. and Ram, D. S. (1991), 'Administering Clean and Fair Elections In India', *Indian Journal of Public Administration*, vol. 37, no. 3, pp.311-23.

[115] S. Kohli (ed.) (1978), *Corruption In India*, Chetana Publications, New Delhi, p. 83.

[116] In case of Indian electoral corruption the politicians publish a booklet explaining the performance of their political party to make the black money legal and collect huge fund from the businesspeople in the name of advertisement. In this style the politicians convert the colour of black money into white. See for related information, Kohli, *Corruption In India*, *op. cit.*, pp. 94-95.

[117] Ouchi, M. (1982), 'The Mechanisms of Political Corruption in Japan With Special Reference to Political Donations', *Politics, Administration and Change*, vol. VII, no. 2, pp. 8-9.

[118] Weingrod, A. (1968), 'Patrons, Patronage and Political Parties', *Comparative Studies in Society and History*, vol. X, July p. 380.

[119] Akhter, 'Patron-client Relations in Bangladesh Organization', *op. cit.*, pp. 28-41.

[120] See, *The Bangladesh Observer*, July 2,1994.

[121] *Pan* is very popular among the common people in the Indian sub-continent. People eat it in a chewing style with betel-nut, *jarda* (a preparation of tobacco, generally scented) and other ingredients.

[122] See for related information, Akhter, M. Y. (1989), 'Electoral Politics in Rural Bangladesh: A Case Study', included in authors' *Political Culture And Socialisation: Bangladesh Perspective* (in Bengali), Nibedan Publications Limited, Dhaka, pp. 99-124.

[123] Scott, *Comparative Political Corruption*, *op. cit.*, p. 100.

[124] Polling and presiding officers in remote rural areas in Bangladesh go to their constituencies the night before the election day to ensure that they are present at the polling stations before the fixed time for voting.

[125] For relevant information, see, Akhter, M. Y. (1985), 'Electoral Politics in Rural Bangladesh: A Case Study' (in Bengali), *Chittagong University Studies*, vol. VIII, no. 1, pp. 209-34.

[126] The terminology of interim governments varies: caretaker government, provisional government, interim government or other names are used. For example, in South Africa in 1993, Klerk's administration and Nelson Mandela's African National Congress established a multi-party Transitional Executive Council or TEC. TEC's main objective was similar to that of a caretaker governments in many countries including Pakistan and Bangladesh, namely to pave the way for free and fair elections for a national government and constituent assembly by all South Africans. For details of the TEC see, Laurence, P. (1993), 'The Diehards and Dealmakers', *Africa Report*, November-December, p. 14.

[127] Shain, Y. and Linz, J. J. (eds) (1995), *Between States: Interim Governments and Democratic Transitions*, Cambridge University Press, Cambridge, p.5.

[128] *Ibid.*, p. 53.

[129] The author examined a number of election reports published by Commonwealth Secretariat and National Democratic institute for this study.

[130] For example, McCallum, R. B. and Readman, A. (1951), *The British General Election of 1945*, Macmillan, London; Butler, D. E. and King, A. (1965), *The British General Election of 1964*, Macmillan, London; Nelson, M. (1985), *The Elections 1984*, CQ Press, Washington D.C.; Mackerras, M. (1975), *Elections 1975*, Angus and Robertson, London; P. Lentini (ed.) (1995), *Elections and Political Order in Russia:*

The Implications of the 1973 Elections to the Federal Assembly, European University Press, New York.

[131] For example see, Reichley (ed.), *Elections American Style, op. cit.*; Lal, S. (1978), *Elections Under the Janata Rule*, India Election Archives, New Delhi; Hakim, M. A. (1993), 'Parliamentary Elections in Bangladesh: Comparative Analysis', *Regional Studies*, vol. XI, no. 2, pp. 87-102; Valla, R. P. (1973), *Elections in India, 1950-72*, S. Chand, New Delhi; Man, A. B., Soong-hoom, K. and Woong, K. K. (1988), *Elections in Korea*, Seoul Computer Press, Seoul; Yadav, K. C. (1981), *Elections in Punjab, 1920-47*, Institute for the Study of Languages and Cultures of Asia and Africa, Tokyo University of Foreign Studies, Tokyo.

[132] For example of this category, see, Tinker, H. (1964), *Ballot Box and Bayonet: People and Government in Emergent Asian Countries*, Oxford University Press, London; Palmer, *Elections and Political Development: The South Asian Experience, op. cit.*; Mackenzie, *Free Elections: An Elementary Textbook, op. cit.*, Harrop, M. and Miller, W. L. (1987), *Elections and Voters: A Comparative Introduction*, Macmillan Education, London; Smith, T. E. (1960), *Elections in Developing Countries*, St. Martin's Press, New York.

[133] See, Taagepera, R. and Shugart, M. S. (1989), *States and Votes: The Effects and Determinants of Electoral Systems*, Yale University Press, New Haven; V. Bogdanor and D. Butler (eds) (1981), *Democracy at the Polls: A Comparative Study of Comparative Elections*, American Enterprise Institute, Washington D.C.; Campbell, P. (1958), *French Electoral Systems and Elections Since 1789*, Faber and Faber, London; Carstairs, A. M. (1980), *A Short History of Electoral Systems in Western Europe*, Allen and Unwin, London; Crains, A. (1968), 'The Electoral System and the Party System in Canada, 1921-1965', *Canadian Journal of Political Science*, vol. 1, pp. 55-80; Blais, A. (1988), 'The Classification of Electoral Systems', *European Journal of Political Research*, vol. 16, pp. 99-110.

[134] For example see, Heidenheimer, *Political Corruption: Readings in Comparative Analysis, op. cit.*, Jackson, B. (1988), *Honest Graft: Big Money and the American Political Process*, Kopf, New York; Jahan, R. (1972), *Pakistan: Failure in National Integration*, Columbia University Press, New York; Hakim, *Bangladesh Politics: The Shahabuddin Interregnum, op. cit.*

[135] Union *parisad* (UP) is the lowest tier of governmental administration in Bangladesh. Nine members and one chairman of a UP is directly elected by the voters of the constituency after every five years. *Upazila* (sub-district) was a medial tier of governmental administration created by the Ershad government in 1984. It was the product of the administrative decentralisation programme of the military government. There were 460 *upazilas* in Bangladesh. The former Khaleda government postponed the *upazila* system. The Hasina government has again reintroduced the system.

[136] For example, see, Sobhan, R. (1968), *Basic Democracies, Works Programme and Rural Development in East Pakistan*, Oxford University Press, Dhaka; Jahan, *Pakistan: Failure in National Integration, op. cit.*, Misra, K. P., Lakhi, M. V. and Virendra Narain, L. (1967), *Pakistan's Search for Constitutional Consensus*, Impex India, New Delhi.

[137] al-Mujahid, S. (1965), 'Assembly Elections in Pakistan', *Asian Survey*, vol. 5, no. 1, pp. 939-51.

[138] al-Mujahid, S. (1965), 'Pakistan: First General Election', *Asian Survey*, vol. 5, no. 6, pp. 280-94; Misra., *op. cit.*, Jahan, *Pakistan: Failure in National Integration*, *op. cit.*; Husain, A. (1972), *Politics and People's Representation in Pakistan*, Feroz Sons, Lahore.

[139] al-Mujahid, 'Pakistan: First General Election', *op. cit*; For further on 1970 elections see, Baxter, C. (1971), 'Pakistan Votes –1970', *Asian Survey*, vol. XI, no. 3.

[140] For example, see, al-Mujahid, 'Pakistan's First Presidential Election', *op. cit.*, pp. 280-94; —— 'Pakistan: First General Elections', *op. cit.*, pp. 159-71; Baxter, 'Pakistan Votes – 1970', *op. cit.*, pp. 197-218; Weinbaum, 'The March 1977 Elections in Pakistan: Where Everyone Lost', *op. cit*; pp. 599-618; Syed, 'The Pakistan People's Party and the Punjab: National Assembly Elections 1988 and 1990', *op. cit*; pp. 581-97; Ziring, 'The Second Stage in Pakistani Politics: the 1993 Elections', *op. cit.;* pp. 1175-85.

[141] Jahan, R. (1980), 'The 1973 National Election in Bangladesh: An Analysis of Partisanship in Two Constituencies', in authors' *Bangladesh Politics: Problems and Issues*, University Press Limited, Dhaka.

[142] Jahan, R. (1974), 'Bangladesh in 1973: Management of Factional Politics', *Asian Survey*, vol. XIV, no. 2, pp. 127-28.

[143] Huque, A. S. and Hakim, M. A. (1993), 'Elections in Bangladesh: Tools of Legitimacy', *Asian Affairs An American Review*, vol. 19, no. 4, p. 249. Also see, Muhit, A. M. A. (1991), *Bangladesh Reconstruction and National Consensus* (in Bengali), University Press Limited, Dhaka, p. 7.

[144] Khan, M. M. and Zafarullah, H. M. (1979), 'The 1979 Parliamentary Elections in Bangladesh', *Asian Survey*, vol. XIX, no. 10, pp. 1023-36.

[145] Rashiduzzaman, M., 'Bangladesh Votes: 1978 and 1979', *op. cit.*, pp. 485-500.

[146] Haque, A. (1980), 'Bangladesh 1979: Cry for a Sovereign Parliament', *Asian Survey*, vol. XX, no. 2, pp.216-30.

[147] Kabir, B. M. (1987), 'Movement and Elections: Legitimisation of Military Rule in Bangladesh', unpublished paper presented at the seminar held on the occasion of the Fifth National Conference of the Bangladesh Political Science Association, 13-14 July, Rajshahi University, Bangladesh.

[148] Hakim, M. A. (1991), 'Legitimacy Crisis and United Opposition: The Fall of Ershad Regime in Bangladesh', *South Asia Journal*, vol. 5, no. 2, pp.181-93.

[149] Islam, M. R. (1996), 'Free and Fair General Elections in Bangladesh Under the Thirteenth Amendment: A Political Legal Post-Mortem', *Politics, Administration and Change*, no. 26, July-December, pp. 18-31.

[150] See, Baxter, C. (1992), 'Bangladesh in 1991: A Parliamentary System', *Asian Survey*, vol. XXXII, no. 2, pp. 162-67; Baxter, C. and Rahman, S. (1991), 'Bangladesh Votes – 1991: Building Democratic Institutions', *Asian Survey*, vol. XXXI, no. 8, pp. 683-93; Hakim, 'The 1991 Parliamentary Elections in Bangladesh: A Review', *op. cit.*; Quadir, F. (1991), 'National Parliament Election 1991: A Review' (in Bengali), *Journal for Human Development*, vol. 3, no. 4, pp.49-62; Amin, S. and Guhathakurta, M. (1991), 'Parliament Election in 1991: Candidate's Opinion on Social and Political Issues' (in Bengali), *Samaj Nirikkhan*, no. 42, November, pp. 14-25.

[151] Huq, M. M. (1994), 'Elections in Bangladesh: Predicaments and Prospects', *Politics, Administration and Change*, no. 22, January-June, pp.12-25.

[152] Zafarullah, H. and Akhter, M. Y. (2000), 'Caretaker Administrations and Democratic Elections in Bangladesh: An Assessment', *Government and Opposition*, vol. 35, no. 3, pp. 345-69.

[153] Farouque, G. (ed.) (1996), *Bureaucratic Rebellion* (in Bengali), Matra Books, Dhaka; — (ed.) (1996), *Election '96: NGO The Bureaucracy Black Money and Corruption* (in Bengali), Mimma Prokashan, Dhaka.

[154] The 1978 election has been thoroughly studied by the academics. For example, see, Baxter and Rashiduzzaman, 'Bangladesh Votes: 1978 and 1979', *op. cit.*; Singammal, M. A. (1979), '1978 Presidential Election in Bangladesh', *Indian Political Science Review*, vol. 40, no. 1, pp. 97-110. For the 1981 election see, Khan, Z. R. (1982), 'Bangladesh in 1981: Change, Stability, and Leadership', *Asian Survey*, vol. XXII, no. 2, pp. 163-70.

[155] Baxter and Rashiduzzaman, 'Bangladesh Votes: 1978 and 1979, *op. cit.*

[156] Singammal, '1978 Presidential Election in Bangladesh', *Indian Political Science Review*, *op. cit.*..; Khan, M. M. and Zafarullah, H. (1986), 'The 1978 Presidential Election: A Review' in S. R. Chakravarty (ed.), *Politics and Society in Bangladesh.* vol. 2, South Asian Publishers, New Delhi, pp. 100-110.

[157] Hakim, M. A. (1994), 'The Mirpur Parliamentary By-Election in Bangladesh', *Asian Survey*, vol. XXXIV, no. 8, pp. 738-47; Mashreque, Md. S. and Rashid, M. A. (1995), 'Parliamentary By-Election in Bangladesh: The Study of Magura-2 Constituency', *Asian Profile*, vol. 23, no. 1, pp. 67-80.

[158] Smith, T. B. (1996), 'Referendum Politics in Asia', *Asian Survey*, vol. XXVI, no. 7, pp. 793-814.

[159] Ahmed, N. U. (1995), 'Party Politics in Bangladesh's Local Government: The 1994 City Corporation Elections', *Asian Survey*, vol. XXXV, no. 11, pp. 1017-29.

[160] Akhter, 'Electoral Politics in Rural Bangladesh: A Case Study', *op. cit.*, pp. 209-34.

[161] Akhter, M. Y. (1994), 'Songs and Politics: the Aspect of Local Government Elections in Bangladesh', (in Bengali), *Bangladesh Political Studies*, vol. 16, pp.79-95.

[162] Akhter, M. Y. (1988), 'Land Politics During Election: A Case of Rural Bangladesh', *The Journal of Local Government*, vol. 17, no. 1, pp. 68-74.

[163] See, Rahman, H. Z. (1990), 'The Landscape of Violence: Elections and Political Culture in Bangladesh', *The Journal of Social Studies*, no.49, July, pp. 83-91; Wahhab, M. A. (1985), 'Attitude of the Rural Leaders Towards Rural Development', *Bangladesh Political Studies*, vol. 8, pp. 66-81; Mizanuddin, M. (1985), ' 'Village-Politics'– A Case Study of Union Parisad Election in Bindopur in 1984', *Bangladesh Journal of Sociology*, vol. 3, no. 1, pp. 198-208.

[164] For related information see, Khan, Z. R. (1997), 'Bangladesh's Experiments With Parliamentary Democracy', *Asian Survey*, vol. XXXVII, no. 6, pp. 575-89.

2 Political Change and Developments in Bangladesh

This chapter focuses on political change and development in Bangladesh by chronologically highlighting the main political developments in Pakistan since independence from Britain in 1947. It examines the role, strategy and governance of the civilian, military, and caretaker governments in the country and the trend towards democratisation and democratic consolidation during their rule.

Background

Contemporary Bangladesh is a small, low-lying, agricultural country watered by rivers, located in South Asia. The country is almost surrounded by India except for borders in the southeast with Myanmar, and in the south with the Bay of Bengal. It was known by various names from the ancient times until the emergence of Mughal empire, including Pundra or Pundravarddhana or Paundravaraddhana, Vanga, Samatata and Harikela.[1] Muslim merchants of Arab origin used to refer to as Bangalah from which its present nomenclature is believed to have gradually evolved.[2] During the Mughal period it became known as Suba Bangla, and the British called it Bengal. As part of Pakistan it was familiar as East Bengal, but after the enactment of the 1956 constitution, renamed East Pakistan, which finally was retitled Bangladesh after the independence in 1971. The history of early Bengal is somewhat obscure, although historians claimed that even three thousand years ago the inhabitants of Bengal lived in comfortable houses and made efficient metal tools and attractive pottery. For hundreds of years Bengal was administered by the Buddhists and the Hindus. The political history of early Bengal is available only form the eighth century onward when the Pala and Sena dynasties ruled (750 – 1200 A.D).[3] Although Islamic missionary activities were evident in the area from the eighth century onward, it was not until the thirteenth century that the Muslims rulers gained political power in greater India through the establishment of the Sultanate of Delhi.[4] The Tughlak sultanate was formed in the fourteenth century followed by an Afghan arrival in 1520. Later, Babur, who founded the great Mughul Empire, overthrew the sultanate of Delhi in 1526.

The Mughals ruled India from the 16th to the middle of the 19th century. Direct Mughal rule proved impossible in some areas of the empire as local contenders for power held sway over their regions. This created continual conflict between the central Mughal administration and the distant territories. In such a situation, the Europeans entered India as traders[5] but soon revealed their political ambitions. The British were able to establish themselves as the most potent force against other European interests and successfully adopted a 'divide and rule' policy. The British victory at Plassey in 1757 heralded the decline of the Muslim empire; it was the beginning of a new era with the English gradually gaining ascendancy over the large expanse of greater India.

It took the people of the region almost 200 years to achieve independence from the British, and in this long struggle the Hindus and the Muslims of greater India had to undergo tremendous trials and tribulations. In the early 20th century, the anti-British movement became popular, and the British rulers under pressure gradually liberalised their authority by granting the local population the social and political rights. Lord Curzon, the viceroy of India, partitioned Bengal for administration purposes in 1905 which due to an opposition movement was reunited in 1912. Both Hindus and Muslims were engaged in the movement against the British although the main political party, the Indian National Congress (INC), was Hindu-dominated and deferred little to Muslim interests.[6] Realising their difficulties the Muslim leaders of India formed their own party, the Muslim League (ML), in 1906 to fight for their social and political rights. The ML, although claiming to represent the Indian Muslims, was not acceptable to the majority in the community. This was reflected in the provincial legislature elections of 1937 held under the Government of India Act of 1935 where the ML was able to win only 109 of the 482 Muslim seats and could not obtain a majority of the votes even in the four Muslim-majority provinces.[7] However, within a short time, the ML improved its position and after 1940, when it passed the Lahore Resolution which called for the establishment of one or more independent Muslim states within the sub-continent, it had won the trust of the majority of Muslims as their preferred representative.

The ML proved its popularity and political strength in the 1945-46 central and provincial assembly elections. It won all of the 30 Muslim seats in the central legislature, and 48 percent of the Muslim seats in the provincial assemblies. The ML formed ministries in two provinces, Bengal and Sindh, and its claim to be 'the voice of the majority of Indian Muslims could no longer be ignored or discounted...'.[8] In the early and mid-forties when the British negotiators were engaged in finding a political solution for India, the INC endeavoured to create one greater independent India. The ML leader, Mohammad Ali Jinnah declared that 'the Muslims are not a minority but a nation and self-determination is their birthright...'.[9] His two-nation theory based on religion, was warmly accepted by the Indian Muslims. The Lahore Resolution and the popularity of ML signified the irrevocable shift in favour of an independent Pakistan,[10] which gained independence from the British colonial rule on 14 August 1947.

After experiencing almost 200 years of British colonial rule the people of East Bengal in the name of independence were imprisoned again in Pakistani 'internal colonialism'.[11] Until late 1971, Pakistan consisted of two geographical units 1,600 kms apart, West and East Pakistan, separated by India. The peoples of East and West Pakistan were different in cultural and linguistic identity but uniform in religious beliefs and values.

Political Environment After 1947

The Indian Muslims were delighted to have a separate homeland of their own in 1947 and expected their new country to emerge as a solvent and powerful Islamic state, although the population and even the political leaders did not have any clear conception of an Islamic state.[12] This hope remained unrealised because of the lack of consensus among political leaders who, after the death of Jinnah, the country's first Governor-General, failed to formulate a constitution for the country until 1956. The main political issue of the early 1950s concerned the basis of the constitution. Some of the main issues were the place of Islam in politics and whether Pakistan should have a parliamentary or presidential form of government, the pattern of federal relations, the choice of direct or indirect election for filling the highest political offices in the country, joint or separate electorates,[13] and whether the state language should be Urdu or Bengali.[14] The politicians, the *ulemas* (religious leaders), and civil and military personnel participated in the constitution-making process. The politicians broadly favoured the parliamentary form of government, the *ulemas* were committed to an Islamic state, while the civil service and the military, critical of politicians and political parties, were in favour of a secular state and a strong central government. The politics between 1947 and 1956 was an example of conflict, confusion, mistrust and instability – all resulting from a lack of consensus.

Political leaders failed to solve the early problems of Pakistan. They took eight years to frame a constitution for the country. The leading political party, the ML which had played a prominent role before partition, was unable to face the challenges posed to it by other Muslim dominant political groups like the Unionists in the Punjab, the Red Shirts in the North-West Frontier Province (NWFP), and the Syed Group in Sindh. The role of the ML in the formative years of Pakistan was a 'source of weakness and dissension rather than of strength...'.[15] The party also faced a leadership crisis during this period. After Jinnah's demise, another popular leader, Liaqat Ali Khan, was assassinated soon after.[16] The other leaders of the ML could not control the party's internal conflicts and the dominating influence of the civil-military bureaucracy.

The political leaders in the 1950s totally failed in establishing parliamentary democracy enshrined in the 1956 constitution. They showed no respect for democratic traditions; ignoring the 'rules of the game' they were involved in a ruthless scramble for power that created an anti-democratic culture in the country. Doubts were expressed about the suitability of parliamentary democracy in Pakistan because of continued political instability and lack of tolerance and mutual trust and respect in politics. Political bickering and rivalry, nepotism and bureaucratic corruption increased, black marketeering, smuggling and profiteering became rampant, regionalism and anti-national feelings flourished.[17] This trend continued and increased in late 1950s after disagreements between political parties grew, disregard of parliament and the constitution were flagrant and cabinet reshuffling became common.[18]

The political situation in East Pakistan (later Bangladesh) was also chaotic. Rivalries between political parties, frequent dismissal of ministries, splits in political parties, and regular verbal and physical brawls between government and opposition members in the Assembly featured in provincial politics.[19] In such a situation, when all the efforts of the political leaders failed to deliver to the nation a stable political system, the military which had 'so long maintained traditional aloofness from politics',[20] took over power on 7 October 1958.[21]

Disparity Between East and West Pakistan

Even though the Pakistani rulers (both civilian and military) ruled the country in the name of Islam and democracy, they were not sympathetic to the demands and problems of East Pakistan. This created a sense of deprivation among the majority inhabitants of East Pakistan, the Bengalis. The political elites of Pakistan failed not only to create political stability but also a national identity, which enraged provincial feelings and contributed to the emergence of Bengali nationalism. The Bengalis of East Pakistan, comprising the majority of the country's total population, were under-represented in the military, the civil bureaucracy and the judiciary. The development budget allocated to East Pakistan was always unequal in comparison with other provinces in the Western wing. The lion's share of Pakistan's foreign earnings was obtained from the export of jute produced only in the Eastern province, but its resources and labour were exploited by West Pakistani capitalists for their own (and West Pakistan's) economic development.[22] This disparity was politically used by the AL, the major party of the Bengalis, which in a well-organised way mobilised the population and was successful in rousing a sense of deprivation among them. The six-point formula[23] of the AL was designed to reduce the disparity. Among other things, it demanded greater autonomy for the Eastern wing. It received an enthusiastic response from the Bengalis in the 1970 general elections when it won an overwhelming victory in East Pakistan.

The Ayub Regime

General (later Field Marshal) Mohammad Ayub Khan (Ayub), after assuming power on 7 October 1958, performed the common rituals of Third World military rulers. He abrogated the 1956 Constitution, declared martial law, became the Commander-in-Chief and subsequently assumed the Presidency. He noted the failings of the early politicians of Pakistan in his first national broadcast just after the takeover:

> Ever since the death of the Quaid-i-Azam [Jinnah] and Mr. Liaquat Ali Khan politicians started a free-for-all type of fighting in which no holds were barred. They waged ceaseless and bitter war against each other regardless of the ill-effects on the country, just to whet their appetites. There has been no limit to the depth of their baseness, chicanery, deceit and degradation. Having nothing constructive to offer they used provincial feelings, sectarian, religious and racial differences to set a Pakistani against a Pakistani... The result is total administrative, economic, political and moral chaos in the country.[24]

Basic Democracy

Ayub, who was always critical of the existing parliamentary system of government and party politics, introduced basic democracy, a new brand of democratic system in 1959. His experience 'taught' him that parties only 'divide and confuse people and expose them to exploitation by unscrupulous demagogues...'.[25] Arguing that the parliamentary system could not provide stability in Pakistan, Ayub remarked: '...government after government rose and fell and within a period of five years six Prime Ministers presided over precariously balanced cabinets'.[26] He was always in favour of a strong central government which he believed could establish political stability.

The British parliamentary system which Pakistan inherited and later adopted in its 1956 constitution was, according to Ayub, 'a system of government totally unsuited to the temper and climate of the country...'.[27] He was in favour of democracy, but a democracy of a different brand. He wrote:

> We must ... have democracy. The question then is: what type of democracy? The answer need not be sought in the theories and practices of other people alone. On the contrary, it must be found from within the book of Pakistan itself.[28]

He specified four prerequisites for the success of any democratic system in a country like Pakistan. Democracy

1. should be simple to understand, easy to work and cheap to sustain;
2. should put to the voter only such questions as he can answer in the light of his own personal knowledge and understanding without external prompting;
3. should ensure the effective participation of all citizens in the affairs of the country up to the level of their mental horizon and intellectual calibre; and
4. should be able to produce reasonably strong and stable governments.

These formed the basis of his Basic Democracy (BD). Directly elected basic units – the union council in rural areas and union and town committees in the town and cities were to serve not only as agencies of local government, administration, and development, but also as an electoral college[29] to choose the president of Pakistan and the members of the provincial and national legislatures.

In this four-tier system,[30] the people could only vote in the lowest tier, although Ayub argued that this system had brought democracy to the doorsteps of the people. He compared the local councils to a gigantic parliament where people could vote in a parliament of 80,000 instead of a parliament of 150. He further argued that as people in this system would vote in small constituencies where everybody knew everyone their choice would generally be wise. People who had proved themselves to be dedicated and devoted trustees of the mass interests would be elected and the entire pattern of leadership would change.[31]

This positive interpretation of BD was highly criticised by politicians and academics both within and outside Pakistan. They branded it as basically an undemocratic system where the sub-divisional officer (SDO) – a civil servant – could easily control the local 'basic democrats'.[32] The political opponents of the ML criticised it as 'a clever innovation by the regime to entrench itself in power with the help of bureaucracy's tentacles spread throughout the length and breadth of Pakistan...'.[33] According to other critics, the system 'became the vehicle for military-bureaucratic control over state power'[34] and 'an undisguised attempt to institutionalise bureaucratic control over the political process...'.[35] Ayub, however, ignored these criticisms and continued in power through this system until 1969. He obtained more than 95 percent 'support' of the basic democrats in a referendum in February 1960. This inspired him to appoint in 1962 a Constitution Commission to frame a new constitution, which virtually gave him unlimited power and influence over the entire machinery of government.

Ayub, like other military rulers, was not intentionally slow in organising an election. Although initially he neither formed his own political party nor joined an existing one and preferred to remain above party politics, he was spontaneously supported by the Conventionist Muslim League (CML).[36] He soon realised the necessity of joining a party to give his rule a civilian makeup,[37] and chose the CML as his political platform. A new constitution was framed according to his directions which provided for a presidential system of government with a largely indirect system of elections.

Anti-military sentiment became popular in both wings of Pakistan and political party activists and students initiated an anti-regime movement. In the eastern wing, the regime used its coercive powers to suppress the AL's six point demands leading to serious political disturbances in late 1968 lasting several months. Ayub was forced to hand over power to the army Chief, General Yahya Khan in March 1969. The new military leader abrogated the 1962 constitution and declared martial law.

The Yahya Interregnum

On assumption of office, General Yahya Khan (Yahya), like other military generals, declared: '...I wish to make it absolutely clear that I have no ambition other than the creation of conditions conducive to the establishment of a constitutional government'. However, unlike other military generals, he honoured his intentions to handover power to the elected representatives. He successfully conducted a free and fair election that resulted in the AL's winning majorities in both national and East Pakistan provincial assembly elections in December 1970.

The results of this election created a new political polarisation in Pakistan. Mujib, leader of the AL, was adamant on his six-points, but Z. A. Bhutto, the leader of the Pakistan People's Party (PPP) that won a majority of seats in West Pakistan, had always been critical of Mujib's strategy and was not prepared to concede any of the six points which made negotiation impossible.[38] Both Yahya and Bhutto underestimated Mujib and expected him to soften his stance. Mujib was a dogged politician and was bent upon realising his objectives. He did not believe in token Bengali participation like some other leaders did in the past.[39] He announced that 'none would be able to stop us from framing a constitution on the basis of the six-point program...'.[40] The AL's claim to form the government was not accepted by Yahya and Bhutto,[41] and in the midst of heightening tension and acrimony, Mujib declared complete autonomy for East Pakistan. The result was military action, and after nine months of a bloody liberation war,[42] East Pakistan achieved independence and emerged as a sovereign independent state. An overview of how the political system has developed since 1971 forms the remainder of this chapter.

Political System and Administrative Environment

Bangladesh has a multi-party democratic system with a parliamentary form of government. A sovereign unicameral parliament (*jatiya sangsad*) elected for a five-year term operates as the legislature and approves the national budget. The parliament has the right to appoint the President (Head of State), by a simple majority of the 330 member House, 300 of whom are directly elected while the remaining 30 members are women elected by parliament itself. The parliament can impeach the president and amend the constitution with the support of two-thirds of its members, but passage of a law or the budget requires only a simple majority. The president appoints the prime minister from the majority party. The prime minister selects ministers from among MPs, although he/she can choose up to one fifth of ministers from outside of the House.

The country has six administrative divisions, each composed of a number of districts (*zila*). Divisions and districts are headed respectively by the divisional commissioner and the deputy commissioner. *Upazila* (sub-district) and the union are two other local government administrative tiers excepting four city corporations and 119 municipalities.[43] The union is the lowest tier of local government; each union is composed of several villages. There are 64 districts, 464 *upazilas*, 45,000 unions and over 68,000 villages in the country. All heads of units including *upazila*, union, city corporation and municipality are directly elected by the people.

Bangladesh's judiciary is a civil court system based on the British model. The highest court, the Bangladesh Supreme Court, comprises the Appellate Division and the High Court division. The president appoints the Chief Justice and other judges. The Bangladesh civil service is the descendant of that of Pakistan, which inherited its members from the Indian civil service of British India. The Bangladesh Public Service Commission (PSC) recruits higher civil servants through competitive examination based on merit. The next 28 years were to see both civilian and military rulers governing this small, poor and highly populated country ostensibly under a democratic system of government.

The Mujib Regime and Its Political Environment

The provisional Bangladesh government[44] moved from Calcutta to Dhaka (formerly spelled Dacca), five days after the surrender of the Pakistan Army on 16 December 1971. Mujib, imprisoned in Pakistan during the war, was released by Bhutto who replaced Yahya as president of a disintegrated Pakistan.

Mujib declared his principles of secularism, democracy and socialism as the policies of his regime to which nationalism was added later. During the war a presidential kind of government functioned in which Mujib was the president, but soon after his return he issued a provisional constitutional order changing the political system into a parliamentary form and became the prime minister. Among other changes, provincial and national assemblies were amalgamated into one body and called the Constituent Assembly. Freedom of press and speech and other fundamental rights were reinstated, but the right wing parties, which had collaborated with the Pakistan army during the liberation war, were banned.[45] In the beginning, Mujib planned to introduce an Indian style of politics.[46] His initial performance in running the country was, by and large, satisfactory; based partly on his charisma. His call to the *Mukti Bahini*[47] (freedom force) to surrender their arms was heeded within the ten-day time limit set by Mujib, although it was 'widely suspected that a large portion of their arms and ammunition had been kept back by many guerrilla groups...'.[48]

The AL regime successfully performed the great task of constitution-making within a year.[49] In its first two years (1972-73), it was able to contain a famine, legitimise its position through a 'landslide' victory in a general election, and with the help of massive relief operations aided by the United Nations and other international agencies, successfully rehabilitate 10,000,000 people who had taken refuge in India in 1971. The communication network was restored within a short time, banks, insurance companies, textile, jute and sugar industries were nationalised, and land reform attempted.[50]

The regime's economic performance, however, gradually declined when flood and famine caused destruction and loss of life. The economy of the country by mid-1974 was in such a bad state that the finance minister, Tajuddin Ahmed, publicly stated that 'the implementation of the development plan of 1973-74 would be impossible and the economy of the country had almost broken down...'.[51] A severe flood occurred in mid-1974, which, according to an estimate of the Planning Commission, caused damage to more than one million tons of food-grains and 10 to 15 million US dollars worth of jute exports. Prices of essential goods during the flood rose by almost 800 percent on the 1969-70 figures.[52] Newspapers gave wide coverage to deaths and the situation was described by Mujib himself as approximating 'near famine condition'.[53] The *Jatiya Sangsad* (national parliament) was informed of the death of about 27,500 persons due to starvation and diseases although unofficial figures were much higher.[54]

The regime, using the charisma of Mujib, prevented a clash between different groups of the *mukti bahini*. However, the leftist groups and parties which were all united for a single cause during the liberation war started pursuing their own ideological lines after 1971.[55] The pro-Moscow National *Awami* Party (NAP-M) toed the ruling AL line, but the pro-Chinese National *Awami* Party (NAP-B) and the *Jatiya Samajtantrik Dal* (JSD)[56] challenged the AL for its suppression of the opposition. Other underground leftist parties, manifesting differences in their ideological beliefs, agreed that the 'war of independence left the revolution unfinished...'. They were dogmatic about their duty to complete the revolution.[57] There were at least four underground revolutionary political parties who not only refused to accept the AL rule but looked upon it as a puppet government of India.[58] Most of these left-wing parties including the

Sarbohara Party led by Siraj Sikder and *Sammyobadi Dal* led by Mohammad Toha regarded the *Jatiya Rakkhi Bahini* (JRB)[59] as an extension of the Indian army in Bangladesh.[60] The main purpose of the formation of the JRB was to counter and silence political opposition.[61]

Leftist revolutionary activities increased at an alarming rate after liberation. Secret political killings, smuggling, armed robberies, looting of banks and shops and attacks on police stations became frequent during 1973-74, especially before and during the 1973 parliamentary elections. The exact number of these violent activities is not available and various estimates showed wide discrepancies. One government estimate puts the figure over 6,000 persons killed mostly for political reasons,[62] whereas a private estimate was double that number during 1972-75.[63] The JSD claimed that AL activists killed about 60,000 and arrested about 86,000 of its political workers in the two years following independence.[64] In one sub-division[65] in one year (May 1972 - April 1973) alone, 372 cases of murders, armed robberies and burglaries occurred and the increase over the previous years was 300 percent for armed robberies, 900 percent for burglaries, and 200 percent for smuggling.[66] Looting of banks and shops increased and armed robberies in private homes had become so frequent that a report described that 'the villagers had been passing sleepless nights being afraid of dacoits and miscreants...'.[67] Moreover, according to an official source, 23 police stations were looted by these revolutionary groups.[68]

The ruling AL, National *Awami* Party (NAP-M) and the Communist Party of Bangladesh (CPB) jointly formed *Gono Oikko Jote* (Popular United Alliance) to publicise the four state principles and 'to launch a united movement against the activities of 'anti-socials''. The committees of this alliance, which were formed at the national and district levels, organised seminars to mobilise public opinion against the revolutionary activities, but were not totally successful as the mass of the public were dissatisfied with the performance of the regime because of the high prices of basic commodities as well as the regime's failure to control law and order, smuggling and widespread corruption.

Factionalism, another significant factor, which became prominent in politics and administration after liberation, permeated down to the district and sub-divisional levels and destroyed the strength and unity of both the party and administration. The internal schism within the ruling party[69] was 'balanced' by Mujib through the distribution of political patronage.[70] The administration and the armed forces were also factionalised.[71] Administrators were divided into three factions namely 'Mujibnagar', 'non-Mujibnagar' and repatriates from Pakistan. The conflict between the three groups of armed forces, those who fought in the liberation war, those who were repatriated from Pakistan after the war, and the JRB – was common. The performance of the ruling party, administration and the military was greatly impaired by these factional schisms.

Large-scale smuggling of food-grains and jute to India was one of the main causes of the 300 to 400 percent rise in the prices of all essential consumer goods. Smuggling became so widespread by 1974 that the prime minister had to order the armed forces to conduct 'an all-out operation to recover unauthorised arms, stop smuggling and hoarding, and apprehend anti-social and subversive elements...'.[72] Many officers during this operation discovered that most of the holders of unauthorised arms and the 'ring leaders of smuggling operations' were linked to powerful AL leaders. A few Bangladeshi newspapers commented that 'India was encouraging smuggling to supplement official trade, especially in jute', a claim dismissed by the Indian government.[73] The administrators of the nationalised industries grew rich overnight by smuggling out machinery and raw materials to India.[74] Relief materials were sold in the open market instead of being distributed to the poor people. According to a researcher, only 10 percent of the relief goods sent by the US government went to the poor, for whom they were meant.[75] Even Mujib's family members, including his own brother, were alleged to have been engaged in the misuse of power and practice of corruption, which adversely affected the morale of party workers and the members of the civil-military bureaucracy.[76] The speeches and statements of the opposition leaders of the early seventies also highlighted this issue.[77] Corruption in administration increased at an alarming rate. The attitude and mentality of the administrators of the country remained similar to that before independence. Bureaucratic corruption increased to such an extent that the prime minister threatened the government officials with severe punishment unless they changed their behaviour.[78]

Mujib himself was aware of corruption and smuggling resorted to by his party leaders but failed to control it. He noted: '...Who take bribes? Who indulges in smuggling? Who becomes a foreign agent? Who transfers money abroad? Who resorts to hoarding? It's being done by us - the five percent of the people who are educated. We are the bribe takers, the corrupt elements'.[79] The operation that was mainly undertaken for recovering illegal arms was gradually reduced under the pressure of the party leaders from different regions of the country.[80] Many arrested AL leaders were released, and without formally declaring the end of the operation, the government 'ordered the army to seal the border and stop smuggling...'.[81] This attitude of the government toward the corruption practitioners and smugglers annoyed a section of frustrated and dedicated army officers.

However, by December 1974, the extent of corruption, smuggling, anti-social activities and political violence together was such that Mujib had no option other than declaring a state of emergency.

The government after being unsuccessful in controlling the revolutionary activities of the leftist parties decided to neutralise the situation by releasing 33,000 right-wing prisoners who were arrested under the Collaborators' Act.[82] In February 1974, the government enacted the Special Powers Act that provided for preventive detention and empowered the government to impose a ban on political parties if their activities were considered 'prejudicial to national interest'.[83] To top it all, on 25 January 1975 the ruling AL on the initiative of Mujib and 'against the private sentiments of the majority of the members of parliament belonging to AL' amended the constitution to change the country's political system without any debate or discussion in parliament 'at a speed unprecedented in the history of law making'.[84] The parliamentary form was replaced by the presidential under a one-party framework[85] and Mujib was made the president for five years without election. Another accompanying piece of legislation clothed the government with emergency powers.[86]

The ruling party fully exploited the weakness of the opposition in parliament and successfully established the tyranny of the majority. From January 1972 to April 1973 the ruling party enjoyed almost 'absolute and unaccountable legislative and executive authority' when it ruled the country through presidential orders, which deprived the people of their fundamental rights.[87] Moreover, the AL alienated the civil bureaucracy by proclaiming Presidential Order No. 9 that 'empowered the government to suspend, demote and dismiss public officials without showing any reason and by denying the victim the opportunity to seek legal protection...'.[88] The opposition parties were subject to extreme measures. Siraj Sikder, the leader of a Marxist group was killed by the police while he was in custody. After this incident, Mujib emphatically declared, '...now there is no opposition in Bangladesh'.[89] The working of parliamentary democracy became a form of personal rule by Mujib, and parliament, the cabinet and the ruling party lost their relevance in governance and became his personal institutions.

The failure of Mujib's authoritarian rule to control leftist revolutionary activities, smuggling, corruption and secret killings and to improve the economic condition of the masses, together with the factional conflicts in the bureaucracy and military, the inexperience of ministers, Mujib's nepotism,[90] the creation of a new para-militia JRB, the small budget allocation to the regular defence force, and the introduction of one party rule[91] frustrated the regular army. This propelled a group of young officers collaborating with some right wing AL leaders to take over power in a bloody coup on August 15, 1975.[92] According to Lifschultz, the main cause of this August Coup was Mujib's failure to control the growing revolutionary movement in the country 'which brought the national and international anti-communist forces together'.[93] Elsewhere he argues that the

> motives for the coup were attributed to a combination of personal grudges held by certain of the officers against Mujib and his associates, together with a general feeling of frustration at the widespread corruption which had become (sic) to characterise Mujib's regime.[94]

The coup leaders installed Khondokar Mushtaque Ahmed (Mushtaque), the commerce minister under Mujib, as president. He appeared to be in control of the situation and there was no significant public opposition against the coup. Ten of the 18 members of Mujib's cabinet joined the Mushtaque government.[95] It has been suggested that Mustaque himself, Taheruddin Thakur and Mahbub Alam Chashi were engaged in conspiring with the young officers of the coup.[96] However, on 3 November, Brigadier Khaled Musharraf led a counter coup, put Mushtaque and the chief of army staff, Major General Ziaur Rahman (Zia) under house arrest, promoted himself as a Major General and took over the leadership of the army. Mushtaque was forced to hand over power to the Chief Justice of Bangladesh, A. S. M. Sayem. Four days later another counter-coup, popularly called the 'Sepoy Mutiny' and led by Colonel Abu Taher, killed Musharraf. Zia, and Mushtaque, were released by the mutineers from house arrest. Although Justice Sayem was allowed to continue as president, Zia established himself as the *de facto* ruler.

The Zia Regime

Zia, the first military ruler of Bangladesh, ruled the country until May 1981. Zia was popular among both the soldiers and the masses due to his courageous role in the freedom movement in 1971. Initially, he showed little interest in politics like other military rulers of the Third World and stated, 'I am not a politician', in his first address to the nation, but gradually turned himself into a shrewd politician by adopting strategies commonly followed by most military rulers in Afro-Asian countries.

Constitutional Changes

After obtaining the presidency from Sayem by undemocratic means and consolidating his position, Zia made several constitutional changes. As he had a 'remarkable talent of feeling the pulse of the people', he was aware of the unpopularity of several changes that were undemocratically made by the Mujib government and took the opportunity to alter them. His first reform was the replacement of Mujib's one-party system by a multi-party political framework. He also abolished 'secularism' and 'Bengali nationalism' and reconceptualised 'socialism' — three of the four fundamental principles of state policy. Secularism was replaced by 'absolute faith in the almighty Allah', which gave an Islamic touch to the constitution by adding to its preamble, *Bismillahir Rahmanir Rahim* (In the name of Allah, the beneficent, the merciful). Socialism was redefined as 'economic and social justice', and Bengali nationalism was replaced by Bangladeshi nationalism. It substituted the 'ethnic identity' of the people for a 'territorial identity'.[97] By restoring the multi-party system, Zia attempted to convince the western democracies of his democratic credentials and by introducing Islamic elements he was successful in winning the support of the local religious population and right wing parties as well as some Muslim countries.

Style and Strategies of Zia's Politics

The process of civilianisation of the military regime commenced with a quick Ayubi-style referendum in 1977. Local elections were held in the same year. The ban on the activities of political parties was lifted and a presidential election took place in 1978. The long expected parliamentary election was held in February 1979 followed by the withdrawal of martial law and emergency rule in April and November respectively. Student politics were allowed to revive the same year. Before the presidential election, Zia announced a 19-point program[98] for social and economic development. He worked very hard to involve the masses in this program and strengthened the organisational network of his own political party -- BNP[99] -- to achieve his objective.

Zia was very careful in building up his popularity and extensively toured the country to explain and gain support for his rural mobilisation,[100] *gram sarkar* (village government) and canal digging programs.[101] The regime termed these programs as the 'first phase of the revolution' to involve the rural masses in development activities.[102] Zia spent several days each month in the rural areas,[103] walked miles to reach the villagers, listened to the problems of the masses and the local officials and very often said 'I shall make politics difficult for the politicians...'. What he meant was, '...to be a politician one has to come down to the villages – the heart of the country, in order to meet the masses rather than to participate in what is popularly called 'palace politics''.[104]

Zia became founder and chairperson of the newly emerged BNP. Political figures from diverse and contradictory ideological backgrounds gathered in the party to share power and positions. It recruited retired military personnel, businesspeople, retired civil servants, and political leaders of leftist, rightist, liberal and Islamic orientations. Because of this, the BNP had to suffer factional feuds from the very beginning.

Zia was successful in both splitting major opposition political parties and attracting a reasonable number of opposition political personalities to join his own political party.[105] His strategy was not to eliminate the political parties but to win their support by dividing them. The Islamic rightist political parties, which were banned by Mujib for their anti-Bangladesh role during the liberation war were resurrected and were patronised by Zia to serve as 'a good antidote to both the leftists and the centrists...'.[106] He successfully exploited the Islamic sentiments of the people for his partisan benefit. The religion-based parties kept Zia under constant pressure but he needed their support to strengthen his base. He kept them in good humour by announcing that the country would be declared an 'Islamic republic', and promised the insertion of Islamic provisions in the constitution.[107] This strategy not only achieved the support of the religion-based local parties but also received a favourable response from the conservative Muslim countries.

Zia was successful in using the military and civil bureaucracy for political purposes. He appointed like-minded military personnel in key administrative positions. Military officers involved in the assassination of Mujib were rewarded with diplomatic positions in foreign missions.[108] Although Zia himself was a freedom fighter and personally honest, he tolerated and sheltered corruption by his party-officials[109] and included people in the ministry who were known to be collaborating with the Pakistani military in 1971.[110] On the other hand, he was exceptionally careful about nepotism, as this had been one of the prime reasons for Mujib's failure to control corruption in administration. Zia wanted to prevent his relatives from taking advantage of his position. He disassociated himself even from his brothers so that his political enemies were precluded from accusing him of favouritism – a move which helped him build a favourable image among the common people.

In spite of these accomplishments, Zia was lucky to quash sixteen military coups after coming to power, but ultimately was assassinated by a group of army officers in an abortive coup on 31 May 1981 in Chittagong. Zia's patronage of para-military organisations[111] and attempts to broaden his civilian base, which senior military officials often criticised as 'over-democratisation' of the polity, angered a faction of freedom fighters in the army who carefully plotted his assassination.[112]

The Sattar Interregnum

After the assassination of Zia, Abdus Sattar, his vice president, took over as acting president of the country. Although he won an overwhelming victory[113] in the 1981 presidential election as a BNP candidate, he continued in power for only four months, having failed to satisfy the high political ambitions of military generals. The military demanded a more direct role in politics and in national decision making. Sattar was initially reluctant to accommodate such demands by arguing that 'the army has a role to protect the sovereignty of the country and I do not think any other role is possible...'.[114] However, under extensive pressure from the army he had to give in and attempted to satisfy the military by involving them in the highest national policy making body, the National Security Council, and by dismissing 22 ministers for corruption and incompetence. Yet, these concessions did not satisfy the army, and 'fell far short of the military's expectations'.[115] Sattar was too old to effectively counter the military. He failed to consolidate the gains of the Zia regime and the support of the BNP was weakened by internal conflicts and factionalism within the party. The overall political situation worsened and favoured a military takeover.

The Military Takeover by General Ershad

Observers of Bangladesh politics predicted that after the assassination of Zia the military might take over power again.[116] Their assumption proved correct. After the abortive coup, the chief of army staff, Lt. General Hussain Muhammad Ershad (Ershad) allowed the normal constitutional pattern of political succession to occur and did not attempt to gain power immediately after the assassination. Politically shrewd, Ershad was aware of the popularity of Zia, which increased after his demise, and he therefore allowed the people time to forget their slain leader. His awareness of and eagerness for political power was revealed six months after the assassination, when he proposed a constitutionally-mandated more active role for the military in national decision making. In one of his articles, he argued,

> our military is an efficient, well disciplined, and most honest body of truly dedicated and organised national force. Potentials of such an excellent force in a poor country like ours can be effectively utilised for productive and nation-building purposes in addition to its role of national defence...This concept requires us to depart from the conventional western ideas of the role of the armed forces. It calls for combining the role of nation building and national defence into one concept of total national defence.[117]

He advanced towards political power with the interests of the military in mind as he knew that one of the major causes of Zia's assassination was his (Zia's) efforts at pursuing a strategy of shifting 'his power base from a military-bureaucratic-industrial combine to a mass-oriented institutional frame...'.[118] Ershad knew that Zia's success in obtaining legitimacy and stability, by concentrating on the development of rural people with the help of the donor countries was abhorred by the top military bureaucrats. This policy had been severely criticised in a meeting ten days before Zia's assassination.[119]

It was clear by late-1981 that the military was significantly involved in politics and Ershad, who became vocal after Zia's death, had been trying to become their spokesman by demanding a constitutionally legal role for the military in national decision making so that military coups could be prevented in future. He also emphasised the need for honest administration. Ershad was the most informed person about a large number of military coups during Zia's rule and he for his own political intentions wanted to unite the armed forces under his command. He pressured the Sattar government to meet his demand by suggesting that political stability in a country like Bangladesh would remain unrealised without the co-operation of the army.

Political parties strongly criticised General Ershad's claim, although not in unison.[120] and when Ershad siezed power in a bloodless coup on 24 March 1982 and performed the primary rituals of a Third World military coup, he encountered no marked opposition. The major opposition political party, the AL, led by Sheikh Hasina, Mujib's daughter, unexpectedly lent support to the military[121] while other political parties criticised Ershad for usurping power by unconstitutional means. But there was no immediate movement against the new military regime.[122]

Ershad declared martial law, political parties were banned, the constitution suspended and parliament dissolved. He justified his takeover by such reasons as:

> the national security, independence and sovereignty were threatened due to social and political indiscipline, unprecedented corruption, devastated economy, administrative stalemate, extreme deterioration of law and order and frightening economic and food crisis.[123]

Many of the reasons behind Ershad's coup resembled standard 'military explanations of military interventions in any Third World countries....'[124]

Style and Strategies of Ershad's Rule

Ershad did not have the charisma of either Mujib or Zia, nor was he popular among the common people; nevertheless he ruled the country for almost nine years. The style and strategies he followed to continue in power made this possible. In terms of legitimising his position and building political institutions he trod in the footsteps of Zia, though he had to face strong opposition throughout his tenure. As Zia was the first military ruler of independent Bangladesh, the mass of the people and younger political party activists were unfamiliar with the strategies usually employed by a military ruler.

Ershad emulated Zia's legitimisation process. It started with a referendum in 1985 and ended with parliamentary elections the following year. However, he failed to claim legitimacy because of BNP's boycott of any elections under his rule. He withdrew martial law in late-1986, almost five years after his coup. He announced an 18-point socio-economic reform program,[125] formed implementation committees at national and different regional levels and was successful in accommodating in his political platform opportunists and renegades from parties with varied orientations.

Administrative Decentralisation

The new government like its predecessors undertook a reform program in local government. From the outset, Ershad emphasised the reorganisation of local government along a policy of decentralisation. In his first speech, he stated that,

> we have to make a drastic change in the administration. We have to establish a new public welfare-oriented administrative structure

which will be able to eliminate the existing distance between the people and the administration. We are to ensure mass participation in administration, and overall we have to reorganise local administration as the servant of the people.[126]

Ershad's emphasis on administrative decentralisation received support because previous rural development and administrative reform experiments had failed to produce the expected results.[127] The local government system was reorganised and a new administrative unit, the *upazila* (sub-district), was created.[128] Among local political functionaries, the *upazila* and union chairmen were to be elected. The *upazila* elections were held in May, 1985 and these representatives came to occupy the top position (as chairman) of the *upazila* administration. The decentralised unit of administration thus achieved, at least theoretically, a representative character.

The real motive of the Ershad Government, however, was not to introduce participatory local governance; rather, the government's intention was to use the *upazila* to further its own political interests. The government expanded the bureaucratic machinery at the local level through the new system, and the activities of local-level bureaucrats were tightly controlled by the central bureaucracy. The respective ministers and divisions utilised 'highly centralised control mechanisms to direct and guide the activities of their officers working in *upazilas*...'.[129] The government was successful in attracting the rural population to this new administrative change and tried to involve them in its activities, although in reality, participation was limited to the elite class. Corruption, traditionally related to the bureaucracy and the judiciary, spread to the rural areas and had an impact on rural political culture.[130]

Militarisation of Administration

Ershad, wanting to continue in power with the help of the military and the bureaucracy, granted them a range of benefits. From the very beginning he favoured the former group, and tried to establish himself as a staunch defender of the military's interest and was successful in modernising the military intelligence network, and establishing discipline and chain of command in the politicised and polarised armed forces.[131] Ershad increased the number of military personnel, enhanced their status through promotions and pay increases, and provided them with subsidised rations and improved housing.[132] A large number of military officers were appointed to strategic positions in civil administration, public corporations and foreign diplomatic missions. In 1987 about 15,000 members of the armed forces were employed in high civilian positions in government.[133] In police administration, over 80 percent of superintendents of police (SP) in districts were former military officers.[134] The career bureaucrats were annoyed with this policy but did not protest in fear of reprisals.

The government tried to constitutionally legalise the participation of the army in the national decision making and development process. In 1987, the Local Government (*Zila Parisad*) Amendment Bill sought to restructure the existing *zila parisad*.[135] An officer from the armed services was to join the elected and nominated members and public officials on the council. This would ensure a place for the military in administrative and developmental activities in the district. It could also be perceived as the first phase in a process that would gradually culminate in the representation of the military in all the local councils in Bangladesh. The bill and its passage were condemned by all the leading opposition political parties who argued that the inclusion of armed services personnel in *zila parisad* would prevent the establishment of a democratic system in Bangladesh, and called upon patriotic forces to unite to oppose this move. Most of the opposition political parties and student organisations unitedly opposed the bill.[136] However, the prime minister, the minister for local government and the president himself defended the bill. When the concerted effort of the opposition political parties received a great deal of support from all sectors of the population, the president, sensing the gravity of the situation, withheld his consent and sent the bill back to the house for reconsideration and suggested that it should be thoroughly debated.[137] Thus the effort of the military government to please the armed forces by providing its officials with an opportunity to constitutionally take part in developmental activities failed. However, the government's policy of appointing more and more personnel from the armed services to key positions in the civil administration as well as public corporations continued.

Ershad's Political Ventures and Opposition to Military Rule

Ershad introduced several socio-economic measures. These measures strengthened the state and were to 'protect and flourish private capital and the privatisation process...'.[138] He, like other military rulers, wanted to civilianise his rule through elections and legalise his steps by constitutional means. His civilianisation strategy, similar to that of his military predecessor, was steered by an 18-point Implementation Committee and *Janadal*, a pro-Ershad political platform. But this arrangement of advancing towards civilianisation with the support of a party did not satisfy the military ruler; he floated his own political party, the *Jatiya* Party (JP) in 1983 to obtain legitimacy for his rule. Ershad, like Zia, had little difficulty recruiting a reasonable number of opposition political personalities for his new party. He also was successful in dominating the cabinet by frequently reshuffling it.

Several political alliances were formed in 1983 to challenge the military government. A 15-party alliance headed by the AL emerged early in the year[139] and another 7-party alliance led by the BNP was formed soon after.[140] Two others, a 12-party and an 11-party alliance of lesser significance also emerged known respectively as *Jatiya Oikya* Front (National Unity Front) led by Mushtaq and *Jatiya Jote* (National Coalition) chaired by Ataur Rahman Khan, a former chief minister of East Pakistan. At the same time several civil society groups supported the opposition's movement against the military government.[141] Fourteen labour organisations formed the *Sramik Karmachari Oikkya Parishad* (SKOP) and the lawyers, doctors, engineers, agriculturists, school teachers, and students also established their own committees to mount a strong challenge against the regime.[142]

Ershad began a political dialogue with different political parties to assess their attitude towards a constitutionally guaranteed role for the military. Almost all major political parties responded negatively arguing for 'this sensitive issue' to be resolved by the representative parliament.[143] Although the main 15-party and 7-party alliances had differences of opinion on some major constitutional issues, they agreed on the need to withdraw martial law and transfer power to a civilian government through free and fair elections.[144] They also agreed on a five-point demand which included restoration of fundamental rights, parliamentary elections preceding all other elections, release of political prisoners and the trial of persons responsible for the mid-February (1983) student killings.[145] Several people had died and hundreds of police and students were injured in student-police clashes.

The movement against Ershad gradually became popular and gained momentum. The first serious protest against the military government came from the students in symbolic form against the education policy proposed by the military government.[146] The students, encouraged by the opposition parties, engaged in street demonstrations and strikes. Universities were closed for indefinite periods and student and political leaders were arrested in large numbers.

Ershad tried to pacify the opposition by offering different concessions. His fourth announcement (since 1983) of parliamentary elections in December 1984 was rejected by the major alliances. They categorically refused to participate in any elections prior to the abolition of martial law. To obtain the co-operation of the opposition, he offered five concessions which included:

1. The posts and offices of martial law administrator (MLA) would be disbanded at the district level by early 1985;
2. Martial law tribunals and courts would be dismantled by the same dates;
3. The suspended constitution would be partially restored and those clauses dealing with fundamental rights and the writ jurisdiction of the High Court revived at about the same time;
4. The constitution would be completely reinstated and martial law withdrawn once the new assembly met; and
5. The cabinet would retain no political appointees once the election schedule had been established, and no standing cabinet member would be permitted to run for election.

Ershad agreed to another opposition demand of a presidential election to be held almost immediately after the *Jatiya Sangsad* elections.[147]

The government failed to achieve legitimacy through its electoral strategy as the BNP led 7-party alliance never participated in any elections under the Ershad government. The government however was successful in persuading the 15-party alliance to participate in the 1986 parliamentary elections. As a consequence, the popularity of the alliance, especially its leading member, the AL, plummeted and seven of its component parties withdrew from the alliance in protest against AL's unilateral decision to participate in the elections.

Agitation against the government increased with renewed vigour after the fourth parliamentary election in 1988 which was boycotted by both the major opposition alliances, although some small parties contested it. While Ershad realised his failure of achieving legitimacy by using elections as a tool, he tried to 'widen the regime's support through non-electoral means'. He, like other military rulers of Pakistan and Bangladesh, used religion as the 'trump' card. The Constitution (8th Amendment) Act (1988) was passed which recognised Islam as the state religion of Bangladesh although other religions could be freely practised.[148] Ershad thus wanted to win the support of the majority Muslim population of the country but the major opposition alliances and its leaders unmasked his political motive behind this strategy. The 7-party alliance leader, Khaleda Zia claimed that the 'illegal' parliament had no right to amend the Constitution, while Sheikh Hasina, the 8-party alliance leader, strongly criticised the amendment as 'a heinous move to destroy the spirit of liberation war and reunite Bangladesh with Pakistan...'.[149]

Although the AL and the BNP, the two major opposition parties, were committed to a strategy of non-participation in elections under the Ershad government and were united in demanding the resignation of Ershad, they differed regarding the form of government they wanted to establish if elected. The AL favoured a return to the parliamentary system under the 1972 constitution,[150] while the BNP wanted to retain the presidential system of Khaleda Zia's late husband Ziaur Rahman which was described as 'Ershadism without Ershad' by one analyst.[151] Ershad in 1990 was under pressure from the donor countries to hold free and fair elections 'that would have to be contested by at least one of the major opposition parties...'. Foreign diplomats initiated 'shuttle diplomacy' but were not successful in negotiating the problem. Khaleda Zia was strongly committed to her party's decision not to take part in any election under the Ershad government.

The student organisations formed the All Parties Student Unity (APSU) in November 1990 and pressured their parent parties to forge unity. As the *Economist* stated, they 'shamed the parties into cooperating'.[152] Under pressure from APSU and sensing the feeling of the masses as well as other socio-political groups, the opposition alliances and parties[153] announced the outline of a non-party caretaker government (NCG) and jointly demanded the resignation of Ershad, and a fresh parliamentary poll under an NCG. Three alliances jointly declared a four point formula to overcome the stalemate which included:

1. boycotting and resisting all elections under Ershad by the opposition parties and alliances;
2. the resignation of Ershad and handover of power to an NCG;
3. the restoration of the credibility of the electoral system and ensuring universal franchise by the NCG; and
4. the transfer of power to a 'sovereign parliament' elected through free and fair elections by the NCG.[154]

This joint declaration was supported by the civil society and took the movement to its peak.[155] The repressive measures including the imposition of a state of emergency were not enough to contain the opposition movement. As there was no other way to control the situation, Ershad resigned and handed over power to a government headed by the chief justice of the Supreme Court, Shahabuddin Ahmed, who took charge to hold parliamentary elections. Thus the second military rule in Bangladesh ended after almost nine years of dictatorial rule.

The Khaleda Regime

The BNP government came to power in 1991 through a fairly conducted fifth parliamentary election held under an NCG headed by Shahabuddin Ahmed. The major political parties in the new parliament except the JP agreed to restore parliamentary democracy in the country and passed the 12th amendment of the constitution.[156] Parliament met regularly and the committees worked effectively in the first three years. Although there were often tensions, the speaker was successful in maintaining order in accordance with the norms and traditions of parliamentary democracy.[157] Yet, in 1992, the Khaleda cabinet faced a no-confidence motion in the parliament which was defeated in the house.[158] This motion was supported by seven of the 10 opposition parties in parliament who explained that their motion was prompted by the deteriorating law and order situation and BNP's failure to curb terrorism.[159]

A parliamentary crisis erupted in March 1994, when the then information minister made a derogatory remark about the opposition and offended their religious sentiments. Opposition members took the matter seriously and the leader of the opposition demanded an unreserved apology from the minister. The leader of the opposition was supported by the JI and JP, whose members jointly walked out in protest.[160] This was followed by their continuous boycott of parliament.

Opposition Demand for an Election Under an NCG

In the aftermath of the Magura by-election, the opposition movement gathered momentum almost to the point of demanding the resignation of the government. The demand for an NCG was reiterated. The opposition pressured the government to introduce a measure in parliament to amend the constitution to ensure the establishment of an NCG to conduct future parliamentary elections. The ruling party criticised the opposition's demand and dismissed the proposal as totally against parliamentary norms and values.[161] It also branded the opposition demand as a conspiracy and called upon all democratic and nationalist forces to unite and resist it. The opposition was accused of 'trying to destroy the tradition of parliamentary democracy...'.[162]

The debate for and against an NCG divided the intellectuals and other professional groups. For example, more than 100 teachers of Dhaka University extended their support to the opposition's demand for an NCG to hold future parliamentary elections,[163] whereas another group of 213 teachers from the same university proposed strengthening the EC with more power and relying on the sincerity of the political leaders for free and fair elections.[164]

Other political leaders, professionals and academics also were divided in supporting or opposing the opposition demand. Some focused on the weak, irresponsible, unrepresentative, undemocratic and unelected characteristics of an NCG.[165] The opposition's stand and their programs were criticised as an attempt to depoliticise the country which could create a legal base for military or some other form of autocratic rule.[166] Others accepted the necessity of an NCG in certain situations and argued that the main aim of an NCG was to establish democratic government. The opposition demands were criticised and labelled as anti-democratic because they were being sought under a democratic government.[167]

The mainstream opposition parties presented the outline of an NCG and mobilised support for their proposal.[168] Under an NCG, the incumbent prime minister and the cabinet would resign with the announcement of the election schedules by the EC following the dissolution of parliament by the president according to the constitution. The president would then appoint a new prime minister either from among the serving and relived judges of the Appellate Division of the Supreme Court or a neutral non-partisan person to head the NCG. The caretaker prime minister would act as the chief executive of the government under Article 55 of the constitution, but would not be a candidate in the parliamentary elections. He would form a cabinet with 'neutral' persons who would not be members of any political party and who would not participate in the parliamentary elections. The main responsibility of the NCG would be to ensure free and fair elections and perform only emergency state functions besides its normal duty and responsibility as per constitutional requirements. The newly elected *Jatiya Sangsad* (National Parliament) would legalise this outline by constitutional amendment, which would include the provision of holding at least three parliamentary elections in future.[169]

The proposed NCG was criticised by the prime minister, Khaleda Zia, who condemned it as not being in accordance with the constitution and the principles of democracy.[170] She called upon the opposition to return to parliament and assist in refining the government's bill to strengthen the EC for ensuring fair elections for the sake of stabilising and institutionalising democracy, which was the primary demand of the opposition. The AL continued to rely on street agitation and strikes and the JP and JI supported its efforts to pressure the ruling party to accept what they called the national demand for an NCG. The *Gono* Forum chief, Kamal Hossain did not support the movement for an NCG and, as an opposition leader, criticised the mainstream opposition's claim that their demand was the demand of the whole opposition.[171]

The Left Front also criticised the demand of the NCG and called the proposal the result of an unholy alliance. It expected that the AL would secure its aims by excluding the autocratic JP and the anti-liberation force, the JI. The AL had to face severe criticism for its united stance with these two parties. A group of intellectuals were highly critical of the AL's understanding with JI, which a AL presidium member defended by arguing that it was part of their political strategy to isolate the ruling party.[172] The middle-ranking leaders and the workers of the party were not satisfied with this explanation.[173]

By August 1994, the distance between the ruling and opposition parties widened. The major opposition parties were threatened with court action unless they ceased agitation. The acting JP chief declared that the opposition movement would continue until the NCG was formed.[174] The BNP, applying different tactics, attempted to have the opposition rejoin parliament but without success. For example, in August and September, 1994 the deputy leader of the house held discussions with the deputy leader of the opposition, and also communicated with top JP and JI leaders in an effort to persuade them to return to parliament.[175] The conflict intensified when the opposition announced a program to blockade the capital. Hundreds of opposition political activists were injured in clashes between police and demonstrators. The AL leaders promised not to return home without achieving their demand, while the prime minister in a national broadcast over the state-owned electronic media urged the opposition to solve all problems through negotiation in parliament.[176] Strikes became more frequent which affected the country's economy alarmingly.

Political Stalemate and the Mediation Process

The ruling party and the opposition were firm in their stand which created a political stand-off in the country with profound implications for the country's economy. A mediation process by distinguished local and foreign personalities was unsuccessful. Among these dignitaries were: Emeka Anyaoku (Commonwealth Secretary General), Sir Ninian Stephen (former Governor General of Australia), Lord Wadiril (ex-Speaker of the British parliament), and Robin Raphel (US Assistant Secretary of State for South Asia). Also involved were diplomats from western countries, a group of local political personalities and five distinguished Bangladeshi intellectuals.[177]

Sir Ninian, as an envoy of the Commonwealth Secretary General, facilitated talks between the government and the opposition. Negotiations that lasted for more than a month finally collapsed in early November, when the two sides were unable to reach a consensus on the format of an interim government. The BNP proposed a 10-member interim government headed by the incumbent prime minister to conduct elections, but the opposition argued that the prime minister could not head an NCG as it was contrary to the concept of neutrality.[178] Instead, the opposition proposed an 11-member non-partisan caretaker government. According to their formula the president, in consultation with the leader of the house and the leader of the opposition would appoint an impartial person as head. A judge of the Supreme Court, a retired judge or any dignified person acceptable to both sides might head such a government. Of the remaining 10 members, also to be non-partisan, five each would be nominated by the leader of the house and the leader of the opposition. The head of the proposed NCG and members of his/her cabinet would not be permitted to contest the subsequent election. Their prime responsibility would be to ensure free and unrestricted voting.[179] None of the proposals was acceptable to the contending parties.[180]

Twenty-one different formulae were put forward for breaking the political impasse.[181] One suggestion by the incumbent information minister was for an interim government with the chief justice as prime minister and four judges of the Appellate Division of the Supreme Court as ministers to conduct parliamentary elections on expiry of the term of parliament. This proposal contradicted the official proposal submitted by the ruling party. Although he claimed that his scheme was based on personal views, he was highly criticised within the party and finally had to quit the cabinet.[182]

Another formula proposed by a well-known lawyer, Ishtiaq Ahmed, suggested impartial persons to form the NCG. It was widely discussed within political, diplomatic and intellectual circles before being rejected by both conflicting parties (for the full text of Ishtiaq's formula, see Appendix C).

The Widening Government-Opposition Hiatus

The opposition, after the collapse of the mediation process, intensified its movement. The ruling party, on the other hand, tabled an amendment bill to further empower the EC to hold fair and impartial parliamentary elections, mainly by way of using identity cards by voters.[183] The ruling party tried its best to attract the opposition back to the House but failed, the opposition rejecting its repeated pleas. To intensify their pressure on the government, the opposition legislators decided to resign *en masse* on 28 December unless their demand was met by the previous day. The leader of the opposition left her official residence on 25 December, and the opposition parties (the AL, JP, JI, & the NDP) presented their resignation letters to the Speaker. The prime minister asked the opposition to reconsider their resignations but in response the leader of the opposition demanded the immediate resignation of the prime minister reiterating that the BNP had no right to stay in power.[184]

The speaker delayed the process of accepting the resignations by saying that, 'since the matter is very complicated from constitutional as well as legal aspects and because it is of national importance, it is essential to examine the matter further and in greater details'. After 57 days, the speaker in a 29-page decision rejected 144 of the 147 letters of resignation[185] claiming 'these letters cannot be deemed to have been received by me as contemplated by Article 67(2) of the constitution...'.[186] The opposition leaders termed the speaker's rejection of the resignation letters of the opposition parliament members (MP) as illegal and unconstitutional. They considered his ruling as merely the implementation of a decision of the ruling party and condemned his delayed decision as a dilly-dallying tactic to prolong BNP's 'illegal rule'.[187]

Two petitions challenging the *en masse* resignations were submitted by the ruling party supporters, which according to the petitioners had a malafide intention to create a crisis and to mark time.[188] The petitioners challenged the validity of the resignations of MPs alleging that they had a political motive. The resignation did create a crisis when the speaker did not officially accept the petitions and explained that the resignations were designed to frustrate the democratic process and push the country into constitutional crisis with unpredictable consequences. In the meantime, the opposition's absence from parliament crossed the 90-day deadline and, as per the constitution, the opposition MPs lost their seats.[189] The president sought the opinion of the Supreme Court on this issue. The full bench of the court after hearing from eight top lawyers ruled that the seats of the boycotting MPs were vacant since the 90-day deadline had expired.[190] The speaker then declared the seats of the absentee MPs vacated from 20 June, 1995. Accordingly, the EC took the necessary action for holding by-elections. However, the mainstream opposition parties once again refused to participate in the by-elections and reiterated their resistance to such an 'anti-people' move at any cost. The EC postponed the by-elections when the ruling party also showed little interest.

The Federation of the Bangladesh Chambers of Commerce and Industry (FBCCI) was concerned about the impact of the stalemate on trade and commerce.[191] Street agitation and crippling strikes increased across the country by late 1995. Foreign investment, eagerly sought by the government, suffered and the donor agencies were dissatisfied with the non-implementation of projects they funded.

The overture of the US Assistant Secretary of State for South Asia to end the stalemate also failed.[192] The US Ambassador maintained contacts with top ranking leaders of BNP and AL,[193] and diplomats from six nations met Khaleda and Hasina on 16 January in an attempt to bring the ruling and the opposition parties at the mediating table to resolve the political crisis,[194] but were not successful. While these efforts of the Western diplomats were futile, the US still continued to express optimism. A Department of State spokesperson commented, 'we have no specific formula that we are advancing here for a settlement between the government and the opposition, but we remain hopeful that the political leaders of the country will together work out a resolution that moves democracy forward, that enhances the democratic process'.[195]

The prime minister and the leader of the opposition formally exchanged views but no solution was found. Seeing no way out of the crisis, the president dissolved the fifth parliament on the advice of the prime minister on 24 November 1995. The EC announced the schedule for the sixth parliamentary election and 15 February 1996 was set as the polling date.

A constitutional amendment was necessary to accept the opposition demand for arranging an election under an NCG. As opposition members resigned *en masse* from parliament the Khaleda government had no other constitutional way of accepting the opposition demand except by forming a new parliament through a fresh election. The government staged the sixth parliamentary election amidst opposition threat, won the 'farcical' election and formed government. The new parliament hurriedly passed the 13th constitutional amendment bill that paved the way for constitutionally forming the NCG. The president dissolved parliament, the prime minister resigned and a new NCG was formed to conduct the seventh parliamentary elections.

The Present Hasina Government

The AL, the single largest party in the seventh parliament, formed the government after 21 years in the wilderness with the support of the JP and the JSD (Rab faction). Hasina assumed the prime ministership and attempted to form a so-called 'government of consensus' and the JP and the JSD (Rab faction) responded to her invitation. The main opposition, the

BNP, and another major opposition party the JI, considered such a consensus, divorced from an ideological basis, absurd. Later, in late 1998, the JP withdrew its support by expressing solidarity with the main opposition although a faction of JP MPs continued to support the government splitting them from the main stream of the JP.

The repressive attitude of the government towards political opposition, and the frequent use of the electronic media for the benefit of the ruling party have not changed.[196] The opposition MPs have frequently complained about the partisan role of the state-controlled television. The bureaucracy has become highly politicised with partisan senior civil servants rewarded for their support for the regime. The law and order has deteriorated and human rights violations have increased significantly.[197] The US State Department in its Human Rights Report on Bangladesh accused the Hasina government of abusing the Special Powers Act (SPA) to harass its political opponents and restricting or denying fundamental rights of the people.[198] The report depicts Bangladesh as a lawless, violent and crime-ridden country where there is no security of life. The government rejected the report while the major opposition defended it.[199]

On the hustings, political violence reached alarming proportions; the 1997 local elections took the life of 84 people and over 4,000 were injured.[200] Police arrested a ruling party MP in mid-1999 for sheltering terrorists in his residence.[201] Electoral breaches continued unabated. Ministers violated the electoral code of conduct by openly campaigning for the ruling party candidates during by-elections.[202] The EC, under pressure from the opposition, had to take stern action against a section of the bureaucracy for its partisan role in conducting elections.[203]

Like its predecessors, the opposition BNP used *hartals* (strikes) as a weapon of protest against government repression and abuse of power.[204] But while its frequency has declined,[205] it continues to frequently paralyse the normal life in the country. The BNP maintains that its infrequent use of *hartal* is a token of its cooperation with the government, but until the middle of 1997 it did not use strikes as a political weapon mainly because of the apathetic attitude of the people towards such action.

The deteriorating relationship between the government and the opposition has been reflected in their statements, counter-statements and parliamentary debates. This relationship between the ruling and opposition parties has also been condemned by the members of Bangladesh Aid Group[206] who voiced their concern over the absence of good governance and political stability caused by growing intolerance, violence and confrontational politics, which were adversely affecting development.[207]

The AL government, despite its stated intention of deciding all national issues in parliament, has practically ignored the body on such matters. The government, for example, signed the Ganges Water Treaty with India and a Chittagong Hill Tracts (CHT) Peace Accord with *Parbattya Chattagram Jana Sanghati Samity* (PCJSS), the political wing of the separatist rebels, better known as the *Santibahini* ('peace force'), bypassing the parliament.[208] It further ignored the parliament or the parliamentary standing committee concerned when deciding upon matters of national interest including natural resources oil and gas, and purchasing MIG-29 jet fighters. The opposition has responded with a concerted campaign against the AL government, accusing it of 'misrule' and 'suppression'. An attempt by the opposition to force a mid-term election has become the main opposition issue since mid-1998. In another attempt in late November 1998, the ruling party initiated a 'no strike' deal with the opposition, which has straight away been rejected by the opposition parties. In January 2000, four major opposition parties have formed an alliance and started anti-government movement.[209] The opposition parties consider the AL government weak and compliant to Indian dictates, and by using anti-Indian sentiment the opposition has been trying to gain the support of the people.[210] They are gradually moving towards the extreme position of calling for the 'ousting of the government'.

Nor has the political situation been facilitated by the mid-1999 mud slinging between treasury and opposition bench members, personal attacks and counter-attacks and the use of un-parliamentary, provocative and abusive language on the floor. This lack of democratic relationship between ruling and the opposition parties was widened by the prime minister's irrelevant vituperative personal attack on the leader of the opposition in late November 1999, while she delivered the concluding speech in the fifteenth parliamentary session.[211] These new lows in parliamentary standards have damaged the image of both the House and the legislators. Moreover, such behaviour both exacerbates and reflects the confrontational culture of Bangladeshi politics and the consequent instability.

In July 2000, in the absence of opposition in the parliament, the government passed the Zila Parisad Bill which made provisions for indirect election and nominated administrators in this local body. Political analysts criticised this Act and branded it as undemocratic and unconstitutional.[212] A few columnists tinted the ruling party for what they called 'deceitful purpose' in this endeavour. They emphasised government's 'evil design' of exploiting the *zila parisad* to ensure ruling party's victory in the coming elections. One of them, highlighting the negative aspects of this Act, has underlined the violation of articles 9, 11, 59 and 60 of the constitution,[213] while another critic labelled the Act 'a farce' and claimed that it would ensure the influence of physical force and black money in the elections.[214] The major opposition leaders expressed their firm determination to initiate a mass movement for the scraping of the Act. Thus the recent trend of Bangladeshi politics points at further disagreement between the ruling and opposition parties, which might contribute to the deterioration of existing political violence and instability.

Election Commission

Like many other Asian countries the Election Commission (EC) in Bangladesh is the constitutionally recognised body for conducting elections. The EC is an independent, quasi-judicial body created under article 118 of the constitution consisting of a Chief Election Commissioner (CEC) and election commissioner(s) appointed for a five-year term. No minimum qualifications for appointment are needed, nor is the president required to consult anyone in the exercise of his power of appointment. Once appointed, the Commissioners like the judges of the Supreme Court are protected from arbitrary removal. Articles 118 and 119 of the constitution describe the composition and functions of the EC, its management, direction and control of the preparation of the electoral rolls and the conduct of the elections.[215]

The EC secretariat is the main office of the EC based at the capital. It is like any other secretariat or division of the government and is functionally an assisting executive division under the supervision and control of the prime minister's secretariat. The EC secretariat has one secretary, one additional secretary, two joint secretaries, five deputy secretaries, 17 assistant and senior assistant secretaries, one public relations officer (PRO), one assistant PRO and a research officer. The EC administers the elections through returning officers at the district level, assistant returning officers at the sub-district level and presiding and polling officers at polling centres. A training institute function to train those who conduct elections. Constitutionally the EC is an independent body but functionally it is dependent on the executive department of the state. The CEC cannot appoint, transfer or exercise any sort of administrative control over the officials of the EC.

Although the EC has the constitutional power of working freely as an autonomous body and it always proclaims its neutrality, allegations of the EC playing a partisan role is very common. This sort of allegation started since the first parliamentary election when JSD leaders demanded the resignation of the CEC. The neutrality of the EC was frequently challenged by the opposition parties during military rule when according to their claim the EC machinery was working under the dictation of the military juntas. Even after civilian succession, the EC had to face similar allegations. During a few by elections and the 'controversial' sixth parliamentary elections under the Khaleda regime and during by-elections in 15 constituencies during the present government the EC again was severely criticised for its partisan role.

The Landscape of *Hartal* and Confrontational Political Culture

The *hartal* (strike) is one of the prominent features in Bangladesh political culture that highlights disagreement between parties and damages economic development and political stability. It is a political instrument used frequently by the opposition to protest against the government or achieve selected demands by generating political pressure.[216] A *hartal* may be called by a single political party or jointly by a number of parties. Those organised on a specific issue at the regional level, such as a demand for constructing a bridge or road, sometimes may have the support of all political parties including even the indirect support of local level ruling party unit.

Student and labour fronts of parties play a leading role in organising a *hartal*. They promote a *hartal* through loudspeaker addresses, posters and by graffiti. Closing down shops, creating blockades on rail, roads and waterways, lighting fires on prominent road roundabouts and spreading terror by detonating home-made bombs are common events during a *hartal*. Organising processions, chanting anti-establishment slogans and direct clashes with the uniformed forces are some of the important characteristics of *hartal* politics. Congratulating the people after any anti-government *hartal*, irrespective of its outcome, has become a familiar tradition in *hartal* culture with the opposition claiming its success and the ruling party arguing that it was a failure.

Newspaper reports claim that the loss due to one day of *hartal* totals about *taka* 2,500,000,000 (US $52,083,333 at the present exchange rate).[217] The opposition parties recently (mid 1999) organised a few *hartals* to force a mid-term election accusing the ruling party of 'misrule' and 'suppression' of the opposition. Students and office staff are accustomed to *hartal* and plan in advance to utilise the break. The positive side of *hartal* is that it mobilises the leaders, workers and supporters and strengthens both links in the chain of command and organisational strength of the *hartal* organising party.

Conflict and confrontation play an important role in political socialization in Bangladesh, which contributes to shaping its political culture. As the Bengalis were ruled by different foreign nations including the Mughal, British and the Pakistanis, their lengthy struggle for freedom made them by nature comfortable in opposing any issue rather than agreeing to it. The history of Bengal reveals that the inhabitants and administrators of Bengal often opposed central domination, while more recent events display the failure of the Pakistani rulers to continue their political domination and economic exploitation of the Bengalis.

Both anti-British and anti-Pakistani movements were popular with the Bengalis. Many of them sacrificed their lives instead of accepting subjugation. This rebellious, uncompromising mentality of the Bengalis has not changed even after achieving independence in 1971. The popularity of opposition politics in post-1971 Bangladesh is a testimony to such obduracy. Opposition politics led by the NAP (B) and the JSD in the 1970s, anti-military movements headed by major opposition parties in the 1980s and anti-BNP and anti-AL movements during the 1990s were all supported by a large section of population. On the other hand, any initiative to build national consensus on major problems was virtually ignored by the political leaders nor did the people seriously support it. For example, in 1998 and 1999, the President of the country frequently proposed to ban violent student politics – which had resulted in many deaths – for the benefit of the nation, but neither the political parties nor the student leaders supported the President's proposal despite a literate section of the population supporting the ban.

Constructive criticism and compromise are important characteristics of a vital parliamentary system; indeed they contribute significantly to democratic decision making. Strong opposition not only plays a crucial role in the democratic performance of state affairs, it also inhibits the exercise of autocratic power on the part of the ruling authority. In Bangladesh, however, both the ruling and opposition parties show little respect for parliamentary 'rules of the game' and neither is willing to make reasonable compromises. Criticising a rival party's programs and policies, even when apparently beneficial for the country, is a standard practice for Bangladeshi politicians. Ruling and opposition party MPs maintain their antagonisms both within and outside of the parliament. A reading of the parliamentary proceedings reveals continual confrontation between rival party legislators which, in most cases, results in walkouts. Publishing statements and counter-statements in newspapers has become a routine affair while destructive and vituperative personal attacks and counter-attacks in a provocative style are a routine feature of the Bangladesh parliament. The hostility between the PM and the Leader of the Opposition has not only been mirrored in the attitudes and behaviour of their respective party members and followers, but it has also exacerbated the problems of political stability and institutionalisation of democracy in Bangladesh. Lack of tolerance and mutual respect among national leaders, opposition demonstrations, strikes, counter-strikes and political violence etc., contribute to the continuation of confrontational political culture in Bangladesh.

Summing Up

The undemocratic policies by the Pakistani rulers towards East Pakistanis contributed to the emergence of Bengali nationalism. The military junta's suppression of the Bengalis accelerated the disintegration of the country. The post-independent *Awami* League government's failure to control revolutionary activities, smuggling, corruption and its authoritarian attitude towards opposition took the country back to military rule.

The success of the first military ruler in using the military and bureaucracy, splitting opposition political parties and changing urban-based politics helped him consolidate his rule. His rural mobilisation policy, multi-party system, pro-Islamic and anti-Indian stand helped him strengthen his support base and legitimise his power. On the other hand, the second military ruler, Ershad, failed to civilianise his regime. By applying his policy of administrative decentralisation and militarisation of administration he did obtain some semblance of support from the local level but he failed to gain people's acceptance and thus political legitimacy. Although he ruled for nine years, the growing opposition to his regime ultimately forced him out of power.

The incoming BNP government faced allegations of poll rigging in several by-elections by the opposition, which demanded elections under an NCG and initiated an anti-regime movement. The government's 'undemocratic and unconstitutional' response to the opposition's demand for an election under an NCG and frequent general strikes caused the near-collapse of the economy. The government finally accepted the opposition demand through an amendment to the constitution.

The AL prevailed over the BNP in the seventh parliamentary elections but its attempt to form a government of consensus did not materialise. The law and order situation deteriorated, violence in local government elections increased, politicisation of the bureaucracy is more extensive and the dignity of the parliament decreased. The attitude towards opposition, the role of the electronic media, the politics of *hartal* and the landscape of confrontational political culture remains the same.

Notes

[1] Chakrabarti, D. K. (1992), *Ancient Bangladesh: A Study of the Archaeological Sources*, Oxford University Press, Delhi, pp. 22-30.
[2] See, 'The Permanent Mission of Bangladesh to the United Nations', internet home page.
[3] Chaudhury, A. M. (1967), *Dynastic History of Bengal*, The Asiatic Society of Pakistan, Dhaka, pp. 3-5.
[4] Huque, A. S. and Akhter, M. Y. (1987), 'The Ubiquity of Islam: Religion and Society in Bangladesh', *Pacific Affairs*, vol. 60, no. 2, p. 215. For the arrival and activities of the Islamic *sufis* in Bengal, see, Karim, A. (1959), *Social History of the Muslims in Bengal* (Down to A. D. 1538), The Asiatic Society of Pakistan, Dhaka; Haq, M. E. (1975), *A History of Sufism in Bengal*, Asiatic Society of Bangladesh, Dhaka; Rahim, M. A. (1963), *Social and Cultural History of Bengal*, Pakistan Historical Society, Karachi, pp. 72-73.
[5] As early as 1651 the British East India Company had established a factory in Bengal.
[6] Congress was mentioned as a Hindu-dominated political party by several researchers. For example, see, Choudhury, G. W. (1959), *Constitutional Development in Pakistan*, Longmans Green And Co., London, p. 137.
[7] Palmer, N. D. (1975), *Elections and Political Development: The South Asian Experience*, C. Hurst, London, p.178.
[8] Sayeed, K. B. (1967), *The Political System of Pakistan*, Houghton Mifflin, Boston, pp. 34, 44-45, quoted in Palmer, *Elections and Political Development: The South Asian Experience, op. cit.*, p. 322.
[9] Lumby, N. W. R (1955), *The Transfer of Power In India*, George Allen and Unwin Ltd., London, p. 72.
[10] Ziring, L. (1980), *Pakistan: The Enigma of Political Development*, Westview Press, Dawson, pp. 19-40.
[11] The new left writers used the term 'internal colonialism' in their writings, which mean the process of domination and exploitation of one ethnic group by another within a country. Later, a large number of academics used this term. For example, see, Jahan, R. (1973), 'Bangladesh in 1972: Nation Building in a New State', *Asian Survey*, vol. XIII, no. 2, 1973, p. 199.
[12] See for related information, Choudhury, *Constitutional Development in Pakistan, op. cit.*, p. 65.
[13] Under the separate electorate system, the voters were divided on a religious basis. Separate constituencies were set up for the different religious communities. Thus, Hindus, Muslims, Sikhs, Europeans, Anglo-Indians could vote under this system in the constituencies reserved for their religious communities. The Indian Act of 1935 retained the system of separate electorates which had been in operation in India since 1909. For detail, see, Choudhury, *Constitutional Development in Pakistan, op. cit.*, p. 45.

[14] For related information, see, Misra, K. P., Lakhi, M. V. and Narain, V. (1967), *Pakistan's Search for Constitutional Consensus*, Impex India, New Delhi, p. 7.

[15] Quoted in, Misra, Lakhi and Narain, *ibid.*, p. 15.

[16] Mohammad Ali Jinnah who was honoured with the title Quaid-i-Azam (the greatest leader) died on September 11, 1948, and Liaquat Ali Khan was assassinated in October, 1953.

[17] For related information, see, Choudhury, *Constitutional Development in Pakistan, op. cit.*, p. 262.

[18] For example, the disagreements between the leading political parties especially the Muslim League, Republican Party and national *Awami* Party came to a head in 1956-57. The Muslim League withdrew its support from Dr. Khan Shahib, although the Republican Party was able to maintain its majority in the Assembly and reshuffle the cabinet. Khan Shahib's ministry had lost its majority in the Provincial Assembly in March 1957. President Mirza suspended the constitution on March 21; Abdur R. Khan of the Republican Party became the new Chief Minister and continued until March 1958 when the NAP withdrew its support for the Republicans in favour of the opposition ML.

[19] For detail, see, Keesing's Research Report, *Pakistan: From 1947 to the Creation of Bangladesh* (1973), Keesing's Publications, New York, pp. 67-71.

[20] General Mohammad Ayub Khan claimed after his takeover on 7 October, 1958, '...we solemnly decided to build a true national Army free from politics', and he confirmed that Ghulam Muhammad when Governor General on several occasions asked the Army to take over the country, but the Army refused such offers in the hope that some politicians would rise to the occasion and lead the country to a better future.

[21] On the same day a few hours before Mr. Noon, the Prime Minister announced a cabinet reshuffle. AL decided to recall its six representatives in the government as a protest against this reshuffling and criticised his partisan attitude. See, Keesing's Research Report, *Pakistan: From 1947 to the Creation of Bangladesh, op. cit.*, p. 72.

[22] For related information, see, James, Sir M. (1993), *Pakistan Chronicle*, C. Hurst, London, p. 175.

[23] AL's six-point Programme included: a federal, parliamentary government for the country, transfer of all subjects except defence and foreign affairs to the provinces; separate but convertible currencies for each wing; all taxing power in the provinces which would make grants to the central government to fund its operations; separate accounting of foreign exchange earnings for each wing; and a separate militia for East Pakistan. See, Baxter, C. (1971), 'Pakistan Votes – 1970', *Asian Survey*, vol. XI, no. 3, p. 207. For a detail analysis of six-point programme, see, Jahan, R. (1972), *Pakistan: Failure in National Integration*, Columbia University Press, New York, p. 167-68; Rizvi, H. (1987), *The Military And Politics In Pakistan 1947-86*, Progressive Publishers, Lahore, pp. 180-81.

[24] For the full text of the address of General Mohammad Ayub Khan, see, *The Pakistan Observer*, 8 October, 1958.

[25] Quoted in, Singhal, D. P. (1962), 'Democracy with Distrust', *Australian Journal of Politics and History*, November, p. 203.

[26] Khan, M. A. (1960), 'Pakistan Perspective', *Foreign Affairs*, vol. 38, no. 4, p. 59.

[27] *Ibid.*, p. 550.

[28] *Ibid.*, p. 551.

[29] The number of the members of the electoral college was 80,000, 40,000 from each wing of Pakistan.

[30] The structure of Basic Democracy was four tier namely the Union Council, the Thana Council, the District Council, and the Divisional Council. For detail, see, Jahan, *Pakistan: Failure in National Integration, op. cit.,* p. 115.

[31] Misra, *Pakistan's Search for Constitutional Consensus, op. cit.,* p. 31.

[32] For related information and a criticism of Basic Democracy system, see, K. J. Newman, 'The Constitutional Evolution of Pakistan', *International Affairs,* July 1962, p. 359.

[33] Misra, Lakhi and Narain, *Pakistan's Search for Constitutional Consensus, op. cit.,* p. 31.

[34] Wallace, P. (1978), 'Centralization and Depoliticisation in South Asia', *The Journal of Commonwealth and Comparative Politics,* vol. XVI, no. 1, 1978, p. 8.

[35] Jalal, A. (1990), *The State of Martial Rule: the Origins of Pakistan's Political Economy of Defence,* Cambridge University Press, New York, p. 302.

[36] The Muslim League which had been banned with other political parties after the military takeover in October, 1958, was revived in June 1962, when the new National Assembly passed the Political Parties Bill, legalising the formation of political parties and their participation in elections. The ML split into three factions, one of which the 'Conventionists', favoured the party's revival on a broad basis and supported President Ayub Khan's government. The other two factions, the 'Council group' and the non-revivalists', maintained that the party could not be re-established pending the restoration of full democracy and allied themselves with the other opposition parties in demanding the democratisation of the new constitution. The Council Muslim League, however, joined the National Democratic Front formed in October 1962 and also supported by *Awami* League, the National *Awami* Party, the *Krishak Shramik* Party, and the *Nizam-i-Islam* Party. The Convensionists Muslim League assumed the title of the Pakistan Muslim League (PML) in order to become the sole inheritor of the parent body.

[37] When the National Assembly passed the Political Parties Bill on July 14, President Ayub Khan held a press conference on 20 July, at which he called on 'right-minded' Pakistanis to form a broadly-based nationalist political party with a progressive outlook, indicating that he himself might join such a party. For related information, see, Keesing's Research Report, *Pakistan: From 1947 to the Creation of Bangladesh, op. cit.,* p. 81.

[38] For Bhutto's outlook regarding negotiations, see, Bhutto, Z. A. (1971), *The Great Tragedy,* A People's Party publication, Karachi, pp. 21-26.

[39] For example, leaders like Nazimuddin, Mohammad Ali, Nurul Amin etc. believed in token Bengali participation. See, Jahan, *Pakistan: Failure in National Integration, op. cit.,* p. 193.

[40] *Pakistan Observer,* 4 January, 1971.

[41] In this process, Bhutto claimed that if a durable constitution was to be framed, there must be a broad consensus between the different regions of the country. No one party or region should impose its majority. Mujib declared that the constitution should be based on the six points alone. See, James, *Pakistan Chronicle, op. cit.,* p. 174.

[42] The struggle for independence of East Pakistan was called a liberation war by the East Pakistanis (Bengalis), but in the government controlled media in Pakistan it had been considered as civil war.

[43] See, *1997 Statistical Yearbook of Bangladesh* Bangladesh Bureau of Statistics, Statistics Division, Ministry of Planning, Government of the People's Republic of Bangladesh, 1998, Dhaka, p. 24.

[44] On 17th of April, 1971, the leaders of the AL who evaded arrest and the members of Parliament elected in the 1970 elections formed a Constituent Assembly in the small village of Baddayanatala (it had then been given the name Mujibnagar) near the Indian border in Kustia district. The Constituent Assembly adopted the Declaration of Independence and officially declared the independence and sovereignty of the People's Republic of Bangladesh and formed Provincial Government of Bangladesh. See for detail, Puchkov, V. P. (1986), *Political Development of Bangladesh 1971-1985*, Patriot Publishers, New Delhi, pp. 12-13.

[45] These parties were: *Jamaat-e-Islami*, the several factions of the Muslim League, the Pakistan Democratic Party, the *Nizam-i-Islam*, and the *Jamiat-e-Ulama-e-Islam*.

[46] The four major features of Indian model were (a) parliamentary democracy (b) a single dominant party system (c) a socialist pattern of economy, and (d) a secular ideology. See, Jahan, R. (1976), 'Bangabandhu and After: Conflict and Change in Bangladesh', *The Round Table*, no. 261, January, p. 74.

[47] The number of the *Mukti Bahini* was 100,000 – 200,000 belonging to various *Bahini*s (armed bands) owing loyalties to different parties and factions. See, Jahan, 'Bangabandhu and After: Conflict and Change in Bangladesh', *op. cit.*, p. 76.

[48] Maniruzzaman, T. (1975), 'Bangladesh: An Unfinished Revolution?', *Journal of Asian Studies*, vol. XXXIV, no. 1, p. 892.

[49] In the process of constitution making the Constitution Assembly Order was promulgated on March 23, 1972. The Constituent Assembly created a thirty-four member special committee headed by Law Minister Kamal Hossain and given the responsibility of drafting a constitution. The committee drafted a constitution within six months which was passed by the Constituent Assembly on October 12 and became effective on December 15. See, Jahan, 'Bangladesh in 1972: Nation Building in a New State', *Asian Survey, op. cit.*, pp. 202-203.

[50] Land holdings were limited to 100 bighas (1 bigha = 1/3 acre) per family.

[51] See, *Holiday*, June 9, 1974, quoted in, Maniruzzaman, T. (1975), 'Bangladesh in 1974: Economic Crisis and Political Polarization', *Asian Survey*, vol. XV, no. II, 1975, p. 119.

[52] *Ibid.*, p. 119.

[53] *Ibid.*, p. 119.

[54] *Ibid.*, p. 119.

[55] For a detailed discussion on the role of the leftist parties, see, Khanam, J. (1995), 'The Leftist in Bangladesh Politics: Crisis and Sequences', *Asian Profile*, vol. 23, no. 5, pp. 407-14.

[56] The *Jatiya Samajtantrik Dal* (JSD) formally emerged on October 31, 1972 under the leadership of A. S. M. Abdur Rab and Major (Retd.) M. A. Jalil. The party worked for the revolution through existing parliamentary institutions.

[57] Maniruzzaman, 'Bangladesh: An Unfinished Revolution?' *Journal of Asian Studies, op. cit.*, p. 903.

[58] About these four underground political parties, their activities and ideologies see, *ibid.*, p. 900.

[59] There were 26,500 men in the armed forces and the paramilitia were 29,000 strong. See, Janowitz, M. (1975), 'Military Institutions and Coercion in the Developing Nations', unpublished paper, quoted in Jahan, 'Bangabandhu and After: Conflict and Change in Bangladesh', *The Round Table*, op. cit., p. 76.

[60] *Jatiya Rakkhi Bahini* (JRB) or National Security Force, was a para-military force, the members of which were drawn from the AL-affiliated organisations. Sheikh Mujib created the JRB to provide support to the police or Bangladesh Rifles (BDR) to improve the law and order situation although in practice this force acted as a protective weapon of the ruling party and had suppressed the revolutionary opposition by its coercive means.

[61] See, Chaudhury, M. H., Hakim, M. A. and Zafarullah, H. (1996), 'Politics and Government: The Search for Legitimacy', in H. Zafarullah (ed.), *The Zia Episode in Bangladesh Politics*, South Asian Publishers, New Delhi, p. 21.

[62] See, *Morning News*, 5 November, 1973, quoted in Rahman, A. T. R. (1974), 'Administration and Its Political Environment in Bangladesh', *Pacific Affairs*, vol. 47, no. 2, p. 182.

[63] Akter, S. (1989), 'Political Murder Occurred During Each Government' (in Bengali), *Ashe Din Jai*, 27 August, p. 22.

[64] *The Bangladesh Observer*, 19 July, 1973, cited in Zafarullah (ed.), *The Zia Episode in Bangladesh Politics, op. cit.*, p. 21.

[65] Sub-divisions were later upgraded into Districts.

[66] *Morning News*, 16 August, 1973, quoted in, Rahman, 'Administration and Its Political Environment in Bangladesh', *Pacific Affairs, op. cit.*, p. 183.

[67] *Morning News*, 14 November, 1973, quoted in Rahman, *ibid.*, p. 183.

[68] *Morning News*, 3 August, 1973, quoted in Rahman, *ibid.*, p. 183.

[69] Factional schism both between old and young party leaders of the AL was visible in 1972 which became acute by 1973. The factional leaders were aware of Mujib's personal popularity and did not break away from the party as they believed that it would have been very difficult to survive as Mujib's opponent.

[70] For example, in September 1993, the AL regime appointed fourteen state ministers to 'keep the support of some of the factional leaders...'. In December, two more ministers were added to the cabinet for the same cause. See, Jahan, R. (1974), 'Bangladesh in 1973: Management of Factional Politics', *Asian Survey*, vol. XIV, no. 2, p. 129.

[71] For different divisions within the military, see, Hakim, M. A. (1998), 'Bangladesh: the Beginning of the End of Militarised Politics?', *Contemporary South Asia*, vol. 7, no. 3, p. 88.

[72] As a result of this operation 1,945 persons were arrested and 7,674 arms and 371,036 rounds of ammunition were recovered. See, Maniruzzaman, 'Bangladesh in 1974: Economic Crisis and Political Polarization', *Asian Survey, op. cit.*, p. 123.

[73] Wright, D. (1968), *Bangladesh: Origins and Indian Ocean Relations (1971-75)*, Starling Publishers, New Delhi, p. 140.

[74] Maniruzzaman, 'Bangladesh in 1974: Economic Crisis and Political Polarization', *Asian Survey, op. cit.*, p. 118.

[75] McHenry, D. F. and Bird, K. (1977), 'Food Bungle in Bangladesh', *Foreign Policy*, 27, Summer, pp. 72-88.

[76] For example, Mujib's own brother Sheikh Naser was engaged in relief corruption. See, Mamoon, M. and Roy, J. K. (1988), *Inside Administration* (in Bengali), Pallab Publishers, Dhaka, the chapter on Mujib regime. Also see, Lifschultz, L. (1975), 'Sheikh Mujib Pays the Ultimate Price', *Far Eastern Economic Review*, vol. 89, no. 35, August 29, p. 10.

[77] For example, see the speeches and statements of the General Secretary of NAP (Muzaffar faction) Pankaj Bhattacharya, NAP (Mozaffar faction) chief Mozaffar Ahmed, and another opposition leader Matia Chaudhury. For their statements criticising the Mujib government's attitude toward corruption, see, Alam, J. (1990), *The Trend of Leftist Politics in Bangladesh 1948-89* (in Bengali), Proteek Prokashona Shonghtha, Dhaka, p. 77.

[78] Barua, T. K. (1978), *Political Elites in Bangladesh: A Socio-Anthropological and Historical Analysis of Processes of their Formation*, Peter Lang, Bern, p. 80.

[79] See, Ziring, L. (1992), *Bangladesh: From Mujib to Ershad, An Interpretive Study*, Oxford University Press, Oxford, p. 93.

[80] As most of the 'arrested belonged to the AL and its affiliated organisation, district level AL leaders put pressure on the government to terminate the operation...'. See, Maniruzzaman, 'Bangladesh in 1974: Economic Crisis and Political Polarization', *Asian Survey, op. cit.*, p. 123.

[81] Maniruzzaman, *ibid.*, p. 123.

[82] The AL government on 29 November, 1973 announced a general amnesty for all the prisoners arrested under the Collaborators' Act. It is widely believed that such action was politically motivated.

[83] Chaudhury, Hakim and Zafarullah, 'Politics and Government: The Search for Legitimacy', in Zafarullahin (ed.) *op. cit.*, p. 21.

[84] Ahmed, M. (1983), *Bangladesh: Era of Sheikh Mujibur Rahman*, University Press Limited, Dhaka, p. 235.

[85] Maniruzzaman has learned from authoritative sources that the idea of a single party system was first sold to Sheikh Fazlul Haque Moni (Mujib's nephew and Chairman of the *Awami Jubo* (youth) League) and to Mansoor Ali (the Home Minister of the Mujib cabinet) by the USSR embassy. The pressure of these two, AL as well as other pro-Moscow leaders and Mujib's desire to subordinate the administrators propelled him to introduce a single party system. See, Maniruzzaman, T. (1976), 'Bangladesh in 1975: The Fall of the Mujib Regime and Its Aftermath', *Asian Survey*, vol. XVI, no. 2, p. 119-20.

[86] Most of the controversial Bills during the AL regime were passed without either eliciting public opinion or being sent to the Select Committees. For example, the Printing Presses and Publications (Declaration and Registration) Bill, 1973; the *Jatiya Rakhi Bahini* (Amendment) Bill, 1974; the Special Powers Act, 1974; the Special Powers (Amendment) Act, 1974; all were passed through unparliamentary means. See for detail, Choudhury, D. (1994), *Constitutional Development in Bangladesh: Stresses and Strains*, Oxford University Press, Oxford, pp. 120-21.

[87] Khan, A. K. (1972), 'People Deprived of Fundamental Rights', *Holiday*, August 20, quoted in Banu, U. A. B. R. A. (1981), 'The Fall of the Sheikh Mujib Regime – An Analysis', *The Indian Political Science Review*, vol. XV, no. 1, p. 9.

[88] Chaudhury, Hakim and Zafarullah, 'Politics and Government: The Search for Legitimacy', in Zafarullah (ed.), *The Zia Episode in Bangladesh Politics, op. cit.*, p. 20.

[89] Cited in, Zafarullah (ed.), *The Zia Episode in Bangladesh Politics, op. cit.*, p. 22.

[90] Favouritism and corruption of the Mujib family and regime received world-wide publicity. For related information, see, Mattern, W. (1975), 'Mighty Mujib's New Brand of Democracy', *Far Eastern Economic Review*, February 7. Syed Sirajul Islam also gave another description of Mujib's favouritism which shows Mujib's close relatives occupied significant political and administrative positions through

favouritism. See, Islam, 'The Rise of the Civil-Military Bureaucracy in the State Apparatus of Bangladesh', *op. cit.*, p. 32.
[91] Some academics called it a 'switchover to naked dictatorship'. For example, see, Banu, 'The Fall of the Sheikh Mujib Regime-An Analysis', *ibid.*, p. 16.
[92] Six junior officers led by Majors Rashid, Farooq and Dalim with three hundred men under their command staged the coup. See, Lifschultz, L. (1979), *Bangladesh: The Unfinished Revolution*, Zed Press, London, pp. 100-101.
[93] Lifschultz, L. (1979), 'The Intrigue Behind the Army Coup which Toppled Sheikh Mujib', *Guardian*, August 15, quoted in, Banu, *op. cit.*, p. 16.
[94] Lifschultz, *Bangladesh: The Unfinished Revolution, op. cit.*, p. 101.
[95] Maniruzzaman, T. (1975), 'Bangladesh: An Unfinished Revolution?' *Journal of Asian Studies*, vol. 34, no. 1, p. 123.
[96] For detail, see, Lifschultz, *Bangladesh: The Unfinished Revolution, op. cit.*, pp. 100-103; also specially see for the August coup, Maniruzzaman, T. (1980), *The Bangladesh Revolution and Its Aftermath*, Bangladesh Books International, Dhaka, pp. 178-91.
[97] Hakim, M. A. and Huque, A. S. (1994), 'Constitutional Amendments in Bangladesh', *Regional Studies*, vol. 12, no. 2, p.80.
[98] The 19 point programme included such objectives as (1) making the nation self-relient in every possible way, (2) ensuring the participation of the people at all levels of the administration, in development programmes and in maintaining of law and order, (3) strengthening the economy by according top priority to agricultural development, (4) ensuring that no one went hungry by making the country self-sufficient in food, (5) ridding the country of illiteracy, (6) curbing population growth, (7) giving women their rightful place in society, and (8) organising and inspiring the youth for building the nation. For detail, see, *Keesing Contemporary Archives*, 13-19 October, 1975, p. 28484; also cited in Zaman, M. Q. (1984), 'Ziaur Rahman: Leadership Styles and Mobilization Policies', *The Indian Political Science Review*, vol. XVIII, no. 2, pp. 194-203. For the full text of the 19-point programme see Appendix – D.
[99] Zia in September 1978 floated his own party the Bangladesh Nationalist Party (BNP). Earlier, he was associated with two political forums *Jatiyatabadi Ganotantrik Dal* (JAGODAL) and *Jatiyatabadi* Front (JF). Leaders of these platforms as well as of the BNP were a blend of political personalities from different and often contradictory backgrounds.
[100] General Zia undertook a number of measures to encourage rural reform toward the end of the 1970s and in the early 1980s. The most important measures were the establishment of a new Thana Development Committee (TDC) in each thana, composed only of elected Union *Parisad* Chairmen, the member of parliament for each district as District Development Coordinator (DDC), and the *Gram Sarkar* (Village Government) in each village of Bangladesh. For achieving self-sufficiency especially in food production President Zia undertook a nation-wide canal digging programme on self-help basis where he himself was 'usually the first man to start the spade'. Zia met thousands of villagers as well as members of the local bureaucracy through this scheme. See, Kamaluddin, S. (1980), 'Bangladesh: A Spadeful of Revolution', *Far Eastern Economic Review*, January 18, p. 24.
[101] For details on *Gram Sarkar*, See, Huque, A. S. (1984), 'The Problem of Local Government Reform in Rural Bangladesh', PhD dissertation, The University of British Columbia, Canada.

[102] Kamaluddin, 'Bangladesh: A Spadeful of Revolution', *Far Eastern Economic Review, op. cit.*, pp. 26-27; also quoted in Zaman, 'Ziaur Rahman: Leadership Styles and Mobilization Policies', *The Indian Political Science Review, op. cit.*, p. 201.

[103] One source cited by M. Franda remarked that in most months Zia was 'out of Dhaka for at least 15 days usually leaving the capital by helicopter after an early breakfast and returning just before dusk'. See, Franda, M. (1981), 'Bangladesh After Zia', *Economic and Political Weekly*, vol. XVI, no. 34, p. 1387.

[104] Zaman, 'Ziaur Rahman: Leadership Styles and Mobilization Policies', *The Indian Political Science Review, op. cit.*, p. 1.

[105] For example, among others Shah Azizur Rahman from the Muslim League and Mashiur Rahman Jadu Mia from the National *Awami* Party joined the BNP. Among the major political parties the National *Awami* Party (Bhasani), National *Awami* party (Muzaffar), *Awami* League, Muslim League, *Jatiya Somajtantrik Dal*, United Peoples Party etc. split during Zia's time.

[106] Ved, M. (1981), 'Bangladesh Under Ziaur Rahman: An Analytical Survey', *Foreign Affairs Reports*, vol. XXX, no. 9, p. 182.

[107] Zia made this announcement at an Islamic Conference in Dhaka. See, the *Daily Sangram*, 1 June 1979. Also cited in Ved, *ibid.*, p. 184. For both Zia and Ershad's strategy in using Islam as a political legitimisation tool, also see, Hakim, M. A. (1998), 'The Use of Islam as a Political Legitimization Tool: The Bangladesh Experience, 1972-1990', *Asian Journal of Political Science*, vol. 6, no. 2, pp. 98-117.

[108] For related information, see, Huque, A. S. and Akhter, M. Y. (1989), 'Militarisation and Opposition in Bangladesh: Parliamentary Approval and Public Reaction', *The Journal of Commonwealth and Comparative Politics*, vol. 27, no. 2, pp. 172-84.

[109] Zia tolerated political and economic corruption among his supporters. He tolerated abuse of power by some of his followers in 'such matters as procurement, electoral manipulation and allotment of residential plots'. See, Khan, Z. R. (1983), *Leadership in the Least Developed Nation: Bangladesh*, Maxwell School of Citizenship and Public Affairs, Syracuse University, Syracuse, p. 163.

[110] For example Senior Minister Mashiur Rahman Jadu Mia, Prime Minister Shah Azizur Rahman, Home Minister Lt. Col. Mustafizur Rahman, Textile Minister Abdul Alim, Dhaka Mayor Abul Hasanat, all were collaborators and played an anti-Bangladesh role during the liberation war. Mashiur had been arrested by the Mujib government after liberation, and Shah Aziz was a 'member of the Pakistani delegation to the United Nations where he vociferously opposed the liberation movement...'. For detail, see, Ved, 'Bangladesh Under Ziaur Rahman: An Analytical Survey', *Foreign Affairs reports, op. cit.*, pp. 183-84.

[111] By 1981, the paramilitary forces were approximately 150,000 strong. Cited in, Ahmed, S. (1989-1990), 'Politics in Bangladesh: The Paradox of Military Intervention', *Regional Studies*, vol. 8, no. 1, fn, 50.

[112] For related information, see, Franda, M. (1982), *Bangladesh: The First Decade*, South Asian Publishers, New Delhi, pp. 308-09.

[113] Justice Abdus Sattar won a landslide victory in the 1981 Presidential Election obtaining 65.5 per cent of the votes cast.

[114] Sen, D. (1981), 'Bangla Army Chief Insists on Role in Government', *Hindustan Times*, November 22, cited in Rahman, Md. A. (1982), 'Bangladesh in 1982: Beginnings of the Second Decade', *Asian Survey*, vol. XXIII, no. II, p. 150.

[115] Rahman, 'Bangladesh in 1982: Beginnings of the Second Decade', *op. cit.*, p. 150.

[116] For detail on Zia's assassination, see, Mascarenhas, A. (1986), *Bangladesh: A Legacy of Blood*, Hodder and Stoughton, London.

[117] See, Ershad, Lt. General H. M. (1981), 'Role of the Military in Bangladesh' *Holiday*, December 6. Also see, Ershad, H. M. (1979), 'The Role of the Military in Underdeveloped Countries', *Bangladesh Army Journal*, vol. 2, no. 2, pp. 1-12.

[118] See, Khan, Z. R. (1984), 'Bangladesh in 1981: Change, Stability, and Leadership', *Asian Survey*, vol. XXII, no. II, p. 165; also cited in Hakim, M. A. (1993), *Bangladesh Politics: The Shahabuddin Interregnum*, University Press Limited, Dhaka, p. 10.

[119] Several Major Generals in that meeting criticised Zia for his 'over-democratising' policy 'playing politics too much' and demanded that he reimposed martial law. For detail, see, Franda, M. (1981), 'Bangladesh After Zia: A Retrospect and Prospect', *Economic and Political Weekly*, vol. XVI, no. XXXIV, p. 1387.

[120] For criticism by different political parties over Ershad's proposal see, *Sangbad*, 30 November, 1, 2, and 3 December, 1981; *Holiday*, 3 January, 1982, cited in Hakim, *Bangladesh Politics: The Shahabuddin Interregnum, op. cit.*, p. 11.

[121] Zafarullah (ed.), *The Zia Episode in Bangladesh Politics, op. cit.*, p. 37.

[122] Kabir, B. M. M. (1985), 'Bangladesh Politics 1981-84: Military Rule and the Process of Civilianization', *The Chittagong University Studies* (Social Science), vol. VIII, no. 1, pp. 171-208.

[123] See, the first address of Lt. General H. M. Ershad, *The Bangladesh Observer*, 25 March, 1982.

[124] Rahman, 'Bangladesh in 1982: Beginnings of the Second Decade', *op. cit.*, p. 151.

[125] For the full text of Ershad's 18 point programme see Appendix E.

[126] See the first address of the Chief Martial Law Administrator Lt. General H. M. Ershad, *The Bangladesh Observer*, 25 March, 1982.

[127] Previous rural development and administrative reform programmes included the Community Development Programme of 1950, the Village Agricultural and Industrial development Programme (V-Aid) of 1953, the Green Revolution of 1960, the Integrated Rural Development Programme (IRDP) of 1962, the Food For Works Programmess (FWP) of 1972, the Area Development Approach of 1976 (the programme was aimed at the employment of poor women), and the Self-Reliance Movement of 1976. For detail, see, Nazem, N. I. (1985), 'Approach to Decentralise Development in Bangladesh: An Examination of Its Efficacy', unpublished Masters Thesis, The Asian Institute of Technology, Bankok, pp. 27-28, quoted in Nazem, N. I. (1978), 'Strategy For Rural Development in Bangladesh: A Review', *BISS Journal*, Bangladesh Institute of International and Strategic Studies, vol. 8, no. 1, pp. 110-11.

[128] Upazila Parisad and Upazila Administrative Reorganisation (Third Amendment) Ordinance, 1983, provided details of the structure and functions of the new council.

[129] Khan, M. M. (1987), 'Politics of Administrative Reform and Reorganization in Bangladesh', *Public Administrative and Development*, vol. 7, no. 4, p. 361.

[130] For related information see, Akhter, M. Y. (1990), 'Socio-political Impact of Administrative Decentralization in Bangladesh', *Asian Profile*, vol. 18, no. 3, pp. 265-77.

[131] It is relevant here to mention that armed forces were split 'along many cleavages such as those between the officers and the jawans (ordinary soldiers), junior and senior officers, pro-Indians and anti-Indians, freedom fighters and repatriates stranded in Pakistan during the liberation war...'. See, Hakim, M. A. (1991), 'Legitimacy crisis

and United Opposition: The Fall of Ershad Regime in Bangladesh', *South Asia Journal*, vol. 5, no. 2, p. 183.

[132] Islam, S. S. (1988), *Bangladesh: State and Economic Strategy*, University Press Limited, Dhaka, p. 164.

[133] Hasanuzzaman (1991), *Militarisation of State and Government* (in Bengali), University Press Limited, Dhaka, p. 41, cited in Hakim, *Bangladesh Politics: The Shahabuddin Interregnum, op. cit.*, p. 13.

[134] Huque and Akhter, 'Militarisation and Opposition in Bangladesh: Parliamentary Approval and Public Reaction', *op. cit.*, p. 184.

[135] The *Zila Parisad* (district council), one of the oldest local government institutions in the country is entrusted with mainly administrative and developmental tasks within a district. At present there are 64 districts in Bangladesh.

[136] The political parties called for a general strike on 13 July, 1987 and observed a 'black day' on 14 July. Twenty-two student organisations observed strikes and announced their opposition to the bill.

[137] For related information, see, Akhter, M. Y. (1991), 'The Politics of Decentralization in Bangladesh', *Indian Journal of Politics*, vol. XXV, no. 2-3, pp. 124-25.

[138] For related information, see, Kabir, B. M. M. (1987), 'Movement and Elections: Legitimisation of the Military Rule in Bangladesh', unpublished paper presented at the seminar held on the occasion of the Fifth National Conference of the Bangladesh Political Science Association, 13-14 July, Rajshahi University, Bangladesh, p. 2.

[139] The 15-party alliance included among others, National *Awami* Party (NAP-Muzaffar), Communist Party of Bangladesh (CPB), Bangladesh *Krishak Sramik Awami* League (BKSAL), *Ganatantri Dal*, Workers Party, *Shammabadi Dal* and *Jatiya Ekota* Party. All the constituent parties of this alliance were centrist and leftist parties. See, Hakim, *Bangladesh Politics ; The Shahabuddin Interregnum, op. cit.*, p. 19.

[140] The 7-party alliance included both leftist and rightist parties. The United People's Party (UPP-Arefin) and Communist League were left-wing and the *Jatiya* League and *Krishak Shramik* Party were rightist parties. See, *ibid.*, p. 19.

[141] For example, the Supreme Court Bar Association in October 1982 took a stand against the judicial decentralisation policy of the military government. Several student organisations formed the Student Action Committee (SAC) which protested against the education policy of the government and launched an anti-martial law mass movement. Fourteen labour organisations formed *Sramik Karmachari Oikkya Parishad* (SKOP) in early 1984 which strengthened the movement of the opposition alliances by participating in their activities. See, Kabir, 'Movement and Elections: Legitimisation of the Military Rule in Bangladesh', *op. cit.*, p. 6.

[142] Kabir, 'Movement and Elections: Legitimisation of the Military Rule in Bangladesh', *op. cit.*, pp. 8-9.

[143] See, Rahman, Md. A. (1984), 'Bangladesh in 1983: A Turning Point for the Military', *Asian Survey*, vol. XXIV, no. II, pp. 240-49.

[144] The 15 party alliance advocated parliamentary system of government as it was before the fourth amendment of the constitution while the 7 party alliance wanted the revival of the pre-martial law presidential system. See, Hakim, *Bangladesh Politics: The Shahabuddin Interregnum, op. cit.*, p. 19.

[145] Rahman, 'Bangladesh in 1983: A Turning Point for the Military', *op. cit.*, p. 242.

[146] The proposed education policy made Arabic and English compulsory subjects at primary and secondary levels. See, Ziring, *Bangladesh: From Mujib to Ershad, An Interpretive Study, op. cit.*, p. 157.

[147] See, Bertocci, P. J. (1986), 'Bangladesh in 1985: Resolute Against the Storms', *Asian Survey*, vol. XXV, no. II, pp. 224-34.

[148] For related information, see, Hakim, 'Legitimacy Crisis and United Opposition: The Fall of Ershad Regime in Bangladesh', *op. cit.*, p: 189.

[149] *Far Eastern Economic Review*, 23 June, 1988, p. 14, cited in Hakim, *ibid.*, p. 189.

[150] In 1975 Sheikh Mujibur Rahman, the father of Sheikh Hasina installed one party rule and the presidential system of government through the 4th Amendment of the constitution.

[151] Baxter, C. (1991), 'Bangladesh in 1990: Another New Beginning?', *Asian Survey*, vol. XXXI, no. II, p. 148.

[152] Baxter, *ibid.*, p. 150.

[153] The main alliances were a 7-party, a 8-party and a 5-party alliances respectively led by Khaleda Zia, Sheikh Hasina and Rashed Khan Menon, and independently *Jamaat-e-Islami* Banglasesh also played a strong role against Ershad.

[154] *The Bangladesh Observer*, 20 November, 1990. Cited in Hakim, 'Legitimacy Crisis and United Opposition: The Fall of Ershad Regime in Bangladesh', *op. cit.*, p. 190.

[155] For example, journalists, doctors, lawyers, engineers, artists, civil servants, university teachers and professional groups supported the joint declaration. See, Hakim, *ibid.*, p. 190.

[156] For a detail discussion on 12th amendment, see, Hakim, M. A. (1992), 'Twelfth Constitutional Amendment: Bangladesh's Reversion to Parliamentary System', *Asian Profile*, vol. 20, no. 3, 1992, pp. 251-61.

[157] For related information, see, *Bangladesh Parliamentary Elections June 12, 1996, The Report of the Fair Election Monitoring Alliance (FEMA)* (1996), FEMA, Dhaka, p. 96.

[158] Salauddin Kader Chowdhury of the National Democrat Party (NDP), *Islami Oikkyo Jote* (IOJ) member Maolana Obaidul Haq, two other independent members, five members of AL, four members of JP, and the *Jamaat-e-Islami* with its 20 members were absent during voting. Besides, two seats were vacated due to death of two AL MPs. A BNP MP was abroad and BNP's Sheikh Razzak Ali, being the Speaker could not vote. See, Q A Tahmina, P. Gain and S. Moral (eds) (1995), *The Reporters Guide: Handbook on Election Reporting*, Society for Environment and Human Development (SHED), Dhaka, p. 136.

[159] Sarker, A. and Begum, D., 'Fifth Parliament at a Glance', included in Tahmina, Gain and Moral (eds), *ibid.*, pp. 136-37.

[160] The AL MP was Abul Hasan Chowdhury. Chowdhury also demanded that the House discuss the killing of Palestinian Muslims by an Israeli settler on the West Bank. The Deputy Leader of the House Badruddoza Chowdhury requested the speaker to expunge the comment of the Information Minister but failed to bring the opposition members back to the parliament.

[161] The Minister for Home and Works Rafiqul Islam Mia expressed such a view while he was interviewed by BSS. See, *Inquilab*, 11 May, 1994.

[162] It was Energy and Mineral Resources Minister Khondokar Mosharraf Hossain. He expressed such views on June 3, 1994 in his address as the chief guest of a discussion meeting on 'The Future of Parliamentary Democracy in Bangladesh', organised in connection with the observance of the 13th death anniversary of President Ziaur Rahman at Dhaka. See, *The Bangladesh Observer*, 4 June, 1994.

[163] *The Bangladesh Observer*, 4 June, 1994.

[164] *Inquilab*, 5 June, 1994.

90 Electoral Corruption

[165] See, Hossain, F. (1996), 'Caretaker Government and the Possibility of Democracy in Bangladesh'(in Bengali), *Lokaoto*, vol. XVI, no. 3, July, pp. 21-25; Huq, M. M. (1994), 'Elections in Bangladesh: Predicaments and Prospects', *Politics, Administration and Change*, no. 22, January-June, pp. 12-25.

[166] *Ibid.*, p. 23.

[167] Chowdhury, A. N. M. M. (1994), 'The Aspect of Caretaker Government, Election and Election Commission: Bangladesh Perspective' (in Bengali), an unpublished paper presented in a seminar organised by the Chittagong University Research Council, 12 June at Chittagong District Council Auditorium, p. 9; for further criticism of the NCG as a permanent institution for holding elections, see, Akhter, M. Y. (1997), 'Caretaker Government and Election: A New Crisis (in Bengali), *Swadesh Barta*, 25 April.

[168] The mainstream opposition outlined of the NCG in a press briefing on June 28, 1994. AL chief and the leader of the opposition Sheikh Hasina was the chief spokesperson while Abdus Samad Azad, Tofail Ahmed and Rahmat Ali of AL; Moudud Ahmed, Kazi Zafar Ahmed and Anwar Hossain of JP; Maulana Matiur Rahman Nizami, Maolana Abdus Sobhan, Sheikh Ansar Ali and Latifur Rahman of JI; Salauddin Kader Chowdhury of NDP and Suranjit Sengupta of *Gonotantrik* Party were present. The MPs of Gono Forum, Workers Party and *Islami Oikko Jote* were absent during the press briefing. The GF had 3 and WP and IOJ each had one member in the parliament. See, *Inquilab*, 29 June, 1994.

[169] *The Bangladesh Observer*, 29 December, 1994.

[170] *Inquilab*, 30 June, 1994.

[171] *Inquilab*, 28 June, 1994.

[172] See, *Sangbad*, 12 August, 1994.

[173] *Sangbad.*, 15 August, 1994.

[174] *Sangbad*, 12 August, 1994.

[175] See, *Sangbad*, 4 September, 1994.

[176] *Sangbad*, 22 September, 1994.

[177] These five Bangladeshi intellectuals were: a distinguished journalist Faiz Ahmed, a constitutional expert Ishtiaq Ahmed, an ex chief justice Kamaluddin Hossain, an ex bureaucrat and adviser of the Shahabuddin caretaker government Fakruddin Ahmed and a member of Planning Commission under the Mujib Government, Rehman Sobhan. This group also known as G-5 was not acceptable as a negotiating agent to JI and JP, the two major political parties of the mainstream opposition.

[178] Beside the PM, five members of the proposed cabinet would be nominated by the government and the opposition would nominate the remaining four members.

[179] *The Bangladesh Observer*, 18 November, 1994.

[180] Sir Ninian, although he came with an optimistic attitude, left Dhaka on 21 November, his attempts at mediation having failed. See, Ahmed, S. (1995), 'Opposition's Cold Response to Dialogue Offer', *Dhaka Courier*, vol. 11, issue, 42, 19 May, p. 8.

[181] See, *Deshchinta*, vol. 1, no. 4, 17 July, 1995.

[182] See, *The Bangladesh Observer*, 6 November, 1994.

[183] Under the identity card system no ballot paper would be issued to a voter in a polling station unless the voter presented a genuine identity card issued by the EC.

[184] *The Bangladesh Observer*, 30 December, 1994.

[185] The Speaker accepted three resignation letters of former President and JP chairman H. M. Ershad, lone member of the NDP Salauddin Kader Chowdhury and AL member Dabirul Islam.

[186] Article 67 (2) of the constitution of the People's Republic of Bangladesh runs as follows: 'A member of parliament may resign his seat by writing under his hand addressed to the Speaker, and the seat shall become vacant when the writing is received by the Speaker or if the office of the speaker is vacant or the Speaker is for any reason unable to perform his functions, by the Deputy Speaker'. For the full text of Speaker's ruling, see, *The Bangladesh Observer*, 24 and 25 February, 1995.

[187] *The Bangladesh Observer*, 24 February, 1995.

[188] The petitions were filed by advocates Towfiqul Hossain and Alauddin Khaled.

[189] For related information, see, Article 67 (1) b of the Bangladesh Constitution; also cited in *Dhaka Courier*, 'Parliament: The 90 Day Crisis', 23 June, 1995, p. 8-9.

[190] The full bench of the court comprised Justice ATM Afzal, Chief Justice, Justice Mustafa Kamal, Justice Latifur Rahman, Justice Muhammad Abdur Rauf, and Justice Ismailuddin Sarker. The top 8 lawyers were: Attorney General of Bangladesh, the President of the Supreme Court Bar Association, S. R. Pal, Asrarul Hossain, Syed Ishtiaq Ahmed, Kamal Hossain, Khondokar Mahbubuddin Ahmed and Rafiqul Huq. See, *The Bangladesh Observer*, 7 July, 1995.

[191] The conference was presided over by FBCCI President Salman F. Rahman.

[192] Robin Raphel had extensive talks with both the PM and the leader of the opposition in the first week of September, 1995.

[193] David Merill had a long discussion with Commerce and Information Minister Shamsul Islam and AL presidium member Amir Hossain Amu on 3 January, 1996. He also spoke with AL leader Tofail Ahmed on 10 January, 1996.

[194] They were: US Ambassador, British High Commissioner, Japanese Ambassador, Canadian High Commissioner, Australian High Commissioner and Italian Ambassador. See, *The Bangladesh Observer*, 17 January, 1996.

[195] *The Bangladesh Observer*, 19 January, 1996.

[196] The parliamentary debates of the late 1996 and early 1997 contain such allegations. The Mayors of Khulna and Rajshahi City Corporations in a joint press conference at Khulna Press Club on 1 November 1997 alleged that their interview earlier taken for BTV was wrongly presented on 28 October. They condemned the interviewer's political motive and stated 'none had any right to put the neutrality of BTV on question mark (*sic*) by twisting the truth'. See, *The Daily Star*, 2 November 1997.

[197] Police torture increased at a horrifying rate; 85 persons died due to police torture in police custody in two years of AL rule. See, *The Independent*, 28 and 29 July, 1998. Also see, Chowdhury, R. (1998), 'Police Brutality', *Dhaka Courier* (internet edition), vol. 15, issue 1, July 31; Also see the reports of the Coordinating Council for Human Rights in Bangladesh (CCHRB).

[198] The Home Minister informed parliament that the government arrested 692 people under the SPA till 1 October, 1998. See *The Daily Star* (internet edition) 16 November, 1998.

[199] Bangladesh protested the release of the report by US embassy at Dhaka in a press conference without prior permission of the government. The US ambassador was summoned to the foreign office and handed the protest in an aide memoir on 4 February 1998. On the other hand the major opposition, the BNP, defended the report. The BNP's Secretary General in a statement said, 'the US report on Human Rights situation in Bangladesh has reflected only a small portion of the human rights abuses resulting from the government sponsored killings, harassment, persecution and oppression against political opponents, and extreme deterioration of law and order in the country'. See, *The Daily Star* (internet edition), 5 and 9 February, 1998.

[200] See, Rahman, H. Z. (1998), 'Union Elections ! A Postscript', *Holiday*, 13 January. Also see, the report of the FEMA (1998), Union Parisad Elections, 1997, FEMA, Dhaka; and the report of the Coordinating Council for Human Rights in Bangladesh (CCHRB) on UP elections.

[201] See, *The Daily Star*, 29 May, 1999.

[202] For example, the CEC expressed his dissatisfaction with the involvement of the ministers in campaigns during the Barisal and Pabna by-elections. See, *The Daily Star* (internet edition), 7 December, 1998.

[203] The CEC found the returning officer of the Pabna-2 by-election playing a partisan role and removed him from his responsibility. See, *The Daily Star* (internet edition), 8 December, 1998. Irregularities of similar nature were detected in November 1999 during the by-election at Tangail-8. See, *Prothom Alo*, 19 November, 1999.

[204] Arresting the opposition activists by using the Special Powers Act and filing a large number of court cases were two widely used strategies of government repression. The prime minister Hasina announced that 69 corruption cases were being filed against former prime minister Khaleda Zia, members of her family, and former ministers of her cabinet. See, *Keesing's Record of World Events*, vol. 44, no. 4, 1998, p. 42198.

[205] It has been reported that in the first year of the BNP rule the AL organised 57 days of strikes (the AL in total had 173 days of strikes during the BNP rule) whereas in the first year of AL rule the BNP observed 2 days. See, *The Daily Star* (internet edition), 29 August, 1997 and 20 November, 1998. Later, the BNP raised the rate of strikes during 1998- 1999.

[206] The Group comprised 15 countries and 12 international development agencies. See, *The Daily Star* (internet edition), 6 November 1997.

[207] World Bank Vice President for South Asia Meiko Nishimizu expressed such comments. See, *The Daily Star* (internet edition), *ibid.*; The donors in a joint statement were of a similar view. The statement was signed by heads of the delegations of US, UK, Japan, European Commission, Australia, Belgium, Canada, Denmark, France, Germany, Italy, Netherlands, Norway, Sweden, and Switzerland.

[208] For a detail analysis of the CHT peace accord see,. Rashiduzzaman, M. (1998), 'Bangladesh's Chittagong Hill Tracts Peace Accord: Institutional Features and Strategic Concerns', *Asian Survey*, vol. XXXVIII, no. 7, pp. 653-70.

[209] These four parties are the Bangladesh Nationalist Party, *Jatiya* Party, *Jamaat-e-Islami* Bangladesh and the *Islami Oikya Jote*.

[210] BNP Chairperson and former prime minister Khaleda Zia alleged that the government was trying to hand over the Chittagong Hill Tract by signing a treaty with PCJSS. Such move should be stopped, if needed, at the cost of blood, she added. Begum Zia was addressing a grand rally at the Chittagong outer stadium organised by the *Sammalito Birodhi Dal* (united opposition). She said 'AL government, whenever it had the scope, signed anti-people and anti-state agreements with India. This government is run under the dictation of India as it wanted to remain in power with that country's blessing...'. See, *The Daily Star* (internet edition), 12 November, 1997.

[211] Prime minister's speech was highly criticised in the print media. For Example of some features published in Bengali, see, Khan, A. (1999), 'Please Don't Speak Like This' (in Bengali), *Prothom Alo*, 15 November; Hossain, S. (1999), 'We are Ashamed, the Nation Astonished, What About You?'(in Bengali), *Sangbad*, 12 November; Hossain, M. (1999), 'Sick Politics and the Educated Class' (in Bengali), *The Daily*

Ittefaq, 14 November; Kaium, A. (1999), 'The Prime Minister has Actually Disrespected Herself' (in Bengali), *Prothom Alo*, 15 November; Musa, A. B. M. (1999), 'Manners have Weathered Away from Politics' (in Bengali), *Bhorer Kagoj*, 14 November.

[212] Ahmed, E. (2000), 'Why Zila Parisad Act is Anti-constitutional?' (in Bengali), *The Daily Ittefaq*, 20 July; —— (2000), 'The Zila Parisad Act 2000', *Dhaka Courier*, vol. 17, issue 52, 21 July, pp. 22-23; Mia, R. I. (2000), 'The District Council Act is Anti-constitutional: The Judicious Mind of the President Faces Question Consenting the Bill' (in Bengali), *Inquilab*, 19 July.

[213] Mia, *ibid*.

[214] Muhit, A. M. A. (2000), 'The District Council Farce' (in Bengali), *Prothom Alo*, 28 July.

[215] *The Constitution of the People's Republic of Bangladesh*, published by the Ministry of Law Judiciary and Parliamentary Affairs, People's Republic of Bangladesh, Dhaka, 1994.

[216] For detail, see, Rashiduzzaman, M. (1997), 'Political Unrest and Democracy in Bangladesh', *Asian Survey*, vol. XXXIII, no. 3, pp. 254-68; Shehabuddin, E. (1999), 'Bangladesh in 1998: Democracy on the Ground', *Asian Survey*, vol. XXXIX, no. 1, pp. 148-54.

[217] Rahman, M. S. (1995), 'Ethics of Hartal', *The Daily Star*, 14 November, 1995.

3 Problems of Democratisation Before Independence (1947-1970)

This chapter examines elections and electoral corruption in united Pakistan from its creation in 1947 to the general elections of 1970 to show their effect on the process of democratisation in that country before its disintegration in 1971. Electoral politics and electoral corruption under both military and civilian rule will be discussed separately to ascertain whether the nature of corruption and politics in these two types of regime differed.

Elections Under Civilian Rulers

Background

In British India, elections were held under the restricted franchise and separate electorate provisions of the Government of India Act, 1935. The members of the constituent assembly were elected indirectly by the provincial assemblies according to a formula of separate representation for each of the major religious communities.[1] Before the military takeover in 1958, in Pakistan, the political system was closely modelled on the British type of parliamentary democracy. During the first military rule both national and provincial assemblies were elected indirectly by BD members. During the second military interregnum, West Pakistan government was divided into four provinces and the direct election system on the basis of universal suffrage introduced.[2] After the disintegration of Pakistan the Bangladesh constitution introduced a British parliamentary system of government with unicameral legislature, which was changed into a one-party presidential system through the fourth amendment of the constitution in 1975.[3] The military rulers preferred the presidential system although after the 1991 election the pre-1975 parliamentary system was reintroduced through the twelfth amendment of the constitution.[4]

Crisis in political leadership and lack of consensus on fundamental constitutional issues hindered the consolidation of democracy and led the country towards political turmoil. The civilian political leadership in united Pakistan ruled the country for 11 years (1947-58) without calling an election at the national level, although there were several direct provincial elections during this time. In the elections in the Punjab and the North West Frontier Province (NWFP) held in 1951 and in Sindh two years later, the ML won convincingly. There were charges of severe ruling party malpractices in these elections, which were 'anything but free and fair'.[5] Elections of this type made democracy a farce according to President Ayub who, writing in *Foreign Affairs*, briefly commented:

> Whatever elections were held, they could be easily manipulated to return candidates with power to influence, money to bribe and nuisance value to coerce. Conditions such as these reduce the practice of democracy to a farce.[6]

The observations of the Electoral Reforms Commission were very similar: 'It was widely and persistently complained that these elections were a farce, a mockery and a fraud upon the electorate'.[7]

East Bengal Provincial Election, 1954

The first provincial elections in East Pakistan (previously called East Bengal) were held from March 8 to 12 in 1954, in a political climate characterized by opposition to the centralisation of power in West Pakistan and demands for a greater measure of provincial autonomy. The election was contested by sixteen political parties to elect a 309-member East Bengal Legislative Assembly.[8] The main contest originated between the ruling ML and the United Front (UF), an opposition alliance of *Awami Muslim league* led by Hussain S. Suhrawardy (a former premier of pre-partition Bengal) and Maulana Abdul Hamid Khan Bhasani and the *Krishak Sramik* Party of A. K. Fazlul Haq (the first premier of pre-partition Bengal). The religious rightist *Nizam-e-Islam* party joined the UF later.[9]

Campaign

The ML campaigned on the issue of integrity and solidarity of Pakistan. It demanded more power for the central government and an Islamic constitution for the country. The PML president in an election meeting at Dhaka stated:

> The Muslim League was the only organization which could maintain national unity and solidarity of the two far-flung wings of the country. If God forbid any other party came to power in this province in the coming elections, the House would be divided and solidarity of country would be put into jeopardy.[10]

The ML leaders emphasised the religious bondage between the people of the two wings of the country and portrayed themselves to the voters as the defender of religion and national unity. They criticised the opposition as working in the interest of India to weakening Pakistan. The UF in their 21-point manifesto demanded Bengali as the state language of Pakistan and full provincial autonomy leaving only defence, external affairs and currency with the centre.[11] By strongly increasing the sense of deprivation among the voters the UF leaders drew their attention to denial of their rights by the national leaders. Two popular Bengali leaders, Fazlul Haq and Maulana Bhasani criticised the centralisation of power, successfully mobilised voters against the ML and created enthusiastic support for their alliance's programmes. The language issue was their main weapon in the campaign which convinced the voters to decide in their favour. The almost 65 percent turnout confirmed the interest in the election.

Results and Impacts

The 1954 election produced an outcome surprisingly different from the previous provincial contests.[12] The ML was virtually wiped out and it was never able to recover its position in East Pakistan. In the end, the verdict of the election was a clear manifestation of the people's grievances against the central government. A Dhaka newspaper labelled the election results as a peaceful revolution[13] whereas the *Economist* (London), sensing the protest of the Bengalis, published an article titled 'One Pakistan or Two?'. The election results gave the Bengalis strength to fight for their own interest.

The election was free and fair and there was no evidence of major rigging by the contesting parties. Generally, candidates campaigned without intimidation and voters freely exercised their franchise. Published sources do not indicate any rigging or malpractice and the election results were accepted by the contenders. A large majority of voters was in favour of the UF which could have deterred the ruling ML activists from becoming involved in corrupt practice.

Elections and Corruption Under Military Rule in United Pakistan

Ayub and Yahya, the two military generals in united Pakistan, ruled the country for almost 12 years from 1958 to 1970 while civilians were in power for 11 years. Ayub's reign was longer, lasting more than a decade, while Yahya was in power for only 33 months. Ayub used elections to legitimise his rule and Yahya's initial intention was to transfer power to a civilian government after the first-ever general elections in the country. But, as we have seen, he deliberately prevented the victorious AL from forming government.

The Ayub Regime

Background

During the Ayub regime (1958-69), elections were held at the local, provincial and national levels. These elections were organised under the Basic Democracy (BD) system. The people chose their respective union council members who collectively served as an electoral college for other elections. Table 3.1 provides information on the different elections held during the regime.

The table shows that most of the elections were indirect in type except those for the lowest tier of the government – the union council. In the referendum, national and provincial assembly polls and the presidential elections the mass of people could not vote. The members of the electoral college were the voters. Ayub legitimised his position through these indirect elections. The main thrust of his policies was economic development through private enterprise, but he was also aware of the Islamic dimension and tried to satisfy the *ulema* by granting several concessions.[14]

Table 3.1 Elections and Types of Voting in Ayub Khan Era

Year	Month/Months	Name of Election	Type of Voting
1959-1960	Dec-Jan	Union Council* Members	directly elected by the people
1960	February	Referendum	indirectly elected by the MECs**
1962	April	National Assembly	indirectly elected by the MECs
1962	May	Provincial Assembly	indirectly elected by the MECs
1964	Oct-Nov	Union Council Members	directly elected by the people
1965	March	National Assembly	directly elected by the people
1965	May	Provincial Assembly	directly elected by the people

Source: The table has been compiled by the author using information from standard secondary sources. *Union Councils were named Town Committees in the urban areas. **Member of electoral college.

Basic Democracy Elections

Background

Although generally local government elections are outside the scope of this study, a brief analysis of these elections is justified here because of the special importance of the basic democracy system under the Ayub regime. Ayub used the BD system to create a 'new cadre of rural political leaders' who would recruit support for the regime. Two BD elections were held during his time, the first in 1959 and the second in 1964. The first created little interest among the people, but the second was vigorously contested. The low turnout rate and the high number of uncontested seats revealed the unpopularity of the first election.[15] The lower income group was heavily represented in the first, whereas in the second, the higher income group, especially traders and contractors, won a significant number of seats. Significantly, the younger and more literate people assumed rural leadership through this system.[16] Ayub himself claimed 85 percent literacy rate among the 'basic democrats' and argued that they would be able to elect better presidents and legislators.[17]

The Nature of the Campaigns

The campaign in the BD elections was new in type. The old tactic of winning mass support by holding mammoth public meetings and rallies, and issuing party manifestos on a wide variety of regional, national and international issues was no longer applicable. The new politics minimised the importance of party affiliations and national politics. As the number of electors was small, '...face-to-face contact, local issues, and money were important factors'.[18] Empirical studies reveal that BD members were elected more on the basis of personal ascription than on party affiliations or ideologies.[19]

Irregularities and Malpractices

These elections were not totally free of political malfeasance. Comparatively, however, the rate of corruption and malpractice in the first BD election was much less than the second. It is possible that the keen competition and interest in the election (evidenced by the high turnout rate) contributed to the rate of corruption.[20] In West Pakistan, the election created much excitement, tension, disorder, and fighting between rival groups causing numerous casualties.[21] In East Pakistan, in some areas where opposition to the regime was stronger, religious minorities blamed the CML for terrorising the voters. Such allegations in West Pakistan were voiced strongly by the opposition parties who accused the ruling party of 'organising large-scale intimidation and impersonation of voters, with the connivance of the police...'.[22] Tension was so high in some cities that the district magistrates banned processions and public meetings for two months.

The opposition, from the very beginning, was apprehensive that the general elections would not be free and fair because of the government's political control against which they were protesting.[23] The opposition charged that the delimitation of constituencies for the elections to the electoral college had not been done on the basis of the provisions laid down in the Electoral College Act, 1964. It was alleged that the principles like 'territorial contiguity' and the population limit on the number of voters for each unit were often violated by the EC in order to provide special favours to some persons. The high number of objections received by the EC on the delimitation task supported the allegation of the opposition.[24]

The voters' list was highly inaccurate and was strongly challenged by the opposition.[25] The large number of objections and claims against the electoral rolls reveal that it contained gross errors.[26] The opposition leaders branded the electoral rolls erroneous and unreliable. Khwaja Nazimuddin, one of the prominent opposition leaders considered the roll 'beyond rectification and therefore useless' and demanded fresh lists of voters to ensure a fair election.

The electoral college polls suffered from large-scale ghost voting and all manner of corrupt practices as a result of faulty polling procedure. The voters were not asked to sign their names or to give their thumb impression before receiving their ballot papers from presiding officers and the identity of a voter was testified by a polling agent. Although any agent could question the identity of a voter, the challenged vote however, was taken into account for the purpose of counting. An English daily commented:

> bogus voting by hired professionals was complained of. In fact, batches are believed to have gone round in urban localities day after day from one station to another to vote in the name of different persons at the same station. Women from red light areas were used to impersonate ladies' votes.[27]

The techniques of false voting showed that it had been done in a planned way.[28] Several decisions of the EC and newspaper reports reveal the substance of the allegations of false voting.[29]

Referendum, 1960

The 80,000 'basic democrats' elected in the first BD election were asked to vote on the following resolution in a referendum held under secret ballot.[30]

> If the majority of the votes is cast in the affirmative, it should be treated as mandate for the President to take the necessary steps forthwith for setting up constitutional machinery in Pakistan, and he should also be deemed to have been elected President of Pakistan for the first term of office under the constitution to be so made.[31]

Almost all members of the electoral college cast their votes and the official result showed the president had received 95.6 percent affirmative votes.

There was neither a massive campaign for this referendum nor did it produce great interest among the people. Thus, Ayub was able to legitimise his position through this risk-free referendum and establish himself as the first elected president of the country.

Assembly Elections

The first of the two elections during the Ayub regime was held in 1962 and the second in 1964. As both these elections were of the indirect type and only the members of the electoral college were the voters, the populace remained largely apathetic. The first National Assembly (NA) election was ostensibly party-less although in the second political parties openly participated. The turnout in NA elections was 96.6 percent, and 97.8 percent voted in the Provincial Assembly (PA) elections. The absence of political party activities and demonstrations as well as a considerable number of uncontested seats resulted in a calm electoral environment which failed to excite popular interest.[32]

The second NA election was not competitive, even though parties participated. The number of candidates was 419, although 18 (16 in West Pakistan and two in East) were elected unopposed. The Combined Opposition Party (COP) contested 25 seats in the West, and in collaboration with the National Democratic Front (NDF), 71 seats in the East. The number of independent candidates was 148 (West 71, East 77).[33] Both the PML and the COP attacked each other during the campaign although the former's chief, Ayub, tactfully 'maintained sobriety, restraint, and largely forget-and-forgive attitude...'.[34]

Campaign, Results and Impact

The campaign in the NA elections was limited in scope, intensity and duration. Ayub did not campaign extensively, although he was anxious to get a two-thirds majority in the house. He appealed to the members of the electoral college (MEC) as president and transformed his receptions into 'campaign meetings'. The opposition challenged his participation in the campaign and asked him to 'make a clear distinction between his position as a head of the state and as a party chief...'. Ayub's ministers and party leaders were also active in the campaign. Bhutto, the foreign minister, consistently attacked the opposition. He argued that the sole purpose of the COP was begging for votes and ultimately to undo the BD system; hence, it was in the interest of the MECs themselves not to commit suicide by supporting the opposition.[35]

The opposition, not believing in the BD system, did not strongly contest the position of the ruling PML in the campaign. Their poor organisation and the misunderstanding among the components of the alliance forced their candidates to organise their own campaigns. However, in the last stage of the campaign charges and counter-charges heated the political environment. Large-scale arrests of MECs and opposition leaders, harassment of workers, raiding of opposition election camps, coercion and intimidation were frequently alleged by the opposition candidates. Chaudhury Muhammad Ali, a *Jamiat-e-Ulema* Pakistan (JUP) leader, after visiting a few districts in West Pakistan, claimed that 'it was the police who were fighting the election with police methods...'. The opposition also accused the PML of using official machinery and pressure tactics in 'wooing the MECs', using government transport for their political purposes and government officials (for example, sub-divisional officer [SDO]) for arranging election meetings scheduled to be addressed by the prominent PML leaders. The PML also charged the COP with intimidating and misleading the MECs.

The election results gave PML an overwhelming majority of 120 seats. The opposition secured 15 seats (COP 10, NDF 5) in East, and 1 in West Pakistan, and the rest were independents. The PML, winning 80 percent of the seats, secured only 54.8 percent (East 49.64% and West 61.31%) of the votes cast, the opposition a little more than 25 percent (34% in the East), the rest being gained by independents.[36] These independent candidates played a crucial role in this election; they not only gained a good number of seats, but also prevented a straight fight between the PML and COP candidates in more than half of the constituencies.

After the defeat in the referendum and NA elections the opposition was demoralised and considered contesting PA elections as 'an exercise in futility...'. The country, the COP contented, was being taken, step by step, towards 'naked authoritarianism', in defiance of the people's mandate and popular sentiments. Hence, it should explore other ways to prepare the country for the ultimate restoration of democracy of the people.[37] The PML was so confident that it did not bother to campaign in the PA elections. However, in the end the PML obtained 96 seats in the West, the independents 49 (4 of whom were opposition candidates) and the *Jamaat-e-Islami* (JI) one seat. The ruling PML secured 11,834 votes (48.78%) from a total of 24,425 votes cast. In East Pakistan, PML obtained 14,144 votes (38%) out of 37,233, the opposition parties 5,863 (16.33%) and the independents 16,284 votes (45.35%). The voters in the provincial elections judged candidates as individuals rather than by their party affiliations.

Presidential Election, 1965

Background

Among all the elections held in the Ayub era, only the 1965 presidential election overcame the apathy of voters despite their exclusion from electing the head of the state. This was the first and only time when President Ayub had to face a candidate supported by the combined opposition party.[38]

The COP selected a national figure as their combined candidate, Fatima Jinnah, the sister of Pakistan's founder, Jinnah. The ruling party from the very beginning was critical of the COP and criticised it as an 'odd conglomeration of tried and discredited leaders...', and 'frustrated politicians', who above all, were actuated by nothing except the desire to seize power.[39] The COP, according to PML, was composed of members who were 'anti-social', their activities were 'nefarious' and their mission was 'to create chaos'.[40]

Campaign

Voters followed the campaign closely, although only the newly elected 80,000 BD members could vote in this election. A series of ten confrontation meetings was held in the main cities and towns where the two major and some unknown candidates addressed the members of the electoral college. The candidates, through these meetings, had an opportunity to project their programmes and policies. The press was allowed to report these meetings but the public was not admitted to them.[41]

The leaders of the ruling PML and COP campaigned vigorously. Ayub claimed that his regime gave the country progress and stability. He argued that Miss Jinnah lacked the capacity for the leadership of the nation, and frequently stated his view that women were generally unsuitable to head any state and obviously encouraged such a feeling in the electorate. But the more orthodox Muslim religious leaders openly declared that 'supporting a women as the head of the state would be contrary to the principles of Islam...'.[42]

In his campaign, Ayub had an advantage among the MECs because it was he who had created the BD system. The MECs were repeatedly told, for instance, that they were the 'custodians of this system', and that it was their responsibility to guard it against those [who were out to] destroy it and their position in it.[43]

Miss Jinnah, an outspoken critic of Ayub, whom she called a dictator, alleged that his regime had created an 'atmosphere laden with fear and reeking with corruption'.[44] She promised to establish a parliamentary system and direct adult franchise which was widely supported by students, intellectuals and other professional groups. Both candidates[45] extensively toured the country and were warmly received everywhere.[46] Various campaign techniques were used by both, chief of which were projection meetings, receptions for the newly elected BD members, campaigning through committees highlighting the grievances of the people, issuing statements, publishing full page advertisements in newspapers, using the official media for publicity (especially radio broadcasts) and distribution of propaganda literature.[47]

Results

The election result gave Ayub a convincing victory and the opposition was stunned by the enormous defeat it experienced. Ayub secured 49,951 (62.7%) of the 79,700 votes cast, and Miss Jinnah 28,691 (36%), West Pakistan gave Ayub great support – 28,939 (73.3%) compared with Jinnah's 10,257 (26.7%). In East Pakistan Ayub received 21,012 votes (52.9%) and Miss Jinnah 18,434 (46.5%). Miss Jinnah defeated Ayub in only three of the country's sixteen divisions by small majorities.[48] Two insignificant independent candidates, Kamal and Bashir, polled a total of 183 and 64 votes respectively, and another 810 votes were declared invalid.[49]

Irregularities and Malpractices

Both PML and the COP accused each other of misleading the MEC members. The PML tried to attract opposition leaders and tempted them to join the ruling party. There were instances of important office-bearers of the opposition parties being persuaded by ministers to join the PML. It was alleged by the opposition that the ruling party was conspiring with its members and holding out bribes (in the form of a seat in assemblies or a significant position in the party) in return for their support.[50] Another malpractice of the ruling party during the campaign was to arrest its opponents, workers and leaders, especially in East Pakistan and some areas in the West where the ruling party had certain weakness.[51]

The government machinery, the opposition complained, was used by the PML for its electoral campaign and the government controlled media openly favoured the ruling party. Miss Jinnah in one of her addresses to the voters said, '...the most unfortunate aspect of the presidential election is that the administrative machinery of the country is being identified with Mr. Ayub Khan's election campaign'.[52] It was pointed out that radio and television worked as a mouthpiece of the ruling party and blacked out the opposition's viewpoint and personalities. The official press agency doctored all its news to favour the interest of the ruling party before releasing items to the newspapers. The Telephone, Telegraph and Police departments, and the members of the bureaucracy were alleged to have displayed a partisan attitude during the campaign and favoured the ruling party. The postal authorities withheld and burnt Miss Jinnah's letters posted to the members of the electoral college.[53] The ruling party misused public money and resources to promote its election campaign. The deputy commissioners at certain places arranged meetings where they canvassed for the party in power.[54] The governors, ministers, provincial and central parliamentary secretaries drew money from the public exchequer as travel allowances to meet the expenses of their campaign tour.[55]

The COP strongly criticised the entire electioneering process and rejected the result. Its steering committee termed the elections a 'farce' as the government permitted all sorts of malpractices to occur. Miss Jinnah claimed that the elections had been rigged. 'I am sure that the so-called victory of Mr. Ayub Khan is his greatest defeat...'.[56] The popular will became distorted and the 'electoral system produced a result which was directly contrary to the will of the people'.[57]

Nonetheless, Ayub was able to consolidate his position through the BD system and obtain additional legitimacy through this election. However, the continuous unrest and disturbances among students, intellectuals, labour and other groups, growing demands for a greater measure of autonomy for East Pakistan, rising popularity of Mujib in the Eastern wing and Bhutto in the West and declining support of the civil and military bureaucracy challenged his grip on power. He resigned in March 1969 in favour of Yahya, his military chief, who imposed martial law in Pakistan.

Yahya Khan Era: First General Election

Background and Preparation

Yahya in his speeches and statements emphasised the need for a smooth transfer of power to the representatives of the people, elected freely and impartially on the basis of adult franchise.[58] He took a series of steps to achieve these aims. Justice Abdus Sattar, a Supreme Court judge of Pakistan was appointed chief election commissioner on 28 July 1969 to prepare electoral rolls and draw up constituencies. He played an appreciable role in arranging a free and fair election. The country in this short interregnum moved from the proclamation of martial law on 25 March 1969, through the restoration of public political activity in January 1970, to the parliamentary elections in December, though martial law remained in force until 1971.

The Legal Framework Order (LFO), issued on 30 March 1970, provided the guidelines for the general elections and outlined the principles for framing a new constitution[59] (for these principles, see, Appendix – F). Earlier in March 1969, political parties in a Round Table Conference with Ayub before he was forced to resign came to a consensus about a parliamentary form of government and direct elections.

Campaign

The political parties had enough time for the campaign when the resumption of full political activity was permitted. Although 24 parties participated, the *Awami* League (AL) and the Pakistan People's Party (PPP) led by Mujib and Bhutto respectively were the most popular and attracted wide national attention. Each party had its strength and popularity in one of the two wings of the country and the two leaders had a 'long record of mutual antipathy and distrust...'.[60] Party leaders addressed public meetings and toured extensively, and the whole process of campaigning went peacefully although 'personal attacks and sensational charges were not absent...'.[61] On the whole, the political parties were able to campaign in a democratic climate and it has been appropriately labelled 'the first and last general election' in united Pakistan.[62]

AL's campaign was mainly based on its six-point programme which marshalled mass support in East Pakistan. AL favoured 'a moderately socialist economic programme' which was embodied in its manifesto. It did not ignore the religious sentiments of the majority of people and designed the manifesto in that light, as the following quote illustrates:

> Islam is the deeply cherished faith of the overwhelming majority of the people. The *Awami* League affirms that a clear guarantee shall be embodied in the Constitution to the effect that no law repugnant to the injunctions of Islam as laid down in the Holy *Quran* and *Sunnah* shall be enacted or enforced in Pakistan.[63]

PPP's campaign, on the other hand, was summed up in the slogan: 'Islam is our faith; Democracy is our polity; Socialism is our economy; all power to the people…'. The PPP manifesto highlighted radical changes in the economic system, rejected capitalism and emphasised Islamic socialism.[64] Both parties distributed a series of pamphlets elaborating their policies. The PPP leader himself wrote a book in which he explained his vision of the country's future.[65] The attacks and counter-attacks between the political leaders of the two wings of Pakistan enlivened the campaign.[66] The elections passed off peacefully in all parts of the country and all parties, including those which were defeated, agreed that the elections were both free and fair and carried out with complete freedom, order, and almost no complaint of irregularity.[67]

Results and Impacts

AL secured a simple majority in the NA and an overwhelming majority in the East Pakistan PA elections. The AL was successful in mobilising the Bengalis to vote in its favour, winning 162 seats in the national, and 288 in the provincial assembly elections. This result established AL as the single major party in East Pakistan. PPP, on the other hand, won 81 seats in the national, and 144 in the provincial assembly elections and obtained a large majority in West Pakistan. Neither AL, nor PPP won a single seat in West and East Pakistan respectively. Tables 3.2 and 3.3 show the party position in the provincial and national assemblies.

The results of the 1970 election created a new political polarisation in Pakistan. The West Pakistani leaders, with their regional political interest in mind, did not allow the AL to form government on the basis of its six points. The AL, on the other hand, was adamant that it would not compromise this mandate from the voters. The ensuing political deadlock was followed by military action to suppress the Bengalis, finally resulting in the disintegration of the country.

Table 3.2 The Results of Pakistan National Assembly Election, 1970-1971

Party	Punja	Sindh	NWFP	Baluch-istan	West Pakistan	East Pakistan	Total
AL	–	–	–	–	–	160	160
PPP	62	18	1	–	81	–	81
PML(Q)	1	1	7	–	9	–	9
CML	7	–	–	–	7	–	7
JU(H)	–	–	6	1	7	–	7
MJU	4	3	–	–	7	–	7
NAP(W	–	–	3	3	6	–	6
JI	1	2	1	–	4	–	4
PML(C)	2	–	–	–	2	–	2
PDP	–	–	–	–	–	1	1
Ind	5	3	7	–	15	1	16
Total	82	27	25	4	138	162	300

Source: Craig Baxter (1971), 'Pakistan Votes – 1970', *Asian Survey*, vol. 11, no. 3, p. 211.

The nature of corruption in elections under the military regimes of Ayub and Yahya was different in degree and style. Table 3.4 gives a crude comparison and estimate of corruption in these elections. Measuring electoral corruption in quantitative terms is not easy; indeed analysts often brand an election fair or corrupt without any attempt at measurement. However, on the basis of qualitative findings and observations, it is possible, even if imprecisely to assign an ordinal category to the degree of corruption.

In this study, we focus on seven dimensions of electoral corruption: rigging; violence/intimidation; restrictions on campaign/party activities; improper use of electronic media; bureaucratic bias and inappropriate use of religion. Each was assigned on a seven-point scale ranging from very low (VL) to very high (VH) to provide a composite picture of electoral corruption for each of the regimes of the country under study. While this may not be a perfect method, it does provide an understanding of the extent of electoral corruption.[68]

Table 3.3 The Results of Pakistan Provincial Assembly Elections, 1970-1971

Party	Punja	Sindh	NWFP	Baluchistan	West Pakistan	East Pakistan	Total
AL	–	–	–	–	–	288	288
PPP	113	28	3	–	144	–	144
PML(Q)	6	5	10	3	24	–	24
NAP(W)	–	–	13	8	21	1	22
CML	15	4	1	–	20	–	20
MJU	4	7	–	–	11	–	11
JU(H)	2	–	4	2	8	–	8
PML(C)	6	–	2	–	8	–	8
PDP	4	–	–	–	4	2	6
JI	1	1	1	–	3	1	4
Others	1	1	–	2	4	1	5
Indepen:	28	14	6	5	53	7	60
Total	180	60	40	20	300	300	600

Source: Craig Baxter (1971), 'Pakistan Votes – 1970', *Asian Survey*, Vol. 11, No. 3, 1971, p. 211. *Note*: Others include one member each from *Jamiat-i-Ahl-i-Hadees* (Punjab), Sind Karachi Punjabi Pathan *Muttahida Mahaz* (Sind), National *Awami* Party (Achakzai) (Baluchistan), Baluchistan United Front(Baluchistan) and *Nizam-i-Islam* Party (East Pakistan).

A Review

All elections under the Ayub regime in Pakistan suffered from political malfeasance but the 1970 general election under Yahya who was apparently sincere in his intention to hand over power to the elected representatives had a democratic character. Although both the military rulers initially disavowed any political ambition, it was only Yahya who meant it. Ayub became politically ambitious and adopted Machiavellian methods to stay in power. He took power by unconstitutional, although peaceful, means and legitimised his position by a risk-free referendum. Ayub was well-organised in his programmes and policies and arranged the referendum within one and a half years after his take over. Through his economic development policies, he tried to mobilise the people to obtain their support for regime legitimisation. He exploited the BD members to hold on to power.

Table 3.4 The Degree of Corruption in Elections Under Military Rule in Pakistan

Electoral Exercise	Rigging	Violence/ Intimidation	Restrictions on campaign/ party activities	Use of electronic media	Bureaucratic bias	Use of religion
Ayub Khan Regime						
BD* Election 1959	M	M	MH	ML	L	L
BD Election 1964	H	MH	MH	ML	L	L
Referendum 1960	L	ML	MH	ML	H	L
Assembly 1962	L	L	MH	MH	H	L
Assembly 1964	L	H	M	MH	MH	L
Presidential 1965	ML	ML	MH	MH	ML	H
Yahya Khan Regime						
Assembly 1970	L	L	L	L	L	MH

Index: *BD = Basic Democracy. VL= Very Low; L= Low; ML= Moderately Low; M = Medium; MH= Moderately High; H = High; VH= Very High.
Source: Based on primary and second sources.

Although Ayub advocated democracy, civil rights were curtailed during his regime. All the national elections under the Ayub regime were indirect in type where the people had no voting rights. Freedom of the press, publication and association were restricted and tightly controlled by the military government. He ruled with a constitution for a long period but also amended it in the light of his political motives. He made the presidency an extraordinarily powerful institution, and it has remained so in Pakistan since disintegration in 1971. The trend of forming alliances during elections emerged as a common political practice in the country. The bureaucracy and the government-controlled electronic media played a partisan role during electoral campaigns and favoured the government. Both Generals used Islam, particularly Ayub, for his partisan benefit. Ayub resorted to intimidation and all sorts of repressive measures, including arrests and imprisonments, to weaken the opposition instead of facing them politically. He gave the highest facilities to the civil-military bureaucracy to obtain their support to continue in power.

Summing Up

Political leaders under united Pakistan experimented with various forms of constitutional structure and government following independence. Lack of unity and consensus among political leaders took the country to military rule in 1958 which continued up to 1971. The political leaders presented a constitution in 1956 which advocated the British parliamentary system, but this was refused by the military government under whose direction another constitution was promulgated that made both the central government and the presidency powerful.

Ayub experimented with a new democratic system – basic democracy, which reduced civil rights and made the national elections indirect in type. Yahya, for the first time in the country, organised a national general election. His government took military action in East Pakistan in 1971 when the *Awami* League, after winning the 1970 elections, wanted to form government and frame a constitution on the basis of its six-point programme.

The nature of electoral corruption under civilian or military rule was similar although elections in these two types of rule were totally different. All the four national elections under the Ayub regime were indirect in type where only the MECs instead of the people, had voting rights. The first Assembly elections under the Ayub regime were held on a non-party basis but in the second Assembly elections political parties participated. In the referendum in 1962, only the MECs were the voters. The only exception was the 1970 general elections which had all the characteristics of a democratic election although it was arranged by a military government.

All national elections had malpractices and corruption except for the 1970 national assembly elections. The 1970 elections were judged fair both by the contesting parties and local and foreign observers. Other elections were more or less influenced by violence, rigging and other traditional malpractices, such as bogus voting. The process of democratisation in united Pakistan which was always a main goal of the civilian political leaders was hampered by chronic military rule. The military rulers claimed to promote democracy, but this was in rhetoric only. The civilian and military governments of the country possessed a similar outlook toward their political opposition as well as on the use of media and press and publications. However, political party activities, which had been highly restricted during the military regimes, increased considerably during civilian rule. The nature of opposition and the character of campaigning in both East and West Pakistan were similar despite the cultural and linguistic difference of the populace.

Notes

[1] Baxter, C. (1971), 'Pakistan Votes – 1970', *Asian Survey*, vol. XI, no. 3, pp. 198-99.
[2] *Ibid.*, p. 200.
[3] For detail, see, Hakim, M. A. and Huque, A. S. (1994), 'Constitutional Amendments in Bangladesh', *Regional Studies*, vol. XII, no. 2, pp. 73-90.
[4] For twelfth constitutional amendment, see, Hakim, M. A. (1992), 'Twelfth Constitutional Amendment: Bangladesh's Reversion to Parliamentary System', *Asian Profile*, vol. 20, no. 3, pp. 252-61.
[5] Palmer, N. D. (1975), *Elections and Political Development: The South Asian Experience*, C. Hurst, London, p. 181.
[6] Khan. M. A. (1960), 'Pakistan Perspective', *Foreign Affairs*, vol.38, no.4, p. 550.
[7] Gazette of Pakistan (extraordinary), 24 April, 1956, p. 922, quoted in Palmer, *Elections and Political Development: The South Asian Experience, op. cit.*, p. 181.
[8] The parties were: Muslim League, the United Front, Pakistan National Congress, Communist Party, *Ganatantri Dal*, *Gana Samity*, Scheduled Castes Federation, Revolutionary Socialist Party, *Nizam-i-Islam* Party and *Khilafat-e-Rabbani* Party.
[9] For further information, see, Murshid, G. (1986), 'East Bengal Provincial Elections of March 1954: Origin of Separatist Movement in East Pakistan', in S. R. Chakravarty and V. Narain (eds), *Bangladesh: Volume One, History and Culture*, South Asian Publishers, New Delhi, pp. 119-32.
[10] *Dawn*, 4 January, 1954. Cited in Murshid, *ibid.*, pp. 123-24.

[11] The main items in the UF's 21-point programme were as follows: (1) Recognition of Bengali as an official language on a parallel with Urdu. (2) Rejection of the draft constitution, the dissolution of the Constituent Assembly, and its replacement by a directly elected body. (3) Complete autonomy for East Pakistan in all matters except defence, foreign policy and currency, which would be reserved to the Central Legislature. (4) Complete freedom from the centre with regard to export of jute. (5) Consultation between the centre and East Pakistan on the allocation of foreign exchange for imports. (6) Abolition of the Indo-Pakistan passport and visa system and of existing restrictions on trade between East and West Bengal, and (7) Devaluation of the Pakistani rupee.

[12] The UF secured 223 seats out of a total 237 seats marked for the Muslims in the 309-member legislative assembly. See, *Dawn*, 5 April, 1954.

[13] *The Mail*, 13 March, 1954. Cited in, Ziring, L. (1962), 'The Failure of Democracy in Pakistan: East Pakistan and the Central Government 1947-58', PhD dissertation, Columbia University, p. 172.

[14] He set up an Advisory Council on Islamic Ideology to advise the government regarding the Islamic aspect of its policies and an Islamic Research Council to conduct research on the Islamic aspects of social, educational and legal matters. Religious political parties especially *Jamiat-ul-Ulema-e-Islam*, *Nizam-i-Islam*, and *the Jamaat-e-Islami* were critical of his policies and agitated for the implementation of *Shariah* (Islamic law).

[15] In East Pakistan the turnout was close to 52 percent, although in West Pakistan it was close to three quarters. See, Government of West Pakistan, *Democracy at the Doorstep*, pp. 14-19, quoted in Ziring, L. (1971), *The Ayub Khan Era: Politics In Pakistan 1958-1969*, Syracuse University Press, Syracuse, pp. 17-18. About 25 percent of the seats were uncontested in the first BD election. See, Voys, K. V. (1965), *Political Development In Pakistan*, Princeton University Press, Princeton, p. 201.

[16] Jahan, R. (1972), *Pakistan: Failure in National Integration*, Columbia University Press, New York, p. 119

[17] Misra, K. P., Lakhi M. V. and Narain, V. (1967), *Pakistan's Search for Constitutional Consensus*, Impex India, New Delhi, p. 31.

[18] Jahan, *Pakistan: Failure in National Integration, op. cit.*, p. 125.

[19] Sobhan, R. (1968), *Basic Democracies, Works Programme and Rural Development in East Pakistan*, Oxford University Press, Dhaka; Thomas, J. W. (1968), 'Rural Public Works Program and East Pakistan's Development', PhD dissertation, Harvard University.

[20] The turn-out was 75 and 90 per cent in West and East Pakistan respectively. See, Keesings Research Report (1973), *Pakistan: From 1947 to the Creation of Bangladesh*, Keesing's Publications, New York, p. 83.

[21] In West Pakistan alone 43 persons were killed and 500 injured during BD election. See, Misra, Lakhi and Narain, *Pakistan's Search for Constitutional Consensus, op. cit.*, p. 91.

[22] Kessings Research Report, *Pakistan: From 1947 to the Creation of Bangladesh, op. cit.*, p. 83.

114 Electoral Corruption

23 Of the various measures of political control available to the government, the most important were the Press and Publication Ordinance, the Loudspeaker Ordinance, the Maintenance of Public order Ordinance, and Public safety Ordinance. Some of the sections of these ordinances were used by the ruling PML to control political opposition through government machinery. For example, section 16 of the West Pakistan Maintenance of Public Order Ordinance empowered the administration to arrest a person found guilty or spreading rumours and making speeches against the government. Section 41 of the East Pakistan Public Safety Ordinance laid down: 'Any police officer not below the rank of a sub-inspector or any other officer of the Government empowered in this behalf by general or special order of the Provincial government may arrest without warrant any person whom he reasonably suspects of having done, or of doing or of being about to do a prejudicial act'. See, *Pakistan Observer*, 17 September, 1964 and 2 October, 1964.

24 The total number of objections received by the Election Commission was over 10,000 of which 7,000 were filed in the East and the other 3,000 in West Pakistan. See, *Dawn*, 4 August, 1964.

25 According to the opposition the names of the persons who had been thought to be unreliable in the party in power had been omitted from the voter's list whereas many fictitious names including names of dead and non-existing persons had been included in the voter's list. *Pakistan Times*, 21 November, 1964.

26 For example, the total number of voters in the Karachi District in the draft lists was 1,086,641, whereas the number of objections and claims filed in connection with electoral rolls was 125,822. *Dawn*, 18 September, 1964, quoted in Misra, Lakhi and Narain, *Pakistan's Search for Constitutional Consensus, op. cit.*, p. 178.

27 *Pakistan Observer*, November 6, 1964.

28 The latecomers, consisting mainly of the gazetted officers and members of the intelligentsia, had become the victims of the false voting. Another style of false voting was that some voters smuggled their ballot paper from the polling booths instead of casting it into ballot boxes and sold it to the candidates who later on put it in their own boxes.

29 For example, on November 6, 1964, with only two days left for polling, the election authority of West Pakistan sent a circular letter to all the presiding officers in West Pakistan asking them to obtain on the counterfoil of each ballot paper the signature or thumb impression of the person to whom it was issued. It again after two days, directed the presiding officers to put down the date of polling on the ballot papers issued to the voters in order to ensure that ballot papers could only be used on that day. *Jamaat-e-Islami Amir* claimed in *Dawn* that 'never in the history of Pakistan such flagrant tampering with elections was restored to. Never was there such a large-scale bogus voting. There are instances where even 70 to 90 percent votes cast in favour of the Conventionists candidate have been bogus. Never was there such widespread and shame-faced goondaism as has been perpetrated on this occasion'. *Nawai waqt*, an Urdu daily reported that 'the electoral college elections have proved to have beaten all records of earlier gerrymandering of pre-Martial Law elections'. About the fairness and freedom in these election it said, 'fairness was noticed by few while freedom was rampant: freedom to violate the law, freedom to cast bogus votes without fear, freedom for the polling staff to ignore all malpractices, freedom for the helpless honest candidates to withdraw from the contest. ... And every kind of freedom was so widespread that everywhere respectable law-abiding and democratically disposed people were bewildered'. See, 'Polls Gerrymandering in

West Wing has Beaten All Previous Records', *Pakistan Observer*, 12 November, 1964.
[30] According to S. A. Saeed, it was Manzur Qadir who suggested to Ayub Khan the need of a vote of confidence. See, Saeed, S. A. (1960), *President Without Precedent*, Lahore Book Depot, Lahore, p. 7.
[31] Kissings Research Report, *Pakistan: From 1947 to the Creation of Bangladesh*, op. cit., p. 77.
[32] For related information, see, Ziring, *The Ayub Khan Era: Politics In Pakistan1958-1969*, op. cit., p. 29.
[33] For a detail discussion, see, al-Mujahid, S. (1965), 'Assembly Elections In Pakistan', *Asian Survey*, vol. 5, no.1, pp. 539-51.
[34] Ayub too, said his opponents, had 'served the cause of democracy'. He urged that a sharp distinction be made between 'political opposition' and 'political enmity', if the opposition wished to 'build up a healthy democratic set-up in the country'. Political enmity, he argued, might lead to 'civil war' and democratic institutions such as elections were meant to prevent this. Sharif appreciated Ayub's liberal appeal made in a situation of post-election uncertainty and opposition threat of boycotting the elections. See, al-Mujahid, 'Assembly Elections In Pakistan', *op. cit.*, p. 543.
[35] *Dawn*, March 18, 20, 1965.
[36] al-Mujahid, 'Assembly Elections In Pakistan', *op. cit.*, p. 547.
[37] *Pakistan Observer*, 3 April, 1965.
[38] On July 21, 1964, five opposition political parties merged into a Combined Opposition Party (COP). These five parties were: Council Muslim League headed by Khawaja Nazimuddin, National *Awami* Party (NAP) headed by Maolana Abdul Hamid Khan Bhashani, *Awami* League (AL) headed by Nwabjada Nasrullah Khan (President) and Sheikh Mujibur Rahman (General Secretary, East Pakistan AL), *Nizam-i-Islam* Party (NIP) headed by Choudhury Mohammad Ali, and *Jammat-e-Islami* (JI), headed by Maolana Moudoodi.
[39] *Dawn*, October 7, 1964.
[40] *Dawn*, October 5, 1964.
[41] See, Kessings Research Report, *Pakistan: From 1947 to the Creation of Bangladesh*, op. cit., pp. 83-84.
[42] See, Palmer, *Elections and Political Development: The South Asian Experience*, op. cit. p. 185.
[43] al-Mujahid, S. (1965), 'Pakistan's First Presidential Election', *Asian Survey*, vol. 5, no. 6, pp. 280-94.
[44] Palmer, *Elections and Political Development: The South Asian Experience*, op. cit., p. 184.
[45] There were two other insignificant candidates (Mian Bashir Ahmed and K. M. Kamal) who were virtually ignored by the voters.
[46] For example, when the Kheyber Mail train carrying President Ayub Khan embarked upon its 210 miles run from Lahore to Multan, crowds gave him a warm welcome to him all along the route. Miss Jinnah had a similar experience when her 'Green Arrow' took thirty hours instead of nine hours, as scheduled, to cover the distance between Dhaka and Chittagong. Mammoth crowds made it impossible for the train to leave the stations, and stopped the train in almost all the forty stations on the way. There were also innumerable unscheduled stoppages where the candidate and other COP leaders had to address the crowds. According to the railway authorities, the 'Green

Arrow' was stopped 'not less than 300 times' between Dhaka and Akhaura. 'Then we stopped counting how many times the chains were pulled,' they added. See, *Pakistan Observer*, October 18, 1964.

[47] Misra, Lakhi and Narain, *Pakistan's Search for Constitutional Consensus, op. cit.*, p. 83-87.

[48] These three divisions were Dhaka and Chittagong in East Pakistan and Karachi in West Pakistan.

[49] See for detail, al-Mujahid, 'Pakistan's First Presidential Election', *op. cit.*, p. 292.

[50] The Convener of the Lyallpur *Nizam-i-Islam* Party revealed that he had been offered unopposed election to the National Assembly if he joined the PML. See, *Pakistan Times*, 30 June, 1964.

[51] For example, in the last week of December, in East Pakistan alone 100 persons belonging to the opposition were arrested. On December 31, 1964, with just one day left for the elections, 50 arrests were made in Noakhali, while several important local leaders of the COP were arrested at Pabna and Madaripur. See, *Times of India*, 1 January, 1964, quoted in, Misra, Lakhi and Narain, *Pakistan's Search for Constitutional Consensus, op. cit.*, pp. 63-64.

[52] *Dawn*, November 11, 1964.

[53] The press statement of J. Ahmed, Chairman of the COP Central Committee, *Dawn*, December 24, 1964, quoted in Misra, Lakhi and Narain, *Pakistan's Search for Constitutional Consensus, op. cit.*, p. 189.

[54] *Pakistan Observer*, 28 December, 1964, quoted in, Misra, Lakhi and Narain, *Pakistan's Search for Constitutional Consensus, ibid.*, p. 190.

[55] Misra, Lakhi and Narain, *Pakistan's Search for Constitutional Consensus, ibid.*, p. 190.

[56] *Pakistan Times*, January 4, 1965, quoted in, Misra, *Pakistan's Search for Constitutional Consensus, ibid.*, p. 191.

[57] The Press Release of the COP, *Dawn*, January 5, 1965, quoted in, Misra, Lakhi and Narain, *Pakistan's Search for Constitutional Consensus, ibid.*, p. 191.

[58] For Yahya Khan's first address to the nation see, *Pakistan Observer*, 27 March, 1969.

[59] Rizvi, *The Military And Politics In Pakistan 1947-86, op. cit.*, p. 173.

[60] Palmer, *Elections and Political Development: The South Asian Experience, op. cit.*, p. 188.

[61] Baxter, 'Pakistan Votes – 1970', *op. cit.*, p. 210.

[62] Choudhury, G. W. (1974), *The Last Days of United Pakistan*, C. Hurst, London, Chapter 5.

[63] For the full text of the AL manifesto, see, *Bangladesh Documents*, published by the Ministry of External Affairs, Government of Pakistan, n.d., vol. 1, pp. 66-82, quoted in Choudhury, *The Last Days of United Pakistan, op. cit.*, p. 131.

[64] See, *Election Handbook 1970*, quoted in, Choudhury, *The Last Days of United Pakistan, op. cit.*, p. 123.

[65] Bhutto, Z. A. (1969), *The Myth of Independence*, Oxford University Press, Karachi.

[66] The West Pakistani leaders expressed doubts about the patriotism of the East Pakistani leaders who in turn 'called candidates of the West-based parties 'anti-people', and 'political touts''. Few West Pakistani political leaders alleged that Mujib, Quamruzzaman and other AL leaders could address undisturbed, well-attended meetings in West Pakistan's major cities, but Mujib's *'Joy Bangla'* (victory of Bengal) chanting supporters had attacked JI and PDP meetings in Dhaka, addressed by West Pakistani leaders. *Pakistan Observer* (editorial), 'Hooligan Politics', 20

January, 1970, and *ibid.*, 2 February, 1970, quoted in, al-Mujahid, 'Pakistan: First General Elections', *op. cit.*, p. 167.
67 Baxter, 'Pakistan Votes-1970', *op. cit.*, p. 217. The national and provincial assembly elections were held on 7 and 17 December, 1970 respectively.
68 Zafarullah, H. and Akhter, M. Y. (1998), 'Military rule, Civilianization and Electoral Corruption: Pakistan and Bangladesh in Perspective', unpublished paper.

4 Military Rule, Elections and Civilianisation

Introduction and Background

The purpose of this chapter is to discuss electoral politics and corruption under military rule in Bangladesh. It analyses elections organised by the military regimes of Zia and Ershad, particularly their use of elections in the process of legitimising their rules. Finally, it estimates the degree of corruption in different elections and discusses how military rule and corruption affected the process of democratisation.

Electoral rules as well as irregularities and malpractices in Third World countries do not have a uniform pattern. For instance in South Asia, the parliamentary elections in Bangladesh and Pakistan are quite different in character and nature from those in India. The main reason for this is the prolonged military rule in these two countries. The military rulers there used elections as a tool to legitimise and civilianise their rule, despite the fact that they came to power in the name of filling a temporary political vacuum or crisis.

The two military leaders, Zia and Ershad, ruled Bangladesh for almost 15 years, more than half the time of Bangladesh's existence as an independent state. They followed a similar strategy in civilianising their regimes and used referenda and presidential and parliamentary elections in the process of legitimising their rule, as well as establishing their own political parties. Both of them were ostensibly reluctant to be involved in politics when they first came to power, but later continued in politics for long periods. They initiated political and administrative reforms and attempted to involve the mass of the people in those schemes.

The First Military Regime

Background

After taking over the presidency from Justice Sayem in April 1977, Zia began to civilianise his regime. Sayem had earlier resigned on the grounds of ill health from his position and designated Zia as his successor.[1] However, there were reports of a power-tussle between the two.[2] Sayem was disinclined to postpone the elections promised earlier. He also despised Zia's style of dealing with his opponents in the armed forces and in public life. Allegedly, Zia took power from Sayem in a 'coup'.[3] Be that as it may, after becoming the president of the country, Zia was keen to legitimise his position through a national referendum. This was in accord with the style generally followed by Third World military rulers.

Before holding the referendum, the regime organised local elections, the results of which concerned Zia. The former AL supporters won a large number of seats.[4] Although the ML claimed between 65 and 75 percent of the newly elected union *parishad* (UP) members were linked with it,[5] Zia did not accept this exaggerated estimate. One report suggested a rightist resurgence through this UP election which showed 77 percent of the elected members and chairmen in some selected councils to be politically aligned to the right and centre; about 21 percent of them were moderately left and about one percent were radicals.[6] The survey also demonstrated that 23 percent of the elected leaders professed to be supporters of the ML and other right-wing parties.[7] Zia wanted to use these village leaders as his political support base and was successful in doing so. Soon after the election, he called upon them to implement his 19-point programme for rural development and population control and arranged a massive training programme for the UP leaders in family planning and managing local administration. Thus by involving them in developmental activities and assuring them of resources and the government's co-operation, Zia was largely successful in winning their support.

1977 Referendum

The referendum has become a popular and widely used technique for obtaining legitimacy by military rulers who come to power through coup and do not initially have a popular support base. Zia was no exception. He announced the first national referendum for 30 May 1977, soon after capturing the presidency. The electorate was asked to approve him as president and to endorse his 19-point programme of development and reform. The referendum resulted in a massive 16,374,175 votes in favour of Zia while only 232,492 voted in the negative. The turnout was claimed to be 85 percent and Zia received 98.88 percent of the 'yes' votes.[8]

Cynics were suspicious of such a massive victory although there were no serious challenges to the validity of the referendum. According to some, '...Zia could easily have won 60-70% of the vote'. One analyst attributes such an overwhelming vote of confidence to several factors:

1. participation of the bureaucracies in mobilising public support;
2. unqualified support of a majority of the newly elected union *parisad* (village councils) leaders;
3. active help from the moderate and right wing forces;
4. influence of the officially controlled media; and
5. absence of any other candidates.[9]

Some newspaper reports were highly critical of the referendum. One such report points out that shutters of offices and shops and movie theatres were closed and sports and social activities cancelled to 'enable the people to participate in the referendum...'.[10] The same report underscored the effect of discipline in the referendum and states that 'although rush in the polling centres was considerable, there was no indiscipline anywhere...'. Extensive publicity by the radio and television continually reminding the people to exercise their franchise was also crucial. The wide use of the machinery of government to persuade the people to vote affected the credibility of the referendum. Official figures showed a very high turnout but in reality the referendum was only partially successful. The opposition camp claimed the figures to be exaggerated.[11] The phrasing of the referendum question: 'Do you have confidence in president Major General Ziaur Rahman and in his policies and programs enunciated by him?'[12] confused many people. There were many who were opposed to military rule but supported Zia's programmes; it was also the reverse for many voters.

As there were no activities of other political parties, it was easy for Zia's supporters to work and influence freely the voting of the referendum. Criticisms of the high voter turnout did not worry Zia who simply wanted to legitimise his position and was successful in doing so.

1978 Presidential Election

Background

Zia was not satisfied with the massive victory in the referendum as it was neither widely accepted nor a contested election. He was not able to demonstrate a strong support base and was in a dilemma whether he should return to the barracks or become a full-time professional politician. Several coup attempts in 1977 showed that his support within the army was dwindling.[13] Although Zia was lucky and successful in crushing the rebellion by the air force officers, it exposed his critical position within the army.[14] Opposition political parties including the AL were demanding an early parliamentary election. Zia decided to join a political party. With his blessings a new political party, *Jatiyatabadi Gonotantrik Dal* (Nationalist Democratic Party, better known as *Jagodal*) was formed by Abdus Sattar (the chief election commissioner in the 1970 parliamentary elections), the then vice president, to support Zia. Most of the members of this new party were either politically unknown or long since disassociated from politics.[15] Political analysts viewed the new party critically. *Jagodal* failed to recruit 'political heavy weights',[16] and 'its members were either second ranking leaders or people with very poor credibility...'.[17]

Political Alliances and Candidates

When political parties were preparing for the next parliamentary elections scheduled to be held in December 1978, Zia surprised everyone by suddenly announcing a presidential election for 3 June 1978, only a year after his massive victory in the referendum. The following comment on this move is appropriate:

> Ziaur Rahman probably saw an ideal opportunity of another massive Presidential victory before opposition political parties gained strength. It is quite possible that he wanted to strengthen his political position before the proposed legislative elections scheduled for January 1979.[18]

Two political alliances – the government-backed *Jatiyatabadi* Front (JF) and AL-led *Gonotantrik Oikyo Jote* (GOJ) were formed to contest the presidential poll.[19] President Zia contested as a candidate of the JF while the GOJ nominated retired General M. A. G. Osmani, who led the 1971 war as the commander-in-chief of the liberation forces, to oppose Zia.

Campaign

The campaign reactivated the political parties whose activities had been restricted since the military takeover in 1975. In his campaign Zia re-emphasised his 19-point socio-economic programme, presidential system, 'Bangladeshi nationalism' instead of 'foreignism', 'people's democracy' in place of 'palace politics', and 'economic self-reliance' instead of dependence on foreign aid. Indeed, '...the election campaigns of Zia were reminiscent of Ayub Khan's notion of political development'.[20] Zia called the Front the first stage of forming national unity[21] and indirectly attacked the opposition platform, especially its main component AL by saying:

> those who once had sacrificed our independence and sovereignty at the altar of expansionist designs of external forces and had established one party rule betraying the verdict of the people ... have appeared in a new garb.[22]

The opposition alliance – GOJ, on the other hand, supported a parliamentary form of government and emphasised the original four state principles including secularism, which Zia had dropped. The opposition alliance accused Zia of being a military dictator[23] and strongly criticised him for concentrating all powers in his hands by 'holding the office of the President, the Commander-in-Chief of the Armed Forces, the Chief of Army Staff, the Chief Martial Law Administrator – all together right through the balloting...'.[24] GOJ also promised to protect the country's freedom movement, resist attacks on the liberation war and to ensure basic rights.

Results and Reactions

Zia won the election securing 76.63 percent of the votes to Osmani's 21.70. The remaining 1.67 percent went to the other eight little-known candidates. There were allegations that the election was 'rigged' and the opposition candidate asserted publicly that it was 'grossly unfree and unfair'.[25] Political parties operated openly for the first time through this presidential election since the August coup in 1975 and Zia was successful in legitimising his position through a contested election. This early presidential election benefited Zia as he 'stole a march on his opponents and met the opposition with ease...'.[26]

The Second Parliamentary Election, 1979

Background, Opposition Boycott and Participation

After the massive victory in the 1977 referendum and the 1978 Presidential election, it was natural to complete the process of legitimisation by holding a widely contested parliamentary election and Zia did so in a planned way. JF, the alliance which had supported Zia in the presidential election was arbitrarily dissolved by Zia because of division and conflict among its components.[27] Similarly the GOJ, the opposition alliance which supported Osmani, disintegrated after its candidate's defeat in the presidential contest. Before authorising the parliamentary election, Zia formed his own political party, the Bangladesh Nationalist Party (BNP) in September 1978 and became its chairman. In November 1978, he repealed the Political Parties Regulation Order (PPR)[28] and in December 1978, decreed a fifth amendment of the constitution which made the presidential position extraordinarily powerful. The amendment empowered the president to appoint a prime minister from parliament even if he/she was short of majority support in the house; appoint one fifth of his cabinet from among people who were not members of parliament; ensure the subservience of the judiciary to the power of the president; and unilaterally enter into any international treaty in the 'national interest' even without informing parliament.[29]

After legitimising his position and concentrating power in his hands, Zia announced 27 January 1979 as the date of the parliamentary election, having twice postponed it earlier. This date was also rescheduled and finally the election was held on 18 February 1979 with the opposition political parties sharply reacting to the rescheduling and criticising the president for not creating what they termed a 'conducive and congenial atmosphere for the elections...'.[30] Twelve political parties decided to boycott the election unless their five demands were met.[31] The demands were:

1. withdrawal of martial law and restoration of fundamental rights;
2. restoration of parliamentary democracy by repealing the fourth amendment to the constitution;

3. unconditional release of all political prisoners;
4. Zia's retirement from the army if he continued in politics; and
5. restoration of press freedom.[32]

The boycotting party leaders stated that the election would be 'a farce and total waste of public and private funds...' if their demands were not accepted.[33] The BML, People's League-Razee, National *Awami* Party-Independents, *Jatiya Gonomukti* Union (JAGMU), and Communist Party of Bangladesh (CPB) for similar reasons, decided not to participate in the elections and strengthened the stand of the boycotting group. On the other hand, several political parties, including the government-blessed BNP, took a pro-election stand and requested the boycotting parties to participate in the elections.[34] The president conceded to the demands of the election-boycotting parties and finally they participated in the country's second parliamentary elections.[35]

Parties, Candidates and Manifestos

Table 4.1 Party Nominations in 1979 Parliamentary Election

Party	Nominations
Bangladesh Nationalist Party (BNP)	298
Awami League-Malek Ukil (AL-MU)	295
Bangladesh Muslim League-Islamic Democratic League-Rahim (BML-IDL-R)	265
Jatiya Samajtantrik Dal (JSD)	240
Awami League-Mizan Chaudhury (AL-MC)	183
National *Awami* Party-Muzaffar (NAP-M)	89
United People's Party (UPP)	70
Gono Front (GF)	46
National *Awami* Party-Nurur-Zahed (NAP-NZ)	37
Jatiyatabadi Gonotantri Dal (JAGODAL)	30
National *Awami* Party-Naser (NAP-N)	28
Bangladesh *Sammyabadi Dal*-Toaha (BSD-T)	19
Bangladesh *Jatiya* League (BJL)	14
Communist Party of Bangladesh (CPB)	14
Other Parties	81
Total	1,709

Source: Bangladesh Election Commission.

A total of 2,125 candidates, 1,709 from 30 political parties and 416 independent contested the 300 seats (for the 300 constituencies, see appendix G). None of the major parties nominated candidates for all seats although some of them nominated a large number of candidates. Table 4.1 shows the number of candidates nominated by the different major political parties.

Three electoral alliances were formed to counter two major parties — the BNP and the AL-MU.[36] The component parties of first two alliances decided to contest the elections under a single election symbol while the parties in the third front fought the elections with their respective party symbols.[37] The parties did not emphasise any significant policy issues. Some major parties issued their election manifestos only few weeks before the election and were not able to influence the electorate. The BNP manifesto expressed determination 'to consolidate people's unity and establish democracy of the masses based on nationalism', pledged 'to free the nation from the clutches of imperialism, neo-colonialism, expansionism and racialism through the attainment of economic self-sufficiency',[38] and advocated a presidential form of government with a sovereign parliament.[39] The AL-MU manifesto emphasised the 'restoration of the constitution of 1972 in its pre-fourth amendment form, the implementation of the administrative, economic and social programmes of the 'second revolution', opposition to any policy of disinvestment in the nationalised sector; and repeal of all black laws...'.[40] Other political parties such as JSD, BML, IDL-R, AL-MC also published their manifestos.[41]

Campaign

The BNP campaigned for Bangladeshi nationalism, a production-oriented democracy, and a presidential form of government with a sovereign parliament; the AL-MU for the implementation of the programmes of Mujib's 'second revolution', the restoration of the 1972 constitution (prior to the fourth amendment); the leftists for people's democracy; the rightists for parliamentary democracy and social justice based on Islam.[42] The opposition electoral campaign was not as effective as that of the government party. They lost much time because of their continued boycott of the election while the BNP and Zia utilised the same time for campaigning. Fragmentation weakened the major opposition parties and they were not successful in countering the campaign of the BNP. Zia, the physically strong 'soldier-turned politician', used the government resources and covered five to six districts in a day while he visited the remotest corners of the country.

Results

The BNP won 207 seats out of 300, which gave it a clear two-thirds majority in parliament. The AL-MU won 39 seats and its rival faction AL-MC only two. The BML-IDL secured 20 and the JSD 7 seats. Table 4.2 details results of the election. How did a new party like the BNP win a two-thirds majority in its first electoral contest? Zia's honesty and popularity have been emphasised by most observers. The personal image of Zia as an honest and hard-working leader, the lack of unity among the opposition parties, Zia's pro-Islamic and anti-Indian stance, and the general satisfaction of the people with the performance of his government contributed to this formidable victory for the BNP.[43] Zia's popularity in the

Table 4.2 Results of 1979 Parliamentary Election

Parties	Number of Seats Won	% Seats Won	Number of Votes Received	% Votes Received
BNP	207	69.00	7,934,236	41.17
AL (Malek)	39	13.00	4,734,277	24.56
BML	20	6.66	1,941,394	10.07
JSD	8	2.66	931,851	4.83
Other Parties	10	3.33	1,762,266	9.98
Independents	16	5.33	1,963,345	10.19

Source: Bangladesh Election Commission. BNP = Bangladesh Nationalist Party, AL (Malek) = Bangladesh *Awami* League (Malek), BML = Bangladesh Muslim League, JSD = *Jatiya Samajtantrik Dal*.

rural areas gave BNP the absolute majority.[44] The AL-MU won only 39 seats because of its split and unimpressive performance when it was in power from 1971-75 under the leadership of Sheikh Mujib. The AL's result indicated that the 'voters remembered the famine, corruption, mismanagement and social tension suffered under the first AL government...'.[45] The rightist ML which was banned under the Mujib regime for its anti-Bangladesh role during liberation and soundly defeated in the 1970 election, won 20 seats and became the third largest party in the parliament. The performance of the leftist parties was very poor although they had been active in politics for a long time.

Rigging Allegations

Almost all opposition political parties alleged poll-rigging after the election.[46] This was strongly denied by Zia. Voters cast their votes freely, and although there were instances of bogus voting, this was not on a large scale.[47] A few opposition leaders alleged rigging and violence on the part of government party leaders and workers who according to them did not allow opposition party agents in some voting centres.[48] The opposition leaders cited several cases with reasonable proof that 'corrupt and irregular practices had been perpetrated by BNP candidates, their supporters and polling agents, and assigned government officials when things turned difficult for ruling party candidates...'.[49] This was found to be 'exaggerated' and far from the truth by the leaders and activists of the ruling party. The opposition also alleged that the rigging in the elections was a pre-planned affair, and the ruling party had decided long before the elections the number of opposition members it wanted in parliament.[50] However, the process of legitimisation which Zia started in 1977 ended through the second parliamentary election in 1979. He was thus successful in obtaining political legitimacy and paid attention to local government reform and other developmental activities.

The Ershad Regime

Background

Ershad faced a serious anti-military movement after coming to power as all political parties knew the meaninglessness of taking part in elections under a military regime. He followed a similar civilianisation strategy as his predecessor and held one referendum, one presidential and two parliamentary elections during his rule. This was possible as he was successful in persuading a major political party and alliance to participate in the third parliamentary elections.

National Referendum, 1985

Ershad changed his legitimisation strategy when opposition parties and alliances criticised his fourth announcement of a parliamentary election in April 1985. The elections were cancelled a month before they were scheduled and all political activities other than the government-sponsored JP were banned. Hasina, the AL chief and Khaleda, the chairperson of the BNP, were placed under house arrest, martial law was tightened and all universities were closed. The opposition parties reacted sharply and argued that Ershad was 'continuing to deprive the people from an elected parliament and government...'.[51] The military leader tried to justify his decision but his explanations failed to satisfy either the main opposition parties or the people. Military officers in his government were also dissatisfied.[52]

Ershad announced a national referendum for 21 March 1998. As political activities and opposition to the referendum were banned, political parties not only urged a boycott of the referendum, but also called a *hartal* (general strike) on the same day. As major political leaders were under house arrest and the universities were closed it was difficult for the opposition to organise demonstrations, and the opposition's call for the poll boycott did not greatly influence the voters. The campaign was muted and completely one-sided and the opposition was blacked-out by the government-controlled electronic media. The voters were urged to support Ershad's 18-point programme. The proposition of the referendum was 'Do you support the policies of President Ershad, and do you want him to continue to run this administration until a civilian government is formed through elections...?' The voters were required to deposit an unmarked ballot in one of the two boxes: one with the General's picture in a military uniform to approve the referendum proposition, and a black box for disapproval.[53] Academics criticised the voting procedure of the referendum. Voters were not asked to mark ballot papers in any way. It was very easy for manipulators to move ballot papers from the black box to the one donning Ershad's portrait. The EC claimed 72 percent turnout in which 94.14 per cent were 'yes' votes. Observers found this figure too dubious and according to many of them the voter turn out was at best 15-20 percent.[54] *The Times* (London) mentioned a two percent turnout in its editorial 'Learning to Live with a Lie' and deemed the referendum a fraud.[55] However, Ershad was successful in conducting this symbolic election which gave him the so-called legitimacy as well as time to strengthen his support structure. This was part of Ershad's strategy 'to discredit the opposition, avoid a possible coup, and postpone elections once more...'.[56]

Third Parliamentary Election, 1986

It appeared by the activities of the opposition alliances and political parties that Ershad would not be able to obtain legitimacy nor would the opposition participate in any elections under his regime. The lack of mutual trust and unity between the political alliances provided Ershad with an opportunity to conduct the third parliamentary elections in which surprisingly one of the major alliances, the AL-led 15-party alliance, announced its participation at the eleventh hour.

Opposition Boycott and Partial Participation

Ershad announced several concessions to woo the political opposition but all major parties refused to participate.[57] The AL and CPB labelled Ershad's concessions as 'incomplete and ambiguous'.[58] Both alliances officially rejected them as they did not include anything about the withdrawal of martial law and the formation of a caretaker government to hold the elections, two major demands of the opposition movement. They also pledged to disrupt the polls by stopping prospective candidates from campaigning. The AL chief, Hasina, declared that those who would contest the mock elections would be considered 'national traitors' and 'people would never forgive them'.[59] Surprisingly on 21 March, a day before the deadline for the submission of nomination papers, the AL and some other parties of the 15-party alliance decided to contest the poll without discussing the issue with the 7-party alliance and other professional groups. The alliance suffered a jolt and seven of its component parties deserted protesting AL's undemocratic decision. Why did the AL take such a damaging decision which favoured Ershad?[60] The CPB and pro-Moscow parties of the 15-party alliance appeared to have influenced the AL to participate in the elections. Foreign embassies of various Western countries played a role before the election but it is not clear whether they advocated a pro-election stance. According to another analysis, '...AL realised that overthrowing the regime would be virtually impossible through processions and rallies, therefore, the party should take part in the election...'.[61] The leader of the AL could gain the status of the leader of the opposition and party leaders would get a legitimate forum for agitation. The AL leaders thought that if they continued to oppose the poll, martial law would be enforced even more severely, opposition leaders would be arrested, the elections would be postponed, and finally the position of the BNP would be better than that of the AL. One analysis strongly rejects all the defending arguments behind AL's sudden decision of contesting the poll and has highlighted the possibilities of a 'seat sharing agreement' between the JP and AL.[62]

Khaleda termed Hasina's decision 'a betrayal' and called her an opportunist. She held strongly to her decision of boycotting the elections. The *Jatiyatabadi Chattra Dal*, the student wing of the BNP supported Khaleda whereas AL's student wing was shocked by the decision of its leader.[63] Khaleda's non-compromising attitude increased her popularity as a leader among the general populace which was reflected later in the fifth parliamentary elections when her party contested the election for the first time after nine years and won convincingly.

Candidates, Campaign and Results

A total of 1,527 candidates – 1,074 from 28 political parties and 453 independents – contested the third parliamentary elections. The six weeks' campaign for the parties created little interest among the voters. The JP emphasised the development activities of the Ershad regime, especially its administrative decentralisation policy for rural development. It also criticised the AL's role particularly the one-party system introduced by it in 1975. The AL branded the Ershad regime as a military dictatorship, promised to restore parliamentary democracy, repeal all black laws, make the judiciary independent of the executive and grant freedom of press. In its campaign the AL used the image of Mujib and the party's major role in achieving independence of the country. The election boycotting parties, especially the BNP, attacked the AL for damaging the anti-military movement by participating in the election, called the election a result of an 'unholy alliance' and repeatedly reminded the electorate that an election under a military dictator could never be free, fair and impartial.

The official turnout was 60.31 percent which was the highest since independence. An election analysis shows that the government-favoured JP, though organisationally weak, won a simple majority (153 out of 300 seats) with the help of the civil bureaucracy and the police, who favoured the ruling oligarchy and manipulated the election results.[64] AL won 76 seats and the *Jamaat-e-Islami* 10 (see table 4.3 for detailed results).

Rigging and Impact

Malpractices and corruption, compared with previous parliamentary elections, advanced one step further in the third parliamentary elections. The major election boycotting party, the BNP had consistently criticised this election. Hasina and Abbas Ali Khan of JI accused the government of 'vote piracy'.[65] AL placed a seven point charter of demands including 're-polling in some polling stations, recounting of votes, and suspending of the announcement of results...'. Ershad defended his government by arguing that 'Hasina had her rigging statement ready before the elections were actually held. She was preparing a ground for her possible defeat...' in the election.[66]

Table 4.3 Results of the 1986 Parliamentary Election

Party/ Independents	No. of Seats Won	Percentage of Seats Won	No. of Votes Received	Percentage of Votes Received
JP	153	51.00	12,079,251	42.34
AL	76	25.33	7,462,157	26.16
JI	10	3.33	1,314,057	4.61
NAP	5	1.66	368,971	1.29
CPB	5	1.66	259,728	0.91
JSD-Rab	4	1.33	725,303	2.54
BML	4	1.33	412,765	1.45
JSD-Siraj	3	1.00	248,705	0.87
BKSAL	3	1.00	191,107	0.67
BWP	3	1.00	151,828	0.53
NAP-M	2	0.66	203,365	0.71
Other Parties	–	–	490,389	1.73
Independents	32	10.66	4,619,025	16.19

Source: Bangladesh Election Commission. Percentage of votes cast: 60.31. JP = *Jatiya* Party, AL = Bangladesh *Awami* League, JI = *Jamaat-e-Islami* Bangladesh, NAP = National *Awami* Party, CPB = Communist Party of Bangladesh, JSD-Rab = *Jatiya Samajtantrik Dal* – Rab, BML = Bangladesh Muslim League, JSD - Siraj = *Jatiya Samajtantrik Dal* - Siraj, BKSAL = Bangladesh *Krishak Sramik Awami* League, BWP = Bangladesh Workers Party, NAP-M = National *Awami* Party – Muzaffar.

Fifteen persons died and 750 were injured in electoral violence on the day of election.[67] According to a press note issued by the Home Ministry, voting was stopped in 284 vote centres due to violence.[68] The EC officially announced the postponement of voting in several centres in 36 constituencies as the situation had escalated out of control of the presiding officers there.[69] A British electoral observation team, the Peoples Commission for free elections, consisting of a former Labour minister, a Conservative MP and a BBC journalist considered the election a 'tragedy for democracy' and a 'cynically frustrated exercise'.[70] Although the EC termed the Peoples Commission illegal and criticised its interference in the electoral process, the team found this election to have totally failed to meet the hope of the participating parties for free and fair elections. Massive rigging and capturing vote centres by force were common practices after mid-morning.[71] The election appeared highly farcical to the foreign reporters, most of whom published reports highlighting the malpractices.[72] The BBC correspondent remarked: 'Voters were very few in the centres which I had visited. Returning officers agreed that voters were coming in a low rate to cast their votes...'.[73] Only five to 10 percent of voters cast their votes according to most reports.[74]

Ershad kept his promise of conducting an election although the results were unacceptable to the contesting parties. The BNP was in a good position to show that an election under a military regime was meaningless. The popularity of the party increased among the general populace for its uncompromising stance *vis-a-vis* the military regime. The AL won 76 seats, many more than it had won in the 1979 election, but lost its standing because of its 'undemocratic' decision to participate in the elections. Perhaps, realising its folly, the AL tried to neutralise the negative public sentiment by staying away from the first session of the new parliament. The BNP on the other hand demanded immediate dissolution of parliament and a fresh, free and fair election. Ershad instead of responding to this demand, shed his military attire, joined JP and became its chairman and called for a presidential election.

Presidential Election, 1986

Opposition Boycott

To strengthen regime legitimacy, a presidential election was held on 15 October, 1986. Ershad contested as JP's candidate. All major political parties, including the AL, apprehensive of the election being encumbered and unfair under the military government, decided to boycott it. Twelve candidates contested of whom only three were formidable contenders. They were Ershad, the 'venerated but old' religious leader Maulana Mohammadullah (Hafizzi Huzur) and Syed Farook Rahman, one of the chief protagonists of the August coup in 1975.

Campaign

The candidates refrained from attacking one another during the campaign; rather the parties, both contending and boycotting, advanced their cases for and against the election. The AL demanded the rejection of Rahman's candidacy as he had been involved in the killing of Mujib and 'also because his manifesto proposed changing the 'national anthem' and 'independence day' from March 26 to August 15' – the day Mujib was assassinated. The BNP maintained its previous stand of boycotting elections. It called this election an attempt to legitimise an illegal regime, demanded Ershad's resignation, dissolution of parliament, the release of political prisoners, and a free and fair election under an NCG. On the other hand, Ershad criticised the opposition by arguing that the people had lost their confidence and trust in both the AL and the BNP and reminded the masses about his development-oriented politics. Both the major candidates, Mohammadullah and Rahman had no support structure to organise a country-wide campaign although they organised a number of electoral meetings in divisional and district towns.

Results and Impact

As anticipated, Ershad won a landslide victory. The EC claimed a voter turnout of 54.23 percent. Ershad obtained 83.57 percent of the votes. His rivals, Mohammadullah, received only 5.69 percent of the votes cast; Rahman 4.5, while another nine candidates received an insignificant percentage. According to opposition sources, fewer than five percent of eligible voters had actually exercised their voting rights. Ershad took the oath as an elected president for a five year term on 23 October, called a 'Black Day' by the opposition. He was successful in passing the seventh amendment of the constitution, which was necessary in order to ratify his assumption of power in 1982 as CMLA and to 'indemnify his government from legal action against decisions made under martial law during the previous four and a-half years...'.[75] Ershad's party members voted infavour of the bill which validated all martial law proclamations and orders since March 1982. The prime minister called the amendment a 'glorious chapter' in the country's constitutional history whereas the leader of the opposition, Hasina, condemned it as a 'black chapter'. However labelled, the event formally transformed Ershad into a politician from a soldier and permitted him to lay claim to his rule being legitimate

The Fourth Parliamentary Elections, 1988

Background

The anti-regime movement increased and became popular in 1987. The main demand of the major alliances continued to centre on the resignation of Ershad, who they insisted, for the umpteenth time had assumed power unconstitutionally in 1982. They also pointed to the 'institutionalisation of corruption at all levels of government and administration, and systematic destruction of the electoral process...'.[76] The anti-Ershad movement obtained support from different professional groups and became popular among students.[77] Strikes, street demonstrations and protest marches were common and some of them were too aggressive for the police to handle. The repeated strikes by the opposition badly affected the economy and the administrative machinery almost collapsed. It appeared by the end of 1987 that Ershad would face difficulty staying in power.

Opposition Boycott, Campaign and Results

Ershad, on his part, dissolved the third parliament on 6 December 1987, and announced 3 March as the date of the fourth parliamentary elections. All major political parties including the AL, BNP and JI decided to boycott the election and reiterated their previous demand for Ershad's resignation and a fresh poll under an NCG. The government was resolute in its decision to proceed with the election by arguing that the legitimacy of an election depended on the participation of the electorate rather than the participation of the opposition political groups.[78]

As the mainline opposition parties boycotted the fourth parliamentary elections there was little eagerness among the electorate. Eight political parties and 764 candidates contested the polls – the lowest numbers since independence.[79] Electors in most constituencies in the country did not vote.

A nation-wide strike was called by the opposition parties on the day of election and the streets appeared empty. No campaign centres were set up nor was there any rush to transport voters to the polling centres. The atmosphere was dramatically different from previous elections. Minor opposition parties that contested the election were unable to compete with the ruling JP, which easily won 251 seats (18 of them were elected uncontested) and obtained 68.48 percent of the votes cast. No other political parties except the Combined Opposition Party (COP) won any significant number of seats[80] (see Table 4.4 for the results). The EC claimed 52.48 percent turnout; the opposition sources believed that only one percent of voters voted in the election.[81]

Table 4.4. March 1988 Parliamentary Election Results

Party/ Independents	No. of Seats Won	% of Seats Won	No. of Votes Received	% of Votes Received of Total Votes Cast
JP	251	83.66	1,76,80,133	68.44
COP	19	6.33	32,63,340	12.63
JSD (Siraj)	3	1.00	3,09,666	1.20
FP	2	0.66	8,50,248	3.29
Other Parties	-	-	2,42,571	0.94
Independents	25	8.33	34,87,457	13.50

Source: Muhammad A. Hakim (1993), *Bangladesh Politics: The Shahabuddin Interregnum,* The University Press Limited, Dhaka, pp. 30-31. JP = *Jatiya* Party, COP = Combined Opposition Party, JSD – Siraj = *Jatiya Samajtantrik Dal* – Siraj, FP = Freedom Party.

Rigging

The election became an absolute farce and a game of capturing election booths by the musclemen of the ruling party, who had no trouble in establishing their dominance in the absence of the two major alliances.[82] The opposition was successful in its boycott call of elections, which were marred by widespread fraud and vote rigging perpetrated by the pro-regime activists who wanted to inflate the number of votes obtained by JP candidates.[83] Violence resulting from the physical confrontation between pro-election and anti-election camps led the postponement of polling in 72

Table 4.5 The Degree of Corruption in Elections Under Military Rule in Bangladesh

Electoral Exercise	Rigging	Violence/ Intimidation	Restrictions on campaign/ party activities	Use of electronic media	Bureaucratic bias	Use of religion
Zia Regime						
Referendum 1977	MH	M	H	H	M	VL
Presidential 1978	M	M	MH	H	M	L
Parliamentary 1979	ML	MH	M	MH	MH	M
Ershad Regime						
Referendum 1985	H	M	H	H	H	L
Parliamentary 1986	MH	MH	MH	MH	H	L
Presidential 1986	H	VH	H	VH	VH	M
Parliamentary 1988	VH	VH	H	VH	VH	VH

Index: VL= Very Low; L= Low; ML= Moderately Low; M= Medium; MH= Moderately High; H = High; VH= Very High.
Source: Based on primary and secondary sources.

vote centres in Dhaka alone. Seven people died and more than 300 were injured in electoral violence in the capital.[84]

The control of media was tight and although restrictions at first were imposed prohibiting comments on the election, the information minister advised the journalists to report objectively.[85] Most of the journalists considered this election horseplay although the home minister called it unfettered, impartial and peaceful as any British election.[86] Table 4.5 shows the estimated degree of electoral corruption under the two military regimes.

Review

All seven elections under two military regimes were characterised by electoral fraud. The degree of rigging in the Zia and Ershad regimes were moderate and high respectively. The rigging reached its peak in the 1988 election and made a mockery of the electoral process. The degree of violence and intimidation were moderate in elections organised by the Zia regime but it was high in elections under Ershad. The use of violence and intimidation in the third and fourth parliamentary elections was extreme. As major opposition parties boycotted the 1988 election, the ruling JP activists had little trouble in capturing vote centres by establishing a reign of terror. Both military leaders severely restricted campaign and party activities. Zia, after strengthening his own party allowed the re-activation of other parties while Ershad was unwilling to lift restrictions upon party activities because of the lack of a support base for his own party. The restriction on the electronic media was tight under both these regimes. The bureaucracy always favoured the ruling party instead of playing a neutral role. It displayed extreme partisanship in all elections under the Ershad regime. The military leaders used religion to their advantage, moderately in the 1979 and 1986 elections but more widely in the 1988 election.

Summing Up

Both Zia and Ershad employed almost similar civilianisation strategies and used elections as a 'tool' to legitimise their rules. Their civilianisation process started with a referendum and was followed by presidential and parliamentary elections. Zia did comparatively better than Ershad in this regard and was successful in making the opposition participate in these elections. His village-based politics and rural mobilisation policies helped his party gain support at the local level. Zia's tactics in using the military and bureaucracy and splitting opposition parties and the exploitation of pro-Islamic and anti-Indian sentiments of the people served his political purpose very effectively. His constitutional reforms, to some extent, were also accepted by the people. His rule thus obtained legitimacy. On the other hand, Ershad was unable to achieve the same degree of legitimacy although he ruled the country for almost nine years. The opposition parties and alliances decided not to participate in elections under his martial law regime. Despite this stance of the opposition, two parliamentary elections were held and Ershad was successful in attracting at least one major opposition alliance to participate in one of these two elections.[87] The BNP's uncompromising attitude was the most important single factor in his failure to achieve legitimation for his rule.

The status of elections as a crucial democratic institution was badly damaged by Ershad. People lost faith in elections and were reluctant to go to the polling booths. The opposition could not campaign freely, nor could the media play an impartial role. The *upazila* (local council) ensured administrative support for the regime that helped him continue in power.

During both regimes, the bureaucracy contributed towards easy victories for the ruling parties. Use of physical force and violence became so common that honest and peace-loving people absented themselves from electoral activities. Thus electoral corruption under military rule which started during the Zia regime reached its peak and made elections a futile exercise during Ershad's autocratic rule.

Notes

[1] The Bangladesh Constitution, as amended during the regime of Sheikh Mujibur Rahman, permits a President to designate his successor.
[2] Ved. M. (1981), 'Bangladesh Under Ziaur Rahman: An Analytical Survey', *Foreign Affairs Reports*, vol. XXX, no. 9, p. 186.
[3] Smith, T. B. (1986), 'Referendum Politics in Asia', *Asian Survey*, vol. XXVI, no. VII, p. 795.
[4] Ved, 'Bangladesh Under Ziaur Rahman: An Analytical Survey', *op. cit.*, p. 186.
[5] *Azad*, 7 February, 1977.
[6] M. Rashiduzzaman conducted this survey of 51 selected village councils and 201 members and chairmen in the summer of 1977. Cited in, Rashiduzzaman, M. (1978), 'Bangladesh in 1977: Dilemmas of the Military Rulers', *Asian Survey*, vol. XVIII, no. II, p. 127.
[7] *Ibid.*, p. 128.

[8] Baxter C. and Rashiduzzaman, M. (1981), 'Bangladesh Votes: 1978 and 1979', *Asian Survey*, vol. XXI, no. IV, p. 486. According to Franda the percentage of 'yes' votes was 98.99, and according to Khan it was 98.89. See, Franda, M. (1979), 'Ziaur Rahman's Bangladesh: Political Realignment', *AUFS Report*, p. 1; Khan, Z. R. (1983), *Leadership in the Least Developed Nation: Bangladesh*, Maxwell School of Citizenship and Public Affairs, Syracuse University, Syracuse, p. 147.

[9] Rashiduzzaman, 'Bangladesh in 1977: Dilemmas of the Military Rulers', *op. cit.*, pp. 126-27.

[10] *Bangladesh Times*, 31 May, 1977.

[11] Maniruzzaman, T. (1980), *Bangladesh Revolution and Its Aftermath*, Bangladesh Book International, Dhaka) p. 217.

[12] Khan, *Leadership in the Least developed Nation: Bangladesh, op. cit.*, pp. 147-48.

[13] There were 26 coup attempts against President Zia during his stay in power. See, Haque, A. (1980), 'Bangladesh in 1980: Strains and Stresses — Opposition in the Doldrums', *Asian Survey*, vol. XXI, no. II, p. 192; also cited in Huque, A. S. and Akhter, M. Y. (1989), 'Militarisation and Opposition in Bangladesh: Parliamentary Approval and Public Reaction', *The Journal of Commonwealth and Comparative Politics*, vol. XXVII, no. II, pp. 172-84.

[14] More than 130 persons died during the rebellion and many more in the backlash. See, Ved, 'Bangladesh Under Ziaur Rahman: An Analytical Survey', *op. cit.*, p. 188.

[15] See, Baxter, C. (1984), *Bangladesh: A New Nation in an Old Setting*, Westview Press, London, p. 65.

[16] Jahan, R. (1980), 'The Zia Regime: Once Again at the Starting Point', included in her *Bangladesh Politics: Problems and Issues*, University Press Limited, Dhaka, p. 212.

[17] Zaman, M. Q. (1984), 'Ziaur Rahman: Leadership Styles and Mobilisation Policies', *The Indian Political Science Review*, vol. XVIII, no. II, p. 199.

[18] Rashiduzzaman, M. (1979), 'Bangladesh 1978: Search for a Political Party', *Asian Survey*, vol. XIX, no. II, p. 191.

[19] There were six political parties in JF. They were JAGODAL, NAP (Bhashani), Bangladesh Muslim League, United People's Party, Bangladesh Labour Party and Bangladesh *Tapshili* Fedararion. The GOJ was consisted of *Awami* League, the pro-Moscow National *Awami* Party, People's League, *Jatiya Janata* Party, *Krishak Sharamik* Party and *Jatiya* League.

[20] Jahan, 'The Zia Regime: Once Again at the Starting Point', in her *Bangladesh Politics; Problems and Issues, op. cit.*, quoted in, Zaman, 'Ziaur Rahman: Leadership Styles and Mobilisation Policies', *op. cit.*, p. 199.

[21] *Bangladesh Times*, 9 May, 1978.

[22] Cited in , Ved, 'Bangladesh Under Ziaur Rahman: An Analytical Survey', *op. cit.*, p. 189.

[23] *Keesing Contemporary Archives*, 15 September, 1978, p. 29197, quoted in, Zaman, *op. cit.*, p. 199.

[24] Zaman, 'Ziaur Rahman: Leadership Styles and Mobilisation Policies' *op. cit.*, p. 199; for related information also see, Franda, M. (1979), 'Ziaur Rahman's Bangladesh: Political Realignment', *AUFS Report*, p. 3.

[25] For rigging allegation in the election see, Rizvi, G. (1985), *Bangladesh: the Struggle for the Restoration of Democracy*, Bangabandhu Society, Europe, London, p. 52; Franda, 'Ziaur Rahman's Bangladesh: Political Realignment', *op. cit.*, p. 3, cited in Zaman, 'Ziaur Rahman: Leadership Styles and Mobilisation Policies' *op. cit.*, p. 199.

[26] Baxter and Rashiduzzaman, 'Bangladesh Votes: 1978 and 1979', *Asian Survey, op. cit.*, p. 487.

[27] For detail on this division and confrontation, see, Khan, M. M. and Zafarullah, H. M. (1979), 'The 1979 Parliamentary Elections in Bangladesh', *Asian Survey*, vol. XIX, no. X, pp. 1023-36.

[28] The Political Parties Regulation Order (PPR) was promulgated in July 1976. Political parties under this regulation were required to submit their constitution and programmes to the government for its approval. For related information, see, Khan and Zafarullah, 'The 1979 Parliamentary Elections in Bangladesh', *op. cit.*, p. 1025.

[29] See, Franda, M. (1981), 'Bangladesh Nationalism and Ziaur Rahman's Presidency, Part 1', *AUFS Report*, p. 5.

[30] Khan and Zafarullah, 'The 1979 Parliamentary Elections in Bangladesh', *op. cit.*, p. 1025.

[31] The name of these parties were: the Bangladesh *Jatiya* League (BJL), *Jatiya Janata* Party (JJP), *Jatiya Somajtantrik Dal* (JSD), *Gono Azadi* League - Tarkabagish fraction (GAL-T), Democratic League (DL), National *Awami* Party-Naser (NAP-N), Bangladesh *Gonotantrik Andalan* (BGA), *Sramik Krishak Somajbadi Dal* (SKSD), National Front For Democracy (NDF), *Awami* League-Malek Ukil (AL-MU), *Awami* League-Mizan Chaudhury (AL-MC), and United People's Party (UPP). See, Khan and Zafarullah, *ibid.*, p. 1025.

[32] See, Haque, A. (1980), 'Bangladesh 1979: Cry for a Sovereign Parliament', *Asian Survey*, vol. XX, no. II, p. 218.

[33] *The Daily Ittefaq*, December 8, 1978.

[34] *The Bangladesh Observer*, 11 and 13 December, 1978, *The Daily Ittefaq*, 15 and 24 December, 1978, cited in, Khan and Zafarullah, 'The 1979 Parliamentary Elections in Bangladesh', *op. cit.*, p. 1026. These parties were: the BNP, Islamic Democratic League-Rahim (IDL-R), Islamic Democratic League-Siddiki (IDL-S), Bangladesh Labour Party-Matin (BLP-M), Bangladesh *Jatiya Dal*-Huda (BJD-H), Bangladesh Democratic Party (BDP), *Gono Azadi* League-Rabbani (GAL-R), Bangladesh *Sammyabadi Dal*-Toaha (BSD-T), and National *Awami* Party-Nurur-Zahid (NAP-NZ).

[35] For a detail list of these concessions, see, *ibid.*, pp. 1026-27.

[36] BML and IDL-R formed a rightist alliance. IDL-S, *Krishak Sramik* Party (KSP), Bangladesh *Jatiya Dal*-Amena (BJD-A), National *Awami* Party-Sattar (NAP-S), and People's Democratic Party (PDP) formed the second alliance. The third alliance was a six-party 'leftist-centrist combine composed of the JSD, UPP, BJL, NAP-NZ, BGA and SKSD. For detail, see, Khan and Zafarullah, 'The 1979 Parliamentary Elections in Bangladesh', *op. cit.*, p. 1028.

[37] In many Third World countries where a large number of voters are illiterate the EC allocates symbols to political parties. The candidates are known by their symbols. Sometimes in rural areas, the symbols become so prominent that the voters forget about the candidate and rely only on the symbols. It is a feature of Bangladeshi electoral culture. The slogan immediately prior to the fifth parliamentary election '*nauka thekao*' (oppose boat), the electoral symbol of the AL, greatly influenced the illiterate voters.

[38] *Ibid.*, p. 1029.

[39] *The Bangladesh Observer*, 2 February, 1979, cited in *ibid.*, p. 1029.

[40] The most prominent of these black laws was the Special Powers Act, 1974, promulgated by the AL government. This Act provides for the detention by the government of any person without formal charge to prevent him/her from committing any prejudicial act. It was enacted with the intention of oppressing political opposition as it provides authority to arrest political leaders. This law has been criticised by every political party while in opposition but these same parties have used it to weaken the opposition after assuming power. See, Hakim, M. A. (1991), 'Legitimacy Crisis and United Opposition: The Fall of Ershad Regime in Bangladesh', *South Asia Journal*,

vol. 5, no. 2, 1991, p. 195, fn. 18; Khan and Zafarullah, 'The 1979 Parliamentary Elections in Bangladesh', *op. cit.*, p. 1029; Zafarullah, H. (1998), 'Consolidating Democratic Governance: One Step Forward, Two Steps Back', a paper presented at the 12 Biennial Conference of the Asian Studies Association, Australia, University of New South Wales, Sydney, 28 September – 1 October.

[41] For a brief description on their manifestos, see, *ibid.*, pp. 1029-30.

[42] Haque, 'Bangladesh 1979: Cry For a Sovereign Parliament', *op. cit.*, p. 219.

[43] Huque, A. S. and Hakim, M. A. (1993), 'Elections in Bangladesh: Tools of Legitimacy', *Asian Affairs An American Review*, vol. 19. no. 4, p. 252; Haque, 'Bangladesh 1979: Cry For a Sovereign Parliament', *op. cit.*, p. 219.

[44] Zaman, H. (1983), 'The Role of Military in Bangladesh and Pakistan: A Comparative Study', *Asian Profile*, vol. 11, no. 4, p. 386.

[45] Huque and Hakim, 'Elections in Bangladesh: Tools of Legitimacy', *op. cit.*, p. 252.

[46] Maniruzzaman, T. (1980), *The Bangladesh Revolution and Its Aftermath*, Bangladesh Book International, Dhaka, p. 227.

[47] See, Akhter, M. Y. (1991), *Search for the Nature of Corruption: Bangladesh* (in Bengali), Nibedan Publications Limited, Dhaka, pp. 142-43.

[48] The alleging opposition leaders were President, General Secretary and Organising Secretary of then AL Abdul Malek Ukil, Abdur Razzak and Tofail Ahmed respectively; ML leader Khan A. Sabur; AL-MC President Mizanur Rahman Chaudhury, and Shahjahan Siraj of JSD. See, *The Daily Ittefaq*, 19 and 23 February 1979.

[49] *Weekly Bichitra*, March 2, 1979, cited in Khan and Zafarullah, 'The 1979 Parliamentary Elections in Bangladesh', *op. cit.*, p. 1035.

[50] *Ibid.*, p. 1035.

[51] Cited in Bertocci, P. J. (1986), 'Bangladesh in 1985: Resolute Against the Storms', *Asian Survey*, vol. XXV, no. II, p. 228.

[52] See for detail, Smith, 'Referendum Politics in Asia', *op. cit.*, p. 797.

[53] Smith, *ibid.*, p. 797.

[54] For example, see, Bertocci, 'Bangladesh in 1985: Resolute Against the Storms', *op. cit.*, p. 229.

[55] Gain, P. (1995), 'General Elections in Bangladesh', in, Q. A. Tahmina, P. Gain and S. Moral (eds), *The Reporter's Guide: Handbook on Election Reporting*, Society for Environment and Human Development (SHED), Dhaka, 1995 p. 119.

[56] Smith, 'Referendum Politics in Asia', *op. cit.*, p. 797.

[57] These concessions were: the ministers who might contest the poll would resign prior to the election; use of state facilities for election campaigning would be prohibited, and abolition of military courts and offices of regional martial law administrators. See, Islam, S. S. (1987), 'Bangladesh in 1986: Entering a New Phase', *Asian Survey*, vol. XXVII, no. II, p. 164, also cited in Hakim, M. A. (1993), *Bangladesh Politics: The Shahabuddin Interregnum*, The University Press Limited, Dhaka, p. 38, Fn. 46.

[58] See, Kabir, B. M. (1987), 'Movement and Elections: Legitimisation of Military Rule in Bangladesh', unpublished paper presented at the seminar held on the occasion of the Fifth National Conference of the Bangladesh Political Science Association, 13-14 July, Rajshahi University, Bangladesh, p. 14.

[59] Ziring, L. (1992), *Bangladesh: From Mujib to Ershad, An Interpretive Study*, Oxford University Press, Oxford, p. 193.

[60] Why 15-party alliance contested in 1986 parliamentary elections has been analysed among others by Hakim, Islam and Kabir. See for their analysis, Hakim, *Bangladesh Politics: The Shahabuddin Interregnum*, *op. cit.*, pp. 23-27; Islam, 'Bangladesh in

1986: Entering a New Phase', *op. cit.*, pp. 163-68; Kabir, 'Movement and Elections: Legitimisation of the Military Rule in Bangladesh', *op. cit.*, pp. 14-18.
61. Islam, 'Bangladesh in 1986: Entering a New Phase', *op. cit.*, p. 165.
62. Hakim, *Bangladesh Politics: The Shahabuddin Interregnum*, *op. cit.*, p. 24.
63. See, Ziring, *Bangladesh: From Mujib to Ershad, An Interpretive Study*, *op.cit.*, p. 195.
64. Hakim, *Bangladesh Politics: The Shahabuddin Interregnum*, *op. cit.* p. 24.
65. *Robbar*, 11 May, 1986, p. 11.
66. Cited in Islam, 'Bangladesh in 1986: Entering a New Phase', *op. cit.*, p. 166.
67. *Weekly Bichittra*, 16 May, 1986, p. 20.
68. *Ibid.*, p. 21.
69. *Ibid.*, p. 20.
70. Cited in Islam, 'Bangladesh in 1986: Entering a New Phase', *op. cit.*, p. 166; see also for related information, Huque and Hakim, 'Elections in Bangladesh: Tools of Legitimacy', *op. cit.*, p. 256.
71. See, Akhter, *Search for the Corruption: Bangladesh*, *op. cit.*, p. 143.
72. Some of the foreign reporters were: Bon Tamest, correspondent of *Los Angeles Times*, Michael Hamylon of *Times*, John Elliott of *Financial Times*, Eric Silver of *Guardian* and Stephen R. Wiseman of *New York Times*.
73. The report of Mark Tali was broadcast from the BBC on the night of May 7, 1986.
74. *Robbar*, 10 May, 1986, p. 11.
75. Islam, 'Bangladesh in 1986: Entering a New Phase', *op. cit.*, p. 169.
76. Hakim, 'Legitimacy Crisis and United Opposition: The Fall of Ershad Regime in Bangladesh', *op. cit.*, p. 188.
77. For related information, see, Ziring, *Bangladesh: From Mujib to Ershad*, *op. cit.*, p. 209.
78. See for related information, Rahman, S. (1989), 'Bangladesh in 1988: Precarious Institution Building Amid Crisis Management', *Asian Survey*, vol. XXIX, no. II, p. 218; also see, *Far Eastern Economic Review*, 25 February, 1988, p. 20.
79. Hakim, 'Legitimacy Crisis and United Opposition: The Fall of Ershad Regime in Bangladesh', *op. cit.*, p. 188.
80. Combined opposition party was an alliance of 76 small parties and factions.
81. Hakim, 'Legitimacy Crisis and United Opposition: The Fall of Ershad Regime in Bangladesh', *op. cit.*, p. 188.
82. The 1988 election has been branded as a game of capturing election booths. See, *Robbar*, 11 March, 1988, p. 9.
83. See the reports of Derek Brown and Arshad Mahmud, *The Guardian*, 4 March, 1988. Also see, the report of the Bruce Palling, *The Independent*, 4 March, 1988.
84. *Robbar*, 6 March 1988, pp. 15-16.
85. *Ibid.*, pp. 15-16.
86. *Weekly Purnima*, 9 March, 1988, p. 21.
87. The 15-party alliance, which later became 8-party alliance, participated in the 1986 parliamentary election.

5 Electoral Politics and Corruption Under Civilian Rule

Introduction

This chapter analyses the electoral politics and corruption under civilian governments in Bangladesh, namely the Mujib, Sattar and Khaleda regimes. It focuses in detail on the first and sixth parliamentary elections, 1981 presidential election, and the 1991 referendum. The chapter also investigates the city corporation election and the Magura-2 constituency by-election because of their special importance in the country's politics. Finally, it examines the degree of corruption in different elections during civilian rule and estimates whether civilian rule lessened electoral corruption.

The civilian rulers in Bangladesh operated in a political-electoral culture that had been created and nurtured by the military rulers in Pakistan before Bangladesh's independence. They found it difficult to imbue the masses with the values of democracy in spite of their being elected democratically. The chapter will also consider why and how the civilian rulers failed to democratise society, their approach to elections, media, and the bureaucracy as well as highlighting their undemocratic attitude to opposition and in running state affairs.

The Mujib Regime (1972-75)

The AL on the basis of its mandate in the 1970 elections under united Pakistan, formed government after independence. In the formative phase, opposition to the new regime was weak but gradually crystallised in the wake of the undemocratic behaviour of the political leadership, use of coercive instruments, irrational policies, maladministration and undisguised political patronage.

Mujib ruled with an iron hand. He created the *Jatiya Rakkhi Bahini* (JRB) and enacted draconian laws like the Special Powers Act ostensibly to control law and order but in practice used it for the purpose of suppressing political opposition. The parliament ran according to his dictates and passed whatever proposals he recommended. It rarely deliberated on important national issues, failed to enforce accountability of the administration and thus made a mockery of parliamentary democracy. Mujib declared a state of emergency in late-1974 to deal with a declining social and economic situation. If that was not enough, he transformed the format of the country's political system by introducing a one-party presidential system, centralised the administrative apparatus, strangled the press, and made the state a pawn of his dwindling charisma. Before Mujib could fully implement his one-party system, he was assassinated by a faction of the army. The country was subject to military-cum civilianised rule from August 1975 until another assassination -- that of the first military ruler Zia in May 1981. Elections under this regime have been discussed in the previous chapter.

Opposition parties were critical of AL's performance in managing state affairs. The newly emerging opposition, the *Jatiya Samajtantrik Dal* (JSD), questioned the legality of the AL to govern as the law under which it was elected in 1970 had become invalid after the country's independence. To silence his opponents and to obtain complete legitimacy, Mujib decided to hold an early election before his party's popularity declined. This was the first parliamentary election in independent Bangladesh, held on 7 March 1973.

The First Parliamentary Election, 1973

One of the remarkable achievements of the Mujib regime was the enactment of the country's constitution within a year of the country's independence. In Pakistan, by way of contrast, it took the political leaders almost nine years to frame the country's foremost legal document. It was on the basis of this 1972 constitution that the first parliamentary election was held four months after it was adopted by the Constituent Assembly.

Candidates, Campaign and Results

Fourteen political parties and 1,075 candidates contested the elections. The opposition political parties were not sufficiently organised to counter the AL. The outstanding opposition leader was the octogenarian firebrand Maulana Bhashani who was able to bring six political parties and eight front-organisation under the umbrella of the All Party Action Committee (APAC) with 201 candidates. The committee did not include the major opposition parties like the pro-Moscow National *Awami* Party (NAP-M) and JSD. The latter, headed by liberation war hero Major M. A. Jalil and student leader, A. S. M. Abdur Rab, emerged as the biggest single opposition contender with 237 candidates, closely followed by NAP-M with 225. Another important feature of this election was the absence of religious-based parties, which were banned by the regime for collaborating with the Pakistani junta during the liberation war.

The voters showed little interest in the election, well aware of its outcome, but there was plenty of bitterness among the different political groups. Frequent outbreaks of violence occurred during the election campaign in which 50 people were killed.[1] The JSD chief was wounded early in February when ruling party activists opened fire on a party meeting. According to press reports, the opposition conducted its campaign under many disadvantages, as all but one of the 16 newspapers were controlled by or supported the regime.[2]

None of the political parties presented alternative policies. Campaigning took the form of parties branding one another conspirators bent upon destroying the country. Indeed 'conspiracy' was the common issue in the campaign. The ruling AL singled out the opposition parties as agents of 'US-Chinese imperialists, conspiring to undermine the sovereignty and integrity of Bangladesh...'. The NAP-M and the Communist Party of Bangladesh (CPB) also called other parties agents of 'US-Chinese imperialism', engaged in conspiracy against the socialist policy of Bangladesh. The pro-Chinese NAP led by Bhasani (NAP-B) and the JSD labelled the AL, NAP-M, and the CPB as 'tools of Soviet-Indian social imperialists'.[3]

As predicted, the AL won a major victory. It secured 293 seats out of 300. The JSD and the *Jatiya* League (JL) won one seat each; five seats went to the independents. The turnout was 54.91 percent and the AL secured 73.16 percent of the votes cast.[4] The dissensions among the opposition groups virtually assured the ruling party of victory, but the AL also used Mujib's charisma in winning the election. According to an analyst, people voted for the AL because they saw 'Mujib himself in every *Awami* League candidate'.[5] This overwhelming win for the ruling party created parliamentary imbalance and transformed the house into a one-party entity.[6]

AL's electoral strategy of 'overkilling the opposition', which almost wiped out its political adversaries from parliament, had a dysfunctional impact on the democratic system. The rigging by the ruling party raised doubts about the credibility of the election results both at home and abroad.[7] The AL's hold on 11 seats without contest brought forth loud protests from opposition parties who alleged that their candidates were physically prevented from filing their nominations in some of those constituencies.[8] Some of the defeated opposition leaders complained that the ruling party intimidated their workers and used unfair means to win the election.[9] JSD leaders alleged that several of their candidates were threatened by the ruling party and were not allowed to submit nomination papers. They also questioned the neutrality of the chief election commissioner and demanded his resignation.[10] Government transport units intended for relief operations were used in the ruling party's campaign.[11] Relief goods meant for free distribution among the poor and the destitute were used to bribe voters to obtain their support. Rumours were rife about people being transported from across the border to cast false votes for ruling party candidates. Irregularities were not uncommon during the counting of ballots and the announcement of election results. The electronic media were heavily influenced by the regime to suppress any news of opposition candidates leading in some constituencies. The JSD chief, who was leading by a huge margin against an incumbent minister was mysteriously declared defeated long after the media had suddenly stopped relaying results from the constituency.[12] This baffled many electoral analysts and the opposition. The ruling party in collaboration with the police administration and the JRB instigated violence and ensured the defeat of potential opposition candidates. AL supporters who were placed in key positions in the nationalised enterprises also did their fair share of politicking for the party. All and all, the dominant role of the ruling party leaders and activists prevented a free, fair and democratic electoral exercise which had an impact on the future parliamentary elections in the country.

Local Government Elections

Nine months after the parliamentary elections, the Mujib government organised local elections. This was the first opportunity in independent Bangladesh for the people to elect their representatives to positions on local councils in both the rural and urban areas. These elections, spread over two weeks in 4,249 union *parisads* and 69 *paurashavas* (municipalities), were different from those in the past as for the first time chairmen and vice chairmen of these grassroots bodies were directly elected by the people. A total of 18,558 candidates vied for the union *parisad* chair, while the number contesting the vice chairmanship was 17,860. Another 38,326 nominated for general membership of the councils.[13] This high rate of participation displayed the ebullience which the people brought to these elections. As they were held on a non-party basis, none of the parties nominated candidates. Village politics, kinship bondage, patron-client relationships and local level groupings were more important in electioneering and outcome. However, in the post-election milieu, the ruling AL adopted a strategy of winning over the elected representatives.

No rigorous analysis of the first local government elections was undertaken. One study, however, noted the absence of any major rigging or violence before or during the elections.[14] As the election was held on non-party basis and the majority of rural voters were concentrating on their financial recovery after the liberation war, village politics and local level groupings were not characterised by their usual violence. However, the election was not free of irregularities; the degree of rigging and other malpractice was balanced by rival candidates' equal strength in resorting to electoral fraud and violence.

The Sattar Interregnum: 1981 Presidential Election

After Zia's assassination, Sattar took over management of the affairs of the country in an acting capacity until his election to the presidency in 1981. He wanted to be a civilian ruler to the dismay.

Candidates and Campaign

The BNP successfully exploited people's sympathy following the brutal killing of Zia and decided to seek an early mandate from voters. Sattar was the automatic choice of the BNP to contest the poll. Eighty two other candidates filed nominations of which 72 were valid. After withdrawals the number was reduced to 39, although only five candidates were successful in attracting support. Sattar's principal opponents were AL's Kamal Hossain, retired General M.A.G. Osmani, sponsored by a citizens' committee, M. A. Jalil proposed by the JSD-led three party alliance, and an independent candidate Maulana Mohammadullah (Hafezji Huzur). Other known political figures who contested the race included Mozaffar Ahmed, Mohammad Toaha, Aleem Al-Razee, Maulana Abdur Rahim, and Selina Majumder.[15] However, the contest became a straight fight between the two candidates belonging to the ruling BNP and the main opposition party, the AL.

The electoral fight of the two prominent candidates centred on the issues bequeathed by two dead charismatic leaders, Zia and Mujib. Sattar campaigned on Zia's successes, especially his 19-point programme.[16] The

BNP manifesto included the building of a self-reliant economy, ensuring people's participation at all levels of administration, the initiating of new development programmes and the maintenance of law and order. It also emphasised the increase of production in different sectors to make the country self-sufficient. Sattar claimed that he was Zia's chosen heir and appealed to the voters to give him the opportunity to complete the unfinished programmes and policies initiated by the slain leader. Sattar's reputation as an 'astute political negotiator' and a 'sensible administrator' proved significant in the defeat of his main opponent, Hossain. Sattar successfully utilised the grass root support of the BNP that had been created by Zia through his extensive tours in remote areas and institution building programmes.

Kamal Hossain was the only opposition candidate who was successful in attracting both the Bangladeshi elite and masses. Hossain, a respectable political leader and a close confidant of Mujib, had won in the elections of 1970 and 1973 but lost in the next four parliamentary elections contested by the AL. Nevertheless, the AL found him the most suitable person for the job because of his vast experience as a lawyer and constitutional expert. The AL focused on a multi-party parliamentary system as envisaged in the original 1972 constitution before its amendment by the AL itself in 1975. Hossain wanted to win the support of the anti-BKSAL (Bangladesh *Krisak Sramik Awami* League) voters by introducing a multi-party system while at the same time trying to capture the support of pro-BKSAL elements by stressing Mujib's approach towards statecraft. A literate section of voters was confused when Hossain, after including a multi-party system in his party's 17-point programme, said, '...this system would not be in contradiction with any administrative policies adopted by Mujib's one-party government in January 1975'.[17]

Two other issues had an impact on the electoral campaign: first, the critical comment of the army chief of staff, H. M. Ershad, on the role of the BNP, and secondly, the acceptability of the AL as an alternative government. BKSAL and Osmani prompted speculation about a military takeover and created uncertainty about the outcome of the election.[18] Ershad clarified his statement later and finally settled the issue by saying that all controversy regarding his statements would be decided by the people in the democratic tradition. He asserted that the verdict of the people in the next presidential election would be honoured by the army.[19] Moreover, the rival groups of the *Chattra* League, one supported by AL's president and the other by the party's secretary clashed frequently during the campaign which had a negative impact on the electioneering of the AL. Pre-election violence especially between AL and the BNP was severe.

The campaign reached its climax by the first week of November when all the five major candidates addressed big public rallies. AL president Hasina attracted surprisingly large and enthusiastic crowds. Hossain tried to impress the voters by his measured, smooth and simple delivery described by one journalist as 'professorial' instead of electioneering in the manner of fiery speeches of other party candidates.[20] In the final stage of the campaign, both parties attacked each other in the language of weaponry and raised the possibility of poll rigging by the rival party. The AL candidate probably could anticipate the results and declared that any election result other than a victory for him would only indicate rigging. He also hinted at launching a mass movement in such a situation.

The BNP candidate in a similar fashion accused the AL of rigging the 1973 parliamentary election and called it a master of the rigging game. He said that as the AL had no chance of winning in a straight fight, they would try hard to rig the election. The BNP candidate instructed the government officials and his party workers to check any attempts by the AL to rig the election. The AL president also asked her followers to form 'rigging resistance bodies' throughout the country to prevent electoral manipulation by the ruling party.

Other major opposition candidates criticised both the AL and the BNP of being two sides of the same coin. Rab, the chief campaign coordinator of Jalil, encapsulated the criticism of the BNP and the AL by other major candidates. He argued:

> BNP's continuance in power will mean more corruption, higher prices, military influence over politics and frequent coups. The Awami League's return to power will mean murder and looting.[21]

Rigging, Results and Impact

The turnout was 54.47 percent and Sattar won comprehensively receiving 66 percent of the votes cast. He won 14 million votes to Hossain's 5.6 million. As predicted, the AL promptly accused the ruling party of extensive poll-rigging and announced plans for demonstrations and nationwide general protest.[22] Hossain in a post-poll press conference alleged that most of his polling agents had been driven out of polling stations and ballot boxes were stuffed in their absence. He further alleged that the minority Hindu voters, whom he considered his supporters, had been intimidated and, in a large number of cases, even prevented from voting. He claimed that the election results were 'manufactured' in Bangabhaban (the president's residence) and commented on the role of the EC as 'neither impartial nor fair'.

The BNP, on the other hand, rejected the rigging allegations of the opposition and claimed their victory as a clear verdict in favour of the continuing process of democratisation and economic development initiated by Zia. One analyst termed BNP's win as 'largely due to the fear of AL's misrule' which was 'still fresh in people's minds'.[23] Others argued that as the AL candidate was a close follower of Mujib and his programmes and policies, 'voters were not prepared to return to days of Mujibism'.[24] The allegations of political corruption, economic wastefulness and administrative mismanagement against the ruling party by the opposition did not alter the verdict of the people.[25] The election results showed strong grass roots support for the ruling party.

The election, however, was not totally free from irregularities, although the ruling and opposition parties enjoyed almost equal opportunities to use different techniques to persuade and intimidate voters. There were reports of some rigging and limited violence by both the parties, which according to an analyst of the election had a 'neutralising effect on the total electoral outcome', and it was as fair as possible under the conditions prevailing in a developing country like Bangladesh.[26] The causes of BNP's victory and the nature of rigging in the election were correctly stated in an editorial of an independent daily. It commented:

> although charges of rigging against the government have been levelled -- and some rigging here and there might have been resorted to -- there is no evidence of massive rigging. The electors' verdict is clear and cannot be disputed, although on deeper analysis it will be apparent that the verdict was more against the Awami League rather than in support of the BNP.[27]

The result of the presidential election again showed that Zia had been able to mobilise the rural population during his more than five years' rule – a legacy which Sattar utilised in his favour during the election. Sattar wanted to civilianise politics and emphasised that 'the army's job is to defend the borders. No other role for the army is conceivable in any democratic country...'.[28] He appointed M. N. Huda, a former professor of economics and adviser to both Zia and Sattar, as the vice president. The highly ambitious army did not like Sattar's attitude and only two days after his comment on the army's role, a group of generals trooped into the president's office to demand a share of power. Under extensive pressure from the army, Sattar agreed to compromise by involving the military chiefs in the National Economic Council, a move that failed to appease the dissatisfied generals. Thus, the civilian regime of Sattar ended four months after its installation when army chief-of-staff, H. M. Ershad, seized power in a bloodless coup.

Civilian politicians had to wait nine years to regain power when, after the forced resignation of Ershad, the BNP again formed government under the leadership of Khaleda Zia, the widow of President Zia. Khaleda ruled the country for almost five years and a number of elections were held during her tenure.

The Khaleda Regime: National Referendum 1991

Background

After the fifth parliamentary elections, the BNP took over the reins of power but avoided taking any step to change the form of government. Although preferring the existing presidential system, the BNP did not commit itself to any particular form of government during the election campaign. The BNP chairperson only once said that the future form of government would be decided by the elected parliament.[29]

The third national referendum was held in 1991. It was necessary to endorse the Twelfth Constitution Amendment Bill which replaced the existing presidential system with a parliamentary one. This referendum decided a constitutional issue for the first time in the political history of the country. The other two referenda held in 1977 and 1985 'had been an extra-constitutional device to legitimise the unconstitutional assumption of state power' by Zia and Ershad.[30]

The main opposition AL favoured a parliamentary system, which could be reinstated only if supported by two-thirds of the members of the new parliament and confirmed by a referendum.[31] The AL and other opposition parties that advocated a parliamentary system in their election manifestos reminded the ruling party to honour the 1990 joint declaration of the main three alliances which committed them to establish a 'sovereign parliament'. The opposition pressure was intensified by the speech of the caretaker president in the inaugural session of the parliament which stressed the need to consider the promises of the joint declaration and its political significance.[32] A number of opposition members from different parties also argued in favour of a parliamentary system during the first session of parliament. Many professional groups including the Supreme Court Bar Association, the Combined Action Committee of Professionals, and a number of cultural and student organisations also supported the opposition.

The ruling party considered the issue although a small section of BNP leaders opposed the idea of amending the constitution.[33] In both the BNP's parliamentary party and its central executive committee meetings a majority of members supported a parliamentary system through a constitutional amendment. The top decision makers of the BNP could sense the public's views and decided to revert to a parliamentary system.

Both BNP and AL put forward constitution amendment bills. After several days of heated discussion, the parliament sent both bills to a 15-member select committee comprising members from the treasury and opposition and headed by the law and justice minister.[34] The committee reached a consensus on the contentious issues of the bill and placed it before the House on 28 July. The bill was passed unanimously on 6 August and was finally approved by the voters through a national referendum on 15 September.

Nature of Voting and Results

As none of the political parties opposed the constitution amendment bill, obviously none campaigned against the referendum. According to secondary sources, the voting was free and fair; the administration, the political parties and the electoral machinery played their proper role. There were no allegations of rigging or any of the other malpractices that were common during the previous two referendums. The turnout was 34.93 percent, low in comparison to the last parliamentary election (55.35%). Table 5.1 shows the results of the referendum.

It is clear from the turnout rate that the referendum had not generated much interest among the voters. The campaign was calm and almost limited to the media. A flood in some parts of the country and the ignorance of the rural voters on the technicalities of the constitutional issues on which the referendum was held, were two major causes of the low turnout. Nevertheless, the people endorsed the Twelfth Constitution Amendment Bill through this referendum which made a number of changes in the constitution including the major change in the form of government.

City Corporation Election, 1994

Background

The first City Corporation (CC) election in the country, although a local government election, resulted in the predicted high level of voter participation. Four mayors and 192 ward commissioners were for the first time directly elected by the people of Dhaka, Chittagong, Khulna and

Rajshahi, the four largest cities in the country. Until the elections were held, the corporations were headed by government-appointed mayors and consisted of three categories of members: elected commissioners, appointed officials and nominated women commissioners.

Table 5.1 Referendum Results

Total voters	62,204,118
Total votes cast	21,919,003
Total invalid votes	190,408
Total valid votes	21,728,595
Percentage of votes cast	34.93
Total 'yes' votes	18,342,882
Total 'no' votes	3,385,513
Percentage of 'yes' votes	84.82
Percentage of 'no' votes	15.58

Source: The Daily Sangram, 17 September, 1991. Cited in Muhammad A. Hakim (1992). 'Twelfth Constitutional Amendment: Bangladesh's Reversion to Parliamentary System', *Asian Profile*, vol. 20, no. 3, p. 259.

Commissioner elections in four cities were first held in March 1988 although the response of the voters and candidates was muted. More than 20 percent of the 177 ward commissioners were elected unopposed, only 127 seats were contested and elections in 15 seats were postponed due to a lack of candidates. Needless to say, the voter turnout also was extremely low. Two main causes of this apathetic attitude were the repressive policies of the Ershad military government towards the opposition and the positive response of the people to the call by the mainstream opposition parties to boycott all elections held under the Ershad government. An analyst of local government elections in Bangladesh branded the 1988 election of commissioners and mayors as an inner-party affair of the ruling JP.[35] The BNP government, after assuming power in March 1991, nominated their party members to be mayors of the four cities.[36] But in July 1992, when the Supreme Court directed the government to hold elections in all local councils within six months, the government took the initiative to revise the existing laws regulating the affairs of local councils. For this purpose the government introduced four identical bills in the 1993 winter session of parliament.[37] The proposals of those bills included direct election of mayors, abolishing the posts of deputy mayors and the election of women commissioners by direct elections rather than by the previous system of nomination. After debate these bills were passed on 28 February 1993. The government took time to update the voter list and delineate the ward boundaries in the four CCs and planned to hold the first CC election by January 1994.

Candidates

One thousand four hundred and fifty-seven candidates contested the first CC election. The competition was high as all the major political parties participated. The number of candidates for four mayoral and 192 commissioner seats were 48 and 1,409 respectively. The seat-candidate ratio and voter turnout were much higher in Rajshahi than in other three cities. Table 5.2 shows detail of candidates in the CC elections of 1994.

The ruling party BNP and the main opposition AL nominated candidates for all mayoral and ward commissioner's seats whereas other parties like JP and JI nominated mayoral candidates in all cities but did not contest commissioner elections in all wards. The majority of ward commissioner candidates were independents. The BNP nominated their party loyalists who had already served as appointed mayors in four cities. These nominees resigned one month before the election in response to the demand of the opposition parties, although the electoral laws did not disqualify a sitting mayor or commissioner from contesting the polls. The number of female candidates was discouraging. There were no woman among the 48 mayoral candidates and only 12 (3.13%) among 1,409 candidates for ward commissioner positions.

Table 5.2 Candidates in City Corporation Elections, 1994

City	No. of Wards	No. of Candidates Filing Nomination		Contestants		Seat-Candidate Ratio	
		Mayor	Comsr:	Mayor	Comsr:	Mayor	Comsr:
Dhaka	90	26	916	24	675	1:24	1:7.2
Chittagong	41	17	418	12	301	1:12	1:7.4
Khulna	31	12	270	05	176	1:05	1:5.7
Rajshahi	30	07	287	07	257	1:07	1:8.5
Total	192	62	1,891	48	1,409	1:12	1:7.5

Source: Nizam U. Ahmed. (1995). 'Party Politics In Banglaadesh's Local Government: The City Corporation Elections'. *Asian Survey.* vol. XXXV. no. II. pp. 1017-29. The table has been condensed by the author.

Campaign

The campaign of the CC election created considerable contest as the voters for the first time had a chance to vote after the BNP formed government in March 1991. Although the union *parisad* election of 1992 was held under this government, the people of the divisional cities who lived in metropolitan areas were not voters in that election. The major parties also took the CC poll seriously for measuring the strength of their support.

The EC declared that any sort of campaign 22 days before the election was illegal and punishable. As the fight for space on the walls of public buildings for painting symbols of candidates and graffiti in their support was one cause of violent clashes between rival groups, the EC imposed a ban on the fixing of any poster, notice, placard or advertisement in places other than those determined for the purpose by the city corporations.

Most of the contesting candidates in the 1994 CC polls stressed their service-oriented qualities and experience, their honesty and integrity and identified a number of problems that needed immediate attention in their respective cities. They also promised to end terrorism, corruption and other anti-social activities, and pledged to upgrade the quality of all municipal services.

All national level political leaders including the prime minister and the leader of the opposition took part in the campaign in support of their party candidates. They addressed a series of public meetings and also took part in door-to-door campaigns to explain their programmes and policies. The prime minister appealed to voters to elect her party's candidates who already had served as mayors and to give them a chance to complete their unfinished projects. She also promised to provide additional resources to develop the cities in a planned way.[38]

The AL president and the leader of the opposition, Sheikh Hasina, strongly criticised the PM for 'indulging in the pork-barrel politics of promising new development funds...' and other facilities on the eve of the election. She strongly objected to the content of the prime minister's speech in which she warned that if opposition candidates were elected the speed of development would be disrupted. A widely used technique of AL was to claim that the election of its candidates would 'ensure effective checks and balances in the country's politics and administration', which was necessary to institute democracy.[39] Other party candidates also stressed their particular policies. JP candidates criticised the government for abandoning development programmes that had been introduced by the Ershad regime (1982-90) and made a commitment to reinstate these programmes if elected. JI candidates stressed the honesty and personal qualities of their candidates, while the mayoral candidate of the left alliance in Dhaka emphasised the rights and welfare of the people as well as a number of other issues such as problems of women and environmental degradation.

The actions of the ruling party were severely criticised by both the AL and the JP. The AL president blamed the ruling BNP for violating election rules in all four constituencies. She argued that the government had become isolated from the people by its unbridled corruption, misrule and terrorism and was violating election rules.[40] Others alleged that the former mayor of Dhaka used official transport for his campaign.[41] JP leaders in a similar fashion attacked the ruling party's role before the CC election. They alleged that the government had disrupted 82 JP public meetings by imposing section 144 of the penal code in 1993. The 'repressive attitude' of the ruling party was strongly criticised and they warned that democracy was not safe in the hands of a BNP government.[42]

Criminals, miscreants and trouble-makers[43] involved themselves in the electoral activities. The production and purchasing of illegal arms in underground markets alarmingly increased before the election. The police published a list of holders of illegal arms twice between 1991 and 1994 but failed to recover their weapons. A former inspector general of police alleged that there were one million illegal arms in Bangladesh. Nevertheless, the election campaign went peacefully except for a few minor occurrences. *The Daily Star* commented that the CC polls marked the beginning of a new trend in the electoral heritage of Bangladesh.[44]

Preparations

The EC undertook a number of measures to make the CC election free, fair and impartial. The commission announced a 12-point code of conduct for candidates and supporters that included 'prohibition on contributions and commitments to contribute during the election campaign, provocative and indecent speeches against rival candidates, arranging transport for voters, and disturbing campaign programme of rivals...'.[45] The EC also directed candidates to report their sources of personal income and expenditure and fixed the limit on election spending.[46] However, these provisions were violated by all major candidates.[47] A commission composed of the representatives of 16 human rights organisations commented that the average expenditure of a mayoral candidate exceeded Tk 20,000,000, forty times more than the EC had fixed. The total of electoral expenses was said to have exceeded Tk 600 million, six times more than specified.[48]

The EC received a large number of allegations of breaches of electoral rules by ministers. A mayoral candidate for Khulna CC accused the speaker of parliament for his indirect participation in the election campaign of the

BNP candidate. There were also allegations against several ministers as well as the prime minister. These allegations claimed that ministers used official transport and influenced the campaign by using their official status – a breach of the code of conduct.[49] The chief election commissioner (CEC) delivered orientation speeches in different city corporations and informed the concerned officials and candidates about the preparations taken by the EC against anticipated violence during the CC polls.[50] The CEC repeatedly cautioned candidates to abide by electoral rules and threatened to apply laws severely against violators. This could result in imprisonment for at least two years in addition to a fine. The commissioner emphasised the need to build a transparent electoral process.[51] The EC declared all types of entertainment related to electioneering punishable under section 171 (E) of the Bangladesh Penal Code.[52]

Results

Out of the 2.87 million enrolled voters 1.66 million exercised their franchise. The turnout was 57.9 percent, and the result gave the AL big wins in Dhaka and Chittagong, the two principal cities in the country. The other two mayoral positions in Rajshahi and Khulna went to the ruling BNP. In the race for positions as ward commissioner the AL won 37.5 percent of all seats while BNP followed with 28.64. The JP won nine commissioner posts while JI secured two. Table 5.3 shows party affiliation of mayors and commissioners.

The BNP, which during the last parliamentary election had won all the MP seats in Dhaka city and secured 52.62 percent of the votes cast, lost the mayoral seat in 1994 and its vote declined to 38.36 percent. Similarly in Chittagong, the BNP's vote declined by more than nine percent.[53]

Causes of Success and Failure

Electoral analysts have identified intra-party conflict, lack of coordination in the campaign, alienation from other political parties and social groups, rising unemployment, over dependency on the bureaucracy, an increasing distance between ministers and the party, and overconfidence as major causes of BNP's defeat in the CC poll. The AL's victory, on the other hand, was grounded on its submissive appeal, more personalised approach and exclusive door-to-door campaigning. The AL's argument of electing its candidates for creating checks and balances in government was well taken and influenced a section of the voters to support the party.

Table 5.3 Partisan Affiliation of Mayors and Commissioners

City	% of Voter Turnout	No. of Mayors	No. of Comsr	Partisan Affiliation of Commissioners					
				AL	BNP	JP	JI	Indepen:	Total
Dhaka	54.19	1(AL)	90	42	33	–	–	15	90
Chittagong	59.39	1(AL)	41	21	12	03	–	05	41
Khulna	63.64	1(BNP)	31	06	08	–	01	16	31
Rajshahi	80.30	1(BNP)	30	03	02	06	–	19	30
Avr./Total	57.89	4	192	72	55	09	01	55	192

Source: *The Daily Star*, March 9, 1994.

Reactions

The AL was highly pleased with the results and described the election as free and fair, although the AL president had alleged before the election that the ruling party planned to stuff ballot boxes with false votes of absentee voters.[54] In an interview with Voice of America she claimed that AL would always win in any fair polls.[55] The JP, although it did not do well, accepted the result and claimed it as its victory. JP leaders in a post-election meeting of the party congress said, 'people voted against the BNP, which is our victory'. The JI leaders were disappointed in the performance of their candidates. In a pre-poll estimation, they expected around 70,000 votes in favour of their candidate for Dhaka City Corporation, but its candidate obtained only 34,430 votes.[56] They saw an 'international conspiracy' as well as the conspiracy of the ruling party as the main causes of JI's poor performance in the election.

Rigging Allegation

None of the contending parties made allegations of rigging and major malpractices in the voting; six people however died in post-poll violence in Dhaka.[57] The role of the Bangladesh Television (BTV) in announcing the election results was partisan and was criticised by the opposition political parties. The BTV declared that it would announce election results from 9:30 pm. to 2:00 am. on election night, but failed to do so before 10:45 pm. It also intentionally focused on centres where the ruling party was leading, thus contravening its proper role.[58]

Impact

The main opposition gained strength by winning two mayor seats and were confident in winning the next parliamentary elections. The success of the AL jolted the overconfidence of the ruling party, and was a severe set back as its popular support base dwindled considerably. The BNP had won 50 percent of the popular vote in the 1991 parliamentary polls in the metropolitan areas, but it secured only 39 percent in the 1994 CC polls. In contrast, the AL's vote surged from 34 percent in 1991 to 42 percent in 1994. The AL, gaining confidence from the CC poll results, set a new strategy which emphasised a strong anti-government focus.

The Magura-2 Constituency By-Election

Background

The Magura-2 constituency by-election deserves special review because of the controversy surrounding it. The Magura-2 constituency seat was held by an AL MP, which fell vacant on his death. The election was scheduled for March 1994, a crucial time both for the ruling BNP and the main opposition AL when they were both competing to display their electoral strengths. AL regained its position through the CC polls and wanted to continue this trend by retaining the Magura seat, whereas the BNP was bent upon restoring its image after its losses in the same election. It was the 17th out of 23 by-elections held during the Khaleda regime (for a detailed list of 23 by-elections see appendix H). Among the 16 by-elections which were held before the Magura election, the BNP had won seven, AL five and the JP four. None of these 16 by-elections was totally free of irregularities and a few local poll monitors had reported violence, terrorism and intimidation.[59] Newspaper reports show that there were strong indications of gross irregularities in the Mirpur and Magura by-elections.[60]

Candidates and Campaign

Five major parties nominated candidates to contest the Magura by-election[61] and all parties mustered their full strength in the campaign. Almost all prominent leaders of the major parties visited the constituency. The BNP chairperson and the AL president held several public meetings in Magura while the central leaders of JP and JI also campaigned in favour of their candidates. In one month alone, 28 ministers of the ruling party campaigned in the constituency.[62] The AL accused the BNP government of corruption and appealed to voters to support its candidate. The ruling party, on the other hand, urged voters to reject the destructive policies of the opposition and to strengthen the hand of the government so that it could push forward with its development projects across the country.

Preparation

The EC took several actions to ensure a free and fair election. As the AL president had alleged to the EC that BNP was planning to rig the election, the CEC together with some of his senior officials went to Magura to observe the polling. He had several meetings with the representatives of the major political parties before polling day. The CEC instructed the government officials, law enforcing agencies as well as presiding and polling officers to fulfil their role without fear or favour, but he himself left Magura before the polling day. It appeared from the confusing newspaper reports that the CEC was not satisfied with the outcome of his meeting with the representatives of contending parties at Magura. He also faced another critical affair, namely the AL chief's stay at Magura Circuit House, which was formally declared as the office of the EC. It was not clear why the CEC left Magura; although he informed journalists on his way to the capital that his press secretary would make everything clear, it is still a mystery. A few investigators presume that the CEC probably realised how tense the situation had become and wished to avoid any unexpected incidents in his presence.[63]

Results, Reactions and Rigging

The BNP candidate won the election defeating the AL candidate by a big margin of 33,626 votes.[64] The opposition parties voiced allegation of rigging allegations against the ruling BNP, calling the election grossly unfair and influenced by violence. Most newspaper reports supported this allegation. The AL chief, Sheikh Hasina, demanded a fresh election. She also demanded the resignation of the government and the transfer of power to a caretaker administration pending a national election. The opposition leader accused the BNP of unprecedented vote dacoity in a planned way by using the administrative machinery. She also criticised the role of the EC.[65] The main opposition called strikes for two days. The AL chief in an interview claimed that if she were able to talk on electronic media she would abandon the tactic of strikes although she did not demand such an opportunity.[66]

The JP and the JI leaders expressed similar sentiments and declared that they would not participate in any election under the BNP government. They also condemned the way the election was conducted, rejected its results and demanded a fresh election under the management of a neutral authority. JI leaders alleged that ministers and the entire administration were engaged in the election campaign using government transport and facilities.[67] The acting chairman of the JP said that the BNP government had rigged the election and manipulated the results by unleashing a reign of terror.[68] He also emphasised the necessity of an NCG for holding free and fair elections. The opposition members in parliament had earlier walked out and boycotted its proceedings on a critical religious issue (this will be discussed in detail in the next section) but related the controversial Magura-2 constituency by-election issue to their boycott. They alleged that the ruling party nakedly rigged the by-election and demanded its cancellation and a fresh poll under an NCG. The AL's choice of street demonstrations instead of taking legal action by lodging a complaint with the election tribunal was also criticised.[69]

The BNP secretary congratulated the people of Magura for electing the BNP candidate. He asserted that the victory of the BNP was a demonstration of the political awareness of the people of Magura and he hoped that the leaders of the AL would accept the verdict of the electorate and demonstrate their confidence in democratic values. He also criticised the activities of the AL leaders in attempting to mislead the people through false and fabricated propaganda. He condemned AL's planned terrorism and cited several examples of terrorist activities by AL activists during electioneering.[70]

A report on the by-election also shows how ministers and even the prime minister influenced the electioneering, although it did not criticise the opposition leaders.[71] A few JSD and eight left-leaning parties in different statements condemned the allegations and counter-allegations between government and opposition political parties and condemned the silence of the EC on this issue. This prompted the CEC to issue a statement explaining that the polling in Magura had been completed in accordance with the rules. Furthermore, the reports of officials engaged in conducting the polls did not suggest that the voting was held in violation of the relevant election rules, except in three centres where polling had been postponed.[72]

Foreign observers, especially the American Embassy's monitoring team, did not support the opposition's allegation of vote rigging only by the ruling party. The members of the team visited 20 vote centres at Mohammadpur and Shalikha Thana and did not find any significant irregularities. The report of this team blamed the major contending political parties including the BNP and AL for the violence and the postponement of voting in three centres.[73] The author's own assessment based on reviews of secondary sources and interviews with a cross-section of people during a personal visit to the constituency also does not totally support the findings of some analysts and opposition allegations blaming only the ruling party. Rather, it corroborates the findings of the election observation team of the US Embassy. The statement of the presiding officer of a vote centre, one of the three centres where voting was officially postponed, described how one group of armed youths brandishing firearms was able to mark the ballot papers and stuff the boxes whereas the other group in a similar fashion broke the ballot boxes and burnt the ballot papers. The statement clearly showed that both the ruling and opposition parties were engaged in violent actions (for the full text of the statement of the PO see, Appendix I).

The Sixth Parliamentary Election, 1996

Background

The political deadlock between the Khaleda government and the opposition continued for two years. The ruling BNP rejected the opposition's demand for election under an NCG which it branded undemocratic and unconstitutional and emphasised the necessity for an amendment of the constitution to fulfil such a demand. As all opposition political parties resigned en masse from parliament, the government had only the option of passing the required constitution amendment bill in a new parliament with two thirds majority. The sixth parliament election was arranged by the BNP government to have a new parliament to pass the constitution amendment required for accepting opposition demand.

Opposition Boycott

The liaison committee of the three major opposition political parties decided to boycott the election[74] and announced a six-day action programme of protest.[75] The leader of the opposition called upon different professionals including administrative and election officials, college and school teachers, members of armed forces, Bangladesh Rifles (BDR), Police and *Ansar*[76] and NGO workers not to cooperate in staging the 'farcical one-party' election. She urged the people to stay away from polling centres on election day and observe a 'people's curfew' as a token of support for the opposition's programme. Professional groups and intellectuals were divided; one group supported the opposition demand, issued statements in favour of an NCG and called the sixth parliamentary election a farce. The other group issued counter-statements defending the stand of the ruling party, argued in favour of constitutional continuity and pleaded for participation in the sixth parliamentary polls as a crucial and mandatory obligation.

The Candidates and Campaign

The EC finalised a code of conduct after discussions with the representatives of all political parties on 25 September 1995, although the EC failed to take action against those who broke the code (for the full text of the code of conduct, see Appendix J). The ruling party, having failed to obtain the participation of the major opposition parties, encouraged the smaller parties, many of which were almost unknown, to contest the elections. Forty-one such small political parties responded (for the name of those 41 political parties and their number of nominations, see Appendix K). Only four parties were able to nominate more than 50 candidates each for a 300-seat parliament.[77] The ruling party was the only party to nominate candidates in all 300 constituencies. Almost one-fifth of the total candidates withdrew their nomination papers.[78] The opposition boycott and threats to resist the election were the main causes of the high-rate of withdrawals.

The campaign based on a single issue: the pro-election group upheld the significance of the election and campaigned supporting it, whereas the anti-election group campaigned to boycott and resist it. The campaign was limited only to newspaper statements, public meetings and speeches by the ruling party candidates. The leader of the AL said, 'holding a mock election and ignoring people's demands is totally undemocratic and illegal...'. She called upon the people and all involved in the electoral process to resist the government's conspiracy to snatch the people's franchise through a mock vote. She added that the government was desperate to stage a 'farce' in the name of an election to continue in power and appealed to voters to stop this one-party farcical election at any cost.[79] The ruling party, on the other hand, was determined to complete the election. The prime minister said parliamentary polls should not be disrupted by organised strikes.[80] She asked the voters to remain patient and peaceful in the face of anti-election provocation and to exercise their right of franchise. The prime minister underlined the importance of the election to overcome the constitutional crisis and maintain a democratic process in the country. In response to the serious opposition threat, the army was deployed in addition to the para-military, police, and para-police to help ensure a peaceful election.

Violence and Corruption

Despite these precautions the election was held amid widespread violence. During the campaign, anti-election violence spread all over the country. Bomb blasts, violent street demonstrations, clashes between pro-and anti poll activists and strikes became almost an everyday event. Anti-election activists assaulted several candidates, set fire to district BNP offices, and burnt a district election office in Chittagong. They were successful in creating an atmosphere of terrorism.[81] The boycotting opposition parties in many places used physical intimidation to prevent polling. Thirteen people were killed on election day and hundreds were injured across the country and the election was postponed in at least 1,000 polling centres.[82] The election was poorly administered and voter turnout was also low, with the people in many places scared to go to the voting centres despite the deployment of the armed forces to maintain law and order. In many election centres, presiding and polling officers were unable to perform their duties because of security hazards.[83] In different parts of the country anti-election activists snatched ballot papers and boxes in polling booths.[84] The pro-election activists in many constituencies were successful in increasing the turnout, but through unfair means, and authorities reported unbelievable figures of voter turnout.[85] The EC initially was able to declare results in 210 seats, followed by another 79. In the remaining 11 constituencies no election could be conducted.[86] Anti-election activists were so successful that the EC had to arrange re-polling in 80 constituencies. Forty eight ruling party candidates including the prime minister and a dozen ministers were declared elected unopposed.

Results, Reactions and Impact

The EC had difficulty declaring the results, as it had to arrange re-polling in 84 constituencies on different dates. After more than a month, the EC published the final results of 285 constituencies in which one NDP, eight independents and 276 BNP candidates won.[87] Prominent opposition parties and several organisations rejected the election results, branded them farcical and meaningless, and demanded once again a fresh poll under a non-partisan government. The main opposition parties – the AL, JP and the JI, after a meeting of their liaison committee, took a decision to *gherao* (besiege) the *sangsad bhaban* (parliament house) and warned that any attempt to form a parliament with the 'vote bandits' would be resisted. The Federation of Bangladesh Chambers of Commerce and Industry (FBCCI), the highest forum of the nation's traders and industrialists, was critical of the election, which they labelled as anything but free and fair. Most of the local newspapers as well as the foreign press acknowledged a low voter turnout, violence, irregularities in the process of voting, kidnapping of polling officers and candidates, ballot box snatching and other sorts of malpractices.[88] The US State Department also found serious flaws in the administration of the election.[89] The prime minister stated that in rural areas elections were peaceful, a claim that was totally rejected. According to reports, the situation in the rural areas on the election day was more turbulent and violent than in urban areas.[90]

The opposition demanded an immediate cancellation of the election, called the parliament illegal, declared indefinite non-cooperation from 9 March, and pressured the president to form an NCG. The President after discussions with the major political parties and drawing upon the expert opinion from leading lawyers of the Supreme court said, '...it appears that the constitution is required to be amended to make provision for the formation of an NCG followed by a country-wide referendum'.[91] He also appealed to the opposition political parties to lift their strikes and programme of non-cooperation and to allow free movement to restore normalcy to civil life. In his address at the inaugural session of the sixth *Jatiya Sangsad*, the president said the February 15 election was necessary for maintaining constitutional continuity. He also expected that the government would make the necessary constitutional amendments to provide for the formation of the NCG.

The government through the 13th amendment of the constitution made the necessary constitutional changes for an NCG to oversee all future parliamentary elections. The president assented almost immediately and on the advice of the prime minister dissolved the sixth parliament. The prime minister resigned on 30 March. The opposition welcomed the prime minister's resignation and claimed it as the people's victory. The NCG was promptly formed and thus a two year long political impasse ended.

It Was Rigged But Benefited All

No doubt the sixth parliamentary election was rigged and was farcical but it contributed towards maintaining constitutional continuity and thereby benefited all. The opposition parties were able to mobilise their workers through anti-election programmes. The AL gained maximum benefit from anti-election demonstrations and won the support of many voters. The JP also increased the mobilisation of its workers at the local level through organisational activities prior to the election. The JI was in the forefront with the AL and JP, the main anti-election forces, and shrewdly tried to be more acceptable to the voters by suppressing its anti-liberation role. The election gave the ruling party a means of accepting the opposition demand of an election under an NCG. It also helped the opposition election boycotting parties to participate in the seventh parliamentary election as it was held under an NCG. Thus the election contributed to end a two year long political deadlock between the government and the opposition. It gave both the conflicting parties some satisfaction of success. The ruling party took it as its victory because it was able to maintain constitutional continuity by amending the constitution in parliament to provide for an NCG. The election boycotting parties also claimed victory as their main demand of a parliamentary election under an NCG materialised through this election. Although the opposition branded the sixth parliamentary election as 'farcical' and the sixth parliament as 'illegal', it accepted the formation of an NCG conceived and validated by this parliament. Thus all political parties participated in the seventh parliamentary election under an NCG which was indeed the contribution of the previous parliamentary election, however flawed.

The Hasina Regime

As there is no possibility of another parliamentary election before 2001, little may be said about electoral corruption under the present AL (Hasina) government that came to power in June 1996. It is, however, relevant to note that this government played an unfair role in conducting by-elections in 15 vacant constituencies held on 5 September 1996.[92] The opposition and poll observers successfully documented planned rigging by the ruling party. The BNP observed a demonstration day to protest the abuses and also demanded the resignation of the CEC and re-election in two constituencies.[93] The Fair Election Monitoring Alliance (FEMA), an NGO-based organisation, in its report on the by-elections admitted widespread rigging especially in Lakkhipur-2 and Chittagong-1 constituencies,[94] and the BBC supported this allegation in its news coverage.[95]

The Barisal by-election in mid-1998 was relatively fair and generally free of violence except for one centre where polling had to be postponed due to the hijacking of three ballot books by unidentified armed youngsters.[96] The winning candidate retained the seat for the opposition BNP signifying, to some extent, the ruling party's increased tolerance in accepting an opposition win.

In another keenly contested by-election at Pabna in late 1998, the partisan role of the civil bureaucracy was so high that the CEC removed the DC from his duties as a returning officer after testifying his involvement in favouring the ruling party.[97] As the substitute returning officer was one of the subordinates of the DC, who was allowed to function in his administrative position, it was not hard for him to play the same partisan role by influencing the new appointee through his official position. The campaign period was marked by violation of election rules and the code of conduct, particularly by the ruling party, which used intimidation and violence in many areas where BNP's support was strong. The polling personnel in many centres, worked for the ruling party candidate and in a few centres, election observers were turned out by the presiding officers. The results of this by-election show that in 22, out of all 81 polling stations, 80% or more votes were cast.[98] In five polling stations, votes cast ranged between 82 to 94% of which votes received by the BNP candidates ranged between 1-9%, whereas votes polled by the AL candidates ranged between

89 to 99%.[99] All contesting parties except the winning AL rejected the results, demanding a fresh election and the resignation of the CEC.

In another by-election in mid-November 1999 at Tangail-8, the situation worsened. Ruling party terrorists confirmed the defeat of the independent candidate. Terrorist activities, intimidation, violation of the code of conduct and the bureaucratic bias made the election unacceptable to both the independent candidate and the electorate. Kader Siddiqui, the independent candidate, rejected the election results even before counting started and demanded a fresh election.[100] The EC instead of announcing the election results formed a four-member judicial inquiry team to investigate allegation of violence and other irregularities. The EC tribunal in an election review meeting suspended presiding officers and magistrates who worked in the four polling stations where voting was postponed. On the other hand, the returning officer in a press conference surprisingly branded the election 'free and fair' except a few minor occurrences.[101] The US ambassador, British high commissioner and the Dutch ambassador met the CEC after having reports from their election observers and expressed dissatisfaction about the electioneering process.[102]

The situation during Jhalakathi-2 by-election in July 2000 was almost similar to Pabna or Tangail by-elections. The ruling party activists applied the same technique to confirm the victory of their candidate and the administration and the EC failed to win the trust of the electorate.[103]

The government, ignoring the opposition demand for an early parliamentary election, staged the Chittagong City Corporation elections in January 2000, which was boycotted by all major political parties except the ruling party and became a one-party show. The four-party alliance called a curfew strike on the day of the election. In some centres, the turnout was less than five percent; albeit, Bangladesh Human Rights Commission claimed a fifteen percent turnout and branded the election 'an electoral farce'.[104] The Commission advised the EC to cancel the election results and rearrange a fresh election ensuring the participation of all political parties. A number of terrorists sheltered by the ruling party won the election among other AL candidates.

The style of conducting elections by the AL government in its first four years has thus been no different from its civilian and military predecessors who manifested a more or less similar repressive attitude towards the opposition.

The degree of corruption in elections under civilian rule in Bangladesh varies from election to election as is reflected in table 5.4. It shows that most of the elections under civilian regimes were rigged. The degree of rigging among six elections was very high in one, high and moderately high in one each, low and moderately low in one each and medium in one.

Table 5.4 The Degree of Corruption in Elections Under Civilian Rule in Bangladesh

Electoral Exercise	Rigging	Violence/Intimidation	Restrictions on campaign/party activities	Use of electronic media	Bureaucratic bias	Use of religion
Parliamentary 1973	MH	H	M	MH	M	L
Presidential 1981	M	M	ML	M	ML	M
Referendum 1991	L	VL	VL	MH	L	VL
C. Corporation 1994	ML	L	ML	M	L	M
Magura By-El: 1994	H	H	ML	L	ML	M
Parliamentary 1996F*	VH	H	L	H	MH	L

Index: VL= Very Low; L= Low; ML= Moderately Low; M= Medium; H= Moderately High; H = High; VH= Very High. *Two parliamentary elections held in 1996 respectively in February and June. 'F' indicates February.
Source: Based on primary and secondary sources.

The 1991 referendum was basically fair as all political parties supported the referendum proposal. The Magura by-election was highly rigged as contending parties, especially the major three, campaigned strenuously to win the seat and applied all legal and illegal means to attract voters. The sixth parliamentary election was very highly rigged only by the ruling party as other major political parties boycotted and campaigned against it. The rigging in the 1973 parliamentary elections was moderately high while that in the 1981 presidential election was moderate. The ruling parties in these two cases were able to mobilise majority support by utilising the charisma of their respective leaders Mujib and Zia which discouraged the workers from taking extreme action. The CC poll was comparatively fair in terms of rigging.

The use of violence and intimidation was high in the 1973 and 1996 parliamentary elections and in the 1994 Magura by-election. It was moderate in the 1981 presidential election and low in the 1994 CC poll, and was absent in the 1991 referendum as it was supported by all parties. The opposition was aware that during the presidential election of 1981 the ruling party candidate could win by using the image of Zia after his brutal death, which inhibited more extreme forms of corruption. The major parties in the 1994 CC poll were hopeful of success and this contributed to the low level of violence and intimidation.

There were moderate restrictions on campaigning and other opposition activities during the 1973 parliamentary election, but in the 1981 presidential election, and in the CC poll and Magura by-election the nature of such restrictions was moderately low. All parties were encouraged to vote in the 1991 referendum, and as the 1996 election was boycotted by mainstream opposition parties, the government-controlled media as well as the ruling party encouraged the opposition to campaign and participate.

The use of electronic media was moderately high in 1973 and in 1991, moderate in the 1981 presidential election and the 1994 CC poll and low and high in Magura by-election and 1996 parliamentary election respectively. During presidential and parliamentary elections the media were biased in favour of the ruling party although it encouraged the voters generally to participate. As the 1996 election was boycotted by the major opposition, the media urged the political parties and the voters to participate in the elections.

The neutrality of the bureaucracy was high in the 1991 referendum and the 1994 CC polls. Its neutrality was moderately high in the 1981 presidential and 1994 Magura by-election, moderate and moderately low in the 1973 and 1996 parliamentary elections. Extensive pressure from the party in power precluded the neutrality of the bureaucracy during the 1973 and 1996 parliamentary elections and in the 1994 Magura by-election. The bureaucracy was relatively impartial during the 1981 presidential and 1994 CC polls when the party in power was confident of a positive result and did not pressure the bureaucracy to work in its favour. The bureaucracy played a neutral role in the 1991 referendum.

Religion was not a dominant issue in the campaigns of the 1973 and 1996 parliamentary elections and in the 1991 referendum. As the JI, the main religious fundamentalist party was banned by the Mujib government and a secular tendency in politics was strong after liberation, religion was not a significant factor in this election. In the other three elections, religion, although not to a high degree, was used in the campaign. In the 1981 presidential election two major candidates emphasised religion in their campaigns.[105] However, in the 1994 CC poll and the Magura by-election the fundamentalist JI participated and religion was one of the main issues in the campaigns of the major parties.

Summing Up

Elections under civilian governments in Bangladesh were not free and fair. Three civilian rulers, Mujib, Sattar and Khaleda, although ruled the country for almost nine years, were unable to establish a democratic trend in politics. They were also unsuccessful in introducing a stable electoral system which could bring transparency to the elections. All three governments faced legitimacy problems and followed the same technique as their military counterparts to retain power. While they were in opposition they were critical of the strategies of the military governments, but were not able to change them after coming to power. They controlled the media, used the bureaucracy for their benefit and followed the same suppression techniques as did the military rulers, although, in terms of allowing political activities, they were more liberal.

The level of corruption in the first parliamentary election in 1973 increased because of the ruling party's strategy of swamping the opposition. The dominant role of the AL leaders and workers stifled the atmosphere of a free, fair and impartial election which impacted on latter parliamentary elections in Bangladesh. The ruling party activists in many places intimidated opposition candidates and institutionalised violence in collaboration with the administration.

During the campaign in the 1981 presidential election, the main contestants, the BNP and the AL, accused each other of formulating rigging plans. The ruling party and the opposition enjoyed equal opportunities to attract voters, although the election was not totally free from irregularities.

The ruling party's massive win was based on the image of its slain leader Zia. There were rigging and violence on the part of all parties which had a balancing effect on the electoral outcome. President Sattar tried to civilianise politics but was ousted by the military. The 1991 referendum was free and fair as all political parties supported it.

The CC poll in 1994 was comparatively fair in terms of electoral corruption although candidates violated electoral principles set by the EC. Miscreants and criminals involved themselves in electoral activities under political banners and the sale of illegal arms in the underground market increased before the poll. Nevertheless, the total campaign was relatively peaceful except for a few isolated incidents. The results went in favour of the AL; however, all major parties accepted them.

The controversial Magura-2 by-election created an unprecedented contest and conflict between the ruling and the main opposition parties. The ministers broke the code of conduct during the campaign by using public facilities and abusing their official status. The opposition rejected the BNP victory, accused the party of rigging the poll and demanded a fresh poll under an NCG. The ruling party considered the opposition claim undemocratic and unconstitutional and branded their activities as terrorist and directed at misleading the people. Accusations and counter-accusations between the BNP and the AL created confusion among the voters. The CEC defended the election as having been completed in accordance with the election rules. A foreign observation team blamed all the contending parties for condoning violence and malpractices and did not support allegations that only the ruling party was guilty of malpractice.

After the Magura by-election, the mainstream opposition parties continued their parliamentary boycott, demanded the resignation of the government, declared the outline of the NCG, and launched strategies to mobilise public support in favour of their demand. The ruling party stressed strengthening the EC to ensure fair elections. The increased distance between the ruling and opposition parties and frequent clashes between opposition electoral workers and the police intensified the complexity. The PM urged the opposition to solve all grievances in the parliament, but the opposition by repeated strikes and demonstrations pressured the government to accept its demand.

The political standoff continued for a long period and adversely affected the economic sector. A lengthy process of mediation conducted by different distinguished personalities and foreign envoys proved unsuccessful. A large number of proposals were prescribed by different parties and personalities during the political impasse, however, none was acceptable to the contending parties. The opposition MPs intensified their pressure on government by resigning *en masse* from the parliament and demanding the resignation of the prime minister. Academics, intellectuals and other professional groups were divided for and against the opposition demand. The EC postponed the by-election in the vacated seats after finding both the ruling and opposition parties unwilling to participate.

The opposition boycotted the sixth parliamentary election held in 1996, and declared its determination to resist it. A large number of insignificant parties contested the election. After a violent campaign, the election was held under opposition threats and amidst widespread violence. The BNP won almost all seats, formed government, and accepted opposition demands by passing the 13th Constitution Amendment Bill 1996. Both sides welcomed the PM's resignation and claimed it as their own success. The long political impasse ended with the BNP claiming victory in maintaining constitutional continuity. The opposition claimed success in that the settlement endorsed its demand for elections under an NCG. Habibur Rahman was appointed to head the NCG and negotiated the seventh parliamentary election. This will be examined in detail in the following chapter.

Notes

[1] Keesing's Contemporary Archives, vol. XIX, April 9-15, 1973, p. 25823.
[2] *Ibid.*
[3] See, Jahan, R. (1974), 'Bangladesh in 1973: Management of Factional Politics', *Asian Survey*, vol. XIV, no. II, p. 27.
[4] See, Huque, A. S. and Hakim, M. A. (1993), 'Elections in Bangladesh: Tools of Legitimacy', *Asian Affairs An American Review*, vol. 19, no. 4, p. 249.
[5] Kamaluddin, S. (1973), 'Mujib, Of Course ...', *Far Eastern Economic Review*, vol. 79, no. 12, 26 March, p. 22.
[6] For related information, see, Quadir, F. (1991), 'The National Parliamentary Election 1991: A Review' (in Bengali), *The Journal for Human Development*, vol. 3, no. 4.
[7] See, Maniruzzaman, T. (1982), *Group Interests and Political Changes: Studies of Pakistan and Bangladesh*, South Asian Publications, New Delhi, pp. 145-46.
[8] Kamaluddin, S. (1973), 'One Man – Still,' *Far Eastern Economic Review*, vol. 79, no. 10, 12 March, p. 22.
[9] For example, Major Jalil (JSD), Rashed Khan Menon, Kazi Zafar Ahmad, Aleem Al Razee (NAP-B), and Suranjit Sen (NAP-M) made such allegations. See, Jahan, 'Bangladesh in 1973: Management of Factional Politics', *op. cit.*, p. 128.
[10] Alam, J. (1990), *The Trend of Leftist Politics in Bangladesh 1948-89* (in Bengali), Proteek Prokashana Sanghtha, Dhaka, p. 56.
[11] See, Kamaluddin, 'Mujib, of Course ...' *op. cit.*, p. 22.
[12] The BTV election telecast 7 and 8 March, 1973.
[13] *The Bangladesh Observer*, 19 December, 1973.
[14] Jahan, 'Bangladesh in 1973: Management of Factional Politics', *op. cit.*, pp. 125-35.

15. For the party affiliation and supporting source, see, Kamaluddin, S. (1981), 'An Eclectic Election: Leading Candidates Stand to Lose Votes to Minor Contestants in a Crowded Field'. *Far Eastern Economic Review*, vol. 114, no. 44, 23 October, p. 23.
16. For related information, see, Kamaluddin, *ibid.*, p. 166.
17. Kamaluddin, S. (1981), 'The Military One-Step: Political Parties Publish Their Manifestos for the Presidential Election, But the Army Chief's Statements Prompt New Uncertainty', *Far Eastern Economic Review*, vol. 114, no. 45, 30 October, p. 22.
18. In an interview with the weekly *Holiday*, Ershad pointed out the shortcomings of the policies of major political parties. He said, '...the failure of the BNP government in the forthcoming election would help the *Awami* League and lead the country towards political turbulence ... the BKSAL ideology (one-party rule established by late Sheikh Mujibur Rahman, the President assassinated in 1975) would never be acceptable to the people'. He also criticised the policy of Osmani and predicted that political crisis would emerge if he were elected President. For detail, see, all major Bangladeshi newspapers of last week of October, 1981.
19. Cited in, Kamaluddin, 'The Military One-Step: Political Parties Publish their Manifestos for the Presidential Election, But the Army Chief's Statements Prompt New Uncertainty' *op. cit.*, p. 22.
20. For related information, see, Kamaluddin, S. (1981), 'Polling Fist First: As Violence Continues to Mar the Run-Up to the Presidential Election, Fears and Uncertainty Prevail', *Far Eastern Economic Review*, vol. 114, no. 46, 6 November, p. 30.
21. Quoted in, Ali, S. and Kamaluddin, S. (1981), 'Sour Grapes of Wrath: As the Ruling Party Scores a Landslide Election Victory, The Opposition Awami League Vows Revenge' *Far Eastern Economic Review*, vol. 114, no. 48, 20 November, p. 18.
22. See, *ibid.*, p. 17.
23. *Ibid.*, p. 17.
24. Ziring, L. (1992), *Bangladesh: From Mujib to Ershad, An Interpretive Study*, Oxford University Press, Oxford, p. 151; Khan, Z. R. (1982), 'Bangladesh in 1981: Change, Stability, and Leadership', *Asian Survey*, vol. XXII, no. II, pp. 165-68.
25. Khan, 'Bangladesh in 1981: Change, Stability, and Leadership', *ibid.*, p. 166.
26. *Ibid.*, pp. 166-67.
27. Cited in, Ali and Kamaluddin, 'Sour Grapes of Wrath: As the Ruling Party Scores a Landslide Election Victory, The Opposition Awami League Vows Revenge' *op. cit.*, p. 18.
28. *Ibid.*, p. 17.
29. See, *The Daily Ittefaq*, 29 January, 1991.
30. See, Hakim, M. A. (1992), 'Twelfth Constitutional Amendment: Bangladesh's Reversion to Parliamentary System', *Asian Profile*, vol. 20, no. 3, pp. 251-61.
31. See, Baxter, C. (1992), 'Bangladesh in 1991: A Parliamentary System', *Asian Survey*, vol. XXXII, no. II, pp. 162-67.
32. For related information, see, Hakim, M. A. (1993), *Bangladesh Politics: The Shahabuddin Interregnum*, The University Press Limited, Dhaka, p. 73.
33. For example, see, the speech of Nazmul Huda, State Minister for food, in the *Jatiya Sangsad*, *The Daily Star*, 13 May, 1991; cited in Hakim, *Ibid.*, p.84.
34. The Select Committee had 8 BNP and 4 AL members. The JP, JI, and Workers Party had 1 member each in the committee. Cited in, Hakim, 'Twelfth Constitutional Amendment: Bangladesh's Reversion to Parliamentary System', *op. cit.*, p. 257.
35. For related information see, Ahmed, N. U. (1994), 'Party Politics In Bangladesh's Local Government: The 1994 City Corporation Elections', *Asian Survey*, vol. XXXV, no. II, p. 1019.

[36] Mirza Abbas, Mir Nasiruddin, Sheikh Taiyebur Rahman and Mizanur Rahman Minu were appointed Mayors for Dhaka, Chittagong, Khulna and Rajshahi respectively.

[37] Ahmed, 'Party Politics In Bangladesh's Local Government: The 1994 City Corporation Elections', op. cit., p. 1019.

[38] Khaleda Zia in her campaign speeches promised to open new TV channels in Chittagong and Rajshahi, upgrade the Chittagong airport to international standards, and construct a new bridge over the Buriganga river at Dhaka.

[39] For related information, see, *The Daily Star*, January 29, 1994; *The Bangladesh Observer*, 23 January, 1994.

[40] See, *The Bangladesh Observer*, 1 January, 1994.

[41] *The Bangladesh Observer*, 7 January, 1994.

[42] *The Bangladesh Observer*, 1 February, 1994.

[43] They included hijackers, pickpockets, thieves etc.

[44] *The Daily Star*, 1 February, 1994.

[45] Ahmed, 'Party Politics In Bangladesh's Local Government: The 1994 City Corporation Elections', op. cit., pp. 1023-24.

[46] According to EC limit a mayoral candidate could spend *taka* 500,000 and a commissioner candidate *taka* 50,000. See, Babur, S. (1994), 'Some Aspects of City Corporation Election' (in Bengali), *Palabadal*, vol. 3, no. 15, 16-31 January, p. 21.

[47] See, *Ajker Kagoj*, 19 January, 1994.

[48] *Ajker Kagoj*, 19 January, 1994.

[49] For related information, see, *Ajker Kagoj*, 23 January, 1994.

[50] For example, see, the speech of the CEC Justice Abdur Rauf delivered at a gathering of candidates of Dhaka CC election on January 25, 1994. *Inquilab*, 26 January, 1994.

[51] See, *The Bangladesh Observer*, 10, 17 and 18 January, 1994.

[52] The Bangladesh EC in a press release said that any entertainment in the form of food or drink or arranging those would be treated as a bribe. Offering tea, biscuits, betel-leaf and cigarettes for the purpose of election was punishable as per law. See, *The Bangladesh Observer*, 20 January, 1994.

[53] In the 1991 parliamentary election 49.86% votes were cast in favour of BNP where as it secured 40.26% of votes in the CC poll of 1994.

[54] *The Bangladesh Observer*, 23 January, 1994.

[55] *The Daily Purbakone*, 9 February, 1994.

[56] *Sangbad*, 5 February, 1994.

[57] *Inquilab*, 1 February, 1994.

[58] See, *Inquilab*, 1 February, 1994.

[59] For related information, see, Timm, R. W. (1991), *Return to Democracy*, Mimeograph, Dhaka.

[60] For rigging and other irregularities in the Mirpur by-election, see, Hakim, M. A. (1994), 'The Mirpur Parliamentary by-election in Bangladesh', *Asian Survey*, vol. XXXIV, no. VIII, pp. 738-47; for irregularities in the Magura by-election, see, Mashreque Md. S. and Rashid, M. A. (1995), 'Parliamentary By-Election in Bangladesh: The Study of Magura-2 Constituency', *Asian Profile*, vol. 23, no. 1, pp. 67-80.

[61] These five parties and their candidates were, AL: Shafiquzzaman Bacchu; BNP: Kazi Salimul Haq Kamal; JP: Nitai Roy Chowdhury; JI: Golam Akbar; and IOJ: Mahbubur Rahman.

[62] *Ajker Kagoj*, 29 March, 1994.

[63] For related information, see, *Inquilab*, 20 and 21 March, 1994.

[64] BNP candidate secured 73,249 votes and his nearest rival AL candidate received 39,623 votes.
[65] Hasina expressed her opinion in a press conference on the evening of March 20, 1994. For detail on her comments, see, *The Bangladesh Observer*, 21 March, 1994.
[66] See, Sobhan, A. (1994), 'Prisoned by Herself: The Odd Situation of the AL Leader' (in Bengali), *Somoy*, 29 April, p. 5.
[67] The statement was signed by among others JI's Assistant Secretary General and Chief Election Coordinator Ali Ahsan Mohammad Mujahidi, *Jamaat*'s Parliamentary Group Secretary Ansar Ali MP, Magura District *Jamaat Ameer* Abdul Matin and party candidate in the by-election Golam Akbar.
[68] The other JP leaders who addressed in the press conference were Kazi Zafar hmed MP, Moudud Ahmed MP and Shah Moazzam Hossain MP, Major General (Retd.) Mahmudul Hasan, Col. (Retd.) Abdul Malek, Lt. Col. (Retd.) Zafar Imam, Anisul Islam Mahmud, Abul Hasanat, Sheikh Shahidul Islam, Monirul Huq Chowdhury MP and Azam Khan.
[69] For example, see, Alam, A. N. (1994), Corruption-free Election: Is Caretaker Government the Only Guarantee?' (in Bengali), *Weekly Bichittra*, 6 May, pp. 11-13.
[70] He cited examples of damage to a BNP office by the AL activists, burning the shop of a BNP worker, beating the Presiding Officer of Boroichara School centre and snatching away ballot boxes and other papers under the leadership of AL MPs Sheikh Harunur Rashid and Tajul Islam. For detail, see, *The Bangladesh Observer*, 23 March, 1994.
[71] See, Islam, S. T. (1994), *A Post-Poll Survey On Magura-2 Constituency*, Coordinating Council For Human Rights in Bangladesh-CCHRB, Dhaka.
[72] These three centres were: Kullia High School centre of Magura *Sadar* Thana, Boroichara Government Primary School and Hatbaria Government Primary School centres of Shalikha Thana. The author has collected this information from Md. Safiul Islam, District Election Officer, Magura, when he interviewed him on 2 October, 1996 at his office.
[73] For detail, see, *The Daily Ittefaq*, 29 March, 1994.
[74] *The Bangladesh Observer*, 18 January, 1996.
[75] The action programme included a march to the PM's residence on 10 February, rallies, demonstrations and processions across the country on 11, rally of the professional groups in front of the national press club on 12, country-wide rail-road-waterways blockade on 13, and a country-wide 48 hours strike on 14 and 15 February. See, *The Bangladesh Observer*, 6 February, 1996.
[76] BDR and *Ansar* are para-military forces.
[77] Two thousand and forty one candidates nominated and finally after withdrawals 1,498 including 457 independent candidates contested the election.
[78] Four hundred and one candidates withdrew their nomination papers. See, *Media Guide: Bangladesh Parliament Election June 1996* (Dhaka: Press Information Department (PID), Ministry of Information, Government of the People's Republic of Bangladesh, 1996) Annexure – 7.
[79] *The Bangladesh Observer*, 26 January, 1996.
[80] *The Bangladesh Observer*, 9 February, 1996.
[81] For related information, see, R. W. Timm (ed.) (1996), *Election Observation Report*, Coordinating Council for Human Rights in Bangladesh (CCHRB), Dhaka, p. 13.
[82] *The Bangladesh Observer*, 16 February, 1996.
[83] *The Bangladesh Observer*, 16 February, 1996.

[84] *The Bangladesh Observer*, 16 February, 1996.
[85] For related information, see, *Bangladesh Parliamentary Election June 12, 1996, The Report of the Fair Election Monitoring Alliance (FEMA)*, FEMA (1996), Dhaka. p. 10.
[86] In 10 constituencies the EC did not conduct an election because of the tense situation created by the anti-election activists, and in another constituency the reason was legal complications.
[87] See, Timm, Father R. W. (ed.), *Election Observation Report, op. cit.*, p. 30.
[88] Election reports containing rigging and malpractices were published in all local and many foreign dailies. For example, *The Financial Times* of London, *The Times* of India, the *Dawn* of Karachi, *The Washington Post, The Independent, The New York Times*, among others published such reports.
[89] Cited in Timm (ed.), *Election Observation Report, op. cit.*, p. 35.
[90] For example, weekly *Jai Jai Din* published such a report.
[91] *The Bangladesh Observer*, 16 March, 1996.
[92] These 15 seats were Bogra-6, 7, Sirajgong-1, Kurigram-3, Shariatpur-1, Sylhet-4, Lakkhipur-2, Chittagong-1, 13, Bagerhat-1, Rangpur-2,6,5, Pirojpur-2 and Khulna-1.
[93] See, *The Daily Al Mujaddid*, 8 September, 1996.
[94] *By-Election to 15 Constituencies Held on September 5, 1996*, The Report of the Fair Election Monitoring Alliance, FEMA (1996), Dhaka.
[95] The BBC broadcast a coverage of the by-election on 5 September in its afternoon Bengali programme. It mentioned that two journalists returning from the Lakkhipur constituency to Dhaka stated that they did not see any voters in 11 centres out of the total 12 centres they visited between 10:30 am to 3:00 pm. The electoral officials at those centres informed them that the voters had cast their votes before 10 am. The voters, on the other hand, stated that they were intimidated and not allowed to go to the vote centres. Some other journalists reported massive rigging and irregularities in Chittagong-1 and Rangpur-5 constituencies. They also claimed that in Tetulia vote centre AL workers took off the clothes of a JP polling agent and forced him to leave the vote centre naked. Cited in, *Inquilab*, 6 September, 1996.
[96] See, *The Daily Star* and *The Independent* (internet edition), 21 July, 1998.
[97] *The Daily Star*, 8 December, 1998.
[98] See, *Report On By-election Held In National Constituency No. 69 Pabna-2 On 10 December 1998*, Fair Election Monitoring Alliance (FEMA) (n. d.), Dhaka, p. 8.
[99] These five centres were: Mathurapur Govt. Primary School, Durgapur Govt. Primary School, Satbaria Girls High School, Manikhat Govt. Primary School and Char Dulai Govt. Prtimary School. For detail, see, the FEMA report, *ibid.* p. 9.
[100] *Prothom Alo*, 16 November, 1999.
[101] *Prothom Alo*, 18 November, 1999.
[102] *Prothom Alo*, 19 November, 1999.
[103] For details on the irregularities of Jhalakathi-2 by-election, see, Mahmuduzzaman, M. (2000), 'Tactical Election: Indication for the Future' (in Bengali), *Jai Jai Din*. vol. 16, no. 43, 8 August, pp. 4-10; Khasru, A. (2000), 'What the CEC Himself Listened and Observed', *ibid.*, pp. 10-12.
[104] *Inquilab*, 6 January, 2000.
[105] These two candidates were Maulana Mohammadullah (Hafizzi Huzur) and Maulana Abdur Rahim.

6 Caretaker Governments and the Myth of Free Elections

Introduction and Background

This chapter analyses electoral politics and corruption under two non-party caretaker governments (NCGs) in Bangladesh. It analyses the nature and functions of NCG and focuses on their formation, administration and neutrality. The chapter critically reviews their role in conducting fair elections and also estimates the degree of electoral corruption.

The unethical conduct of elections by partisan governments increased under military rule, as we have seen, but continued after civilianisation. After contesting several rigged elections under military regimes the opposing parties realised the futility of the process and refrained from participating in further elections. This also occurred during the Khaleda and Hasina civilian regimes, when the events surrounding a few controversial by-elections brought to the fore the question of electoral integrity of the incumbent governments. The opposition parties lost faith in that democratically-elected regime and its EC machinery to oversee free and fair elections. Their old demand for an NCG was renewed and vigorously pursued. It is ironic that it was Khaleda herself and the BNP which were at the forefront of the movement to oust the authoritarian regime in 1990 for its persistent electoral depravity that made elections a sham. She was eloquent in clamouring for the conduct of elections by an NCG which would be non-partisan, completely neutral, objective and detached in its approach towards electioneering. The BNP itself was returned to power by the people who exercised their franchise in an election supervised by an NCG. But when her government was blamed for malpractices by the opposition and demands for an NCG were made, she defended an elected government's responsibility to conduct elections as the people had reposed their trust in it. She swept aside the forceful entreaties of the opposition but in the end had to relent under tremendous pressure. The NCG as an institution was incorporated in the constitution and became a part of the political process in Bangladesh.

The fifth and the seventh parliamentary elections were held under caretaker governments that were created specifically to conduct fair elections. Both NCGs were headed by judges of the Supreme Court, indicating the confidence of the people in the judiciary. The first NCG was headed by the Chief Justice of the Bangladesh Supreme Court, Shahabuddin Ahmed (Shahabuddin), and the second by Mohammad Habibur Rahman (Habib), a retired Chief Justice of the same court. The members of the NCGs were selected from among different professions including bureaucrats, academics, industrialists and technocrats. The tenure of each NCG was almost three months.

The Fifth Parliamentary Election, 1991

The Shahabuddin NCG was constituted in early December 1990 after the fall of Ershad. It lost no time in formulating a schedule for the fifth parliamentary elections. The EC was restructured and clothed with extra-powers. New voters were registered and the electoral rolls updated.

The Groundwork

The electoral roll used for the 1991 election had been prepared by the previous military regime and was last revised in 1989. While none of the major parties was fully satisfied with this roll and the way it was compiled, there was a consensus among the parties to accept it, subject to the opportunity for further correction by the EC, which updated the rolls within a short time.[1] A report claimed that the EC received over 100,000 applications for inclusion in the roll but had rejected all but a few (0.3%). The EC argued that most applications did not comply with the requirements.[2] A number of election monitoring teams in their reports also identified significant flaws in the electoral roll.[3] (See table 6.1 and table 6.2).

In response to the demand of the political parties the NCG reconstituted the EC with three sitting judges. The Election Officials (Special Act) Ordinance 1990 was promulgated to maintain discipline within the ranks of electoral officials. It empowered the EC to suspend both returning and presiding officers for electoral offences. All government and semi-government officials and employees deployed for electoral work were brought under the jurisdiction of the EC.[4]

Table 6.1 Defects on the Electoral Roll (Dhaka Electoral Constituency 10, Ward No. 65, Baily Road)

Total Voters	1,000
Listed in the roll although moved from the constituency	150
Names of dead in the list	2
No. of voters listed in more than one constituency	10
No. of voters who are in prison	5
No. of eligible voters not listed	89

Source: Father R. W. Timm and Philip Gain (ed.) (1991), *Fifth National Parliamentary Election 1991, Observation Report* (in Bengali), Coordinating Council for Human Rights In Bangladesh, Dhaka, p. 57.

Table 6.2 Defects on the Electoral Roll (Madaripur Electoral Constituency 3, Ward No. 3, Ghatmajhi Union)

Total Voters	4,022 Male: 2,142 Female: 1,880
Listed in the roll after the announcement of the election date	4
Names of dead in the list	28
No. of under-age voters	51
Listed but not living in the constituency	253
No. of eligible voters not listed	112
Voters from outside the constituency	11
No. of voters who were enrolled in more than one place	165
Listed but unknown (phantom voters)	113

Source: Father R. W. Timm and Philip Gain (ed.) (1991). *Fifth National Parliamentary Election: 1991 Observation Report* (in Bengali), Coordinating Council for Human Rights In Bangladesh, Dhaka, p. 59.

To ensure administrative neutrality, the NCG circulated a press release which forbade officials working at government and semi-government offices from attending political meetings. The press release also directed officials not to attend any socio-cultural gatherings that had been arranged for or were to be attended by political leaders.[5]

The NCG increased the limit of election expenses from *taka* 100,000 (about US $ 2,750 at that time) to *taka* 300,000 (US $ 8,250) in order to control the use of black money in the election. Further, candidates were ordered to submit probable sources of their election expenses to the returning officers in a prescribed form within seven days after the deadline for withdrawal of nomination papers. If a candidate was a taxpayer, he/she was also to disclose all debts, annual income, expenditure and a copy of their last income tax return.[6] Moreover, every candidate was asked to submit an account of their election-related expenditure to the EC within 15 days of the election.[7]

The NCG imposed certain special responsibilities on the *union parisads* (lowest tier of local government) and *pourashavas* (Municipalities) to maintain law and order within their respective jurisdictions. The Union Parisad and Pourashava (Special Responsibilities) Ordinance, 1991 required these bodies to resist all activities directed against the holding of a fair election, including any attempt to violate the electoral laws and rules, and any step that might harm electoral peace. The Ordinance empowered the government to suspend or dissolve any *union parisad* or *pourashava* where peace was disrupted.[8]

The EC after consulting with the representatives of almost all political parties formulated a 16-point code of conduct (for the full text of the code of conduct, see Appendix L). The basic principles of the code to be observed by the parties highlighted the maintenance of mutual respect, the recognition of the democratic rights of others and a congenial atmosphere.

The members of the EC visited different regions of the country and reviewed the preparations for holding a fair election. Secretaries (highest-ranking civil servants) of ministries were also sent to different regions to ensure administrative impartiality in the elections. In order to reduce the influence of violence in the election the NCG launched a countrywide drive to recover illegal arms. The Arms Law was amended to this end and the maximum punishment for possession of illegal arms was raised to life imprisonment.

The NCG decided to deploy the military in addition to the police and other para-militia forces to maintain law and order on polling day. Mobile security units were created in every *upazila*, town and city. The metropolitan police installed 150 check posts and searched doubtful persons on election day. A restriction was imposed upon taking motorbikes and other motor vehicles within 400 yards of voting centres. All these measures ensured that voters could freely participate in the campaign and then vote for the candidate of their choice.

Parties and Candidates

Immense enthusiasm among parties and voters were noted in the fifth parliamentary election. As the people had long sought an election under an impartial government, they took the opportunity of exercising their franchise and enjoyed the event as a carnival. The political parties were also very active in their attempts to enhance their strength and popularity through this election.

Seventy-six political parties, a few with a grass-roots base and most without, contested the election, breaking the previous record. However, the main competition was limited to four major parties.[9] Altogether, 2,360 candidates (of whom 32 were women[10]) and 424 independents stood for the 300-seat *Jatiya Sangsad*.[11] The BNP was the only party to nominate candidates in all 300 constituencies. The AL fielded 264 candidates and supported candidates of other parties making up an eight-party alliance, which jointly with the AL, had played an active role in the anti-Ershad movement. The JP, JI and *Zaker* Party nominated more than 200 candidates. Table 6.3 shows the number of candidates nominated by political parties and independents.

Manifestos and Campaign

One study notes that as in previous elections,

> the campaign was marked by direct verbal attacks by the two leading contenders against one another. Each accused the other of wrongdoings in the past when in government, of violating democratic norms, and of unpatriotic behaviour. At times the insinuations became very sordid, often bordering on personal innuendos. Both the AL and the BNP exploited the image of their slain paramount leaders, Sheikh Mujib and Ziaur Rahman, who were still very popular among different segments of the population, and extolled the virtues of their rule.[12]

The AL's manifesto was a blend of old and new commitments. It promised to restore a democratic parliamentary system, although Mujib, Hasina's father, had instituted a presidential, one party civilian authoritarian system in early 1975. The AL manifesto also advocated secularism and Bengali nationalism and committed itself to bring the murderers of Mujib to trial if voted to power.[13] The party used its *'Joy Bangla'* (victory of Bengal) slogan which aligned the party closely with India. This was seen by AL detractors as 'less nationalistic' than the 'Bangladesh *Zindabad*' (long live Bangladesh) slogan used by the BNP and some other parties.[14] The AL manifesto also pledged to restore the constitution to its pre-fourth amendment form, providing for the full independence of the judiciary, freedom of the press, the autonomy of electronic media and to repeal all repressive laws (also known as black laws). The AL also supported a market economy, foreign investment and a productive public sector.

Table 6.3 Number of Candidates by Political Parties/Independents

Party/Independents	Number of Candidates
Bangladesh Nationalist Party (BNP)	300
Jatiya Party (JP)	272
Bangladesh *Awami* League (AL)	264
Zaker Party	251
Jamaat-e-Islami Bangladesh (JI)	222
Jatiya Samajtantrik Dal (JSD-Rab)	161
Bangladesh *Krishak Sramik Awami* League (BKSAL	68
Jatiya Samajtantrik Dal (JSD-Inu)	68
Freedom Party	65
Bangladesh Muslim League (Quader)	62
Islami Oikyo Jote	59
Bangladesh *Janata Dal*	50
Communist Party of Bangladesh (CPB)	49
Bangladesh *Khelafat Andolan*	43
Other Parties	429
Independents	424
Total	2,787

Source: Election Commission, Bangladesh.

The AL manifesto aimed to strengthen the country's relations with the Organisation of Islamic Countries (OIC) and the South Asian

Association for Regional Cooperation (SAARC), and the party promised to establish a corruption-free administration and build strong and disciplined armed forces. Although advocating secularism, the AL was careful not to offend the Islamic religious sentiment of the majority population and its president declared that it would not ban any religion-based party. However it would not allow them to use religion as a tool for achieving political ambitions — a technique which was criticised by an electoral analyst.[15] He meant that if a religious fundamentalist party is allowed to function, it obviously would use religion for its political benefit.

As in the 1979 parliamentary elections, the BNP in its campaign stressed 'Bangladeshi nationalism', 'absolute trust and faith in Almighty Allah', and 'social and economic justice'.[16] It indirectly favoured the continuation of the presidential system although the party manifesto tactfully 'avoided the debate over the future form of government by simply pledging a multi-party democracy'.[17] The BNP leaders tried to utilise the religious and anti-Indian sentiments of the majority of the population in its campaign speeches, posters and graffiti.[18] The party used the 'Bangladesh Zindabad' slogan and underlined cultural integrity. The BNP leaders referred to its six years rule as a 'golden era' in contrast to the three and a half years AL regime which it labelled as a 'nightmare' and the Ershad regime (1982-1990) as an 'era of conspiracy'.

Manifestos of all major parties highlighted their past successes in government and spelled out future plans. Not surprisingly, none of the parties who had ruled before recognised any of its past mistakes or shortcomings. The two main contestants, AL and the BNP, directly attacked each other during the campaign. Khaleda Zia, in more than 2,000 public electoral speeches always criticised her main rival the AL and did not hesitate to declare that the AL would sell the country and delete *bismillah*[19] from the constitution if voted to power. She also blamed the AL for supporting the military regime of Ershad. In a similar vein, Hasina attacked the BNP and declared that democracy would be confined to the military if the BNP regained power. She also alleged that there had been no democracy during the last 15 years and criticised both Zia and Ershad equally. Overall, the campaign was dull. It was

> remarkable for the bankruptcy of ideas in all the parties. The manifestos of all the parties were a rehash of old promises and clichés. There was little to distinguish between the programme of the (several) parties that fielded candidates. Indeed, every party was careful not to omit a promise made by its rival so as not to be

outdone in its populist commitments, but little thought was given to consistency or coherence.[20]

Use of Media

The media played a relatively neutral role during this election in contrast to those under military regimes when radio and television were used only by the ruling party and access was denied to the opposition. Television provided coverage to all political parties according to the number of their candidates. From early February television allocated 45 minutes to each party fielding at least 30 candidates to make their presentations. However, the *Jatiya* Party and the Freedom Party, for example, although nominating more than 30 candidates were not allocated any television time.[21] The *Jatiya* Party complained to the EC about such treatment by the media. The other party leaders on this point argued that as the JP regime had previously abused its use of the media and had been removed from power by a widespread popular movement, allowing equal access to television was too sensitive an issue.[22] The TV authority worked with a fair degree of impartially under the NCG and produced a number of electoral programmes to educate the voters on fair polling. Tables 6.4 and 6.5 highlight the election-oriented programmes on the TV during the election. Newspapers provided adequate coverage of the manifestos and views of all parties. The English language press maintained a balance between the two main alliances and played a neutral role. As most of the Bengali newspapers favoured certain political parties, they strongly advocated the interests of those parties. However they also allocated space for news of other parties. All newspapers gave equal prominence to the news and statements of the NCG and the EC.

Violence and Corruption

The fifth parliamentary election was, by and large, held in a peaceful atmosphere, barring a few isolated cases of violence. A large number of local and foreign teams from the UK, Japan, Malaysia, and the USA, who monitored the elections, found it peaceful and recognised the election as impartial, free, fair and successful. The same positive sentiment was reflected in the report of the European Community election observation group. Another team from the Association for South Asian Regional Co-operation (SAARC) countries also praised the election and recommended that the standard established at this election should be followed by other SAARC countries.[23] Liberty Forum and the Coordinating Council for

Human Rights in Bangladesh (CCHRB) were two local institutions which also attested to the fairness of the election.

Table 6.4 Programme Time Allocation of Total Telecast Hours (9 February - 1 March)

Programmes	Duration			% of Total Tele-cast Time
	Hours	Minutes	Seconds	
Total telecast time	182	11	08	100
Total time devoted to election programems	19	49	33	10.88
Total time devoted to announcement of election results	14	01	40	07.70
Total time devoted to regular/general programmes	119	58	54	65.86
Total time devoted to newscasts	28	21	01	15.56

Source: Father R. W. Timm (ed.) (1991), *Fifth National Parliamentary Election, 1991: Observation Report* (in Bengali), Coordinating Council for Human Rights in Bangladesh, Dhaka, p. 67. Slightly modified in designing and translated by the author from Bengali.

Table 6.5 Time Distribution of TV Programmes on Election (9 February - 1 March)

Programmes	Duration			% of Time Devoted to Election Programmes
	Hours	Minutes	Seconds	
Total time devoted to speeches of the Acting President, CEC and political leaders	9	55	45	50.08
Time devoted to documentary films on election	2	57	30	14.92
Time devoted to short dramas on election	1	21	00	6.81
Announcements on elec: rules, regulations, voting slogans and duties of the election officials	1	37	53	8.23
Time devoted to advertisements, slogans, telops on election	2	12	10	11.11
Time devoted to discussions and dialogue on election	1	45	15	8.85
Total	19	49	33	100

Source: Father R. W. Timm (ed.) (1991), *Fifth National Parliamentary Election, 1991: Observation Report* (in Bengali), Coordinating Council for Human Rights in Bangladesh, Dhaka, p. 68. Slightly modified in designing and translated by the author from Bengali.

The author personally observed the elections in two constituencies of Khulna, visiting a number of centres in the Khulna-2 (Kotowali) and Khulna-3 (Khalishpur, Daulatpur) constituencies. People were seen to vote freely without any impediment. A number of voters in Khulna-2 constituency were interviewed, most of whom expressed their satisfaction with the voting procedure and arrangements.[24] Only a few voters indicated irregularities in the voter list. The absence of rigging and widespread violence was the most striking feature of this election. Nevertheless, the EC postponed voting in 21 centres in four constituencies where the situation got beyond the control of the presiding officers. Altogether 48 persons died in electoral violence; most of the deaths were the result of bombing and gun fights, and attacks on the electoral processions of the rival groups, and other violent actions.[25] Utilising the Union Parisad and Pourashava (Special Responsibility) Ordinance 1991, the NCG suspended 5 union *parisads* for their failure to maintain law and order during voting in their areas.[26]

Results and Reactions

In the final count, the BNP with 140 seats emerged as the single largest party belying all pre-election speculations and surveys. Political analysts had predicted the AL to emerge as the largest party in the fifth parliament. A pre-election survey showed that the AL might win as many as 178 seats and that the BNP would finish a distant second with 67 seats.[27] But the AL only managed to win 88 seats. The JP which political observers predicted would be totally rejected by the voters surprisingly secured 35 seats, despite being deprived of equal opportunity in the campaign. The JI won 18 seats, well below its expected figure. Table 6.6 shows the parties and their positions in the fifth parliament.

Table 6.6 shows that the 4 major parties won 281 of the 300 seats although 76 political parties contested the elections. None of the major parties won an absolute majority. Among the remaining 19 seats, 16 were shared by eight political parties and three seats went to independent candidates. Sixty-four political parties (about 84% of the total contestant parties) failed to win a seat.

The results surprised political observers who had not expected such a quick rehabilitation of the JP, nor did they expect the defeat of the AL-chief in two constituencies in Dhaka by politically unknown BNP candidates. The JI's 18 seats, although fewer than its expectation, was far better than the performance of the leftist parties. The CPB won only five and other left wing parties together obtained just eight seats which indicated their poor support in the predominantly conservative Muslim society of Bangladesh. While the BNP and the AL received a similar percentage of votes (BNP 30.81 and AL 30.08), the percentage of seats won by the BNP was much higher (BNP 46.66%, AL 29.33%). A similar result was the case with JI and JP. JI received more votes than the JP (JI 12.13%, JP 11.93%), but won almost 50 percent fewer seats than the JP. The reason for this discrepancy was that BNP candidates won by a slim margin while the AL support was more concentrated; and JI candidates although defeated in many constituencies received a high proportion of votes whereas the JP's support in many parts of the country was so negligible that the candidates lost their deposits.

Table 6.6 Results of 1991 Parliamentary Elections

Parties/Independents	No. of Seats Won	% of Seats Won
Bangladesh Nationalist Party (BNP)	140	46.66
Bangladesh *Awami* League (AL)	88	29.33
Jatiya Party (JP)	35	11.66
Jamaat-e-Islami Bangladesh (JI)	18	6.00
Bangladesh *Krishak Shramik Awami* League	5	1.66
Communist Party of Bangladesh (CPB)	5	1.66
Other parties*	6	2.00
Independents	3	1.00

Source: Bangladesh Election Commission. *Six parties won 1 seat each. They were: National *Awami* Party (NAP-M), *Ganatantri* Party (GP), Workers Party (WP), *Jatiya Samajtantrik Dal* (JSD-Siraj), National Democratic Party (NDP) and *Islami Oikyo Jote*.

By all standards, the 1991 election was the fairest and best organised since independence.[28] The two major parties were so certain of winning that they did not encourage their activists and supporters to adopt unfair practices to manipulate the elections to their advantage. Election officials were vigilant in preventing any undue influence disrupting fair polling and the law-enforcing agencies worked conscientiously to maintain peace. Almost all the political parties accepted the results. The JP and JI, despite holding the third and fourth positions, accepted both the electoral process and the results. However, the reaction of AL, being second in the race, was ambivalent. AL leader Sheikh Hasina alleged in a published statement that the election was rigged and she made the same allegation during an interview with Voice of America. Hasina claimed that, 'it appears in a wider view that the election was fair, but in actual practice it was tactfully rigged'.[29] Her statement was not supported by other major parties, or even by the leadership of her own party. Senior AL leaders, Abdus Samad Azad and Tofail Ahmed, accepted the results and recognised the election as free and fair. Another central leader and a presidium member of the AL, Kamal Hossain, though defeated, praised the standard of the election.[30] The other alliances and parties were also satisfied with the results.

Causes of Success and Failure

The win for the BNP, which was much weaker organisationally than the AL, was surprising. However, the major cause of BNP's win was centred around the uncompromising role of its leader in opposing the Ershad regime. Under Khaleda Zia's bold decision, the BNP boycotted all elections when Ershad was in power. Even after Ershad's resignation, Khaleda demanded an appropriate trial and punishment for the overthrown president and his associates. She was able to show the people the relevance of her commitments and actions during the anti-Ershad movement. *Jatiyatabadi Chattra Dal* (JCD), the student wing of the BNP, which controlled most of the college and university student unions including the Dhaka University Central Student's Union (DUCSU), played a prominent role in taking the message of the BNP to the remote areas.[31] The party was able to win the support of the younger generation, particularly those born in post-independent Bangladesh and the post-Mujib period. The active involvement of these teen-agers made the BNP campaign stronger than its rivals. Moreover, BNP's policy of strengthening the private sector, a contemporary issue-oriented campaign and its anti-Indian and pro-Islamic stand, and the use of the image of Zia, were well received by the majority of voters.

The debacle of the AL resulted from overconfidence. They did not take their campaign as seriously as their rivals. The AL leaders thought that as the JP was almost absent and the BNP was organisationally weak, they could easily win the election using their strong party network throughout the country. AL badly underestimated the BNP believing that it might win no more than 30 seats.[32] The party also performed poorly in coordinating its activities with allied parties. As a result, in 37 seats allied parties nominated their own candidates and campaigned against the AL.[33] AL's other policies, such as its commitment to the re-introduction of secularism, and its inability to deflect the opposition's accusation that the AL was pro-Indian contributed to the party's defeat. The internal feuds within the party and dictatorial role in the nomination of candidates also weakened unity among the party leaders. Hasina's criticism of Zia and her past-oriented campaign instead of offering positive future plans were disliked by the majority of voters.

The main cause of JP's doing well in the election resulted from the failure of the major parties to build an anti-JP sentiment during the campaign. The AL and BNP were too busy attacking each other and did not view the JP as a strong opponent. Another cause of JP's winning a number of seats was the popularity of some of its leaders in their constituencies. They used their personal image and relationships which were established through development works in their constituencies when in power and were successful in winning the support of the voters.

The Seventh Parliamentary Election, 1996

Background

As the sixth parliamentary election 1996 was opposed and boycotted by almost all major opposition political parties, it could not solve the long political deadlock in the country. The opposition rejected it and strengthened their movement by launching a fresh anti-government programme including a policy of indefinite non-cooperation. The government tried to control the opposition through repressive measures but was not successful.[34]

The central bureaucracy (including many secretaries and high officials) directly favoured the opposition's non-cooperation movement. In March, 1996, officials and employees of the government held meetings within the national Secretariat premises in support of the opposition.[35] They also appeared on the political podium called *Janatar Mancha* (Platform of the People) which was erected by the AL and operated as its political rostrum. Moreover, they began strike action from 30 March, 1996, when they attended their offices but abstained from work and decided to continue this tactic until the formation of an NCG. They also asked government officials and employees to form units of their organisation — the 'Republic Officers Coordination Council', an unknown organisation of government employees, to make their action a success throughout the country. Thirty-seven secretaries gave the president a six-point demand that included the appointment of a caretaker government.[36] This directly partisan role of the civil bureaucracy was tantamount to a 'bureaucratic rebellion' against the government, a move which had its supporters and detractors.[37]

The prime minister declared her intention to introduce a Caretaker Government Bill in parliament, but the opposition termed this 'a move to legalise farcical polls'.[38] Fresh proposals for talks were also rejected by the former leader of the opposition,[39] who responsed by presenting a five-point demand to the prime minister. The demands were:

1. The release of all opposition leaders and workers from jails and the withdrawal of all false warrants of arrest against opposition leaders, workers and others in the democratic movement by March 9.
2. Cessation of all activities related to farcical re-polling, cancellation of the 'one party election' of February 15 and the resignation of the government.
3. The president to form a new NCG by 10 March after meeting with all political parties to ensure a free and fair election for the sixth *Jatiya Sangsad* by May.
4. Compensation for political leaders, workers and members of different professions who were killed, injured and harassed by government forces during the democratic movement and the 'farcical' election on February 15.
5. Restoration of law and order to protect the lives and property of the people.

The prime minister did not retreat from her stand and in response to the opposition demand for cancellation of the February poll asked, 'if this election is cancelled, how will the non-party government bill be passed?'[40]

The BNP was able to form a cabinet and maintained its commitment to constitutional continuity by passing the Constitution Thirteenth Amendment Bill 1996, in the only session of the sixth parliament. The salient features of the Bill were:

1. A non-party caretaker government would govern the country between the period when parliament was dissolved and a new prime minister took over after elections to the new parliament. This government would be constituted within 15 days of dissolution of parliament.
2. This government would be accountable to the president.

3. The caretaker government would perform the routine work of a government but would not make any policy decisions.
4. The members of the caretaker government would be known as advisers and the head of caretaker government as Chief Adviser. The president would appoint the chief adviser and select other advisers in consultation with the chief adviser.
5. The advisers would be below the age of 72, would not be a member of any political party (or their affiliated organisations) and would not contest the parliamentary elections.
6. The President would appoint the chief adviser from amongst the chief justices of the Supreme Court who had retired most recently.
7. The chief adviser would enjoy the rank of prime minister and the advisers, that of ministers.

The mainstream opposition, although recognising neither the sixth parliamentary election nor the sixth parliament, calling them 'farcical' and 'illegal' respectively, nevertheless cooperated with the president in forming the NCG according to the provisions of the Constitution Thirteenth Amendment Bill 1996, passed by the sixth parliament. Thus a long political standoff ended when the president dissolved the parliament, the prime minister resigned and Mohammad Habibur Rahman was appointed the chief adviser to the new NCG for conducting the seventh parliamentary election.

Preparations for Fair Elections

The caretaker government[41] commenced its task by revamping the EC. Earlier, the opposition parties had accused the CEC of facilitating vote rigging in the previous election.[42] A new chief election commissioner and two election commissioners were appointed and the top echelon of the election secretariat was reshuffled.

Major emphasis was given both by the NCG and the political parties to the maintenance of law and order during the campaign. The chief adviser in a broadcast over radio and TV stressed this point and committed the NCG to taking stern measures to this end. The chief adviser also stressed the determination of the government to enable the EC to perform its work smoothly. The leaders of the major parties including Hasina and Khaleda met the chief adviser and also expressed their anxiety about law and order and urged the recovery of illegal arms. The NCG directed the deputy commissioners (DC), the chief executives of districts and superintendent of police (SP), and the chief police officers of districts to jointly prepare special weekly reports for the home ministry outlining the existing situation and noting possible trouble spots and measures taken. The Cabinet Division, acting on a press release issued by the chief adviser's office, asked the DCs and SPs to monitor the use of illegal arms and force, and extortion. It also directed them to visit the *thanas* in their respective districts and classify the areas as either troubled, risky, or normal.

The EC undertook the task of updating the electoral rolls by calling for fresh voluntary registration of voters who missed enrolment before. Availing themselves of this opportunity, 688,646 new voters were able to have their names included in the list.[43] Critics of the scheme described it as unnecessary and contributing to increased false voting because the EC failed to check the eligibility of claimants applying for registration and as a consequence a large number of voters would enrol in several constituencies. Others however praised this effort.[44] It was also argued that during the last voters' registration in 1995, the stress placed on physical presence and the authenticity of address of the voters was so rigid that a number of high government officials and university teachers who were temporarily overseas had been excluded from the roll.[45]

As the central bureaucracy played a partisan role during the anti-BNP movement and participated directly in opposition meetings and other demonstrations, the NCG took measures to ensure administrative neutrality. The chief adviser in a statement underlined the importance of maintaining the reputation of the executive branch of the government at all costs. He maintained that he would not hesitate to take stern action against those who indulged in or allowed intentional wrongdoing. He added that the executive should maintain the continuity of administration as per law and the constitution and discharge their duties under the authority of a lawfully elected government.[46]

Moreover, the NCG made a large-scale transfer of the DCs, SPs, *thana nirbahi* officers (TNO, the chief executive of a *thana*), officers in charge (OCs, the chief of a police station) who although defended by the AL, were severely criticised by the BNP. The secretary general of the party maintained that it would not be possible to hold a fair election merely by re-posting those DCs who had directly involved themselves with a particular political party. He also identified quite a number of currently posted DCs who had expressed their solidarity with a particular political party and joined a political rally. He added that it would be unrealistic to think of holding a fair election with those DCs conducting the election. The central working committee of the AL alleged that the BNP government during its five year rule had politicised the country's administration by installing its party sympathisers in key positions of administration. 'If the administration cannot be completely de-politicised the neutrality of administration cannot be expected', it pointed out.[47] The NCG took additional care to maintain law and order during the election and deployed 40,000 soldiers to help 400,000 police and security forces.

The EC, on the basis of an agreement reached by the major political parties, formulated a code of conduct (for the full text of the code see appendix M). The EC warned five candidates for violating the code and asked all candidates to submit an account of the sources of their electioneering funds within seven days of the date set for the withdrawal of candidature. This was to include: personal income which would be expended for electioneering; the amount of money to be provided by relatives as debt or donation and the sources of income of these relatives; the amount of money to be provided by any other persons as debt or voluntary donation; the amount of money to be provided by any institution, political party or any organisation as voluntary donation and the possible amount of money to be provided by any other sources. In addition, according to the Representation of Public Order, 1972, the contesting candidates had to submit the return of their annual income and expenditure in the prescribed form. If a candidate was an income tax payer, he had to submit a copy of his last income tax return with the statement.[48]

The EC undertook a voter education programme. It distributed voter education posters throughout the country (for sample of such posters see appendix N). Training programmes were organised for election officials. The EC's Election Training Institute arranged a three-day workshop for judicial officers and DCs who were also returning officers, while the presiding officers and assistant presiding officers underwent a short course training to enable them to discharge their electoral duties. Some NGOs organised voter education and training programmes such as those arranged by the Fair Election Monitoring Alliance (FEMA), a NGO-based election monitoring organisation, on the eve of the election.[49] A total of nearly 30,000 persons were trained by FEMA who worked as its local level polling station observers. It also trained 135 district coordinators, and more than 1,000 constituency and *thana* coordinators between May 15 and June 3, 1996. The FEMA programmes were severely criticised as politically motivated by a large number of academics and political party leaders and workers.[50] Both BNP and JI were highly critical of FEMA's role.[51] Several prominent BNP and JI leaders informed the author that all FEMA's activities in the name of voter education were directed to support a particular political party. A defeated JI candidate alleged that NGO workers under the leadership of FEMA indirectly campaigned against his party, and voters who attended its voter education programmes confirmed to the author that the trainers told them to vote for a specific party. On further questioning, they explained that although the trainers did not directly mention the name of a party, their discussion surreptitiously implied support for a particular party. A district coordinator of FEMA, who conducted voter education and training programmes in a south eastern district, confirmed that FEMA's voter education programme was not totally impartial.[52] Impartial voter-education programmes, of course, are essential for characterising an election as fair.[53]

Parties and Candidates

Eighty-one political parties, the highest number since independence, contested the seventh parliamentary elections of 12 June 1996. The politics of nomination in the major parties started vigorously before the announcement of the election date as they attempted to attract influential personalities to stand as candidates. The former members of the civil-military bureaucracy, industrialists and prominent leaders from other parties were the principal targets of all parties and a fair number of former bureaucrats joined the three main political parties AL, BNP and the JP. According to one estimate, the number of former military officers standing in the election totalled 26. The number of retired civil bureaucrats was even higher[54] and party switching by candidates – 36 in all – occurred at a frequency not seen before. Twenty-two out of these joined the BNP, nine joined the AL, four the JP and one the *Islami Oikyo Jote*.[55] Altogether, 3,093 candidates from 81 political parties and independents filed nomination papers. After scrutiny and withdrawals 2,574 candidates finally stood for 300 seats with an average of 8.58 candidates per seat. The number of independent candidates was 281. The four major parties, AL, BNP, JP and JI fielded candidates in all 300 constituencies. The number of female candidates contesting general seats was 47 and candidates from minority communities numbered 74.

Manifestos and Campaign

The manifestos of most parties reflected their past pledges. The AL stressed the formation of a transparent and accountable government on the basis of national consensus, highlighted a participatory administration free from party influence and proposed initiatives to eradicate corruption and terrorism from Bangladesh society. It also committed the party to encourage a free market economy, the modernisation of agriculture and small co-operatives. Ensuring the independence of the judiciary by separating it from the executive, and the creation of a strong, well-equipped army were other plans in the party's platform. Autonomy for the electronic media, decentralisation of administration and the re-introduction of the *upazila* system were three other commitments. A new addition to the manifesto also announced that AL would not renew the 25 years friendship treaty with India but would take steps to have a proper share of the Ganges water.[56]

The BNP manifesto emphasised defence of the four fundamental principles of the constitution, the democratisation of all tiers of administration, the establishment of the rule of law and the sovereignty of the people. It also contained commitments to reform the labour law, to formulate a national policy on land, to maintain the independence of the judiciary and to build a powerful and well-equipped defence force. The manifesto gave priority to industrialisation and the development of a free market economy. It pledged to seek a permanent solution to the problems of the Ganges and other international rivers and to establish special relations with the Muslim countries. The BNP also stood for revitalising and preserving Islamic values and culture, forming *thana* and *zila parisads* and re-introducing *gram sarkar* (village government).[57]

The JP manifesto resembled that of the BNP with extra emphasis on the reintroduction of the *upazila* system. However, the JI manifesto differed markedly from those of the other parties in that it sought to amend the constitution in the light of the Holy Quran and the *Sunnah* and to declare the country an Islamic republic. The manifesto committed the party to ensure the rule of honest people by eradicating bribery, nepotism, corruption and misappropriation. It promised to revise the anti-corruption act to bring everybody within its ambit and stressed the principle of the nourishment of good and the punishment of evil. The party pledged to design the nation's foreign policy in accordance with the ideals of Islam and to build a defence force imbued with the spirit of 'jihad' (crusade). It also planned to democratise local government, reduce educational expenses, and to give rights and status to women as recognised in Islam.[58]

A review of the manifestos of the major four political parties shows that all accepted a free market economy as the guiding principle of their programmes for economic development. The control of corruption, reforms in education and agriculture, strengthening the defence forces and the independence of the judiciary were other common commitments. The differences were not major in the manifestos of the AL, BNP and the JP. Only the JI differed in its stress on religion in the framing of state policy.

While the manifestos contained impressive commitments, none provided plans to implement those promises. A critique dismissed election manifestos as a traditional political ritual for cheating the people, arguing that the parties failed to execute these commitments.[59] According to another political analyst manifestos encouraged movements instead of development.[60]

The election campaign officially ran from 22 May through to midnight of 10 June 1996. The parties circulated posters, pamphlets and bulletins carrying messages and criticisms of their rivals. The major parties also used audio and video cassettes to highlight their positive aspects. Songs supporting candidates were composed and sung by folk singers especially in rural areas and were recorded and played continuously in party campaign offices.[61] Electoral processions, public meetings and door-to-door canvassing were other widely used campaign techniques. In the metropolitan areas several parties formed female campaign teams who approached only female voters to support their parties.

Attacks and counter-attacks were common among the parties. The AL criticised the BNP focusing on the corruption of its ministers, the politicisation of administration, the high price of essential goods and the flooding of Bangladesh market by smuggled Indian goods. The AL attempted to disprove its pro-India image with contrary facts and figures and accused the BNP of being pro-Indian by highlighting the government's relationship with India. AL admitted its mistakes committed during the party's three and a half years in government after independence and sought forgiveness and the opportunity to serve the nation.

Similarly, the BNP campaign attacked the AL portraying it as being a pro-Indian political platform safeguarding Indian interests in Bangladesh and working to convert the nation into a vassal state.[62] The BNP reminded the voters of the 1974 famine and the formation of a one party (BKSAL) state in 1975 by the AL government. It also raised the issue of the 25 years friendship treaty with India negotiated by the AL government after independence and warned the voters against supporting the AL to prevent them from renewing the pact. The BNP tried to unite the nationalist forces and highlighted development work completed during its tenure.

The campaign of the JP was centred on the imprisonment of its chairman, Ershad, and the JI's campaign was almost totally based on religion.[63] The JI workers wooed voters with claims that the JI was the party of Allah and that its supporters would certainly enter paradise in the life hereafter. One of JI's main slogans was '*vote diley pallae khushi hobay*

Allahai' ('voting for the scale (its electoral symbol) will make Allah glad').[64]

Frequent violations of the code of conduct and other irregularities were noticed during the campaign. There were graffiti, colourful posters, banners, an excessive number of loudspeakers and vehicle processions. The EC warned candidates of their violations of the code but was reluctant to take action. At least 20 people died in clashes between rival groups during the campaign.[65]

The Role of Media

The radio and TV authorities had opportunities to work independently as the NCG did not impose any forms of major censorship. It issued a special instruction to the broadcasting authorities that they were not to broadcast party leaders who were in jail or who were not standing as a candidate. This prevented Ershad and Golam Azam (JI chief), two significant political figures, presenting their party political broadcasts on television.[66] Once again BTV provided for representatives of every party fielding a minimum of 30 candidates to make political broadcasts. The JP challenged the decision and the High Court ruled in Ershad's favour, but the NCG appealed to the Supreme Court and the issue became irrelevant as the schedule of time for the campaign was over. This undue intervention of the NCG was labelled undemocratic by analysts. They argued that the leaders who were allowed to address public meetings or stand as candidates should not have been shunned by the electronic media.[67] Party activities were covered by national news broadcasts on radio and television although the time allocated to different parties was not carefully monitored. Table 6.7 shows the allocation of time for the coverage of different political parties in the main news.

The table shows that the allocation of time for party news coverage on television was more balanced than that on the radio. But the time allocated for television news with pictures (see column four) indicates a greater bias towards the AL. The JI was totally ignored in this category and the BNP was also treated unfairly. The analysis of the table indicates only the time but not the content or potency of the coverage.

A number of television programmes were produced covering the election. A widely discussed and influential programme titled '*Sabinaye Jante Chai*' ('Humbly Want to Know') was strongly criticised by the political leaders and campaign workers as being biased towards the AL. Panellists in this live programme interviewed the invited party leaders. Political parties which were represented in the fifth parliament by at least

10 seats were invited to participate in this programme, the only exception being Golam Azam who was barred by the television authority.

Table 6.7 Time Allocated for the Coverage of Party Activities in the Main Bengali News (in percentage)

Party	Radio	TV	TV (Pictorial)
AL	24.1%	17.2	46.8
BNP	20.8%	17.4	18.1
JP	10.2%	13.1	7.5
JI	16.9%	11.7	0.0
Others	28.0%	40.7	27.7
Total	**100.0**	**100.1***	**100.1***

Source: Compiled by the author using information from *Bangladesh Parliamentary Elections June 12, 1996*, the Report of the Fair Election Monitoring Alliance (FEMA) (1996), FEMA, Dhaka, pp. 20-21. AL= Bangladesh *Awami* League, BNP = Bangladesh Nationalist Party, JP = *Jatiya* Party, and JI = *Jamaat-e-Islami* Bangladesh.
*Rounding error.

A number of political observers were also highly critical of this television programme. Alleging bias on the part of the panel one analyst criticised the partiality of the moderator of the programme. The panel made critical comments in cases of JI and BNP rather than questioning its leaders. One columnist criticised the excitable and aggressive attitude of the panel members while asking questions of the representatives of the JI and BNP.[68] Another critic argued that the questions that were asked of AL representatives were secretly supplied beforehand to the AL leaders allowing them to prepare the replies while representatives of other parties were made to answer impromptu. Moreover, the JI and BNP representatives were more critically cross-examined and were deliberately harassed. He also alleged bias on the part of the director general of the BTV.[69] The NCG simply overlooked the discriminatory stance of the television authority.

Nor were the print media totally fair. FEMA, after monitoring four newspapers, reported that Hasina and her party got more coverage with a total of 1,659.3 column inches than Khaleda and her party's 1,368.65 column inches. AL and its leader Hasina also received privileged positions in the layout of news items and photographs. Table 6.8 and table 6.9 show allotted space for political parties and placement of news items and photographs of Hasina and Khaleda.

Both the English dailies (*Bangladesh Observer* and *The Daily Star*) played a neutral role but Bengali dailies (*Ittefaq* and the *Janakhantha*) clearly favoured the AL. The *Janakhantha* was open in its supporting of AL; one stated that 'it was time for a change and voters should support the *Awami* League...'.[70] No other newspapers openly canvassed for the AL although a number of them directly supported it.[71] The BNP and the JI had only one newspaper each to support their cause.[72] The analysis in tables 6.8 and 6.9 indicates allotted space for political parties and news items and photographs of two selected leaders respectively, but not the content or potency of this coverage.

Table 6.8 Allotted Space for Political Parties in the Four Major Newspapers (inches)

Newspaper	Sheikh Hasina	Khaleda Zia
Bangladesh Observer	374.07	404.07
The Daily Star	253.02	231.09
Janakantha	291.01	199.15
The Daily Ittefaq	740.03	532.09

Source: Bangladesh Parliamentary Elections June 12, 1996, The Report of the Fair Election Monitoring Alliance, FEMA (1996), Dhaka, p.22.

Results and Reactions

In the final count AL emerged as the majority party with 146 seats followed by 116 seats for the BNP. JP won 32 while JI secured only 3 seats. JSD (Rab), *Islami Oikyo Jote* and an independent each secured one. The polling was not without irregularities, vote rigging, violence and other malpractices although a large number of foreign and local observer groups termed the election fair.[73] In 123 polling centres in 27 constituencies polling was postponed due to clashes between rival parties.[74] In addition, polling was also postponed in another 85 voting centres in 47 constituencies due to clashes and other disruptions but re-polling was not necessary as the difference between the winner and the runner up was more than the votes at stake. Reports of intimidation, terrorism and the partisan role of presiding officers and other electoral officers were published in the newspapers following the election.

Table 6.9 Placement of News Items and Photographs of Hasina and Khaleda in Four Major Newspapers (22 May-10 June, 1996)

	Name of Newspaper	No. of News Items on Page One	No. of News Items on Page Two	No. of Photographs Printed
HASINA	B. Observer	10	8	17
	Daily Star	9	9	10
	Janakhantha	15	3	7 (2 colour)
	Ittefaq	17	1	11 (2 colour)
	Total	51	21	45
KHALEDA	B. Observer	11	8	13
	Daily Star	10	9	8
	Janakantha	3	15	5 (2 colour)
	Ittefaq	2	17	10 (2 colour)
	Total	26	49	36

Source: Compiled by the author using information from *Bangladesh Parliamentary Elections June 12, 1996*, The Report of the Fair Election Monitoring Alliance, FEMA (1996), Dhaka, p.22.

The 73.19 percent turnout was unexpectedly high and set a record in the history of parliamentary elections in the country. Table 6.10 highlights the turnout rates in different national elections in Bangladesh.

Table 6.10 The Turnout in Different National Elections in Bangladesh (1973-1996)

Type of Election	Year	% of Turnout
Parliament	1973	56
Referendum	1977	88.5
President	1978	53.59
Parliament	1979	50.94
President	1981	55.47
Referendum	1985	72
Parliament	1986	60
President	1986	54.23
Parliament	1988	52.48
Parliament	1991	55.35
Referendum	1991	34.93
Parliament	1996 F*	NA
Parliament	1996 J*	73.19

Source: Muhammad Yeahia Akhter (1991), *Search for the Nature of Corruption: Bangladesh* (in Bengali), Nebedan Publications Limited, Dhaka, p. 148; and some other articles from research journals. *Two parliamentary elections held in 1996. F and J respectively indicates February and June. The February election was boycotted by all major opposition parties and the turnout was very low.

The table shows that the turnout at previous parliamentary elections varied between 50 to 60 percent. With the exception of the turnout for the two farcical referendums held under the military regimes, the percentages even under military regimes varied little. Thus the figure of 73.19 percent in 1996 was unusual and has been criticised by a number of observers, who argue that the actual percentage of votes cast was different from the figure shown in the press. According to one estimate, 58 to 60 percent of eligible voters cast their votes. The remaining 13 to 15 percent of recorded votes were the result of vote rigging.[75] The post-election statements by the BNP, JP and the JI supported such allegations. Mohammad Younus, the Director of the *Grameen* Bank, who also worked as one of the advisers of the NCG, claimed that the contribution of his Bank and other NGOs were responsible for this high turnout. He said that his bank employees encouraged their clients, especially women loan borrowers to participate in the election.[76] Critics appreciated such encouragement by different NGOs prior to the election, but they alleged that the NGOs urged their clients to vote for the AL, which they considered a political crime. The NCG simply overlooked the partisan activities of the NGOs.

The results also differed from pre-election surveys. An opinion poll conducted by Bangladesh *Unnayan Parisad* (BUP) indicated equal support for both AL and BNP at 29 percent followed by five percent for JP, two percent for JI, one percent for other parties, while 34 percent were not sure.[77] A few other surveys conducted by different newspapers also varied considerably and did not reflect the actual results. Table 6.11 depicts the results of some such surveys.

Table 6.11 Results of Pre-Election Survey Conducted by Newspapers (Number of Seats)

Name of Newspaper	AL	BNP	JP	JI	Others
Inquilab	126	83	65	21	5
Millat	76	149	42	17	16
Sangbad	135	106	39	14	6
Rupali	152	83	50	13	2
Samachar	100	130	40	12	15
Janatar Dak	96	158	28	12	6

Source: The table has been compiled by the author using information from an article written by A. B. Siddique, 'Electoral Survey Business' (in Bengali), *Robbar*, 16 June, 1996.

Allegations of widespread rigging and manipulation in the poll were made by the major political parties with the AL[78] alleging poll rigging by the BNP.[79] On the other hand the BNP demanded re-elections in 111 constituencies for 'massive rigging' and called upon the EC not to gazette election results before completion of the re-elections. It also accused the EC of partisan behaviour.[80]

The BNP secretary general accused the NCG and its administrative machinery as well as the EC of having totally failed to ensure fair elections. He accused the AL workers of stuffing ballot boxes, ousting the polling agents of BNP candidates from polling booths, occupying polling centres, and creating a reign of terror at voting centres with the help of the local administration. He claimed that in his own constituency, despite his written allegation, no measures were taken by the administration to stop vote rigging. In some constituencies, he added, the AL candidates with the help of the TNOs, OCs and presiding officers stuffed the ballot boxes and manipulated the election results. The total rigging scheme, he said, 'had been done in a pre-planned way to bring the results in favour of AL'. Another central BNP leader described the poll rigging as 'pre-planned, unprecedented and conspiratorial and had broken all previous records'.[81] The BNP leaders again sharply reacted when the EC officially declared the results of 111 constituencies, ignoring the written protests of the defeated BNP candidates. They described the EC move as totally partisan and unfair and in defiance of the election rules. They pointed to discrepancies in the results announced by the EC and the result sheets submitted by the respective returning officers and likened the result to that of the 1986 rigged election. The BNP Chairperson was also critical of the role of the administration and the EC claiming that her party was not defeated in the election, but was made to suffer defeat although the majority of people had voted for BNP.[82] Seventy cases were filed with the election tribunal and the tribunal after two years of hearing one such case (Dhaka 10 constituency), declared the election results of 51 vote centres out of the total 81 null and void.[83]

The AL and JP also alleged vote rigging in the poll. The political adviser to the AL chief, in a press briefing, accused the BNP of rigging the poll through massive false voting and the use of violence.[84] The AL and JP candidates jointly complained of vote rigging, the hijacking of ballot boxes, violence and intimidation in Chittagong-6 constituency.[85]

The JI leaders claimed that a national and international conspiracy, the partisan role of the EC officials, massive vote rigging and influence of black money were the causes of the JI's debacle in the poll. The party secretary general said that fair elections were held in only a few centres because the administrative machinery engaged in conducting the elections was widely influenced by politics. 'We expected a 1991-style election but we failed to realise the extent of the bureaucratic conspiracy against JI', he added. He bitterly criticised the civil administration for its failure to maintain law and order and some NGOs for playing a direct role against his party.[86] The central *Majlish-e-Shura* (working committee) of JI expressed similar sentiments and complained that the NCG failed to play a neutral role like the NCG in 1991.[87]

Causes of Success and Failure

The AL campaign was superior to those of the other parties. The AL leaders and workers saw the election as a battle for survival and campaigned vigorously. Their management was better than that of the other parties and their recruitment of polling officers was also well-organised. The party was successful in attracting public sympathy by apologising for its past mistakes and asking for another chance to serve the nation. Its submissive campaign strategy and success in gaining the favour of the civil administration, the NGOs and the media contributed to its victory.

The AL's strategy of politically isolating its main rival BNP paid dividends. The party was able to mobilise its workers through a long anti-government movement as well as using religion to its advantage. The party chief's pilgrimage to Mecca and donning of Islamic dress before the election pleased the religious-minded voters. The AL also succeeded in counteracting its pro-Indian image and won the support of the voters by promising not to renew the 25 years friendship treaty with India.

The BNP was overconfident and failed to convince other political forces to work together and thus failed to win the majority of seats. The party was also unable to resolve internal conflicts which was one of the main causes of the defeat of a number of BNP candidates. It also suffered from the violent activities of *Jatiyatabadi Chattra Dal*, the student wing of the party. Its weakness in electoral management, and the quality of its candidates also contributed to its defeat. Knowing the anti-BNP role of the administration and NGOs, BNP failed to take any action or organise public opinion to condemn such bias. The party's effort to unite 'nationalist' forces under its leadership was unsuccessful and its delay in accepting the opposition's demand for an election under an NCG also lost support. Nevertheless, the BNP in winning 116 seats performed better than expected and showed the strength of its grass roots support.

The JP's 32 seats was not a great change from its 35 seats in the 5th parliament. A few JP leaders using their personal standing easily retained their seats. The JP chairman, although contesting the election from prison, won five seats, indicating his popularity in his own constituencies.[88] JP's vote almost doubled although its number of seats decreased.

The JI performed disastrously. It won only three seats against its previous 18, and its share of votes fell from 12 to nine percent. The opportunistic politics of JI was the main cause of the debacle. The party supported the BNP to form a government in 1991 but after only two years supported an anti-BNP movement led by the AL, which upset swinging voters. The JI also failed to take any action against the anti-JI role played by the administration, the NGOs and the media. The party's organisational strength was not adequate to allow it to conduct elections effectively in 300 constituencies. Most of its candidates lacked financial resources and the party provided insufficient campaign funds; nor did the party receive support from other Islamic forces.[89] The negative campaign of NGOs and the other major parties created fear among female voters, many of whom deserted the party and the party's explanation of its political role during the war of liberation in 1971 failed to convince younger voters.

A Comparison

A number of actions by both the NCGs were controversial, but the Shahabuddin NCG appeared to be comparatively more committed and successful in conducting a fair election than the Habib NCG. As the political parties were not confident of their victory during the fifth parliamentary election, they all supported the NCG to conduct the election fairly. Besides, the civil administration and the NGOs did not take a direct role in supporting any particular political party. All contesting political parties and the local and foreign election observation teams agreed on the transparent nature of the electoral process. The situation during the seventh parliamentary election was different. A large number of civil bureaucrats who also had significant electoral responsibilities nakedly supported the AL. Hundreds of NGOs involved their employees in electoral activities and worked for the victory of the AL although they formally claimed that they were only encouraging their workers to participate in the election. The contesting political parties (especially BNP and the JI) reacted sharply after the election and labelled it as 'rigged with the help of administrators and the NGOs' despite the foreign election observers viewing it as free and fair. The first NCG took punitive measures and suspended five *union parisads* for their failure to maintain law and order during voting in their areas. The second NCG did not take any such action although violent clashes between rival parties caused postponement of voting in more than 200 vote centres. The degree of corruption in the two elections under the non-party caretaker

Table 6.12 The Degree of Corruption in Elections Under Caretaker Governments in Bangladesh

Electoral Exercise	Rigging	Violence/ Intimidation	Restrictions on campaign/ party activities	Use of electronic media	Bureaucratic bias	Use of religion
Shahabuddin NCG Parliamentary 1991	L	L	ML	MH	L	M
Habibur NCG Parliamentary 1996*	M	M	L	H	H	MH

Index: VL= Very Low; L= Low; ML= Moderately Low; M= Medium; MH= Moderately High; H High; VH= Very High. *Two parliamentary elections held in 1996 respectively in February and June. 'J' indicates June.
Source: Based on primary and secondary sources.

governments in Bangladesh varied considerably. This is reflected in table 6.12.

The table shows that both the elections held under NCGs were not uniform in terms of rigging, intimidation, violence, restrictions on party activities, bureaucratic neutrality, use of religion and the role of the media. It shows that the NCG is not the only measure needed to control electoral corruption. The fifth parliamentary election held under the Shahabuddin NCG was far better than the seventh parliamentary election held under the Habib NCG. Rigging, intimidation and violence were rare during the 1991 election, but were clearly present in the 1996 election. The bureaucracy in the 1991 election was impartial but during the 1996 election it was highly partisan. In the 1991 election restrictions were placed on the campaigning and political activities of certain parties – specially the JP – but in 1996 all parties had equal opportunities to campaign. The use of the electronic media and the use of religion for political benefit was higher in the 1996 election.

Summing Up

The NCG has become a favoured solution in Bangladesh when people have lost faith in the willingness of civilian and military governments to conduct fair general elections. Both the NCGs in Bangladesh came to power after a prolonged standoff between the ruling and the opposition parties. The first NCG was demanded against a quasi-military ruler Ershad, but the second NCG was forced on a democratically elected civilian Khaleda government. In both cases, the demand for an election under an NCG was first rejected by the ruling party but then granted after tremendous pressure from a united opposition. As the NCGs were technically impartial, they had sufficient opportunity to treat all political parties equally. The composition and performance of both the NCGs were not uniform despite their similar purpose of conducting a transparent election.

The fifth parliamentary election was conducted fairly under the Shahabuddin NCG which took all possible steps to achieve a democratic election. The campaign was relatively free and fair although the code of conduct was frequently violated. All parties except the JP enjoyed equal opportunities during the campaign. The media played a relatively neutral role although BTV did not allow the JP to present its political broadcast. Local and foreign observers considered the election fair, and the results were accepted by all political parties, despite a few alleged irregularities in the process of voter registration. The NCG, administration and electoral officials were seen as having played impartial roles during the election.

The seventh parliamentary election under the second NCG was different. As the central bureaucracy became totally partisan during the movement for an NCG and participated directly in the opposition-led anti-government demonstrations, they played the same partisan role during the election. The AL received maximum support from the administration, the media and NGOs. The voter registration and the role of both the EC and the NCG were not totally impartial and free from controversy. The EC took a number of measures to make the election fair but was unsuccessful. The code of conduct was violated frequently, the role of the media was not totally impartial, and the recorded turnout was unexpectedly high. The BNP and the JI reacted sharply after the election, although other parties made similar allegations of massive rigging. The role of the NCG and the EC was condemned as partisan by a number of the contending parties.

Notes

[1] The Report of the Commonwealth Observer Group (1991), *Parliamentary Elections in Bangladesh 27 February 1991*, Commonwealth Secretariat, London, p. 12.

[2] F. R. W. Timm and P. Gain (eds) (1991), *Fifth National Parliamentary Election 1991: Observation Report* (in Bengali), Coordinating Council for Human Rights in Bangladesh, Dhaka, p. 62.

[3] For example, see the Report of the *Commonwealth Observer Group, Parliamentary Elections in Bangladesh, 27 February 1991, op. cit.*, pp. 12-13; F. R. W. Timm and P. Gain (eds), *Fifth National Parliamentary Election 1991: Observation Report, op. cit.*, pp. 54-62.

[4] For detail, see, *Inquilab*, 28 December, 1990; also cited in, Hakim, M. A. (1993), *Bangladesh Politics: The Shahabudddin Interregnum*, University Press Limited, Dhaka, p. 51.

[5] See, *Inquilab*, 2 January, 1991.

[6] See, *Inquilab*, 10 January, 1991.

[7] Address to the nation by the Acting President and the Chief Election Commissioner on the eve of election. Cited in Quadir, F. (1991), 'Jatiya Sangsad Election 1991: A Survey' (in Benglai), *Journal of Human Development*, vol. 3, no. 4, p. 53.

[8] See, *Inquilab*, 19 January, 1991; also see, *The Bangladesh Observer*, 19 January, 1991.

[9] In the last four parliamentary elections held in 1973, 1979, 1986 and 1988 the number of parties were 14, 29, 28 and 8 respectively. See, *Inquilab*, 26 February, 1991. The four major parties were, the Bangladesh *Awami* League, Bangladesh Nationalist Party, *Jatiya* Party and the *Jamaat-e-Islami* Bangladesh.

[10] *Bangladesh Times*, 11 February, 1991.

[11] Hakim, M. A. (1991), 'The 1991 Parliamentary Elections in Bangladesh: A Review', *Politics, Administration and Change*, no. 17, July-December, p.28.

[12] Zafarullah, H. and Akhter, M. Y. (2000), 'Caretaker Administrations and Democratic Elections in Bangladesh: An Assessment', *Government and Opposition*, vol. 35, no. 3, pp. 345-69.

[13] See, Bangladesh *Awami* League, *Election Manifesto-1991* (in Bengali). For a brief outline of the AL manifesto, see, *The Bangladesh Observer*, 7 February, 1991.

[14] Baxter, C. (1992), 'Bangladesh in 1991: A Parliamentary System', *Asian Survey*, vol. XXXII, no. II, p. 163.

[15] See, Hossain, S. A. (1991), 'Election in the Name of Religion', (in Bengali), *Weekly Bichitra*, 11 April.

[16] See, Bangladesh Nationalist Party, *Election Manifesto, 27 February 1991* (in Bengali).

[17] Also cited in, Huque, A. S. and Hakim, M. A. (1993), 'Elections in Bangladesh: Tools of Legitimacy', *Asian Affairs An American Review*, vol. 19, no. 4, p. 259.

[18] For example, one common slogan on their posters and banners was *'la ilaha illallah, dhaner shishay bismillah'*, which translates as 'Allah is only the master, vote for sheaf of paddy' (the electoral symbol of the BNP). Another writing on a wall in Chittagong, *'desher meye Khaleda, Bharot thake alada'*,(sic) translates, 'daughter of the soil Khaleda is different from India', meaning that Khaleda was a nationalist and not pro-Indian, which spread strong anti-Indian sentiment.

[19] Literally means 'in the name of Allah', a phrase the Muslims usually utter before doing anything in the belief of having blessings of Allah.

[20] Rizvi, G. (1991), 'Bangladesh: Towards Civil Society', *The World Today*, August/September, pp. 155-60.

[21] The *Jatiya* Party and the Freedom Party fielded 272 and 65 candidates respectively.

[22] For related information, see, The Report of the Commonwealth Observer Group (1991), *Parliamentary Elections in Bangladesh, 27 February 1991*, Commonwealth Secretariat, London, pp. 16-18.

[23] Akhter, M. Y. (1991), *Search for the Nature of Corruption: Bangladesh* (in Bengali), Nibedan Publications Limited, Dhaka, p. 157, fn. 50.

[24] The voting centres of Khulna-2 constituency that the author visited were: Lion's School, Pallimangal High School, Pallimangal Girl's High School, Shonapota Maddhamik Biddalai, Baniakhamar Hafijia Madrasha and Shaheed Sohrawardi College.

[25] The numbers of deaths in electoral violence were: 10 in Chittagong, 5 in Raojan and Barisal each, 3 in Gajipur, Khulna, Tangail, Bhola and Faridpur each, 2 in Satkhira, Mymensing, Dhaka and Sirajgong each, and 1 in Kustia, Jessore, Hatia, Swandip and Thakurgaon each. See, Timm and Gain (ed.), *Fifth National Parliamentary Election, 1991: Observation Report* (in Bengali), *op. cit.*, p. 70.

[26] The suspended union *parisads* were Gaibanda, Charputimari and Goalinir Char union *parisads* of Islampur *upazila* under Jamalpur district, Uttar Hamsadi union *parisad* of Laxmipur *sadar upazila* under Laxmipur district, and Harinakundu union *parisad* of Harinakundu *upazila* under Jhenidah district.

[27] *Banglar Bani*, 26 February, 1991, cited in Hakim, 'The 1991 Parliamentary Elections in Bangladesh: A Review', *op. cit.*, p. 33.

[28] For related information see, Ahmed, N. (1997), 'Parliamentary Opposition in Bangladesh: A Study of Its Role in the Fifth Parliament', *Party Politics*, vol. 3, no. 2, p. 149.

[29] Hasina's interview with Voice of America was broadcast by BBC on 4 March, 1991.

[30] Akhter, *Search for the Nature of Corruption: Bangladesh, op. cit.*, p. 146.

[31] See, *Dhaka Courier*, 8-14 March, 1991, pp. 8-9. Cited in Hakim, 'The Parliamentary Elections in Bangladesh: A Review', *op. cit.*, p. 36.
[32] See, *Far Eastern Economic Review*, 14 March, 1991, p. 12. Cited in Hakim, *ibid.*, p. 36.
[33] *Chitrabangla*, vol. 10, no. 39, March 8-14, 1991, p. 7, cited in , Ahsan, S. A. (1992), 'Bangladesh at the Polls: Free and Fair Elections', *Asian Profile*, vol. 20, no. 2, p. 73.
[34] The most common repressive measure was arrest. For example, AL leader Mohammad Nasim, Tofail Ahmed; JP leader Moudud Ahmed; and JI leader Abdul Quader Molla were arrested in the second half of February 1996.
[35] The meetings held under the leadership of Dr. Mohiuddin Khan Alamgir and were addressed by Dr. M. K. Alam, Sirajuddin, Abdul Hye, Shajahan Siddiquie, B. Karim, Dr. Abu Alam Shaheed Khan, Syed Ahmed, Waliul Islam and Alamgir Faruq Chaudhury.
[36] Cited in, Rashiduzzaman, M. (1997), 'Political Unrest and Democracy in Bangladesh', *Asian Survey*, vol. XXXVII, no. 3, p. 255.
[37] For example, see, G. Farouque (ed.), *Bureaucratic Rebellion* (in Bengali), Matra Books, Dhaka; Rashiduzzaman, 'Political Unrest and Democracy in Bangladesh', *op. cit.*, p. 255; Mamoon, M. (1996), 'Legal-Illegal of the Officials of the Republic' (in Bengali), *Janakhantha*, 7 April.
[38] *The Bangladesh Observer*, 4 March, 1996.
[39] The PM in a letter invited the former leader of the opposition to hold discussions.
[40] *The Bangladesh Observer*, 12 March, 1996.
[41] The second NCG was composed of one Chief Advisor and ten Advisors. The Advisors were: Syed Ishtiaq Ahmed, a barrister and constitutional expert; Muhammad Yunus, a former Professor of Economics and founder of Grameen Bank; Shegufta Bakht Choudhury, former Governor of Bangladesh Bank; Wahiduddin Mahmud, Professor of Economics at Dhaka University; Mohammad Shamsul Haq, former Vice Chancelor of Dhaka University; Major General (Retd.) Abdur Rahman Khan; Syed Manjur Elahi, Industrialist; Nazma Choudhury, Professor of Political Science at Dhaka University; Jamilur Reza Choudhury, Professor of Bangladesh University of Engineering and Technology; and AZM Nasiruddin, a former Secretary.
[42] *The Bangladesh Observer*, 7 April, 1996.
[43] According to the electoral rolls prepared in 1995, the total number of voters in the country was 56,028,289 and after the fresh updating the number of the voters stood at 56,716,935. See, The Report of the Fair Election Monitoring Alliance (FEMA) (1996), *Bangladesh Parliamentary Elections June 12, 1996*, FEMA, Dhaka, p. 17.
[44] For criticism of the updating of the voters list by the EC see, Mujahidul Islam, 'The Neutrality and Other Aspects of the Caretaker Government' (in Bengali), included in, G. Farouque (ed.), *Election '96: NGO The Bureaucracy Black Money and Corruption* (in Bengali), Mimma Prokashan, Dhaka, pp. 35-43. For an evaluation the appreciation of the updating of the voters list, see, The Report of the Fair Election Monitoring Alliance (FEMA), *Bangladesh Parliamentary Elections June 12, 1996, op. cit.*, p. 17.
[45] Farouque, (ed.), *Election '96: NGO The Bureaucracy Black Money and Corruption, op. cit.*, p. 36.
[46] See, *The Bangladesh Observer*, 3 April, 1996.
[47] See, *The Bangladesh Observer*, 27 April, 1996.
[48] See, *The Bangladesh Observer*, 6 May, 1996.

[49] Fair Election Monitoring Alliance (FEMA) is a non-partisan, broad based citizens coalition initiated by a number of NGOs in January 1995. It has a membership of 175 organisations (most of which are NGOs including Bangladesh Rural Advancement Committee (BRAC), *Proshika Manabik Unnayan Kendra, Gono Unnayan Prochesta* (GUP) and many more and a large number of individuals. FEMA has observed the sixth and seventh parliamentary elections and by-elections to 15 constituencies held on 5 September, 1996 and the Pabna-2 by-election held in late 1998. The objectives of FEMA's election monitoring were: (a) Encourage large-scale participation of voters in the election by building confidence of the electorate in the electoral process; (b) Deter election fraud, irregularities and manipulation; and (c) Report election fraud and irregularities should they occur. The FEMA activities include a training programme, public awareness programme, voter education programme and briefing international observers. Although FEMA claims it is a neutral and non-partisan election monitoring organisation, a number of political parties including the BNP and JI are critical of its role. For detail about FEMA's organisation, activities and its member organisations, see, *By-Election to 15 Constituencies Held on September 5, 1996*, The Report of the Fair Election Monitoring Alliance, FEMA (1996), Dhaka.

[50] The author interviewed a large number of academics, political party leaders, student leaders and different professionals during August and September, 1996, and almost all of them expressed their anxiety about the role of the NGOs in national politics.

[51] Kamaruzzaman, M., 'Election '96, the Role of Caretaker Government/Administration etc: A Review of Politics of Awami League-BNP-JP-Jamaat', in Farouque (ed.), *Election '96: NGO Bureaucracy Black Money and Corruption, op. cit.*, pp. 17-25.

[52] For detail on FEMA's controversial role, see, G. Farouque (ed.), *Election '96: NGO Bureaucracy Black Money and Corruption, op. cit.*, pp. 26-34, 60-62.

[53] See for relevant information, Elklit, J. and Svensson, P. (1997), 'What Makes Elections Free and Fair?', *Journal of Democracy*, vol. 8, no. 3, p. 37.

[54] For related information, see, The Report of the Fair Election Monitoring Alliance (FEMA) (1996), *Bangladesh Parliamentary Elections June 12, 1996, op. cit.*, pp. 15-16. For a list of ex civil-military bureaucrats who joined the AL see, *The Bangladesh Observer*, 3 and 4 May, 1996. For the names of three former JP ministers who joined the BNP see, *The Bangladesh Observer*, 4 May, 1996.

[55] Khan, M. R., Adnan, M., Mortaza, G. and Mostafiz, B. (1996), 'Election 1996: A Review' (in Bengali), *Weekly Bichittra*, 21 June, p. 38.

[56] In March 1972, the AL government signed a treaty of peace and friendship with India. As this treaty was criticised by the opposition as 'unequal' and 'a treaty of slavery' (golamir dashkhat), the AL strategy was to win the support of the voters by announcing its plan not to renew it again.

[57] For detailed information on *Gram Sarkar* see, Huque, A. S. (1985), 'The Politics of Local Government Reform in Rural Bangladesh', *Public Administration and Development*, vol. 5, no. 3; Khan, M. M. and Zafarullah, H. M. (1981), 'Innovations in Village Government in Bangladesh', *Asian Profile*, vol. 9, no. 5; Akhter, M. Y. (1991), 'The Politics of Decentralization in Bangladesh', *Indian Journal of Politics*, vol. 25, no. 2-3.

[58] For detail of the manifestos of the major political parties, see, The Report of the Fair Election Monitoring Alliance (FEMA), *Bangladesh Parliamentary Elections June 12, 1996, op. cit.*, pp. 27-28.

[59] Umar, B. (1996), *Power in the Hands of the people — Election or Coup?* (in Bengali), Sanskriti Prokashani, Dhaka, pp. 78-81.
[60] Shafiq, M. (1996), 'Election Manifesto and the Expectation of the People' (in Bengali), *Weekly Bichittra*, 7 June, pp. 21-26.
[61] For the influence of songs on elections, see, Akhter, M. Y. (1994), 'Songs and Politics: The Aspect of Local Government Elections in Bangladesh' (in Bengali), *Bangladesh Political Studies*, vol. 16, pp. 79-95.
[62] The Report of the Fair Election Monitoring Alliance (FEMA), *Bangladesh Parliamentary Elections June 12, 1996, op. cit.*, pp. 26.
[63] For detail on the election manifestos of JP and JI, see, *ibid.*, pp. 27-28.
[64] See, Hossain, 'Election in the Name of Religion', *op. cit.*, p. 21.
[65] Pratap, A. (1996), 'Bangladesh Election Tests Future of Young Democracy: Voters Want Peace, Security, Jobs', a CNN report, broadcast on 12 June.
[66] Golam Azam did not contest as a candidate and Ershad was in jail serving a 13 year sentence for corruption and abuse of power. He was allowed to contest in five constituencies but not to address voters.
[67] The author interviewed a number of college principals, professors and university teachers in Khulna, Dhaka and Chittagong during August, 1996 and some of them expressed such opinion.
[68] Islam, 'The Neutrality and Other Aspects of the Caretaker Government, *op. cit.*, p. 96.
[69] Badruddoja, A.K.M., 'Electoral Rigging: '96 Style' (in Bengali), in Farouque (ed.), *Election '96: NGO The Bureaucracy Black Money and Corruption, op. cit.*, pp. 93-96.
[70] Cited in, *The Parliamentary Elections in Bangladesh 12 June 1996*, The Report of the Commonwealth Observer Group, *op. c it.*, p. 16.
[71] For example, *Ajker Kagoj, Bhorer Kagoj, Banglar Bani, Sangbad, Banglabazar Patrika, Rupali* etc. dailies directly supported the AL.
[72] *Dinkal* gave its full support to the BNP and the *Sangram* was the mouthpiece of the JI.
[73] A large number of foreign and local election observation teams monitored the June 12 election. Teams came from National Democratic Institute, USA, Commonwealth, SAARC, Pakistan, India, Nepal, Sri Lanka, Japan, Cambodia, Canada. Observers also came from Denmark, Germany, France, Ireland, Italy, Netherlands, Austria, Sweden, UK. See, F. R. W. Timm (ed.) (1996), *Bangladesh: Parliamentary Election '96 Observation Report*, Coordinating Council for Human Rights in Bangladesh, Dhaka, p. 21.
[74] F. R. W. Timm (ed.), *Bangladesh: Parliamentary Election '96 Observation Report., Ibid.*, p. 17. Also see, *Preliminary Statement of the NDI Observer Delegation to the June 12, 1996 Parliamentary Elections in Bangladesh* (1996), National Democratic Institute For International Affairs, Washington D.C, 14 June, p. 2.
[75] Kamaruzzaman, 'Election '96: The Role of Caretaker Government/Administration Etc.: A Review of the Politics of the Awami League-BNP-Jamaat' (in Bengali), in, Farouque (ed.), *Election '96: NGO Bureaucracy Black Money and Corruption, op. cit.*, pp. 17-25.
[76] Mohammad Younus claimed the contribution of NGO workers to the high turnout in a public lecture on poverty alleviation on 18 March, 1997 at the University of Sydney. The lecture was organised jointly by the Centre for Peace and Conflict Studies, the University of Sydney and the UN Association of Australia.
[77] *The Bangladesh Observer*, 2 June, 1996.

[78] For example, the author interviewed a number of defeated candidates of the AL in July 1996, and all of them alleged rigging by their rivals.
[79] See, *The Bangladesh Observer*, 13 June, 1996.
[80] See for related information, Kochanek, S. A. (1996), 'Bangladesh in 1996: The 25th year of Independence', *Asian Survey*, vol. XXXVII, no. 2, p.138.
[81] *The Bangladesh Observer*, 14 June, 1996.
[82] *The Bangladesh Observer*, 23 June, 1996.
[83] Mia, M. (1998), 'How Free and Fair was 1996 Election?' *Dhaka Courier* (internet edition), issue 17, 20 November.
[84] *Ajker Kagoj*, 13 June, 1996.
[85] See, The Report of the Fair Election Monitoring Alliance (FEMA), *Bangladesh Parliamentary Elections June 12, 1996, op. cit.*, p. 36.
[86] *The Bangladesh Observer*, 16 June, 1996.
[87] *The Bangladesh Observer*, 21 June, 1996.
[88] According to Bangladeshi electoral rules a candidate can contest not more than five seats although he/she can retain only one. The EC then arranges by-elections in the vacated seats. It is a common strategy for the parties to nominate their popular leaders in more than one constituency.
[89] For example, *pirs* (spiritual leaders), *Tableeg Jamaat* and Islamic parties such as *Jaker Party, Khelafat Andolan, Islami Oikya Jote* did not support the JI.

7 Conclusion

This final chapter provides some general observations on the nature of elections in both pre- and post-independent Bangladesh. It also focuses on the peculiar Bangladeshi electoral culture, analyses the character and trends of electoral corruption and examines how electoral malfeasance affects democratic consolidation in that country.

Nature of Elections

Pre-independence Elections

The provincial assembly elections held under civilian governments in united Pakistan were not free from irregularities, except for the 1954 provincial assembly election in East Pakistan which was conducted in a relatively democratic electoral environment. Ayub's 'basic democracy' system introduced indirect elections and scope for only a limited democratic exercise. Electoral fraud and violence influenced the two elections under this system. The high turnout under indirect voting in the 1959 referendum was used to legalise military rule; while in the presidential election of 1965 the ruling party influenced Electoral College members and guilefully suppressed the electioneering of the opposition. The ruling party also secured the services of the bureaucracy by fiat and used the media for its political ends. The results of the two assembly elections under civilianised military rule were manipulated to the advantage of regime.

The first general national election in united Pakistan was free and fair and contending parties accepted the verdict of the people without demur. The election was symptomatic of both transparency of the electoral process and the neutrality of the election machinery. It set new standards. Electioneering was generally free from violence and intimidation, the state-controlled electronic media were largely unbiased in their coverage, and the bureaucratic machine played a neutral role. The military regime, which conducted the election, could maintain its non-partisan and thus disinterested orientation largely because it was not a contesting party in the polls. In many ways, it foreshadowed the non-partisan caretaker government scheme that was to become a reality in both Pakistan and Bangladesh several years later.

Post-independence Elections

The several elections held in independent Bangladesh featured varying degrees of malfeasance. Some, conducted by military or party governments, bore the stigma of being highly manipulated by incumbent regimes while others, like the two parliamentary elections supervised by non-partisan caretaker governments, were relatively free and fair, unhindered by an intimidating environment and afforded all parties almost equal access to state-owned resources, especially the electronic media. Of the three referenda, the 1991 referendum seeking support for or opposition to a return to parliamentary democracy stood out as the most unfettered electoral exercise largely because the issue before the electorate had the complete support of all parties. On the other hand, regime supporters manipulated the two referenda organised to obtain endorsement for military rule. The high turnout figures and the manner in which the polls were conducted clearly demonstrated that the regimes were bent upon proving to the detractors of military rule, both inside and outside the country, that they had the support of the people and thus legitimacy to govern.

In parliamentary elections conducted by party governments, the incumbent government was always returned and in presidential polls their nominees for the presidency victorious by huge margins. The authoritarian tendencies of the first civilian government and its arbitrary handling of the first parliamentary elections set the standards for all elections to follow until 1991. The ruling party employed all available tactics to crush the opposition. Violence, intimidation, media control and conscription of government employees ensured the incumbent government's success in the polls. The election machinery earned the dubious reputation of being an accessory to the electoral high-handedness of the regime.

In the second parliamentary election, the military ruler completely changed the political environment of electioneering. Restrictions on party activities were imposed and the bureaucracy and the media worked as tools of the government. This undemocratic trend continued in all elections that followed. During the third parliamentary election, questionable deals between the regime and one of the major opposition parties profaned the electoral milieu. The election, marred by widespread violence and excessive coercion by activists of participating parties, lost its credibility and was dubbed a great electoral bungle at home and abroad. Both ruling and opposition parties accused each other of high levels of vote rigging and all participants but the governing party rejected the results. The fourth parliamentary election, the second under the second military order, was boycotted by all major opposition parties and thus reduced to a one party farce. The controversial sixth parliamentary election, again boycotted by major opposition parties, was another travesty with extreme violence perpetrated by both pro and anti-election activists. The opposition, while rejecting this election and its outcome, was prepared to accept the Constitutional Thirteenth Amendment Act providing for a non-partisan caretaker government [NCG] to conduct all future elections passed by the sixth parliament, which the election had created.

By-elections, mostly, returned candidates nominated by parties holding the seats before being vacated due to resignations or deaths. Those that did not had to face the wrath of the losing party. The classic case was that of Magura where the scale of rigging by the ruling party was allegedly so high that the candidate of the major opposition party, which had won the constituency in the previous parliamentary election, was defeated. Exceptions to this pattern have been rare. While the major opposition party was equally blameworthy for rigging, Magura set the scene for an opposition backlash, strong enough to ultimately persuade the government to accept its demands for the NCG scheme.

Electoral malpractices were also widespread in the three direct presidential elections, all held under party governments. Neither the incumbent military president nor the candidate supported by the ruling party encountered any real threat from opposition candidates. In reality, they were stage-managed to guarantee the triumph of the person already in power. The degree of election breaches, use of the state apparatus or manipulation of results however varied between them. The first presidential election was won by the ruling military president and labelled as grossly unfair by the main opposition candidate. The civil bureaucracy was called on to support the president, and other suppression techniques commonly used by military rulers to restrict opposition activities were covertly employed. Nonetheless, the military candidate's village-based politics and reform measures did earn him electoral support. In the second presidential election the ruling party candidate, exploiting the charisma of the party's slain leader, won easily. This election, however, was befouled by irregularities, bogus voting and some violence by both the ruling and opposition parties. The third presidential election was conducted in military style and the ruling party had little trouble in winning with the entire opposition boycotting the event.

The electoral climate of national politics has always flowed on to the local scene in Bangladesh with elections at this level characterised by rigging, violence and other irregularities. At this level, unlike national politics where the ruling party enjoys greater advantage, no parties are outright winners or losers, first, because local elections are officially non-partisan and candidates compete on issues such as local allegiances mainly based on village politics. Secondly, candidates encounter one another with equal strength insofar as violence, intimidation and other malpractices influence the outcome of the polls.

Elections Held Under NCGs

The two elections under NCGs were the result of prolonged pressure from the opposition for elections to be held under a non-partisan authority. In both cases, the ruling parties hesitated before accepting the demand. In support of an NCG the opposition parties employed a variety of techniques ranging from public meetings, demonstrations, strikes and blockades, to non-cooperation and en-masse resignations of their MPs from the parliament. The neutral arrangement of the fifth parliamentary elections by the transitory first NCG successfully regained public confidence in the election. Unrestricted campaigning, the impartial role of the EC, the media, the civil bureaucracy and the law enforcing agencies added a democratic dimension to the election. The absence of major vote rigging and the acceptance of the results by the contending parties underlined the transparency of that election.

However, contesting parties and electoral analysts respectively challenged both the fairness of the seventh parliamentary elections and the first constitutionalised NCG. The failure of the second NCG to take action against the partisan role of the civil bureaucracy, the NGOs and the media brought its role into contention. Its weakness in resisting pressure from the major parties and deciding crucial national policies was also criticised. While the major opposition parties were critical of the results, they did enjoy freedom during the campaign. Thus, it will be interesting to see whether the next NCG in its conduct of the coming eighth parliamentary elections will perform a neutral role as demanded by the Constitution.

Bangladeshi Electoral Culture

Electoral Alliances

The electoral culture in Bangladesh reflects its political culture, which is quite similar to that of other countries of South Asia. Smaller parties forming political alliances before an election in most cases with the larger parties is common practice in Bangladesh. The AL always led the so-called pro-liberation camp, while the BNP provided the leadership to the so-called pro-nationalist forces. In the past, major parties formed alliances for strategic reasons especially to contest presidential elections, and, because there was only one candidate representing an alliance in these elections, the question of sharing seats between the constituting parties did not arise. However, in parliamentary elections the alliance mechanism has not really worked. Alliances do not nominate common candidates and constituent parties go their own ways in contesting the elections. They have always suffered from a lack of unity, have had short tenure and withered away after elections.

Changing Party Allegiance

Changing political parties is common among leaders and activists in Bangladesh especially during elections. The major parties attract prominent leaders of their rivals by offering them nominations to contest parliamentary elections in safe constituencies as well as enticing dissatisfied prominent parliamentarians belonging to rival parties by promising them ministerial positions if elected to power. Offering nominations to distinguished bureaucrats, business tycoons or retired military officers has become another political routine. Many top-ranking leaders of the major parties have backgrounds different from and even contrasting with their present position.

Patron-client Relationship

Patron-client relationships significantly influence Bangladeshi elections. Candidates seek the favour of prominent social and political leaders especially in the agrarian rural society. Moneylenders and landowners are approached for their support by the candidates in the hope of thereby having the votes of their clients. Village *matbar* (headmen), and *murubbi* (family heads in a joint family structure) are a common target of all candidates who know that the favour of these patrons includes the votes of their clients. In a situation where the majority of voters are illiterate and suffer chronic poverty, it is usual that they will support the preferred candidate of their patrons if for no other reason than to ensure assistance during economic crises.

The Significance of Symbols and National Icons

As a large number of voters cannot read, the Election Commission allocates electoral symbols to parties. Voters identify candidates by the symbols they represent. They vote for symbols, which become so prominent to voters that they do not care who the candidates are as long as they represent the symbol of the parties of their choice. Some families support a particular symbol and it continues over generations as a tradition of the family. Party symbols get prominence in slogans, posters and graffiti. Further, the parties during an election exploit prominent national political figures. The AL and the BNP respectively use the charismatic political leaders Mujib and Zia (both deceased) for their electoral appeal. Their personality, ideology and various dreams are portrayed to the voters. Their sculptures and life-sized photographs adorn the electoral environment and candidates present themselves to the voters as close followers of their ideals and promise to fulfil their dreams.

The Gender Issue

Male and female voters do not enjoy equal opportunity during elections in Bangladesh although constitutionally their status is alike. As female voters are dependent on their male partners or fathers for cultural and economic reasons, the voting of the wives and daughters is shaped and influenced respectively by their husbands and fathers. Rural female voters, who are the majority in this gender-based division, are in most cases illiterate, politically unaware, and totally dependent on their husbands; they do not think of disagreeing with their choice. The rate of women participation as candidates in parliamentary elections is extremely low due to their illiteracy and political naiveté. Paradoxically, however, women who have led parties and government, in most cases, came to such a position through the politics of kinship.

The Role of Money

Money is the most important issue in Bangladeshi elections. The parties obtain funding from various sources -- legal and illegal -- before contesting elections. Money plays a vital role in the entire electoral process from effective campaigning to vote buying. Business tycoons obtaining nominations after paying substantial donations to party funds has become common. Candidates frequently violate the EC-fixed ceiling on electoral expenses but are never punished as they submit fake statements to the EC showing false expenditure and sources of funding.

Intimidation and Violence

Violence and intimidation are frequently used in most elections in Bangladesh. Use of home-made bombs and illegal arms in attacking and counter-attacking processions of opposing groups, intimidating rival supporters, creating terror among voters to discourage them from casting their votes, hijacking ballot boxes or voting papers are some of the negative aspects of electioneering. Intimidating minority voters is also not uncommon. Declaration of a *hartal* on an election day with its inevitable violence by the election-boycotting party/parties is another tradition in the country's electoral culture.

The Role of the Media

The government controls the electronic media in Bangladesh and during elections, they favour the ruling party. Military rulers unabashedly used these media for their electoral benefit while the opposition was denied access. While the civilian rulers allowed the opposition limited use of the electronic media, they also garnered the advantage of ready access to further their political interest. The print media are mainly independent and enjoy some form of autonomy. Major daily and weekly newspapers are owned by private investors but may have direct or indirect connections with major parties.

The Role of Bureaucracy and Uniformed Services

The civil bureaucracy in Bangladesh is officially neutral and is expected to treat all political parties equally. Yet, in practice it has the dubious record of some of its constitutive components supporting either the regime or the opposition in different political situations. A similar tendency is noticeable in the military, police and other law enforcing agencies/groups who are often found to perform a controversial role during elections.

Restrictions on Opposition Activities

Opposition political activities were not allowed during military rule but partisan governments have also suppressed opposition activities to a certain degree. The opposition parties, which had a positive relationship with the military governments, were allowed to function. The opposition legislators under neither the civilian nor military governments were permitted to enjoy their due status in parliament. The continuous and dysfunctional conflict relationship between the ruling and opposition parties has helped to shape the country's parliamentary culture. The ruling party has always dominated the floor of parliament and any logical arguments raised by opposition MPs are ignored due to the ruling party's strength in the house. The frequent use of the Special Powers Act in bridling opposition by both military and civilian governments has hampered democratic consolidation.

Techniques of Voter Influence

Several techniques are followed to entice voters. Temporary campaign offices are set up, public meetings and processions are organised, and polling centres and crowded market places are decorated with posters, banners and huge party symbols. Offering free tea and cigarettes in campaign offices and continuous playing of patriotic and party songs on loud speakers are some of the popular techniques to attract voters during election campaigns. Door to door campaigning by candidates or their protégés to persuade voters is also popular. Contestants also give away clothing and money to poor voters.

Students, youths and the unemployed are engaged by parties or their candidates to campaign on their behalf. Even known miscreants and criminals are actively involved. They mainly help in organising processions and approaching people to vote for their parties. Children of families in extreme poverty become busy in city streets and join processions for a token fee. All major parties maintain their different supporting branch organisations including farmer, labour, female, youth and student fronts. Student political fronts based in university and college campuses also play their part by working for their respective parent parties.

The sudden spurt of 'public welfare' activities by candidates before an election to impress voters is widespread. Candidates present themselves as benevolent problem-solvers for the common people to attract their support. Their claim before an election of being the custodians of the public interest is abandoned soon after.

They often exploit the religious sentiments of the people by paying extra attention to the problems of religious institutions and participating in religious prayers to display their religiosity to the voters. The religion-based parties attempt to obtain extra benefits from the religious-minded voters by explaining that their parties are closest to Allah and confuse the ignorant voters by implying that supporting their cause would be tantamount to pleasing Allah.

Forms of Electoral Malfeasance

Irregularities and rigging are the two most common characteristics of a Bangladeshi election. False or dual registration, bogus voting, intimidating voters, bribing electoral officials, capturing vote centres, hijacking ballot boxes or ballot papers, manipulation in vote counting and announcing the results in the electronic media, promising false commitments by the contenders, bribing poor voters, etc. are not unusual.

The Role of the EC Machinery

The EC, an autonomous body and expected to be neutral in its political stance, has often violated its constitutional obligations by supporting incumbent governments during elections. After each election, the opposition has challenged the neutrality of the EC and moved for the dismissal of the chief election commissioner. EC's defective preparation of electoral rolls and slow response to post-election rigging allegations by defeated candidates are constantly criticised by opposition parties.

Final Observations

This book has focused on the significance of elections in an ostensibly democratic state, Bangladesh, and portrays how electoral corruption has damaged the process of democratic consolidation. The study has revealed the failure of both civilian and military governments to obtain democratic legitimacy and/or credibility through free and fair elections. It has also examined the relatively democratic, but largely non-transparent nature of electioneering under non-partisan caretaker governments. Finally, it has projected the facilitated role of transparent elections in institutionalising democracy.

Lack of understanding of and consensus as to 'the rules of the democratic game' among political leaders both before and after independence remains one of the main issues in Bangladesh politics. It is a primary cause of political instability as is the lack of mutual respect and tolerance among politicians. These characteristics resulted in eight years of protracted negotiations among political parties and personalities to produce a constitution in united Pakistan; continuing political instability in Bangladesh; the assassination of great leaders; and the destruction of democratic culture both inside and outside parliament. They also provided opportunities for military leaders to takeover and dominate politics and governance. Any positive developments in Bangladesh's political culture for institutionalising fair elections were rendered futile by negative directions, which in turn sabotaged the credibility of electoral undertakings. The persistent discord between ruling and opposition parties and their craving for power inject all forms of malfeasance into the electoral exercise and denigrate democratic values. The electorate is corrupted by dishonest politicians and parties who, by taking advantage of the abject poverty and the political naiveté of the majority population, indulge in fraudulent machinations to influence the outcome of polls in their favour.

Personal charisma and kinship ties play an influential role in politics. The country has frequently faced a leadership vacuum after the demise of charismatic political personalities. The leaders in united Pakistan and independent Bangladesh were successful in utilising their charisma to obtain some degree of political legitimacy. The blind acceptance by citizens of charismatic leaders has been a key factor in restricting democratic discipline within party organisations. Hereditary politics has gripped this country since Fatema, Jinnah's sister, first entered politics in pre-independent Bangladesh. After President Zia's assassination, his wife, Khaleda, a politically uninformed housewife, was catapulted to BNP's top position while Hasina, President Mujib's daughter, a political amateur, was given the mantle of the AL's presidency when the party faced a leadership crisis in the seventies. Such undemocratic political recruitment at the highest levels of party hierarchies has had a debilitating effect on internal democracy in the two major parties in Bangladesh and has blocked avenues for normal leadership succession. Indeed, the electoral campaigns of the two parties have always taken the form of making political capital from the 'greatness' and 'achievements' of their slain charismatic leaders.

Yet, because of such dynastic succession to top party positions, the major political parties have frequently experienced internal conflicts and divisions. Competition for significant party positions was the primary cause of such divisions. Forming a new breakaway faction by dissatisfied leaders of an established party has been common practice since the mid-1970s. The

226 *Electoral Corruption*

change of party allegiance by self-seeking individuals before elections has also emerged as a destabilising factor in party systems.

Military rulers, in their bid to civilianise their rule by forming their own political platforms, attracted renegades from other parties which had the effect of weakening the opposition movement against their regimes. The recruitment by the military-sponsored party of political figures with contrasting backgrounds introduced opportunism in politics. The lure of party tickets in elections as well as powerful positions in both party and government transformed politics into a business-like enterprise. Loyalty and commitment towards party ideology or the national interest became secondary; obtaining private gain out of political capital assumed greater significance. The civil administration was militarised with the intention of consolidating military rule or its civilianised variant. Military rulers after seizing power invariably denied having any political ambitions but all, with the sole exception of Yahya Khan in erstwhile Pakistan, breached their pledges. They were able to achieve their political aspirations with the support of a section of civilian politicians with whom they maintained clandestine relationships under cover of outward antagonism. The opposition was always critical of the oppressive policies of the ruling party but, on assuming power, was not hesitant about playing a similar role. In fact, the total socio-political environment was distorted in a way that was completely unsuited to free and fair elections.

Only a few of the thirty elections that took place in Bangladesh either before or after independence were totally free of electoral fraud. Those that were relatively fair produced other forms of electoral malfeasance. Some elections were competitive with major parties enthusiastically participating; a few were apologies for elections devoid of competitive parties or voters. Fear of loosing political legitimacy compelled ruling regimes, military or civilian, to conduct frequent elections to showcase the extent of democracy in the country. Vote rigging, violence, intimidation and government oppression of the opposition were common during most of the elections that were held under partisan governments. The electronic media and the bureaucracy, in most cases, worked for the ruling parties, especially in mobilising support for their candidates. The use of religion for partisan benefit has been another common technique exercised by both civilian and military governments.

Three military regimes (Ayub, Zia and Ershad) adopted similar strategies for running state affairs and used elections as a tool to obtain political legitimacy. Their attempts to legitimise their rule originated with risk-free referenda and advanced through presidential and parliamentary elections. In each case, the generals either joined an existing political party or established a new party to further their political interests. Restrictions were imposed on electioneering and arrests and intimidation curbed opposition activities, which were labelled as 'anti-state' and 'undisciplined' by the ruling party. The electoral process was manipulated with the bureaucracy, the law-enforcing agencies and the electronic media unabashedly used by the regime. The election machinery was also reorganised and staffed with regime sympathisers to serve regime interests. Electoral manipulation reached its apogee during the second period of military rule in Bangladesh. The people totally lost confidence in the electoral system and deemed voting a meaningless exercise.

An important component of the struggle against anti-authoritarian rule in the late 1980s was the demand for a non-partisan caretaker government (NCG) to conduct general elections in a democratic environment. The first NCG, a purely interim measure, set the standards for free and fair elections that brought to power a democratically-elected government in a pluralist political framework. However, the failure to establish electoral transparency in the aftermath of authoritarian rule served as an obstacle on the road to democratic consolidation in a civilian polity. The repressive attitude of the ruling party towards the opposition, its manipulation of the electoral process to gain and hold power by infringing democratic norms, and capricious control of the electronic media were similar to the methods applied by the military rulers. The persistent violation of the norms of the electoral process led to unequivocal demands for institutionalising the NCG scheme. After prolonged debates, discussions, parleys, threats and counter-threats, overseas intervention and mediation efforts, the NCG scheme was constitutionalised.

Bangladesh, as a matter of fact, is one of a few polities to have in its constitution a mechanism for a caretaker administration to be installed in office after the expiry of the term of an incumbent government and manage state affairs before a duly elected regime assumes power. Restrained from taking significant policy initiatives, the prime task of an NCG is to arrange and oversee an intimidation and violence-free general election in which all participating parties would have equal opportunity to campaign and solicit the support of the electorate and voters would be able freely to make their choices.

Despite this far-reaching change, democratic politics has failed to change the electoral culture shaped by years of undemocratic rule. Healthy democratic competition in the political arena is yet to become a reality. Electoral corruption, violence and intimidation continue to pollute the electoral process. The role of the EC under the two successive civilian regimes since 1991 has been suspect; its partisan attitude and behaviour have stirred the wrath of the opposition, which has always judged it as an instrument of the ruling party. The two civilian governments have failed to comply with the norms of ethical electoral behaviour. The BNP regime's handling of by-elections and the holding of a voter-less general election in 1996 generated considerable political heart-burning and mayhem, an offshoot of which was the clamour for an NCG to conduct all future polls. The AL government also lost its impartiality in handling a few by-elections. Indeed, the prevalent electoral culture has properties that inhibit the development of democratic politics including the electoral process.

Electoral matters cannot be isolated from political or other state affairs. Consequently, the transparency of the electoral process is difficult to realise without installing probity in all aspects of politics, administration and society. Nevertheless, positive experiments including the introduction of effective electoral policies, appropriate electoral laws and other reform measures may help abate electoral corruption. Political stability, which is essential for fair elections to take root in a democratising polity, can become a reality if there is acceptance of the rules of the democratic game by all political parties, mutual tolerance and understanding among them to acknowledge without grudge the outcome of elections and, most importantly, reverence for democratic values.

Hopefully, the analysis of electoral corruption attempted in this study will provide a convenient and comprehensive source of information for politicians and electoral officials in Bangladesh to framing the right electoral policy and other laws pertaining to fair elections and to establish a transparent electoral process thereby contributing towards the consolidation of democracy in the country.

By way of a concluding comment, it is appropriate to retain to the brief mention which was made in chapter 1 of the functions of elections in a democratic society. How will have they been realised in Bangladesh? With mixed success; the main purpose of election, namely selecting representatives of the people by unfettered choice has not been achieved due to the lack of fairness in the electoral exercise. As a large number of elections are rigged, the leaders elected by tainted process are not acceptable to the people. Elections are a tool for rulers to achieve power; they intensify existing and encourage new patron-client relationships; tighten the exchange relationship between political and economic elites; and provide thugs and touts opportunities for unlawful behaviour. On the other hand, in terms of increasing party activities and political awareness of the voters (particularly among the illiterate), elaborating political polarisation and strengthening contact between urban and rural communities they do play a positive role. They spread party activities more widely and increase the contact between the leaders and voters, provide some temporary work – even if for minor reward – for the unemployed and vagabonds and increase voluntary welfare activities in the constituencies. Finally, though for a short while, elections make the leaders dependent on the people for their support and thus remind the voters that they are the ultimate source of all political power.

Post-Script

When military and civilian governments failed to establish electoral transparency and sincere attempts by NCGs were not wholly successful, the country in desperation has undertaken to conduct future parliamentary elections under NCGs. The Khaleda government secured the necessary constitutional amendment to facilitate that arrangement. Nevertheless, the fairness of future elections will depend on the sincerity of the NCG and the cooperation of all political parties. Transparency in elections can only expedite the process of democratic consolidation and bring political stability to Bangladesh. If this attempt fails, Bangladeshis will have to find an alternative method to organise meaningful elections, either by investing the EC with increased constitutional powers or by some other reform, which can satisfy the demands of the populace, and institutionalise a transparent electoral system. It is questionable if a foreign electoral system applied to Bangladesh will provide the answer. As has been demonstrated in many Third World countries, only the people who suffer the problem are able to develop a workable solution to their problem.

Appendices

Appendices

Appendix – A
Different Terms of Bribes

Country	Familiar as	Meaning
U.S.A (in some specific cases)	Protection Money	giving bribe for illegal protection from law
some Asian and some Middle Eastern countries	Baksheesh	gratuity or 'tip'
some Asian countries	Tea Money	to pay for tea
South East Asian countries	Palm Oil	oiling one's palm
India, Pakistan, Bangladesh	Najrana	close to honorarium
India, Pakistan, Bangladesh	Salami	close to honorarium
India, Pakistan, Bangladesh	Vet	close to honorarium
India	Khilana Para	to pay feeding money
Bangladesh	Sommani	honorarium
Bangladesh	Percentage	fixed bribe per cent
Pakistan	Chae Pani	tea-drink
Indonesia	Pelicin	giving money for making the process easier
Indonesia	Sogok	giving money for making the process easier
South Korea	Chun-Chose	quasi-tax
Taiwan	Hung Bao	giving money in red envelopes
Thailand	Kin Money	feeding money
Turkey	Rushvet	same as baksheesh
Japan	Shito Fumekin	unexplained expenses
Japan	Dango	bid-rigging
Latin America	La Mordida	the bite
Australia	Brown paper Bag	giving bribe
Italy	La Bustarella	little envelope
West Africa	Dash	bribe money
Philippine	Lagay	same as speed money
Ghana	Rate-Money	fixed money as bribe
France	Pot-de-Vin	wine jug (bribe)
France	Sous-la-Table	under the table
some parts of India	Speed Money	giving money for speeding up the process
China	Shouhui	use of official position to take in bribes
China	Tequan	A privilege-seeking activities by officials
China	Back Door	giving bribe for illegal benefit
China	Guandao	official speculation
Hong Kong, China	Guanaxi	connections

Appendix – B
Party Symbols

Party Symbols

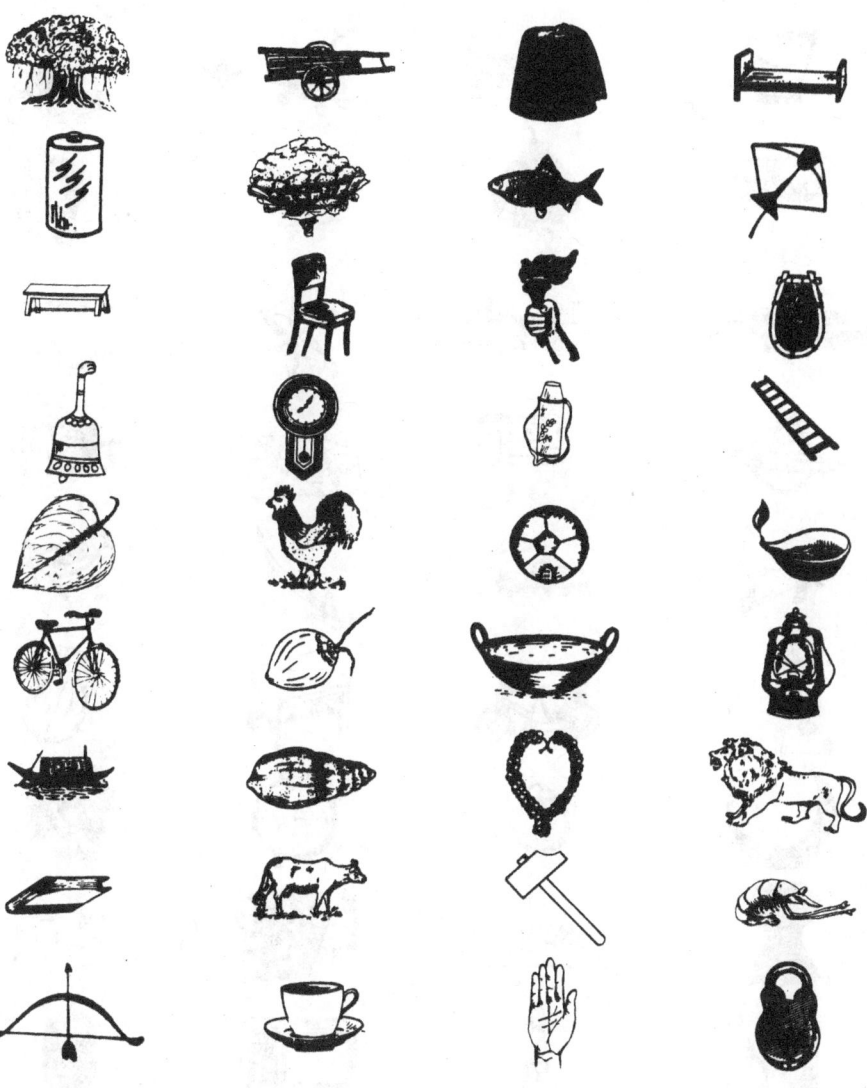

Party Symbols

Party Symbols

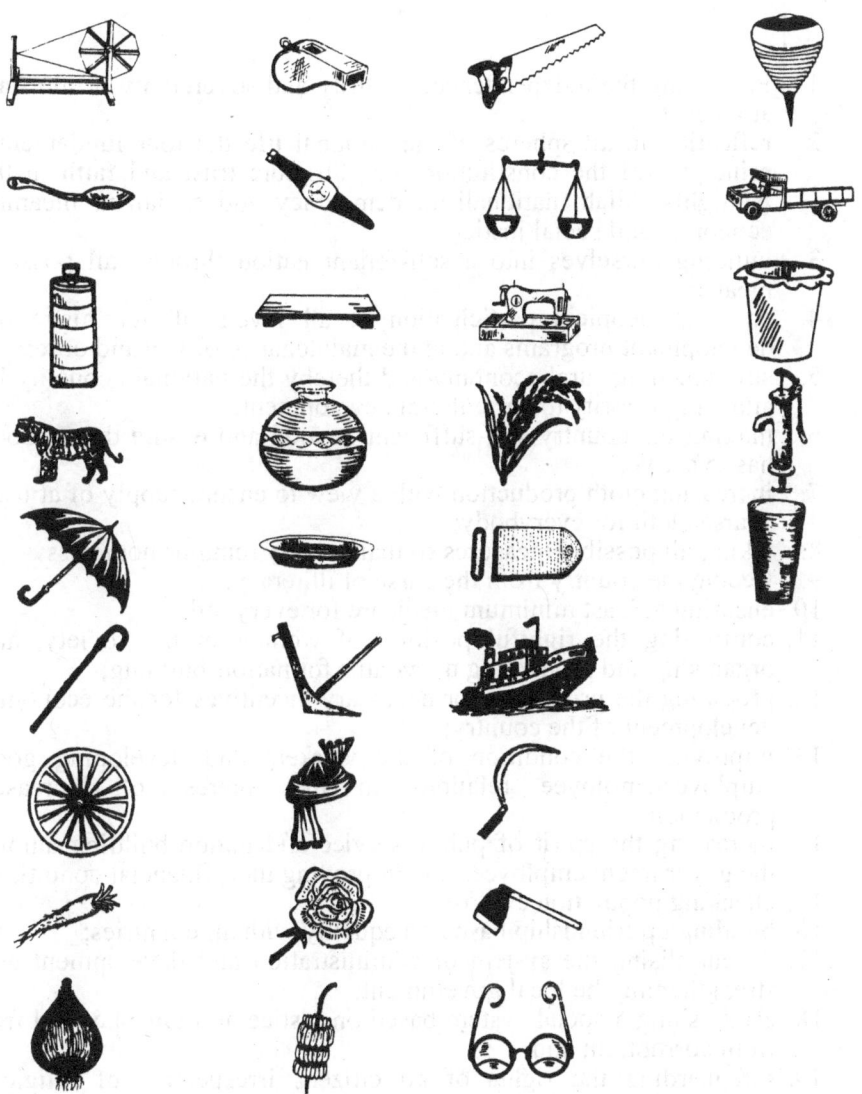

Appendix – C
Zia's 19-Point Programme of Development

1. Preserving the independence, integrity and sovereignty of the state at all cost;
2. reflecting in all spheres of our national life the four fundamental principles of the constitution, i.e., absolute trust and faith in the Almighty Allah, nationalism, democracy and socialism meaning economic and social justice;
3. building ourselves into a self-reliant nation through all possible means;
4. ensuring people's participation at all levels of administration, development programs and in the maintenance of law and order;
5. strengthening rural economy and thereby the national economy by attaching priority to agricultural development;
6. making the country self-sufficient in food and ensure that nobody has to starve;
7. increasing cloth production with a view to ensure supply of at least coarse cloth for everybody;
8. taking all possible measures so that nobody remains homeless;
9. freeing the country from the curse of illiteracy;
10. ensuring at least minimum medicare for everybody;
11. confirming the rightful position of women in the society, and organising and motivating the youths for nation-building;
12. providing the private sector necessary incentives for the economic development of the country;
13. improving the condition of the workers and developing good employer-employee relations in the interest of increased production;
14. increasing the spirit of public service and nation-building among the government employees and improving their financial condition;
15. checking population explosion;
16. building up friendship based on equality with all countries;
17. decentralising the system of administration and development and strengthening the local government;
18. establishing a social system based on justice and fair play and free from corruption; and
19. safeguarding the rights of all citizens irrespective of religion, colour and sect and consolidate national unity and solidarity.

Appendix – D
Ershad's 18-Point Programme of Development

1. Achieving rural development;
2. increasing agricultural production in order to achieve self-sufficiency in food;
3. taking steps for further land reforms;
4. expanding the activities of Grameen bank in rural areas;
5. increasing industrial production;
6. encouraging industries in the private sector and creating atmosphere for investment;
7. developing cooperative system and cottage industries;
8. reducing the gap between the rich and the poor through proper distribution of national incomes;
9. introducing development and production-oriented educational system;
10. creating maximum employment opportunity;
11. ensuring at least minimum medicare for everybody;
12. taking steps for the establishment of Islamic ideals and values in national life;
13. eliminating corruption;
14. decentralising the administrative system and handling over power to the elected representatives;
15. checking population;
16. transforming 'politics' into 'politics of production' and securing political freedom through economic emancipation;
17. reconstructing judiciary in order to ensure justice at all levels; and
18. ensuring the socio-economic rights and status of women.

Appendix – E
Ishtiaq Ahmed's Formula

Considering both government and opposition stand Barrister Ishtiaque Ahmed for solving the long political stand off suggested a course of action at a seminar at the National Press Club on 28 July 1995, which may be more concretely elaborated as follows:

1. A number of neutral non-partisan persons, say ten, acceptable to the government and opposition parties, should be agreed and nominated to form a workable future cabinet. The future PM will be designated from among them.
2. Upon seats in parliament having fallen vacant, by-elections are required to be held within 90 days of the occurrence of the vacancies. This presents an opportunity for nominating the persons, who are to form the agreed cabinet under paragraph 1 above, as candidates to be elected uncontested in the by-elections. By-elections could be announced to fill all the vacant seats or only to fill the number of seats equivalent to the number of persons who are to form the agreed cabinet.
3. If the schedule is announced to fill all the vacant seats, the longest possible date may be fixed as polling day and as early as possible dates may be fixed for nomination, scrutiny and withdrawal. If that is done, it might still be possible to avoid holding of by-elections in all seats which will by agreement be uncontested would be declared elected immediately upon scrutiny. Once their election is notified, parliament may be convened when the persons elected uncontested will take their seats. The holding of the by-elections in the rest of the constituencies may not be necessary, as dissolution of parliament in accordance with the agreement could be follow.
4. To resolve the present constitutional problem, under the Constitution, the following matters must be covered by agreement:
   (a) The names and number of neutral, non-partisan persons, who will form the new cabinet and the name of the person from among them who will be the PM;
   (b) The date on which the new cabinet, consisting of agreed neutral, non-partisan members, shall be installed;
   (c) The date for dissolution of parliament;
   (d) The date for holding of general elections.

Appendix – F
The Principles Outlined by the LFO for the Future Constitution of Pakistan

The LFO outlined five broad principles for the future constitution of Pakistan. These were:

First: The Constitution must ensure the independence, territorial integrity and national solidarity of Pakistan. The territories which now and may hereinafter be included must be united into a federation.

Second: It must preserve the Islamic ideology which was the basis of the creation of Pakistan. The head of the state will be a Muslim.

Third: It must be a democratic constitution in which such basic ingredients of democracy as free and periodical elections on the basis of population and direct adult franchise are included and fundamental rights are guaranteed. Moreover, independence of judiciary must be protected.

Fourth: The division of powers between the centre and provinces shall be effected in such a way that provinces enjoy maximum autonomy, that is to say, 'maximum legislative, administrative and financial powers', but the federal government shall also have adequate powers including legislative, administrative and financial powers, to discharge its responsibilities in relation to external and internal affairs and to preserve the independence and territorial integrity of the country.

Fifth: It must ensure the fullest participation of the people of all areas in national activities, and it must contain a statutory provision to remove all disparities, in particular economic disparities among various provinces of Pakistan within a fixed period of time.

Appendix – G
The Map of Bangladesh and 300 Constituencies for Parliamentary Elections

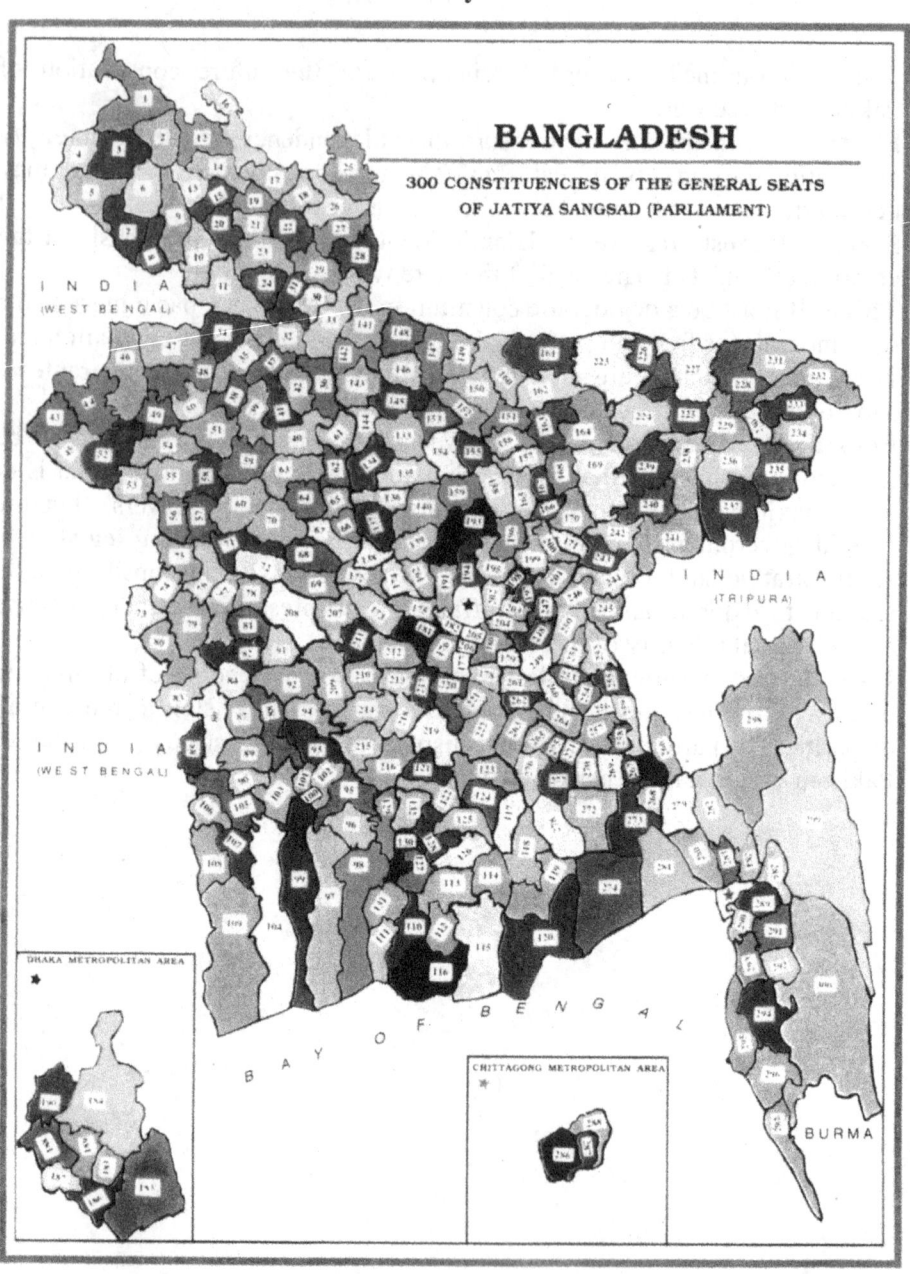

Appendix – H
Parliamentary By-elections Held Under the BNP Government (1991-1996)

Sl. No.	Date of Elections	Constituency	Name of Elected Candidate	Political Affiliation
1	Sept. 11, 1991	19 Rangpur-1	Md. K.U. Bhorasha	JP
2	Sept. 11, 1991	20 Rangpur-2	P. Chakrabarti	JP
3	Sept. 11, 1991	23 Rangpur-5	M. R. Chaudhury	JP
4	Sept. 11, 1991	24 Rangpur-6	S. M. Hossain	JP
5	Sept. 11, 1991	42 Bogra-7	Md. H. T. Lalu	BNP
6	Sept. 11, 1991	198 Bhola-2	M. H. Sajahan	BNP
7	Sept. 11, 1991	184 Dhaka-5	Major (Retd.) Md. K. Islam	BNP
8	Sept. 11, 1991	188 Dhaka 9	J. U. Sirker	BNP
9	Sept. 11, 1991	217 Madaripur-1	Nur-e-Alam Chaudhury	AL
10	Sept. 11, 1991	218 Madaripur 2	S. Khan	AL
11	Sept. 11, 1991	286 Chittagong 8	A. Khosru	BNP
12	Dec. 21, 1991	125 Bakergong-5	M. R. Sarwar	BNP
13	Oct. 12, 1992	207 Rajbari-1	K. Ali	AL
14	Oct, 15, 1992	151 Mymensing-3	R. Begum	AL
15	Dec. 2, 1992	120 Bhola-4	Md. J. U. Chaudhury	AL
16	May 3, 1993	190 Dhaka-11	S. Md. Mohsin	BNP
17	Mar. 20, 1994	92 Magura-2	K. S. Haque	BNP
18	Jul. 7, 1994	39 Bhola-4	Z. H. Mollah	BNP
19	Uncontested	87 Jessore-3	T. Islam	BNP
20	Jan. 25, 1995	59 Natore-3	K. G. Morshed	BNP
21	Jan. 25, 1995	126 Bakergong-6	Md. A. R. Khan	BNP
22	Jan. 25, 1995	148 Sherpur-3	Md. M. Haque	Indepen:
23	Jan. 25, 1995	247 B. Baria-6	S. Mia	BNP

Appendix – I
Statement of the Presiding Officer of Kullia High School Centre, Magura

To
Returning officer
92 Magura - 2
Magura

Subject: postponement of voting

Sir,
As per the above concerned subject, I am writing for your kind information that I, the undersigned Presiding Officer, was in charge of the Kullia centre of the Kullia High School. The polling was continuing smoothly from 8 am. Suddenly, 10/15 armed youths forcefully entered the polling centre, held me in a room by brandishing a pistol and threatened to take my life. They entered different polling booths of the voting centre and forcefully began to stamp (ballot papers) and stuffing the ballot boxes. They also forcefully took some of the counter-foils of the ballot papers. It was heard that at about the same time the honourable State Minister for Textile was present in the nearest market-place. After half an hour of such activity, the honourable Awami League MP, Mr. Mosharraf Hossain (Netrokona) arrived there. After some time, approximately 1500-2000 people once again surrounded and threatened me and took papers out of the sealed ballot boxes and burnt them. After a while, the honourable BNP MP (Mymensing Sadar), Mr. Fazlur Rahman arrived. Ultimately, as the situation went out of control and feeling insecure about my life, I announced at 2 pm. the closure of polling on the basis of article 2, section 30 of the Guideline for Presiding Officers.

It may be mentioned that, because I was held hostage I could not instruct the law enforcing personnel (to take action).

This is forwarded to you for your kind information and necessary action.

Sd/illegible
20-1-1994
MD. Shamim Haider
Presiding Officer
Kullia High School, Kullia
Magura Sadar

Copy forwarded for information:
1. Mr. Md. Mostafizur Rahman
Magistrate.

(English translation of the original in Bengali)

Appendix – J
Sixth National Parliament Election, 1996
(Code of Conduct to be Adhered to by Political Parties and Candidates)

The code of conduct was finalised after a discussion of the Election Commission with the representatives of the political parties on 25 September, 1995. Earlier a draft code of conduct had been circulated among the political parties for comments and opinions. The Election Commission adopted the code of conduct in the hope that the political parties and the candidates would abide by these to maintain a peaceful atmosphere during the election campaign and on the polling day.

1. Democratic Conduct

1.1 All contesting political parties and candidates should be aware not only of their own democratic rights, but also those of others.
1.2 Constitutional and legal rights of the people must be upheld. The land, buildings and any other property of the citizens shall not be abused in any way and no one shall be disturbed by unwarranted occurrences and indecent conduct.

2. Laws and Rules Relating to Elections

2.1 All contesting political parties and candidates should obey the laws, rules and regulations relating to elections.
2.2 After the announcement of the election schedule and till the election day, no candidate or anyone on his/her behalf should promise or give any donation or grant to any organisation openly or secretly in the concerned constituency or make any promise of adopting development projects in the concerned constituency. Of course, the overall development plan of a political party can be presented.
2.3 Any attempts to influence the voting through money or allurement and to hire or use any kind of transport to carry voters other than for self and family are election offences. Everyone should be aware of these offences.

2.4 The election expenses of a candidate shall not exceed taka 300,000 (US$ 7,500) and one shall maintain all expenses through bank account(s) for the sake of auditing.

2.5 The persons, who have taken loans from public banks, investment institutions or the like and have been declared defaulters for failing to repay the loans in time, should be considered illegible to participate in elections.

3. Assistance in Conducting Elections

3.1 Local leaders and workers of the political parties will extend full cooperation to the authorities in preparing Votersí Identity (ID) Cards, especially in collecting votersí photos, signature/thumb impressions and in distributing the ID cards.

3.2 All political and candidates participating in the poll will extend full cooperation to the election officials who are on duty and unitedly will ensure their security until all election activities are over.

3.3 In each district, an Electoral Inquiry Committee will be instituted with officials of the judiciary for submitting reports after inquiring into the pre-election irregularities. On the basis of allegations received, the accused will be fined and measures will be taken to collect such fines.

3.4 All political parties and candidates will get equal opportunity to use government Dakbunglows, Rest Houses and Circuit Houses.

4. Election Campaign

4.1 A fair, healthy and sound election environment will be created through the election campaign so that voters can exercise their right to franchise without fear or intimidation and of their free will.

4.2 It is normal that criticism of opponents will take place during electioneering. However, indecorous and provocative speeches/statements, taunting, ridiculing, religious and communal hatred should be avoided. One party should not make any such statements or comments about another party which might cause unnecessary tension. All parties should exercise moderation and sobriety in speech and show respect to the opinions of others so that electioneering does not turn into a war of words.

4.3   All parties and candidates will have equal opportunity for publicity. Meetings, processions and other campaign activities of opponents cannot be foiled or interfered with.

4.4   Participants of a meeting or rally will not carry any sort of arms and ammunition. All parties and candidates should be careful that any material carried does not cause any harm or is not used for vindictive purposes.

4.5   Prior to organising a mass meeting or rally, a candidate should inform all the opposing candidates from his/her constituency about the date, time and venue of such a meeting or rally.

4.6   No rally or torchlight procession in buses and trucks will be organised for any contesting candidate.

4.7   After the announcement of the election schedule, the Ministers of the sitting government will not use or take help from the government media, officials and employees, transport and other government facilities.

4.8   All political parties contesting in polls will get an opportunity to campaign through the government media after the announcement of the election schedule.

4.9   No poster, banner, leaflet and handbill of a candidate will be pasted over those of another opposing candidate.

4.10 An election camp cannot be constructed on roads or in any placement for public use and movement. Election camps should be as plain as possible. Voters cannot be served any food and drinks in election camps. The number of election camps of a candidate will not exceed the number determined by the Election Commission.

4.11 After the announcement of the election schedule, the contesting candidates and their agents will refrain from erecting expensive arches, printing and publicising multi-coloured posters, exceeding the specified number of banners and from any other expensive publicity.

4.12 No governmental Dakbunglow, Rest House, Circuit House or any other government office can be used as campaign place by any political party or candidate.

4.13 Everybody should refrain from any kind of wall-writing as an election campaign tool.

5. Maintaining Law and Order

5.1 A natural and peaceful law and order situation is a precondition of a free and impartial election. But the efforts of the law enforcing agencies alone are not enough for a well-disciplined election. So all political parties and candidates will extend the necessary assistance to the law enforcing agencies in this regard.

5.2 All political parties will be vocal against terrorist activities. No party will sympathise with terrorist activities to demonstrate its strength or supremacy over another party. All political parties will extend cooperation to the law enforcing agencies in the recovery of illegal arms. No party will make an effort to release anyone captured with arms by the police personnel during election campaign or in and around a polling centre during voting. No armed person will enter the vicinity of a polling centre during voting.

5.3 In the interest of a peaceful atmosphere in the vicinity of a polling centre, all kinds of motor cycles or motorised vehicles, firearms and explosives, movement of the thugs, illegal interference with the government officials or with the local leaders will be stopped.

5.4 The Election commission will stop the election in a centre at any stage outright, if the election is abused or influenced by money, arms, physical force or local influence.

5.5 Assistance of the nearest law enforcing agencies will be obtained to control and resist election offences of any kind.

5.6 A sound and peaceful atmosphere prevailing in a polling centre will not be disturbed by untrue and motivational rumour or conspiracy.

6. Security of the Polling Centre

6.1 Votes cannot be solicited by capturing a polling centre by force or through any other illegal means. In a rigged centre, the Election Commission can cancel polling.

6.2 Election camps cannot be set up close to the polling centre or within the prohibited vicinity of the polling centre and no campaign will be allowed inside a polling centre.

6.3 No placard or badge with a party-symbol can be taken in and around a centre.

6.4 Other than the election officials, only the voters have access to the polling centres. Political party workers will not loiter inside the centre. Only the polling agents will remain seated in places designated for them in the polling centre and discharge their responsibilities.

Appendix – K

The Sixth Jatiya Sangsad (National Parliament) Election, 1996 Contesting Parties and Candidates		
Sl. No.	Name of the Party	No. of candidates
1	Bangladesh Nationalist Party (BNP)	300
2	Seven Party Alliances	98
3	Freedom Party (Farooq)	67
4	Bangladesh *Khelafat Andolon*	54
5	National Democratic Alliance (NDA)	50
6	Bangladesh Muslim League (Jamir Ali)	39
7	National Democratic Party (NDP)	35
8	*Progotishil Ganotantrik* Party (PROGOSH)	34
9	*Janodal*	31
10	*Jatiya Nagorik Sanghaty* (JANAS)	31
11	Bangladesh *Gano Adhikar* Front	31
12	Bangladesh *Jatiyatabadi Awami* League (S. M. Uddin)	27
13	*Jatiya Janata* Party (Sheikh Asad)	27
14	*Islami Shashantantra* Andolon	25
15	*Progotishil Jatiyatabadi Andolon*	24
16	Bangladesh *Jatiya* League	24
17	Other insignificant parties*	146
18	Independents	457

*Other 25 insignificant parties were: *Satero Dalio Ganotantrik Morcha* (Abu Alam), Bangladesh *Bekar Samaj, Jatiyatabadi Ganotantrik Dal* (Zakir Hossain), Social Democratic Party (SDP), *Bhasani Panthi* Alliance, *Jatiya Mukti Dal, Jatiya Palli Dal* and 17 Party Democratic Alliance (S.Zainal), Maolana Bhasani *Adarsha Bastabayan Parisad*, Peopleís Democratic Movement, *Sammilita Islami Sangram Parisad*, Bangladesh *Jatiyatabadi Awami League* (Mostafa Allama), Bangladesh National *Awami* Party (NAP Bhasani), Bangladesh *Jatiya Islami Janata* Party, Bangladesh *Islamic* Party, Bangladesh Peopleís Party, United Democratic Front, United Peopleís Party, *Krishak Jukto* Front, Democratic Republican Party, Peopleís Solidarity Centre, Farraka and *Agrasan Protirodh* Council, Bangladesh *Gano Mukti Andolon*, Bangladesh *Jatiya Sheba Dal*, Bangladesh National Congress and Bangladesh *Mehnaty Party*.

Appendix – L
Jatiya Sangsad (Parliament) Election, 1991
Code of Conduct to be Observed by Political Parties

The code of conduct, finalised after discussions with the representatives of 67 political parties including major ones, is aimed at maintaining a peaceful atmosphere during the election campaign and on polling day. The Election Commission hoped that if all political parties faithfully abided by the code, they would greatly contribute to the holding of a credible election in the country. The legitimacy of a representative government elected through such an election would not be questioned.

Code of Conduct

1. Existing election laws and rules must be adhered to.
2. All political parties and contestants will extend all necessary help and co-operation to the law-enforcing authorities.
3. Everyone should be aware of not only his own rights, but should also respect the rights of others.
4. All political parties and candidates participating in the polls will extend full co-operation to the election officials and ensure their safety and security until the polls are over.
5. Election campaigns should be so organised that a congenial and peaceful atmosphere prevails during polling.
6. Nothing should be done that will create tension and disrupt the congenial atmosphere of the election. All parties should exercise restraint in speech and show respect to the opinions of others so that electioneering does not turn into war of words.
7. It is expected that criticism of opponents will occur during electioneering. However, indecorous and provocative speeches / statements, taunting, ridiculing and innuendos should be avoided. Parties should be careful that statements and comments do not cause unnecessary tension. In a situation where the possibility of a clash arises because of a misunderstanding between contesting parties, then an Election Co-ordination Committee composed of representatives from the concerned parties shall allay tension and settle the dispute.
8. All political parties shall be vocal against violence. No party shall indulge in any kind of violent activity to demonstrate party strength or

to prove supremacy. All political parties will extend co-operation to the law enforcing agencies for recovery of illegal arms. No party will take any initiative for the release of any person arrested by police with arms during election campaign or in the polling centre during voting or in the vicinity of the polling centre during polls.

9. All parties and candidates will have equal opportunity for publicity. Meetings, processions and other campaign activities of opponents cannot be interfered with.
10. Assistance of the nearest law enforcing agencies will be sought to resist and check any sort of election offence.
11. Any attempts to influence voting through money or allurement and to hire or use kind of transport to carry voters other than for self and family are election offences. Everyone should be aware of these offences.
12. Political parties will reach an understanding to resist attempts to procure votes by forcible occupation of polling centres or through illegal activities in the polling centres. Votes thus obtained illegally will be of no use as the Election Commission will cancel polling in such centres.
13. No candidate can commit covertly or overtly any contribution or grant to any institution in his constituency until election day for the purpose of election campaigning and obtaining votes.
14. A congenial and peaceful atmosphere for the election should not be disturbed by spreading untrue and motivated rumour or by recourse to conspiracy.
15. Election camps cannot be set up within the centres and no campaign shall be allowed inside the polling centres.
16. In addition to the election officials, only the voters are entitled to enter the polling centres: the political parties should make sure that their workers do not enter the polling centres and loiter therein. Only the polling agents will remain seated at their designated seats in the polling centre and discharge their responsibility from there.

Appendix – M
The Seventh Parliamentary Election, 12 June 1996
The Code of Conduct for Elections

1. Short title

These rules may be called The Code of Conduct for the Political Parties and Contesting Candidates Seeking Election to the Jatiya Sangsad, 1996

2. Definitions

In these rules, unless there is anything repugnant in the subject or context,
(a) 'pre-poll period' means the period commencing on the announcement of the election schedule and ending on the declaration of results;
(b) 'candidate' means a person nominated by a political party or a person contesting the election independently from a constituency; and
(c) 'political party' includes a group of combination of persons who operate within or outside Parliament under a distinctive name and who hold themselves out for the purpose of propagating a political opinion or engaging in any other political activity.

3. Ban on subscription, donation etc. to any institution

Concerned political parties may announce their overall development planning. But following the announcement of the election schedule till the day of polling, no candidate or any person on his behalf shall, openly or in secret, give any subscription or donation, or make promise for giving such subscription or donation, to any institution of their respective constituency or to any other institution, nor shall commit to undertake any development project in the respective constituency.

4. Use of Dakbangalows and Rest House

All parties and candidates shall be given equal rights for using government dakbanglows, rest houses and circuit houses on the basis of the application first made and in accordance with the existing rules for use of the same. But the officers engaged in the conduct of the election shall get preference to use government dakbanglows, rest houses and circuit houses.

5. Election campaign

5.1 All parties and candidates shall have equal rights with regard to the election campaign. Meetings, processions and other election campaigns of the opponents shall not be disrupted or obstructed.

5.2 The local police administration and the opposite party shall, in advance, be informed of the date, time and place for holding meetings or processions in favour of any contending political party or candidate.

5.3 The local police administration shall, well in advance, be informed of the date, time and place of the proposed holding of meeting by any contending party or candidate, so that the police administration can take necessary steps for unobstructed movement of the public and for ensuring law and order there.

5.4 No meeting shall be held on any through fare creating hindrance to the movement of the public without obtaining permission from the appropriate authority.

5.5 The organisers of any meeting shall have to seek the assistance of the police for taking action against the persons who obstruct the holding of such meetings or create disturbances in such meetings. The organisers shall not themselves take any action against such persons.

5.6 No candidate or political party or anybody on their behalf shall use government media, government officers, employees or transport or other state facilities following the announcement of the election schedule.

5.7 No posters, leaflets or handbills, shall be stuck over the posters, leaflets or handbills of the rival candidates.

5.8 No election camps shall be set up on any road or place meant for the use of the public. Election camp shall as far as possible be simple. No food or drink shall be served to the voters in the election camp.

5.9 No Government dakbanglows, rest houses, circuit houses and government office shall be used by any party or candidate as a place for election campaigning.

5.10 The posters for election campaign shall be printed on paper manufactured in the country and its colour shall be black and white and its size in no case shall be more than 22" x 18".
5.11 No contesting candidate shall use more than three microphones in his constituency and the use of microphones shall be restricted between 2 pm and 8 pm.
5.12 No land, building or movable or immovable properties of any citizen shall be damaged in connection with the election and personal peace of any person shall not be violated by undesirable activities or disorderly behaviour.
5.13 Every person shall refrain from all sorts of wall writings as a means of election campaign.
5.14 In the interest of maintaining law and order, no motor cycle or any other mechanical transport shall be used and no fire arms or explosives shall be carried within the premises of the polling stations. No government officer or influential local person shall make any illegal interference in the election process.
5.15 No procession of buses, trucks or any other vehicles or torch procession shall be held in favour of any contesting candidate.
5.16 All political parties and candidates shall have to render necessary assistance to the officers and employees entrusted with the responsibility of holding elections in order to ensure peaceful and orderly casting of votes independently by the voters without any hindrance.
5.17 During the election campaign, no contesting candidate shall make any bitter or provocative statement or any such statement that may hurt the sentiment of the followers of any religion.
5.18 No contesting candidate shall, under any circumstances, exceed the limit of election expenses.

6. Keeping election free from any influence

The election shall not be influenced by money, arms, physical force or local influence.

7. Access to polling station

Only the polling personnel, contesting candidates, polling agents and voters shall have access to the polling station. Workers of the political parties or candidates shall not enter and move about inside the polling station. Only the polling agents, sitting on their allotted places, shall perform their specific duties.

8. Pre-poll irregularities

Violation of any provision of these rules shall be considered as pre-poll irregularities and any person or political party aggrieved by such violation may apply to the Electoral Inquiry Committee or Election Commission seeking redress. If the application filed with the Election Commission is found by the Commission as tenable, it shall send the same to the concerned or any Electoral Inquiry Committee for investigation. In both the cases, the Electoral Inquiry Committee, after making investigation as per provisions of Article 91A of the Representation of the People Order, 1972 (P.O. No. 155 of 1972), shall submit its recommendations to the Commission.

Appendix – N
Bangladesh Election Commission
Voter Education Posters
Sample 1

English translation from Bengali: Parliamentary election: June 1996. How do you cast your vote? At the vote centre, you will be given a ballot paper and an inked rubber stamp to cast your vote. You must stamp on the space to the right of the symbol of your preferred candidate. It would be convenient for you to know in advance the location of your polling centre and your serial number on the electoral roll. Polling will take place from 8 am to 4 pm without any break. Cast your vote in a disciplined manner before time runs out. You can vote only once. Therefore cast your vote in the proper way after due consideration of your correct choice. Bangladesh Election Commission.

Bangladesh Election Commission
Voter Education Posters
Sample 2

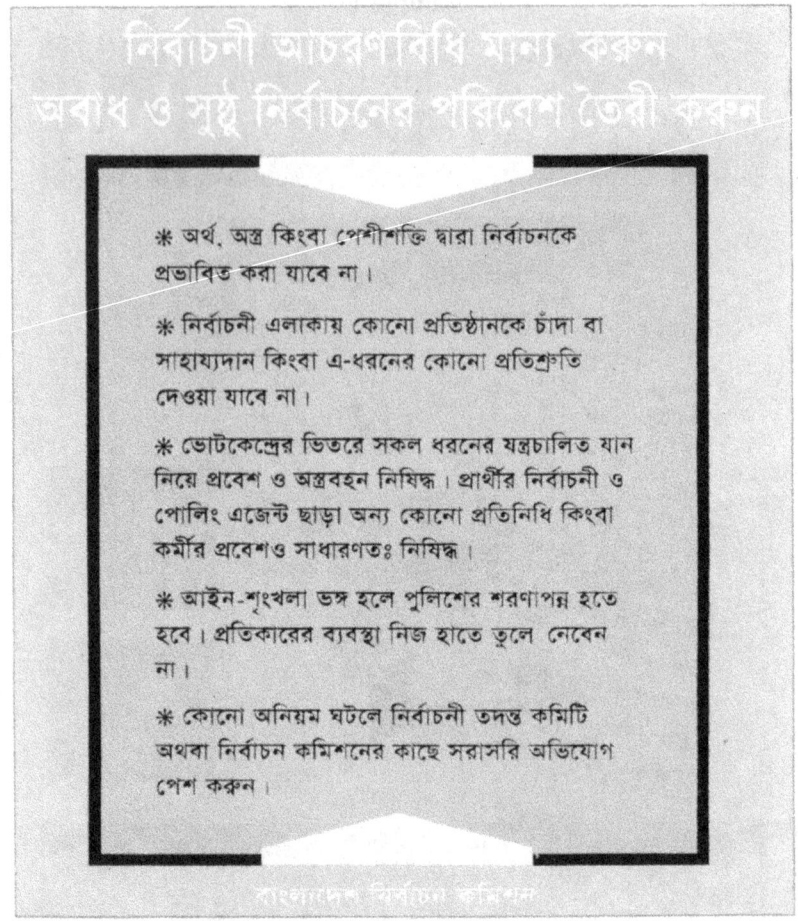

English translation from Bengali: Abide by the electoral code of conduct. Support an environment for a free and fair election. The election cannot be influenced by money, arms or physical force. Making or promising donations to any parties are not allowed. Motor vehicles or arms are not allowed in a vote centre. Entry to the polling centre is restricted to electoral and polling agents of candidates and voters. All others are prohibited from entering. Police should be contacted in case of the failure of law and order. Do not take the law into your own hands. In case of any irregularities, lodge your complaint directly to Election Inquiry Committee or to the Election Commission. Bangladesh Election Commission.

Appendices 259

Bangladesh Election Commission
Voter Education Posters
Sample 3

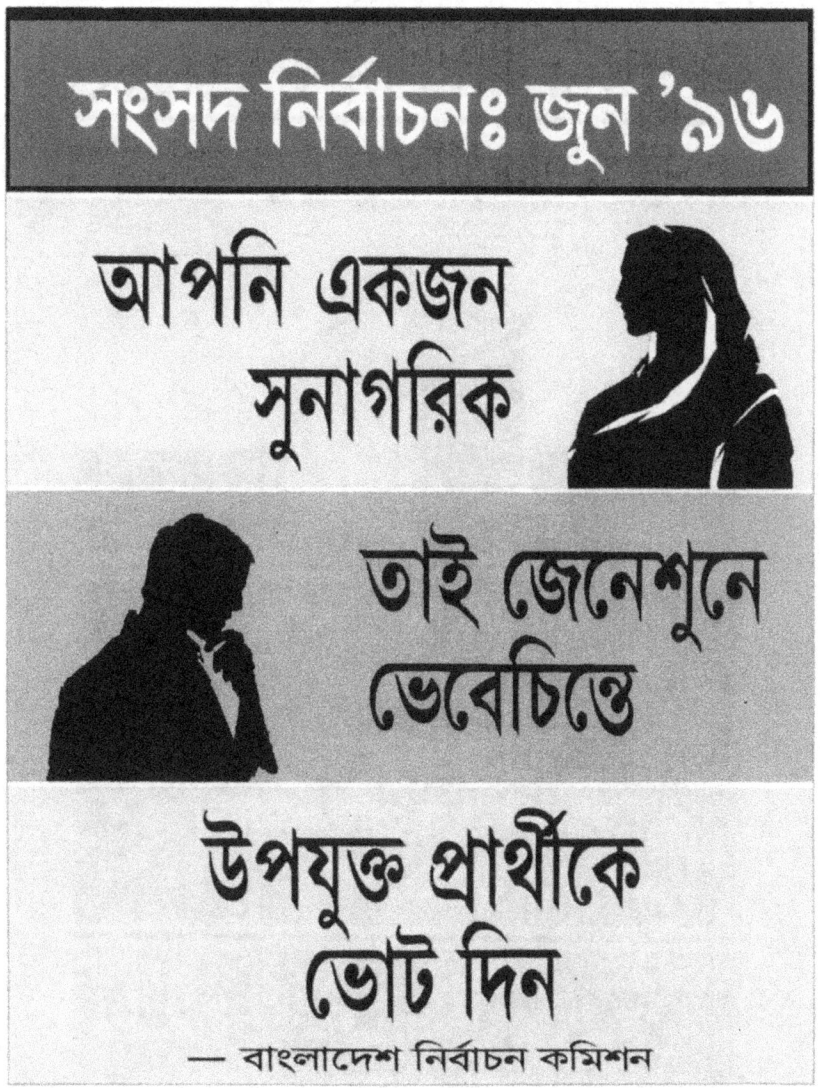

English translation from Bengali: Parliamentary election: June 1996. You are a good citizen. So, cast your vote for the best candidate after proper consideration. Bangladesh Election Commission.

**Bangladesh Election Commission
Voter Education Posters
Sample 4**

English translation from Bengali: The Electoral Code of Conduct, 1996 is the key to a free, fair and peaceful election. Read and discuss it with others and contribute towards its proper implementation. Bangladesh Election Commission.

Bibliography

Books

Ahmed, M. (1983), *Bangladesh: Era of Sheikh Mujibur Rahman*, University Press Limited, Dhaka.
Akhter, M. Y. (1991), *Search for the Nature of Corruption: Bangladesh* (in Bengali), Nibedan Publications Limited, Dhaka.
────── (1989), *Political Culture and Socialization: Bangladesh Perspective* (in Bengali), Nebedan Publications Limited, Dhaka.
Alam, J. (1990), *The Trend of Leftist Politics in Bangladesh 1948-89* (in Bengali), Proteek Prokashana Sangshtha, Dhaka.
Alatas, S. H. (1968), *The Sociology of Corruption*, Donald Moore Press, Singapore.
Barua, T. K. (1978), *Political Elites in Bangladesh: A Socio-Anthropological and Historical Analysis of Processes of their Formation*, Peter Lang, Bern.
Baxter, C. (1984), *Bangladesh: A New Nation in an Old Setting*, Westview Press, London.
Benson, G. (1978), *Political Corruption in America*, Lexington Books, Lexington, M. A.
Berg, L. L. and Schmidhauser (1976), *Corruption in the American Political System*, General Learning Press, Morristown, New Jersey.
Bhan, S. (ed.) (1995), *Criminalization of Politics*, Shipra Publications, Delhi.
Bhargava, G. S. (1974), *India's Watergate: A Study of Political Corruption in India*, Arnold-Heinemann Publishers, New Delhi.
Bhutto, Z. A. (1971), *The Great Tragedy*, A People's Party Publication, Karachi.
────── (1969), *The Myth of Independence*, Oxford University Press, Karachi.
Bienen, H. (ed.) (1968), *The Military Interventions: Case Studies in Political Development*, Russel Sage Foundation, New York.
Bogdanor, V. and Butler, D. (eds) (1981), *Democracy at the Polls: A Comparative Study of Comparative Elections*, American Enterprise Institute, Washington D.C.
Bryce, J. (1921), *Modern Democracies, vol. 2*, Macmillan, New York.
Butler, D. E. and King, A. (1965), *The British General Election of 1964*, Macmillan, London.
Butler, D., Penniman, H. and Ranney, A. (eds) (1981), *Democracy at the Polls: A Comparative Study of Competitive National Elections*, The American Enterprise Institute for Public Policy Research, Washington D.C.

Campbell, P. (1958), *French Electoral Systems and Elections Since 1789*, Faber and Faber, London.

Carstairs, A. M. (1980), *A Short History of Electoral Systems in Western Europe*, Allen and Unwin, London.

Chakravarty, D. K. (1992), *Ancient Bangladesh: A Study of the Archaeological Sources*, Oxford University Press, Delhi.

Chakravarty, S. R. (ed.) (1986), *Politics and Society in Bangladesh*, vol. 2., South Asian Publishers, New Delhi.

Chandra, S. (1978), *Parties and Politics in Mughal Darbar 1707-1740* (in Bengali), K. P. Bagchi, Calcutta.

Chaudhury, A. M. (1967), *Dynastic History of Bengal*, The Asiatic Society of Pakistan, Dhaka.

Choudhury, D. (1994), *Constitutional Development in Bangladesh: Stresses and Strains*, Oxford University Press, Oxford.

Choudhury, G. W. (1974), *The Last Days of United Pakistan*, C. Hurst, London.

────── (1959), *Constitutional Development in Pakistan*, Longmans Green, London.

Clarke, M. (ed.) (1983), *Corruption: Causes, Consequences and Control*, Frances Printer Publishers, London.

Clubb, J. M., William, H. F. and Nancy, H. Z. (eds) (1981), *Analyzing Electoral History: A Guide to the Study of American Voter Behaviour*, Sage Publications, Beverly Hills, London.

Copeman, C. and Mcgrath, A. O. (eds) (1997), *Corrupt Elections: Ballot Rigging in Australia*, Tower House Publications, Sydney.

DeLeon, P. (1993), *Thinking About Political Corruption*, M. E. Sharpe, New York.

Dwivedy, S. and Bhargava, G. S. (1967), *Political Corruption in India*, Popular Book Services, New Delhi.

Ekpo, M. U. (ed.) (1979), *Bureaucratic Corruption in Sub-Saharan Africa: Toward A Search for Causes and Consequences*, University Press of America, Washington.

Etzioni-Halevy, (1979), *Political Manipulation and Administrative Power*, Routledge and Kegan Paul, London.

Farouque, G. (ed.) (1996), *Bureaucratic Rebellion* (in Bengali), Matra Books, Dhaka.

────── (ed.) (1996), *Election '96: NGO The Bureaucracy Black Money and Corruption* (in Bengali), Mimma Prokashan, Dhaka.

Felknor, B. L. (1992), *Political Mischief: Smear, Sabotage, and Reform in U.S. Elections*, Praeger Publishers, New York.

Franda, M. (1982), *Bangladesh: The First Decade*, South Asian Publishers, New Delhi.

Fredman, L. E. (1968), *The Australian Ballot: The Story of An American Reform*, Michigan University Press, East Lansing.

Gardiner, J. L. (1978), *Decisions For Sale, Corruption and Reform in Land-Use and Building Regulations*, Praeger Publishers, New York.

Gong, T. (1994), *The Politics of Corruption in Contemporary China: Analysis of Policy Outcomes*, Praeger Publishers, Westpot.

Hakim, M. A. (1993), *Bangladesh Politics: The Shahabuddin Interregnum*, The University Press Limited, Dhaka.
Haq, M. E. (1975), *A History of Sufism in Bengal*, Asiatic Society of Bangladesh, Dhaka.
Harlan, L. L. B. and Schmidhauser, J. R. (1976), *Corruption in the American Political System*, General Learning Press, Morristown, New Jersey.
Harries-Jenkins, G. and Doorn, J. V. (1976), *The Military and the Problem of Legitimacy*, Sage Publications, London.
Harris, J. P. (1929), *Registration of Voters in the United States*, Brooking Institution, Washington.
Harrop, M. and Miller, W. L. (1987), *Elections and Voters: A Comparative Introduction*, Mcmillan Publication, London.
Hasanuzzaman, (1991), *Militarisation of State and Government*, University Press Limited, Dhaka.
Heard, A. (1960), *The Costs of Democracy*, University of North Carolina Press, Chapel Hill.
Heidenheimer, A. J. (ed.) (1970), *Political Corruption: Readings in Comparative Analysis*, Holt, Rinehart and Winston, New Jersey.
Hume, L. P. (1982), *The National Union of Women's Suffrage Societies 1897 – 1914*, published by the author, USA.
Hurst, J. W. (1980), *The Growth of American Law*, Little Brown, Boston.
Husain, A. (1972), *Politics and Peoples Representation in Pakistan*, Feroz Sons, Lahore.
Islam, S. S. (1988), *Bangladesh: State and Economic Strategy*, University Press Limited, Dhaka.
Jackson, B. (1988), *Honest Graft: Big Money and the American Political Process*, Kopf, New York.
Jahan, R. (1980), *Bangladesh Politics: Problems and Issues*, University Press Limited, Dhaka.
——— (1972), *Pakistan: Failure in National Integration*, Columbia University Press, New York.
Jalal, A. (1990), *The State of Martial Rule: The Origins of Pakistan's Political Economy of Defense*, Cambridge University Press, New York.
James, S. M. (1993), *Pakistan Chronicle*, C. Hurst, London.
Janowitz, M. (1977), *Military Institution and Coercion in the Developing Nations*, The University of Chicago Press, Chicago.
Kabra, K. N. (1986), *India's Black Economy and Mal-development*, Patriot Publications, New Delhi.
Karim, A. (1959), *Social History of the Muslims in Bengal (Down to A. D. 1538)*, The Asiatic Society of Pakistan, Dhaka.
Kennedy, G. (ed.) (1974), *The Military in the Third World*, Gerald Duckworth, London.
Khan, Z. R. (1983), *Leadership in the Least Developed Nation: Bangladesh*, Maxwell School of Citizenship and Public Affairs, Syracuse University, Syracuse.
Kohli, S. (ed.) (1975), *Corruption in India*, Chetana Publications, New Delhi.

Kumar, S. (1978), *The New Pakistan*, Vikas Publications, New Delhi.
Lal, S. (1978), *Elections Under the Janata Rule*, India Election Archives, New Delhi.
LeDuce, L., Niemi, R. G. and Norris, P. (eds) (1997), *Comparing Democracies: Elections and Voting in Global Perspective*, Sage Publications, London.
Lees, K. (1995), *Votes for Women: The Australian Story*, Allen and Unwin, St. Leonards, NSW.
Lentini, P. (ed.) (1995), *Elections and Political Order in Russia: The Implications of the 1973 Elections to the Federal Assembly*, Central European University Press, New York.
Luttwak, E. (1969), *Coup d'Etat*, Penguin, Harmondsworth.
Laski, V. (1977), *It Did Not Start With Watergate*, Dial Press, New York.
Le Vine, V. T. (1975), *Political Corruption: The Ghana Case*, Hoover Institution Press, California.
Lee, P. L. (ed.) (1981), *Corruption and Control in Hong Kong*, The Chinese University Press, Hong Kong.
Lifschultz, L. (1979), *Bangladesh: The Unfinished Revolution*, Zed Press, London.
Lumby, N. W. R. (1955), *The Transfer of Power in India*, George Allen and Unwin, London.
McCallum, R. B. and Readman, A. (1951), *The British General Election of 1945*, Macmillan, London.
McGrath, A. (1996), *The Frauding of Votes*, Tower House Publications, Sydney.
Mackenzie, W. J. M. (1958), *Free Elections: An Elementary Textbook*, George Allen and Unwin, London.
Mackerras, M. (1975), *Elections 1975*, Angus and Robertson, London.
Man, A. B., Soong-hoom, K. and Woong, K. K. (1988), *Elections in Korea*, Seoul Computer Press, Seoul.
Magrath, C. P. (1966), *Yazoo: Law and Politics in the New Republic*, Brown University Press, Providence, R. I.
Mamoon, M. (1983), *Inside Administration* (in Bengali), Pallab Publishers, Dhaka.
Maniruzzaman, T. (1987), *Military Withdrawal from Politics*, Ballinger, Cambridge.
────── (1982), *Group Interests and Political Changes: Studies of Pakistan and Bangladesh*, South Asian Publications, New Delhi.
────── (1980), *Bangladesh Revolution and Its Aftermath*, Bangladesh Book International, Dhaka.
Marilley, S. M. (1996), *Women Suffrage and the Origins of Liberal Feminism in the United States, 1820 – 1920*, Harvard University Press, Cambridge.
Mascarenhas, A. (1986), *Bangladesh: A Legacy of Blood*, Hodder and Stoughton, London.
Matin, A. (ed.) (1986), *Ershad's Election Fraud*, Radical Asia Publications, London.
Misra, K. P., Lakhi, M. V. and Narain, V. (1967), *Pakistan's Search for Constitutional Consensus*, Impex India, New Delhi.
Monterio, J. B. (1980), *Corruption In India*, Sachin Publications, Jaipur.

———— (1966), *Corruption: Control of Maladministration*, P. C. Manaktala and Sons, Bombay.
Muhit, A. M. A. (1991), *Bangladesh Reconstruction and National Consensus* (in Bengali), The University Press Limited, Dhaka.
Nelken, D. and Levi, M. (1996), *The Corruption of Politics and the Politics of Corruption*, Blackwell Publishers, Oxford.
Nelson, M. (1985), *The Elections 1984*, CQ Press, Washington D.C.
Noorani, A. G. (1974), *Minister's Misconduct*, Vikas Publishing House, Delhi.
Nordglinger, E. A. (1977), *Soldiers in Politics: Military and Governments*, Prentice-Hall, Englewood Cliffs, New Jersey.
Palmar, N. D. (1975), *Elections and Political Development: The South Asian Experience*, C. Hurst, London.
Pandhy, K. S. and Muni, R. K. (1987), *Corruption in Indian Politics – A Case Study of an Indian State*, Discovery, New Delhi.
Plato, *The Laws* (translated by Trevor J. Saunders) (1970), Hazell Watson and Viney, London.
———— *The Republic* (translated by Paul Shorey) (1930), William Heinemann, London.
Polsby, N. W. and Wildarsky, A. B. (1968), *Presidential Elections: Strategies of American Electoral Politics*, 2nd ed., Charles Scribner's Sons, New York.
Puchkov, P. (1986), *Political Development of Bangladesh 1971-1985*, Patriot Publishers, New Delhi.
Quibria, M. G. and Dowling, J. M. (eds) (1996), *Current Issues in Economic Development: An Asian Perspective*, Asian Development Bank, Hong Kong.
Quotedin, J. W. H. (1980), *The Growth of American Law*, Little Brown, Boston.
Reeve, A. and Ware, A. (1992), *Electoral Systems: A Comparative and Theoretical Introduction*, Routledge, London, New York.
Richley, A. J. (1987), *Elections: American Style*, The Brookings Institution, Washington D.C.
Rizvi, G. (1985), *Bangladesh: The Struggle for the Restoration of Democracy*, Bangabandhu Society, London.
Rizvi, H. (1987), *The Military and Politics In Pakistan 1947-86*, Progressive Publishers, Lahore.
Rogow, A. A. and Lasswell, H. D. (1963), *Power, Corruption and Rectitude*, Prentice Hall, Englewood Cliffs, New Jersey.
Rose-Ackerman, S. (1978), *Corruption: A Political Economy*, Academic Press, New York.
Rule, W. and Zimmerman, J. M. (eds), *Electoral Systems in Comparative Perspective: Their Impact on Women and Minorities*, Greenwood Press, Westport, Connecticut, London.
Sabato, L. J. and Simpson, G. R. (1996), *Dirty Little Secrets: The Persistence of Corruption in American Politics*, Times Books, New York.
Saeed, S. A. (1960), *President Without Precedent*, Lahore Book Depot, Lahore.
Satori, G. (1967), *Democratic Theory*, Praeger Publishers, New York.
Sayeed, K. B. (1967), *The Political System of Pakistan*, Houghton Mifflin, Boston.

Scott, J. C. (1972), *Comparative Political Corruption*, Prentice-Hall, Englewood Cliffs, New Jersey.
Seligman, E. R. (1931), *An Encyclopaedia of the Social Sciences*, vol. 5, Macmillan, New York.
Seton-Watson, R. W. (1911), *Corruption and Reform in Hungary: A Study of Electoral Practice*, Constable, London.
Shain, Y. and Linz, J. J. (1995), *Between States: Interim Governments and Democratic Transitions*, Cambridge University Press, Cambridge.
Sherman, L. (1978), *Scandal and Reform: Controlling Police Corruption*, University of California Press, Berkeley.
Smis, K. M. (1982), *USSR: The Corrupt Society*, Simon and Schuster, New York.
Smith, B. C. (1996), *Understanding Third World Politics*, Indiana University Press, Bloomington.
Smith, T. E. (1960), *Elections in Developing Countries*, St. Martin's Press, New York.
Sobhan, R. (1968), *Basic Democracies, Works Programme and Rural Development in East Pakistan*, Oxford University Press, Dhaka.
Sorauf, F. J. (1988), *Money in American Elections*, Scott, Foregman, Glenview IL.
Taagepera, R. and Shugart, M. S. (1989), *Seats and Votes: The Effects and Determinants of Electoral Systems*, Yale University Press, New Haven and London.
Tahmina, Q A., Gain, P. and Moral, S. (eds) (1995), *The Reporters Guide: Handbook on Election Reporting*, Society for Environment and Human Development (SHED), Dhaka.
Tinker, H. (1964), *Ballot Box and Bayonet: People and Government in Emergent Asian Countries*, Oxford University Press, London.
Umar, B. (1966), *Power in the Hands of the People – Election or Coup?* (in Bengali), Sanskriti Prokashani, Dhaka.
Valla, R. P. (1973), *Elections in India, 1950-72*, S. Chand, New Delhi.
Voys, K. V. (1965), *Political Development in Pakistan*, Princeton University Press, Princeton.
Welch Jr, C. E. and Smith, A. K. (1974), *Military Role and Rule: Perspectives on Civil-Military Relations*, Duxbury Press, North Scituate.
Winter Jr., R. W. (1974), *Watergate and the Law: Political Campaigns and Presidential Power*, American Enterprise Institute for Public Policy Research, Washington D.C.
Wright, D. (1968), *Bangladesh Origins and Indian Ocean Relations (1971-75)*, Starling Publishers, New Delhi.
Yadav, K. C. (1981), *Elections in Punjab, 1920-47*, Institute for the Study of Languages and Cultures of Asia and Africa, Tokyo University of Foreign Studies, Tokyo.
Zafarullah, H. (1996), *The Zia Episode In Bangladesh Politics*, South Asian Publishers, New Delhi.
Ziring, L. (1992), *Bangladesh: From Mujib to Ershad, An Interpretive Study*, Oxford University Press, Oxford.

——— (1980), *Pakistan: The Enigma of Political Development*, Westview Press, Dawson.
——— (1971), *The Ayub Khan Era: Politics in Pakistan 1958-69*, Syracuse University Press, Syracuse.

Articles

Ahmed, E. (2000), 'Why Zila Parisad Act is Anti-constitutional?' (in Bengali), *The Daily Ittefaq*, 20 July; ——— (2000), 'The Zila Parisad Act 2000', *Dhaka Courier*, vol. 17, issue 52, 21 July, pp. 22-23.
Ahmed, N. (1997), 'Parliamentary Opposion in Bangladesh: A Study of Its Role in the Fifth Parliament', *Party Politics*, vol. 3, no. 2, pp. 147-68.
——— (1995), 'Party Politics in Bangladesh's Local Government: The 1994 City Corporation Elections', *Asian Survey*, vol. XXXV, no. 2, pp. 1017-29.
Ahmed, S. (1989-1990), 'Politics in Bangladesh: The Paradox of Military Intervention', *Regional Studies*, vol. 8, no. 1, pp. 37-65.
Ahmed, S. (1995), 'Opposition's Cold Response to Dialogue Offer', *Dhaka Courier*, vol. 11, issue 42, 19 May, p. 8.
Ahsan, S. A. (1992), 'Bangladesh at the Polls: Free and Fair Elections', *Asian Profile*, vol. 20, no. 2, pp. 71-74.
Akhter, M. Y. (1997), 'Caretaker Government and Election: A New Crisis', (in Bengali) *Swadesh Barta*, 25 April.
——— (1994), 'Songs and Politics: the Aspect of Local Government Elections in Bangladesh', *Bangladesh Political Studies*, vol. 16, pp. 79-95.
——— (1991), 'Controlling Administrative Corruption: Some Suggestion' (in Bengali), *Proshashan Samikkha*, vol. 4, no. 1, pp. 56-86.
——— (1991), 'The Politics of Decentralization in Bangladesh', *Indian Journal of Politics*, vol. 25, no. 2-3, pp. 119-31.
——— (1990), 'Socio-political Impact of Administrative Decentralisation in Bangladesh', *Asian Profile*, vol. 18, no. 3, pp. 265-77.
——— (1989), 'Patron-client Relations in Bangladesh Organisations', *Administrative Change*, vol. 17, no. 1, pp. 28-41.
——— (1988), 'Land Politics During Election: A Case of Rural Bangladesh', *The Journal of Local Government*, vol. XVII, no. 1, pp. 68-74.
——— (1987), 'Styles of Administrative Corruption: The Case of a Bangladeshi Organization', *Politics, Administration and Change*, vol. XII, no. 1, pp. 61-76.
——— (1985), 'Electoral Politics in Bangladesh: A Case Study' (in Bengali), *Chittagong University Studies* (Social Science), vol. 8, no. 1, pp. 209-34.
Akter, S. (1989), 'Political Murder Occurred During Each Government' (in Bengali), *Ashe Din Jai*, 27 August, pp. 22-23.
Alam, A. N. (1994), 'Corruption-Free Election: Is Caretaker Government the Only Guarantee?' (in Bengali), *Weekly Bichittra*, 6 May, pp. 11-13.
al-Mujahid, S. (1971), 'Pakistan: First General Elections', *Asian Survey*, vol. 11, no. 2, pp. 159-71.

———— (1965), 'Pakistan's First Presidential Election', *Asian Survey*, vol. 5, no. 6, pp. 280-94.

———— (1965), 'Assembly Elections in Pakistan', *Asian Survey*, vol. 5, no. 1, pp. 939-51.

Ali, S. K. (1981), 'Sour Grapes of Wrath: As the Ruling Party Scores a Landside Election Victory, The Opposition Awami League Vows Revenge', *Far Eastern Economic Review*, vol. 14, no. 48, 20 November, pp. 17-18.

Amin, S. and Guhathakurta, M. (1991), 'Parliament Election in 1991: Candidate's Opinion on Social and Political Issues' (in Bengali), *Samaj Nirikkhan*, no. 42, November, pp. 14-25.

Babur, S. (1994), 'Some Aspects of City Corporation Elections' (in Bengali), *Palabadal*, vol. 3, no. 15, 16-31 January, pp. 27-28.

Banu, U. A. B. R.. A. (1981), 'The fall of the Sheikh Mujib Regime-An Analysis', *The Indian Political Science Review*, vol. 15, no. 1, pp. 3-19.

Baum, J., Hoon, S. J. and Smith, C. (1995), 'Grease that Sticks', *Far Eastern Economic Review*, March 23, pp. 54-55.

Baxter, C. (1992), 'Bangladesh in 1991: A Parliamentary System', *Asian Survey*, vol. 32, no. 2, pp. 162-67.

———— (1991), 'Bangladesh in 1990: Another New Begining?', *Asian Survey*, vol. 31, no. 2, pp. 146-52.

———— (1971), 'Pakistan Votes - 1970', *Asian Survey*, vol. XI, no. 3, pp. 197-218.

———— and Rahman, S. (1991), 'Bangladesh Votes – 1991: Building Democratic Institutions', *Asian Survey*, vol. 31, no. 8, pp. 683-93.

———— and Rashiduzzaman, M. (1981), 'Bangladesh Votes: 1978 and 1979', *Asian Survey*, vol. 21, no. 4, pp. 485-500.

Bertocci, P. J. (1986), 'Bangladesh in 1985: Resolute Against the Storms', *Asian Survey*, vol. 35, no. 2, pp. 224-34.

Blais, A. (1988), 'The Classification of Electoral Systems', *European Journal of Political Research*, vol. 16, pp. 99-110.

Brasz, H. A. (1963), 'Some Notes on the Sociology of Corruption', *Sociologica Neerlandica*, vol. 1, no. 2, pp. 111-17.

Brownsberger, W. N. (1983), 'Development and Governmental Corruption: Materialism and Political Fragmentation in Nigeria', *Journal of Modern African Studies*, vol. 21, no. 2, pp. 215-33.

Bull, M. J. and Newell, J. L. (1997), 'New Avenues in the Study of Political Corruption', *Crime, Law and Social Change*, vol. 27, no. 3-4, pp. 169-83.

Chander, P. and Wilde, L. (1992), 'Corruption in Tax Administration', *Journal of Public Economics*, vol. 49, no. 3, pp. 333-50.

Chowdhury, A. N. M. M. A. (1994), 'The Aspect of Caretaker Government, Election and Election Commission: Bangladesh Perspective' (in Bengali), an unpublished paper presented in a seminar organised by the Chittagong University Research Council at Chittagong District Council Auditorium, 12 June.

Correa, H. (1985), 'A Comparative Study of Bureaucratic Corruption in Latin America and the U.S.A', *Socio-Economic Planning Sciences*, vol. 19, no. 1, pp. 63-79.
Crains, A. (1968), 'The Electoral Systems and the Party Systems in Canada, 1921-1965', *Canadian Journal of Political Science*, vol. 1, pp. 55-80.
Deysine, A. (1980), 'Political Corruption: A Review of the Literature', *European Journal of Political Research*, vol. 8, no. 4, pp. 447-65.
Elklit, J. and Svensson, P. (1997), 'What Makes Elections Free and Fair?', *Journal of Democracy*, vol. 8, no. 3, pp. 32-46.
Ershad, H. M. (1981), 'Role of the Military in Bangladesh', *Holiday*, December 6.
────── (1979), 'The Role of Military in Underdeveloped Countries', *Bangladesh Army Journal*, vol. 2, no. 2, pp. 1-12.
Findlay, M. and Chor-Wing, T. C. (1989), 'Sugar Coated Bullets: Corruption and the New Economic Order in China', *Contemporary Crises*, vol. 13, pp. 145-61.
Franda, M. (1981), 'Bangladesh After Zia: A Retrospect and Prospect', *Economic and Political Weekly*, vol. 16, no. 39, 22 August, pp. 1387-94.
Gardiner, A. J. (1993), 'Defining Corruption', *Corruption and Reform*, vol. 7, no. 2, pp. 111-24.
Gehlot, N. S. (1991), 'Elections and Role of Money Power In India', *Indian Journal of Public Administration*, vol. 37, no. 3, pp. 437-47.
George, H. (1883), 'Money in Elections', *North American Review*, CCCXVI, March, pp. 201-202.
Gierzynski, A. and Breaux, D. (1991), 'Money and Votes in State Legislative Elections', *Legislative Studies Quarterly*, vol. 16, no. 2, pp. 203-17.
Gillespie, K. and Okvuhlik, G. (1988), 'Cleaning Up Corruption in the Middle East', *The Middle East Journal*, vol. 42, no. 1, pp. 59-82.
Gomez, E. T. (1996), 'Electoral Funding of General, State and Party Elections in Malaysia', *Journal of Contemporary Asia*, vol. 26, no. 1, pp. 81-97.
Gould, D. J. and Mukendi, T. B. (1989), 'Bureaucratic Corruption in Africa: Causes, Consequences and Remedies', *International Journal of Public Administration*, vol. 12, no. 3, pp. 27-57.
Hakim, M. A. (1998), 'Bangladesh: the Beginning of the End of Militarised Politics?', *Contemporary South Asia*, vol. 7, no. 3, pp. 283-300.
────── (1998), 'The Use of Islam as a Political Legitimization Tool: The Bangladesh Experience, 1972-1990', *Asian Journal of Political Science*, vol. 6, no. 2, pp. 98-117.
────── (1994), 'The Mirpur Parliamentary By-Election in Bangladesh', *Asian Survey*, vol. 34, no. 8, pp. 738-47.
────── (1992), 'Twelfth Constitutional Amendment: Bangladesh's Reversion to Parliamentary System', *Asian Profile*, vol. 20, no. 3, pp. 251-61.
────── (1993), 'Parliamentary Elections in Bangladesh: Comparative Analysis', *Regional Studies*, vol. 11, no. 2, pp. 87-102.
────── (1991), 'The 1991 Parliamentary Elections in Bangladesh: A Review', *Politics, Administration and Change*, no. 17, July-December, pp. 24-38.

────── (1991), 'Legitimacy Crisis and United Opposition: The Fall of Ershad Regime in Bangladesh', *South Asia Journal*, vol. 5, no. 2, pp. 181-93.

────── and Huque, A. S. (1994), 'Constitutional Amendments in Bangladesh', *Regional Studies*, vol. 12, no. 2, pp. 73-90.

Haque, A. (1980), 'Bangladesh 1979: Cry for a Sovereign Parliament', *Asian Survey*, vol. 20, No. 2, pp. 217-30.

────── (1981), 'Bangladesh in 1980: Strains and Stresses – Opposition in the Doldrums', *Asian Survey*, vol. XXI, no. 2, pp. 188-202.

Harsch, E. (1993) 'Accumulators and Democrats: Challenging State Corruption in Africa', *Journal of Modern African Studies*, vol. 31, no. 1, pp. 31-48.

Hariharan, A. (1974), 'India, A Common Goal: Get-Rich-Quick', *Far Eastern Economic Review*, vol. 85, no. 35, pp. 25-26.

Harris, P. (1986), 'Socialist Graft: The Soviet Union and the People's Republic of China – A Preliminary Survey', *Corruption and Reform*, vol. 1, no. 1, pp. 13-32.

Hossain, F. (1996), 'Caretaker Government and the Possibility of Democracy in Bangladesh' (in Bengali), *Lokaoto*, vol. 16, no. 3, July, pp. 21-25.

Hossain, M. (1999), 'Sick Politics and the Educated Class' (in Bengali), *The Daily Ittefaq*, 14 November.

Hossain, S. (1999), 'We are Ashamed, the Nation Astonished, What About You?' (in Bengali), *Sangbad*, 12 November.

Hossain, S. A. (1991), 'Election in the Name of Religion' (in Bengali), *Weekly Bichittra*, 11 April, pp. 21-23.

Hughes, C. A. (1998), 'The Illusive Phenomenon of Fraudulent Voting Practices: A Review Article', *Australian Journal of Politics and History*, vol. 44, no. 3, 1998, pp. 471-91.

Huq, M. M. (1994), 'Elections in Bangladesh: Predicaments and Prospects', *Politics, Administration and Change*, no. 22, January-June, pp.12-25.

Huque, A. S. (1985), 'The Politics of Local Government Reform in Rural Bangladesh', *Public Administration and Development*, vol. 5, no. 3, pp. 205-17.

────── and Akhter, M. Y. (1989), 'Militarisation and Opposition in Bangladesh: Parliamentary Approval and Public Reaction', *The Journal of Commonwealth and Comparative Politics*, vol. 24I, no. 2, pp. 172-84.

────── and Akhter, M. Y. (1987), 'The Ubiquity of Islam: Religion and Society in Bangladesh', *Pacific Affairs*, vol. 60, no. 2, pp. 200-25.

────── and Hakim, M. A. (1993), 'Elections in Bangladesh: Tools of Legitimacy', *Asian Affairs An American Review*, vol. 19, no. 4, pp. 248-61.

Islam, M. R. (1996), 'Free and Fair General Elections in Bangladesh Under the Thirteenth Amendment: A Political – Legal Post-Mortem', *Politics, Administration and Change*, no. 26, July-December, pp. 18-31.

Islam, S. S. (1987), 'Bangladesh in 1986: Entering a New Phase', *Asian Survey*, vol. XXVII, no. II, pp. 163-72.

────── (1986), 'The Rise of Civil-Military Bureaucracy in the State Apparatus of Bangladesh', *Asian Thought and Society*, vol. 11, no. 31, pp. 28-36.

Jahan, R. (1976), 'Bangabandhu and After: Conflict and Change in Bangladesh', *The Round Table*, no. 261, January, pp. 73-84.
────── (1974), 'Bangladesh in 1973: Management of Factional Politics', *Asian Survey*, vol. XIV, no. II, pp. 125-35.
────── (1973), 'Bangladesh in 1972: Nation Building in a New State', *Asian Survey*, vol. XIII, no. 2, pp. 199-210.
Janowitz, M. (1975), 'Military Institutions and Coercion in the Developing Nations', unpublished paper.
Johnston, M. (1996), 'The Search for Definitions: The Vitality of Politics and the Issue of Corruption', *International Social Science Journal*, vol. XLVIII, no. 3, pp. 321-36.
────── (1986), 'The Political Consequences of Corruption: Reassessment', *Comparative Politics*, vol. 18, no. 4, pp. 459-77.
────── and Hao, Y. (1995), 'China's Surge of Corruption', *Journal of Democracy*, vol. 6, no. 4, pp. 80-94.
Kabir, B. M. (1987), 'Movement and Elections: Legitimisation of Military Rule in Bangladesh', unpublished paper presented at the seminar held on the occasion of the Fifth National Conference of the Bangladesh Political Science Association, 13-14 July, Rajshahi University, Bangladesh.
────── (1985), 'Bangladesh Politics 1981-84: Military Rule and the Process of Civilianization', *The Chittagong University Studies* (Social Science), vol. 8, no. 1, pp. 171-208.
Kaium, A. (1999), 'The Prime Minister Has Actually Disrespected Herself' (in Bengali), *Prothom Alo*, 15 November.
Kamaluddin, S. (1981), 'Polling Fist First: As Violence Continues to Mar the Run-Up to the Presidential Election, Fears and Uncertainty Prevail', *Far Eastern Economic Review*, vol. 114, no. 46, 6 November, p. 30.
────── (1981), 'The Military One-Step: Political Parties Publish Their Manifestos for the Presidential Election, But the Army Chief's Statements Prompt New Uncertainty', *Far Eastern Economic Review*, vol. 114, no. 45, 30 October, p. 22.
────── (1981), 'An Eclectic Election: Lending Candidates Stands to Lose Votes to Minor Contestants in a Crowded Field', *Far Eastern Economic Review*, vol. 114, no. 44, 23 October, p. 23.
────── (1980), 'Bangladesh: A Spadeful of Revolution', *Far Eastern Economic Review*, vol. 107, no. 3, January 18, pp. 26-27.
Khan, A. (1999), 'Please Don't Speak Like This' (in Bengali), *Prothom Alo*, 15 November.
Khan, M. R., Adnan, M., Mortaza, G. and Mostafiz, B. (1996), 'Election '96: A Review' (in Bengali), *Weekly Bichittra*, 12 June.
Khan, M. A. (1960), 'Pakistan Perspective', *Foreign Affairs*, vol. 38, no. 4, pp. 546-56.
Khan, M. M. (1987), 'Politics of Administrative Reform and Reorganization in Bangladesh', *Public Administration and Development*, vol. 7, no. 4, pp. 351-62.

———— and Husain, S. A. (1996), 'Process of Democratization in Bangladesh', *Contemporary South Asia*, vol. 5, no. 3, pp. 319-34.
———— and Zafarullah, H. M. (1981), 'Innovations in Village Government in Bangladesh', *Asian Profile*, vol. 9, no. 5, pp. 447-54.
———— and Zafarullah, H. M. (1979), 'The 1979 Parliamentary Elections in Bangladesh', *Asian Survey*, vol. XIX, no. 10, pp. 1023-36.
Khan, Z. R. (1997), 'Bangladesh's Experiments With Parliamentary Democracy', *Asian Survey*, vol. XXXVII, no. 6, pp. 575-89.
———— (1982), 'Bangladesh in 1981: Change, Stability and Leadership', *Asian Survey*, vol. XXII, no. 2, pp. 163-70.
Khanam, J. (1995), 'The Leftist in Bangladesh Politics: Crisis and Sequences', *Asian Profile*, vol. 23, no. 5, pp. 407-14.
Khasru, A. (2000), 'What the CEC Himself Listened and Observed' (in Bengali), *Jai Jai Din*, vol. 16, no. 43, pp. 10-12.
Kiser, E. and Tong, X (1992), 'Determinants of the Amount and Type of Corruption and State Fiscal Bureaucracies: An Analysis of the Late Imperial China', *Comparative Political Studies*, vol. 25, no. 3, pp. 300-31.
Klugman, J. (1986), 'The Psychology of Soviet Corruption, Indiscipline, and Resistance to Reform', *Political Psychology*, vol. 4, pp. 76-82.
Kochanek, S. A. (1997), 'Bangladesh in 1996: The 25th Year of Independence', *Asian Survey*, vol. XXXVII, no. 2, pp. 136-42.
Laski, H. J. (1931), '*Democracy*', in Edwin R. A. S. (ed.), *Encyclopaedia of the Social Sciences*, vol. 5, Macmillan, New York, pp. 76-85.
Laurence, P. (1993), 'The Diehards & Dealmakers', *Africa Report*, vol. 38, no. 6, November-December, pp. 13-16.
Lee, P. N. (1990), 'Bureaucratic Corruption During the Deng Xiaoping Era', *Corruption and Reform*, vol. 5, no. 1, pp. 29-47.
Leiken, R. S. (1996-'97), 'Controlling the Global Corruption Epidemic', *Foreign Policy*, no. 105, Winter, pp. 55-73.
Leys, C. (1965), 'What is the Problem about Corruption?' *Journal of Modern African Studies*, vol. 3, no. 2, pp. 215-44.
Lifschultz, L. (1975), 'Sheikh Mujib Pays the Ultimate Price', *Far Eastern Economic Review*, vol. 89, no. 35, August 29, pp. 10-12.
Liu, A. P. L. (1983), 'The Politics of Corruption in the People's Republic of China', *American Political Science Review*, vol. 77, no. 3, pp. 602-23.
Lowi, T. J. (1981), 'The Intelligent Person's Guide to Political Corruption', *Public Affairs*, series 81, bulletin no. 82.
Machipisa, L. (1997), 'Growing Lobby Against Zim State Corruption', *Guardian*, 17 July.
Mahmud, S. (1996), 'Election Manifesto and the Expectation of the People' (in Bengali), *Weekly Bichittra*, 7 June.
Mahmuduzzaman, M. (2000), 'Tactical Election: Indication for the Future' (in Bengali), *Jai Jai Din,* vol. 16, no. 43, 8 August, pp. 4-10.
Mamoon, M. (1996), 'Legal-Illegal of the Officials of Republic' (in Bengali), *Janakhantha*, 7 April.

Maniruzzaman, T. (1976), 'Bangladesh in 1975: The Fall of the Mujib Regime and Its Aftermath', *Asian Survey*, vol. XVI, no. 2, pp.119-29.
———— (1975), 'Bangladesh: An Unfinished Revolution?', *Journal of Asian Studies*, vol. XXXIV, no. 1, pp. 891-911.
———— (1975), 'Bangladesh in 1974: Economic Crisis and Political Polarization', *Asian Survey*, vol. XV, no. 2, pp. 117-28.
Marican, Y. M. (1979), 'Combating Corruption: The Malaysian Experiences', *Asian Survey*, vol. XIX, no. 6, pp. 597-610.
Mashreque, Md. S. and Rashid, M. A. (1995), 'Parliamentary By-Election in Bangladesh: The Study of Magura-2 Constituency', *Asian Profile*, vol. 23, no. 1, pp. 67-80.
Mattern, W. (1975), 'Mighty Mujib's New Brand of Democracy', *Far Eastern Economic Review*, February 7, pp. 11-13.
Mbaku, J. M. (1996), 'Bureaucratic Corruption in Africa: The Futility of Cleanups', *Cato Journal*, vol. 16, no. 1, pp. 99-118.
———— (1994), 'Bureaucratic Corruption and Policy Reform in Africa', *Journal of Social, Political and Economic Studies*, vol. 19, no. 2, pp. 149-75.
McCook, J. J. (1982), 'The Alarming Proportion of Venal Voters', *The Forum*, 14 September, pp. 1-13.
McHenry, D. F. and Bird, K. (1977), 'Food Bungle in Bangladesh', *Foreign Policy*, vol. 27, Summer, pp. 72-88.
McGrath, A. (1998), 'For Many, Its One Man, A Dozen Votes', *Sydney Morning Herald*, 2 October.
Mia, M. (1998), 'How Free and Fair was 1996 Election?' *Dhaka Courier* (internet edition), issue 17, 20 November.
Mia, R. I. (2000), 'The District Council Act is Anti-constitutional: The Judicious Mind of the President Faces Question Consenting the Bill' (in Bengali), *Inquilab*, 19 July.
Mizanuddin, M. (1985), 'Village-Politics'– A Case Study of Union Parisad Election in Bindopur in 1984', *Bangladesh Journal of Sociology*, vol. 3, no. 1, pp. 198-208.
Muhammad, A. (1988), 'Poverty and Underdevelopment in Bangladesh: Historical Perspective' (in Bengali), *Proshashan Shamikkha*, vol. 2, no. 1, pp.50-53.
Muhit, A. M. A. (2000), 'The District Council Farce' (in Bengali), *Prothom Alo*, 28 July.
Musa, A. B. M. (1999), 'Manners have Weathered Away from Politics' (in Bengali), *Bhorer Kagoj*, 14 November.
Nas, T. F., Price, C. and Weber, C. T.(1986), 'A Policy-Oriented Theory of Corruption', *American Political Science Review*, vol. 80, no. 1, pp. 107-119.
Nazem, N. I. (1978), 'Strategy for Rural Development in Bangladesh: A Review', *BISS Journal*, vol. 8, no. 1.
Nelken, D. and Levi, M. (1996), 'The Corruption of Politics and the Politics of Corruption: An Overview', *Journal of Law and Society*, vol. 23, no. 1, pp. 1-17.
Newman, K. J. (1962), 'The Constitutional Evolution of Pakistan', *International Affairs*, no. 3, July, pp. 353-64.

Nye, J. S. (1967), 'Corruption and Political Development: A Cost-Benefit Analysis', *American Political Science Review*, vol. 61, no. 2, pp. 417-27.

Ostergaard, C. S. (1986), 'Experimenting China's Recent Political Corruption', *Corruption and Reform*, vol. 1, no. 3, 209-33.

Ouchi, M. (1982), 'The Mechanisms of Political Corruption With Special Reference to Political Donations', *Politics, Administration and Change*, vol. 7, no. 2, pp. 1-8.

Peters, J. J. and Welch, S. (1978), 'Political Corruption in America: A Search For Definition and a Theory', *American Political Science Review*, vol. 78, no. 3, pp. 974-84.

Pinto-Duschinsky, M. (1976), 'The Survival of Political Corruption in Advanced Democracies', a paper presented in The International Political Science Association, World Congress, Edinburgh.

Quadir, F. (1991), 'National Parliamentary Election 1991: A Review' (in Bengali), *The Journal for Human Development*, vol. 3, no. 4, pp. 49-62.

Rahman, A.T.R. (1974), 'Administration and Its Political Environment in Bangladesh', *Pacific Affairs*, vol. 47, no. 2, pp. 171-91.

Rahman, Md. A. (1984), 'Bangladesh in 1983: A Turning Point for the Military', *Asian Survey*, vol. 24, no. 2, pp. 240-49.

—————— (1983), 'Bangladesh in 1982: Beginnings of the Second Decade', *Asian Survey*, vol. XXIII, no. 2, pp. 149-57.

Rahman, H. Z. (1998), 'Union Elections ! A Postscript', *Holiday*, 13 January.

—————— (1990), 'The Landscape of Violence: Elections and Political Culture in Bangladesh', *The Journal of Social Studies*, no.49, July pp. 83-91.

Rahman, M. S. (1995), 'Ethics of Hartal', *The Daily Star*, 14 November.

Rahman, S. (1989), 'Bangladesh in 1988: Precarious Institution Building Amid Crisis Management', *Asian Survey*, vol. XXIX, no. II, pp. 216-22.

Rashid, A. (1996), 'Delayed Action: President Leghari Bumbles Political Clean-up', *Far Eastern Economic Review*, 19 December, p. 28-29.

Rashiduzzaman, M. (1998), 'Bangladesh's Chittagong Hill Tracts Peace Accord: Institutional Features and Strategic Concerns', *Asian Survey*, vol. XXXVIII, no. 7, pp. 653-70.

—————— (1997), 'Political Unrest and Democracy in Bangladesh', *Asian Survey*, vol. XXXVII, no. 3, pp. 254-68.

—————— (1979), 'Bangladesh 1978: Search for a Political Party', *Asian Survey*, vol. XIX, no. II, pp. 191-97.

—————— (1978), 'Bangladesh in 1977: Dilemmas of the Military Rulers', *Asian Survey*, vol. XVII, no. 2, pp. 126-34.

Reddi, A. E. and Ram, S. D. (1991), 'Administering Clean and Fair Elections In India', *Indian Journal of Public Administration*, vol. 37, no.3, pp. 310-23.

Root, H. (1996), 'Corruption in China: Has It Become Systemic?', *Asian Survey*, vol. XXXVI, no. 8, pp. 741-57.

Roy, J. G. (1991), 'Electoral Violence and Role of Law And Order Administration', *Indian Journal of Public Administration*, vol. 37, no. 3, pp. 383-91.

Schwartz, C. A. (1997), 'Corruption and Political Development in the U.S.S.R', *Comparative Politics*, vol. 11, no. 4, pp. 425-43.

Sen, D. (1981), 'Bangla Army Chief Insists on Role in Government', *Hindustan Times*, November 22.

Shehabuddin, E. (1999), 'Bangladesh in 1998: Democracy on the Ground', *Asian Survey*, vol. XXXIX, no. 1, pp. 148-54.

Singhal, D. P. (1962), 'Democracy With Distrust', *Australian Journal of Politics and History*, vol. 8, no. 2, November, pp. 200-13.

Singmal, M. A. (1979), '1978 Presidential Election In Bangladesh', *Indian Journal of Political Science*, vol. 40, no. 1, pp. 97-110.

Smith, T. B. (1986), 'Referendum Politics in Asia', *Asian Survey*, vol. XXVI, no. 7, pp. 793-814.

Staatts, S. J. (1972), 'Corruption in the Soviet System', *Problems of Communism*, vol. 21, no. 1, pp. 40-47.

Sun, Y. (1991), 'The Chinese Protests of 1989: The Issue of Corruption', *Asian Survey*, vol. 31, pp. 762-83.

Syed, A. H. (1991), 'The Pakistan People's Party And The Punjab: National Assembly Elections 1988 and 1990', *Asian Survey*, vol. XXXI, no. VII, pp. 581-97.

Szeftel, M. (1982), 'Political Graft and the Spoils System in Zambia – The State as a Resource in Itself', *Review of African Political Economy*, no. 24, May-August, pp. 5-21.

Tanner, S. J. (1995), 'Defining 'Political Corruption' in Light of Metherell Inquiry', *Legislative Studies*, vol. 10, no. 1, pp. 48-58.

Thomas, S. J. (1989), 'Do Incumbent Campaign Expenditure Matters?', *Journal of Politics*, vol. 51, pp. 965-76.

Tilman, R. O. (1986), 'Emergence of Black-Market Bureaucracy: Administration, Development and Corruption in the New States', *Public Administration Review*, vol. 28, no. 5, pp. 437-44.

Treisman, D. (1998), 'The Role and Power of Money in Russia's Transitional Elections', *Comparative Politics*, vol. 31, no. 1, pp. 1-22.

Ved, M. (1981), 'Bangladesh Under Ziaur Rahman: An Analytical Survey', *Foreign Affairs Reports*, vol. XXX, no. IX, pp. 175-204.

Wahhab, M. A. (1985), 'Attitude of the Rural Leaders Towards Rural Development', *Bangladesh Political Studies*, vol. 8, pp. 66-81.

Wallace, P. (1978), 'Centralization and Depoliticisation in South Asia', *The Journal of Commonwealth and Comparative Politics*, vol. XVI, no. 1, pp. 3-21.

Weinbaum, M. G. (1977), 'The March 1977 Elections in Pakistan: Where Everyone Lost', *Asian Survey*, vol. XVII, no. VII, pp. 599-618.

Weingrod, A. (1968), 'Patrons, Patronage and Political Parties', *Comparative Studies in Society and History*, vol. 10, July, pp. 377-400.

Welch, W. P. (1981), 'Money and Votes: A Simultaneous Equation Model', *Public Choice*, vol. 36, pp. 209-34.

——— (1976) 'The Effectiveness of Expenditures in State Legislative Races', *American Politics Quarterly*, vol. 36, pp. 336-58.

Werlin, H. H. (1973), 'The Consequences of Corruption: The Ghanaian Experiences', *Political Science Quarterly*, vol. 88, no. 1, pp. 71-85.

Xie, B. (1988), 'The Functions of the Chinese Procuratorial Organ in the Combat Against Corruption', *Asian Journal of Public Administration*, vol. 10, pp. 71-79.

Yang, M. M. (1991), 'The Gift Economy and State Power in China', *Contemporary Studies in Society and History*, vol. 31, pp. 25-54.

Yeh, M. (1987), 'Modernisation and Corruption in Mainland China', *Issues and Studies*, vol. 23, pp. 11-27.

Zafarullah, H. (1998), 'Consolidating Democratic Governance: One Step Forward, Two Steps Back', a paper presented at the 12 Biennial Conference of the Asian Studies Association, Australia, University Of New South Wales, Sydney, 28 September – 1 October.

———— (1987), 'Public Administration in the First Decade of Bangladesh', *Asian Survey*, vol. 27, no. 4, April, pp.468,474-75.

———— and Akhter, M. Y. (2000), 'Non-Political Caretaker Administrations and Democratic Elections in Bangladesh: An Assessment', *Government and Opposition*, vol. 35, no. 3, pp. 345-69.

———— and Akhter, M. Y. (1998) 'Military Rule, Civilianization and Electoral Corruption: Pakistan and Bangladesh in Perspective', unpublished paper.

Zaman, H. (1983), 'The Role of Military in Bangladesh and Pakistan: A Comparative Study', *Asian Profile*, vol. 11, no. 4, pp. 377-96.

Zaman, M.Q. (1984), 'Ziaur Rahman: Leadership Styles and Mobilization Policies', *The Indian Political Science Review*, vol. XVIII, no. 2, pp. 194-203.

Ziring, L. (1993), 'The Second Stage In Pakistani Politics: The 1993 Elections', *Asian Survey*, vol. XXXIII, no. XII, pp. 1175-85.

———— (1991), 'Pakistan in 1990: The Fall of Benazir Bhutto', *Asian Survey*, vol. XXXI, no. II, pp. 111-24.

Reports, theses and other documents

A Background Paper on Bangladesh Fifth Parliament Elections, Press Information Department (1991), Government of the People's Republic of Bangladesh, February.

Bangladesh Documents, Published by the Ministry of External Affairs, Government of Pakistan (n. d.), vol. 1.

Bangladesh Parliamentary Elections June 12, 1996, The Report of the Fair Election Monitoring Alliance (1996), FEMA, 30 July, Dhaka.

By-election Held In National Constituency No. 69 Pabna-2 On 10 December 1998, Fair Election Monitoring Alliance (n. d.), FEMA, Dhaka.

By-election to 15 Constituencies Held on September 5, 1996, The Report of the Fair Election Monitoring Alliance (1996), FEMA, 30 September, Dhaka.

Carino, L. V. and DeLeon, J. H. (1983), '*Final Report of the Study of Graft and Corruption, Red Tape and Inefficiency in Government*, Mimeo, Manila.

Huque, A. S. (1984), 'The Problems of Local Government Reform in Rural Bangladesh', PhD dissertation, The University of British Columbia, Canada.
Indorf, H. H. (1969), 'Party System Adaptation to Political Development in Malaysia During the First Decade of Independence, 1957-1967', PhD thesis, New York University.
Islam, S. T. (1994), *A Post-Poll Survey on Magura-2 Constituency*, Coordinating Council for Human Rights in Bangladesh (CCHRB), Dhaka.
Keesing's Research Report (1973), *Pakistan: From 1947 to the Creation of Bangladesh*, Kessing's Publications, New York.
Media Guide: Bangladesh Parliament Election June '96, (1996), Press Information Department (PID), Ministry of Information, Government of the People's Republic of Bangladesh, 1 June.
Mohan, S. C. (1987), 'The Control of Corruption in Singapore', PhD thesis, University of London.
Nazem, Md. N. I. (1985), 'Approach to Decentralise Development in Bangladesh: An Examination of Its Efficacy', Masters thesis (No. Hs-85-9), The Asian Institute of Technology, Bangkok.
Parliamentary Elections in Bangladesh 27 February 1991, The Report of the Commonwealth Observer Report (1991), Commonwealth Secretariat, London.
Pinto-Duschinsky, M. (1976), 'The Survival of Political Corruption in Advanced Democracies', a paper presented in The International Political Science Association, World Congress, Edinburgh.
Preliminary Statement of the NDI Observer Delegation to the June 12, 1996 Parliamentary Elections in Bangladesh (1996), National Democratic Institute For International Affairs, Washington D.C.
Pratap, A. (1996), 'Bangladesh Election Tests Future of Young Democracy: Voters Want Peace, Security, Jobs', a CNN television report, broadcast on 12 June.
The Parliamentary Elections in Bangladesh 12 June 1996, The Report of the Commonwealth Observer Group (1996), Commonwealth Secretariat, London.
Thomas, J. W. (1968), 'Rural Public Works Program and East Pakistan's Development', PhD dissertation, Harvard University.
Timm, F. R. W. (ed.) (1996), *Bangladesh: Parliamentary Election '96 Observation Report*, Coordinating Council for Human Rights in Bangladesh, Dhaka.
U. S. Department of State, Background Notes: Bangladesh (1996), prepared by the Bureau of Public Affairs, (internet edition) July.
Union Parisad Elections, 1997, The Report of the Fair Election Monitoring Alliance (1998), FEMA, Dhaka.
1997 Statistical Yearbook of Bangladesh, Bangladesh Bureau of Statistics, Statistics Division, Ministry of Planning (1998), Government of the People's Republic of Bangladesh, Dhaka.

278 *Electoral Corruption*

Newspapers and periodicals

English

Asia Weekly (Hong Kong).
Baluchistan Times (Baluchistan daily, Pakistan).
Dhaka Courier (Dhaka weekly).
Economic and Political Weekly (Mumbai, India).
Far Eastern Economic Review (Hong Kong weekly).
Hindustan Times (Indian daily).
Holiday (Dhaka weekly).
Morning News (Karachi daily).
New York Times (New York daily).
The Bangladesh Observer (Dhaka daily).
The Bangladesh Times (Dhaka daily).
The Daily Star (Dhaka daily).
The Dawn (Karachi daily).
The Economist (London daily).
The Financial Times (London daily).
The Guardian (London daily).
The Hindu (South Indian daily).
The Independent (London daily).
The Pakistan Observer (Dhaka daily, now known as *The Bangladesh Observer*).
The Pakistan Times (Lahore daily).
The Statesman (Calcutta daily).
The Sydney Morning Heralds (Australian daily).
The Times (Indian weekly).
The Tribune (Khulna daily).
The Washington Post (Washington daily).

Bengali

Ajker Kagoj (Dhaka daily).
Azad (Dhaka daily).
Banglabazar Patrika (Dhaka daily).
Banglar Bani (Dhaka daily).
Bhorer Kagoj (Dhaka daily).
Chitrabangla (Dhaka weekly).
Deshchinta (Dhaka weekly).
Inquilab (Dhaka daily).
Jai Jai Din (Dhaka weekly).
Janakhantha (Dhaka daily).
Janatar Dak (Dhaka daily).
Palabadal (Dhaka fortnightly).

Prothom Alo (Dhaka daily).
Robbar (Dhaka weekly).
Samachar (Dhaka daily).
Sangbad (Dhaka daily).
Somoy (Dhaka weekly).
Swadesh Barta (Sydney weekly).
The Daily Al Mujaddid (Dhaka).
The Daily Ittefaq (Dhaka).
The Daily Millat (Dhaka).
The Daily Purbakone (Chittagong).
The Daily Rupali (Dhaka).
The Daily Sangram (Dhaka).
Weekly Bichittra (Dhaka).
Weekly Purnima (Dhaka).

Urdu

Nawai Waqt (Pakistani daily).
The Daily Jang (Pakistani daily).
Weekly Takbeer (Pakistan).

Index

administration
    caretaker 27, 161, 227
    Chinese 12
    civil 63, 206
    local 119
    militarisation of 62, 78
    Mughal 44
    non-partisan 6
administrative change 62
administrative machinery 105, 133, 161, 205
administrative mismanagement 150
administrative morality 14
administrative neutrality 180, 194
administrative reform 118
administrative units
    division 51
    district 51
    upazila 51, 138
    union 51
adult franchise 106
Ahmed, I. 70
Ahmed, K. M. (Mushtataque) 56
    Mushtaque government 56
Ahmed, M. 147
Ahmed, N. U. 154
Ahmed, S. 67, 179, 209
Ahmed, T. 52
Akhter, M. Y. 30r, 31r, 35r, 39r, 42r, 79r, 86r-88r, 90r, 117r, 140r, 141r, 203, 211r, 213r, 214r
Al-Rajee, A. 147, 173r
Ali, C. M. 102
amendment of the constitution
    fifth 123
    fourth 94, 123
    thirteenth 27
    twelfth 67, 95
American society 10, 11
anti-Bangladeshi role 58, 126
anti-election activists 164, 218

anti-election group 163
anti-liberation force 69, 166
anti-liberation role 166
anti-national feelings 46
anti-social activities 155
Anyaoku, E. 69
arrests 102
    house 128
Asian Profile 42r, 82r, 87r, 89r, 112r, 140r, 153, 174r, 175r, 212r, 213r
Asian Survey 34r-37r, 41r, 42r, 79r, 82r, 83r, 84r, 87r-89r, 92r, 89r, 109, 112r, 115r, 138r, 140r, 141r, 154, 174r, 211r, 212r, 215r
assembly election(s) 44
    1944 provincial 96, 216
    first national 101, 111
    provincial 101, 107, 216
    second 112
Azad, A. S. 190
Azam, G. 200

ballot boxes 149, 157, 163
    forced staffing of 19
    hijacking of 205, 222, 224
    snatching of 17, 165
    stuffing 205
ballot papers 100, 128, 163
    hijacking 224
Bangabhaban 149
Bangladesh 49, 55, 118
Bangladesh Aid Group 74
Bangladesh Human Rights Commission 168
Bangladesh Penal Code 157
Bangladesh Public Service Commission (PSC) 51
Bangladesh Television (BTV) 159, 199, 209
Bangladesh *Unnayan Parisad* (BUP) 204

Index 281

Barisal 167
basic democracy (BD) 26, 48, 216
basic democrats 49, 100
    literacy of 99
Baxter, C. 37r, 41r, 42r, 89r, 108, 109,
    112, 116r, 117r, 138r, 139r, 174r,
    211r
Bay of Bengal 43
BBC 167
BBC correspondent 131
BBC journalist 130
Bengali 45
Bhasani, A. H. K. 95, 96, 115r, 144
Bhutto, Z. A. 50, 51, 81r, 101, 102, 106,
    116r
bid-rigging 12
Bihar 20, 21
black chapter 134
black day 133
black laws 125, 130, 183
black marketeering 46
bombs 76, 164
borough monger 20
bribery 6, 10, 12, 14, 17
    direct 20
    extent of 12
bribery items 23
bribes 11, 12, 14, 22, 54
    cash 22
    electoral 22, 23
bribing electoral officials 224
British high commissioner 167
Bryce, J. 10, 33r
bureaucracy 62, 143, 157, 216, 219
    central 62,, 191, 194
    civil 3, 47, 55, 58, 130, 167, 192,
        218, 222
    civil-military 46, 54, 111, 196, 218,
        219
    military 105
    Thai 12
bureaucratic bias 108, 167
bureaucratic machinery 62
bureaucratic neutrality 209
bureaucratic partisanship 5
bureaucratic rebellion 192
by-elections 72, 166, 178, 218, 228, 228
    Barisal 167
    Chittagong 167

    Jhalakati 168
    Lakkhipur 167
    Magura 28, 67, 143, 159, 160, 161,
        168, 170, 172, 175r
    Mirpur 28, 175r
    Pabna, 167
    Tangail 168
    Uttar Pradesh 22

Calcutta 51
campaign 108
    door-to-door 155
    election 105, 122
    electoral 21, 105
    influence of songs in the 28
    one-sided 28
    past-oriented 191
campaign fund 19
campaign offices 223
campaign meetings 101, 102
campaign techniques 28, 104, 198
campaign tour 105
Canada 18
Caretaker Government Bill 192
censorship 3,
charisma 52, 61, 144, 145, 168, 218, 225
charismatic leaders 147
Chashi, M. A. 56
check posts 181
Chief Adviser 193
Chief Martial Law Administrator
    (CMLA) 122, 133
Chief Election Commissioner (CEC) 75,
    76, 106, 146, 156, 160, 162, 167,
    168, 193
Chief Justice 179
Chinese society 12
Chittagong 152, 157, 164, 205
Chittagong Hill Tracts (CHT) Peace
    Accord 74
citizens' committee 147
city corporations 51
civil rights 111
civil society 28, 66
civilian autocrat 6
civilian governments 29
civilian makeup 49
civilian rulers 94
civilianisation strategy 64, 127

282 *Electoral Corruption*

civil-military bureaucrats 21
code of conduct 73, 167, 195, 198, 209
    12-point 156
    16-point 181
    violation of the 29, 167
Collaborators' Act 55
commander-in-chief 122
Commonwealth Secretariat (London) 25
Congress Party 14
consensus 4, 95, 152, 179, 224
    national 196
conspiracy 145, 159, 164
    bureaucratic 205
    era of 184
    international 159
constituent assembly 144
constitution
    1946 43
    Bangladesh 94
    Islamic 96
Constitution Commission 49
constitution amendment bill
    thirteenth 72, 165, 173, 192, 193
    twelfth 151, 152
constitutional crisis 71
corrupt officials 10
corruption 21, 55, 58, 59, 62, 78, 103, 118, 126, 131, 143, 155, 164, 170, 178, 196 198
    bureaucratic 46
    concealing 12
    consequences of 7
    defining 7
    degree of 108, 118, 143, 168, 207
    emergence of 9
    estimate of 108
    extent of 9, 55
    high level political 11
    level of 171
    modernisation thesis of 9
    nature of 94
    non-political 10
    organised 10
    political 10, 11, 12, 13, 14, 16
    political and administrative 2, 9
    post-polling 19
    prevalence of 14
    problem of 14
    rampant 9, 12
    teamwork 12
    ubiquity of 14
    unbridled 156
    unprecedented 61
corruption research 29
corruption stories 14
corruption of Hungary
corruption scandals 11
coup(s) 29, 56, 119, 121, 149
    abortive 59
    August 56, 133
    bloodless 150
    bloody 56
    counter- 29, 56
    Ershad's 61
    military 59, 60
criminals 156, 223
culture 8
    anti-democratic 46
    confrontational 75
    democratic 225
    electoral 5, 7, 216, 219, 222, 227, 228
    hartal 77
    hung bao 12
    parliamentary 223
    political 220, 225
    Third World electoral 5
Curzon, L. 44

dango (bid-rigging) 11
Daulatpur 187
decentralisation 43
    administrative 61, 62, 78, 130
democracy 112, 156
    basic 111
    consolidation of 15, 95
    degree of 4
    liberal 3
    parliamentary 29, 46, 55, 68, 94, 144 123, 125, 130, 217
    people's 122, 125
    production-oriented 125
    tragedy for 130
    values of 143
democratic competition 6
democratic consolidation 29, 43, 216, 223, 224, 227, 229
democratic freedom 1.
democratic game 224, 228
democratic norms 182, 227

democratic tradition 148
democratic values 225, 228
democratisation 1, 94, 112, 118, 150
  problems of 94
  process of 30, 94
  over- 59
Deputy Commissioner (DC) 167, 193, 194
Dhaka 51, 152, 156, 157, 157, 205
Dhaka City Corporation 159
Dhaka University 67
dilly dallying tactic 71
diplomatic missions 63
dishonest politicians 225
donations 21, 195, 221
  big 22
  underhand 17
  voluntary 195
dual registration 224
Dutch ambassador 167

East Bengal 43, 45
East Bengal Legislative Assembly 95
East India Company 13, 14
East Pakistan 26, 43, 45-47, 50, 64, 96, 101, 107, 111, 216
economic development 47, 97, 150
economic development policies 109
economic elites 19
economic exploitation 77
economic shelter 5, 22
Economist (London) 96
education ministry 14
ethnic identity 57
election(s) 49, 129, 131, 145, 156, 226
  1960
  American 15, 16
  basic democracy 98
  British 20, 137
  Chittagong City Corporation 168
  city corporation (CC) 152, 155, 157
  democratic 209
  direct 5, 106
  fair 15, 27, 69, 100, 178, 179, 181, 193, 194, 224
  farcical 72, 164
  farcical one-party 163
  first BD 100
  first city corporation 28
  free 6, 130

free and fair 6, 14, 17, 50, 64, 66, 68, 178
general 47, 111, 112
indirect 97, 216
Lebanese 20
local government 28, 78, 98, 146, 152, 153
mid-term 74, 76
mock 129, 164
one-party 192
state-managed 3
symbolic 128
transparent 209
union *parisad* 119
upazila 62
election booth 134
  capturing 135
election camps 102
Election Commission(s) (EC) 20, 68, 71, 75, 76, 100, 128, 130, 133, 150, 155, 156, 160, 162, 164, 165, 168, 171, 172, 179, 183, 185, 188, 195, 199, 205, 210, 221, 222, 224, 227, 229
EC officials 30
EC tribunal 167
election expenditure 20
election machinery 5, 29, 178
election monitoring teams 29, 179
  American Embassy's monitoring team 163
  Coordinating Council for Human Rights in Bangladesh (CCHRB) 185, 186
  European Community election observation group 185
  Fair Election Monitoring Alliance (FEMA) 167, 177r, 195, 196, 200, 201, 213r-215r
  Liberty Forum 185
  National Democratic Institute (NDI) (Washington) 25, 214r
  SAARC 86, 214r
election officials 18
Election Training Institute 195
election tribunal 205
electoral analysts 184, 219
electoral battle 19
electoral climate 17

284 *Electoral Corruption*

electoral college 97, 99, 100,101, 103, 105, 216
Electoral College Act, 1954 99
electoral competition 29
electoral corruption 7, 14, 15, 16, 17, 18, 19, 28, 29, 30, 94, 111, 138, 143, 166, 171, 216, 227, 228
    American 16
    Australian 15
    degree of 178
    measuring 108
electoral deception 22
electoral fairness 26
electoral farce 168
electoral fight 147
electoral fraud 137, 216, 226
electoral laws 16, 17, 181
electoral machine 20
electoral machinery 152
electoral malfeasance 1, 6, 29, 216, 224
electoral manipulation 149, 227
electoral pathology 30
electoral policy 228
electoral processions 188, 198
Electoral Reforms Commission 95
electoral rights 5
electoral rolls 17, 100, 179
electoral strategy 65, 145
electoral symbols 23, 221
    daripallah (scale) 23
    dhaner sheesh (sheaf of rice) 23
    langal (plough) 23
    nauka (boat) 23
electoral transparency 6, 30, 229
electoral victory 19
electorate 125
embezzlement of funds 13
en masse resignation 71, 219
Ershad, H. M. (Ershad) 59, 60, 87r, 118, 129, 132-34, 137, 147, 150, 190, 198, 199, 226
    18-point Implementation Committee 63
    18-point socio-economic programme 61
    Ershad government 62, 65, 66, 153
    Ershad regime 127, 130, 137, 155
    Ershad's portrait 128

Ershad's resignation 134, 190
Ershad's autocratic rule 137
Ershad's legitimisation strategy 128
external threats 2
European scholars 25

faction
    Mujibnagar 53
    non-Mujibnagar 53
    repatriates from Pakistan 53, 54
factionalism 53, 59
falsification of reports 12
falsification of voter identity 17
famine 126
favouritism 7, 58
Federation of the Bangladesh Chambers of Commerce and Industry (FBCCI) 71, 165
female campaign teams 198
five-point demands 64, 123, 192
folk singers 198
Foreign Affairs 95
foreign agent 54
forgery 16
four-point formula 66
fraud 12, 16, 135
    electoral 16, 137, 147
    Yazoo land 10
fraudulent election practices 18
fraudulent practices 15
freedom fighter 58
freedom of press 51, 111, 123, 130, 183
freelance researchers 25
friendship treaty with India 196, 198, 206
fundamental rights 123
fundamentalist party 184

Gain, P. 141r, 180, 210r, 211r
Gandhi, I. 20
Ganges Water Treaty 74
gaps
    cultural 1, 2
    economic 1, 2,
    political 1
    social and cultural 2,
Gartia 12
Ghana 13

gherao (besiege) 165
glorious chapter 134
golden era 184
Gono Forum 68
Good governance 73
government(s)
    AL 168
    BNP 161. 194
    caretaker 43, 129. 179, 192. 193, 224
    central 96
    civilian 25, 29, 97. 128. 143, 171,
        216, 223, 229
    constitutional 50
    interim 24
    international interim 24
    military 64, 111, 112, 133, 153, 171,
        209, 223, 224, 226
    revolutionary provisional 24
Government of India Act, 1925 44, 94
graffiti 76. 155, 184, 199. 221
gram sarkar 197
Grameen Bank 204
Great Britain 18, 20
Greek society 4. 10
guanxi (connections) 12
guerrilla groups 52
gun fights 188
Gupta C. 13

Hakim, M. A. 37r, 38r, 41r, 42r, 83r,
    85r-89r. 112r. 135. 140r-142r.153.
    173r-175r, 210r, 212r
Haq, A. K. F. 95. 96
Hartal (strike) 73. 128. 133. 135. 161.
    164, 191. 222
    curfew 168
    Landscape of 76
    politics of 79
Hasina, S. 60, 65, 72, 89r, 92r, 128. 129,
    133, 149, 155. 161. 189. 193. 201-
    03, 225
    government of consensus 73
    Hasina government 73. 166
    Hasina regime 166
High Court 65. 199
hijacking
    ballot boxes 19, 222
    ballot books 167
hiring taxis for electioneering 20
holy war 20

Home Ministry 131
hooligan groups 20
Hossain, K. 68, 82r, 91r, 147-49
Huda, M. N. 150
Human rights organisations 156
human rights violations 73

illegal arms 54, 156, 171, 181, 193. 194
illegal financing 11
illegal exchange 22
illiteracy 5
imperialism 125
Independent Commission Against
    Corruption (ICAC) 11
India 25, 43-45, 52, 54, 74, 118, 183
    anti-Indian stand 78, 190
    Indian army 53
    Indian Chief Election Commissioner
        22
    Indian election 21
    Indian electoral system 21
    Indian government 54
    Indian National Congress (INC) 44,
        45
Indonesia 3.
    society 12
    corruption 12
information minister 137
institutional autonomy 2,
international donor community 25
intimidation 6, 15. 99, 102. 108. 137,
    160, 170, 205, 209, 216, 217, 219,
    222, 227
    physical 164
Ishtiaq's formula 70
Islam 46, 65. 111, 125, 196
Islami Oikyo Jote (IOJ)
Islamic dress 206
Islamic forces 207
Islamic missionary 43
Islamic Republic 58, 196
Islamic rightist political parties 58
Islamic socialism 107
Islamic state 45
Islamic values 197

Jalil, M. A. 82r, 145, 147, 149
janatar mancha (platform of the people)
    191
Jhalakathi 168, 177r

Jihad 197
Jinnah, F. 103, 105
Jinnah, M. A. 45, 47, 103-05

Kautylla 13
Kenya 13
Khaldun, A. R. I. 13, 64
Khalishpur 187
Khan, A. A. 131
Khan, L. A. 46, 47
Khan, M. A. (Ayub) 47, 81r, 95, 97, 101,
    103, 104, 108, 109, 111, 112r, 115r,
    122, 226
    Ayub regime 47, 97, 101
Khan, Y.(Yahya) 49, 50, 97, 108, 109,
    116r, 226
    Yahya interregnum 50
Khulna 91r, 152, 156, 177r, 187
Kinship 147, 225

Lakkhipur 167, 177r
Lahore Resolution 44, 45
landowners 220
Laski, V. 11, 33r
law and order maintaining forces in
    elections
    Ansar 163
    Bangladesh Rifles (BDR) 163
    Jatiya Rakkhi Bahini (JRB) 53, 54,
        55, 146144
    Metropolitan Police 181
    para-military 164, 181
    Police 163, 181
leadership crisis 46
Leary, C. O' 16
Left Front 69
leftist parties 127
Legal Framework Order (LFO) 106
legitimacy 3, 60, 61, 64, 65, 105, 132,
    134, 138, 144
    democratic 6
    political 78,127, 225, 226
    unofficial 21
legitimacy crisis 26
legitimacy problems 171
liaison committee 163, 165
liberation 170
liberation forces 122
liberation war 50, 53, 58, 122, 147
Lifschultz, L. 56

local government reform 127
Local Government (Zila Parisad)
    Amendment Bill 63
Lok Sabha 21
looting 149
    banks 53
lower income group
Lowi, T. J. 8

Machiavellian methods 109
magistrates 167
Magura 218
Magura Circuit House 160
Majlish-e-Shura 205
Majumder, S. 147
maladministration 143
Malaysian parliament 13
malpractice(s) 118, 131, 147, 152, 165,
    172, 178, 202
    electoral 6, 15, 16, 218
manifesto(s) 124, 125, 182
    21-point 96
    AL-MU 125
    BNP 125, 147, 197
    PPP 107
manipulation of the ballot 19
Marcos 12
martial law 47, 49, 57, 60, 61, 65, 105,
    106, 123, 128, 129, 134
    withdrawal of 129
martial law administrator (MLA) 47, 65
martial law tribunals 65
massive victory 27
Mecapegal 12
Mecca 206
media 143, 152, 185, 199, 207, 216
    autonomy of electronic 183
    electronic 146, 161, 170, 199, 217,
        222, 227, 227
    government controlled 105, 170
    electronic111,
    official 104
    officially controlled 120
    print 222
    state-controlled 5, 216
    state-owned electronic 69
    state-run 2
media reports 9
Meiji University 11
Middle East 8

Middle Eastern States 13
MIG-29 jet fighters 74
military bureaucrats 60
military-bureaucratic control 49
military dictator 6, 122
military interventions 1, 61
military juntas 5, 76
military rulers 6, 26, 28, 56
    Third World 119
military style 218
military takeover 1, 2, 26, 59, 94, 122, 148
military training 3,
miscreants 156, 223
misuse of public office 12
misusing public funds 13
Mitra, D. 13
Mohammadpur 163
Mohammadullah (Hafezji Huzur) 133, 147
money 99
    black 21, 75, 181, 205
    colour of 21
    head 22
    rate- 13
    role of 221
    use of 19
monetary transactions 10
moneylenders 220
movement 178, 198
    anti-British 44
    anti-BNP 194
    anti-Ershad 134, 182, 190
    anti-government 74, 206
    anti-military 127, 130
    anti-Pakistani 77
    anti-regime 27, 49, 79, 134
    democratic 192
    freedom 56, 122
    mass 149
    non-cooperation
    opposition 129
    six-point
Mughal empire 43
mukti bahini (freedom force) 52
municipalities 51
murder 149
murubbi (family heads) 220
muscleman 134
Musharraf, K. 56

Myanmar 3, 43

Narayan, J. 20
national anthem 133
National Economic Council 150
national identity 47
National Parliament (*Jatiya Sangsad*) 50, 52, 68, 165, 182, 192
National Security Council 59
national traitors 129
national unity 122
nationalised industries 54
nationalism 125
    Bangladeshi 122, 125, 184
    Bengali 47, 57, 77, 183
nationalist forces 198, 206
Nazimuddin, K. 81r, 100, 115r
neo-colonialism 125
nepotism 46, 58
New York 20
newspapers (Bengali)
    Inquilab 89r, 90r, 93r, 175r, 177r, 204, 210
    Ittefaq 93r, 139r, 140r, 174r, 176r, 201, 202
    Janakhantha 201, 202
    Janatar Dak 204
    Millat 204
    Rupali 204, 214r
    Samachar 204
    Sangbad 90r, 175r, 204, 214r
    The Daily Sangram 86r, 153, 214r
newspapers (English)
    The Bangladesh Observer 91r, 139r, 140r, 173r, 175r, 176r, 201, 202, 212r-215r
    The Daily Star 92r, 156, 158, 174r, 175r, 177r, 201, 202
    People's Daily 12
    The Times (London) 128
Nigeria 13
nightmare 184
Nil Darpan 13
no-strike deal 74
nomination papers 181
non-governmental organisation (NGO) 25, 204, 206, 207, 210
    NGO workers 163
    partisan activities of the 204

288 *Electoral Corruption*

non-partisan caretaker government
   (NCG) 24, 66-70, 72, 73, 79, 134,
   161, 163, 165, 166, 172, 173, 178,
   181, 185, 188, 192-95, 199, 204,
   206, 207, 209, 210, 217-19, 229
   constitutionalised 219
   first 179
   Habib 207, 209
   Sahabuddin 207, 209
North America 8
North West Frontier Province (NWFP)
   95
Nye, J. S. 7, 8, 31r, 32r

office selling 11
officer(s)
   polling 23
   presiding 23
official investigation 9
one-party entry 145
one-sided victory 26
Organisation of Islamic Countries (OIC)
   183
Orisa 21
Osmani, M. A. G. 122, 147, 148

Pabna 167, 168
Pakistan 43, 46, 49, 94, 96, 100, 106,
   118, 143, 226
   Pakistan army 51
   Pakistani internal colonialism 45
   Pakistani rule 25
   Pakistani rulers 46
   Pakistani society 14
*Parbatta Chattagram Jana Sanghati
   Samity* (PCJSS) 74
parliamentary crisis 67
parliamentary debates 73
parliamentary elections 57, 61, 64, 67,
   68, 70, 106, 118, 123, 131, 138, 146,
   159, 165, 220, 226, 229
   1960 121
   fifth 25, 27, 67, 129, 151, 179, 182,
      185, 207, 209
   first 26, 53, 143, 144, 171, 217
   fourth 27, 65, 134, 137, 218
   second 26, 123, 124, 126, 127, 217
   seventh 25, 27, 78, 166, 173, 179,

   191, 193, 196, 207, 209, 210
   third 27, 65, 127-129, 131, 217
   sixth 27, 72, 76, 143, 163, 165,
      168, 172, 191, 193, 218
parliamentary imbalance 145
parliamentary norms 67
parliamentary proceedings 77
participation
   political 3
party songs 223
party tickets 226
patron-client relationship 5, 21, 147, 220,
   228
pecuniary values 11
Peoples Commission 130
People's curfew 163
physical coercion 6, 21
physical force 138
Pinto-Duschinsky 9
Planning Commission 52
Plassey 44
Plato 10
police 14, 105, 134, 156
police administration 146
political alliances 64, 121, 129, 220
   7-party alliance 64, 65, 66, 129
   8-party alliance 65, 182
   15-party alliance 65, 129
   4-party alliance 168
   All Party Action Committee (APAC)
      144
   Combined Opposition Party (COP)
      101-103, 105, 135
   Gono Oikko Jote 53
   Gonotantrik Oikyo Jote 121, 122,
      123
   Islami *Oikya Jote* 92r, 175r, 183,
      189, 196, 201, 215r
   Jatiya Jote 64
   Jatiya Oikya Front 64
   Jatiyotabadi Front 121, 123
   Left Front 156
   United Front (UF) 95, 96, 97, 109
political analysts 188
political awareness 1, 3
political heavy weights 121
political climate 29
political corruption 150

Index 289

African 13
American 10, 11
Chinese 12
European 11
Japanese 11, 12
Malaysian 13
Philippino 12, 13
South Asian 13
Thai 12
political bickering 46
political crisis 29, 30
political culture 4, 7, 62, 77
   Bangladeshi 29
   confrontational 79
   democratic 3
political deadlock 166, 191
political development 4, 7, 122
political dialogue 64
political elites 8
political ethics 3
political impasse 29, 70, 166, 173
political instability 2, 5, 46, 225
political institutions 1
political leadership 95, 143
political malfeasance 99
political maturity 22
political opposition 144
political participation 1, 4
political parties
   Awami Muslim League 95
   Baluchistan United Front 109
   Bangladesh *Awami* League (AL) 23, 26, 53, 64, 65, 69, 71, 72, 106, 107, 111, 119, 121, 122, 128, 130, 131, 132, 134, 145-50, 154, 155, 158-63, 165, 166, 167, 168, 172, 182-85, 188-92, 194, 196-02, 204, 205, 206-07, 210r-212r, 214r, 220, 221
   Bangladesh *Awami* League – Malek Ukil (AL-MU) 124-26, 128, 129, 139r
   Bangladesh *Awami* League-Mizan Chaudhury (AL-MC) 124, 125, 126, 139r
   Bangladesh *Janata Dal* 183
   Bangladesh *Jatiya* League (BJL) 124
   Bangladesh *Khelafat Andolon* 183
   Bangladesh *Krishak Sramik Awami* League (BKSAL) 88r, 131, 148, 183, 189
   Bangladesh Muslim League (BML) 124-26, 131
   Bangladesh Muslim League (Quader) 183
   Bangladesh Nationalist Party (BNP) 23, 26, 71, 92r, 123-26, 129, 130, 131, 132, 134, 135, 137, 147-52, 154, 155, 157, 159-63, 164, 165, 167, 172, 173, 178, 182-85, 188-92, 194-02, 205, 206-07, 210, 211r, 220, 221
   Bangladesh *Sammyabadi Dal*-Toha (BSD-T) 124, 139r
   Bangladesh Workers Party 88r, 90, 131
   Communist Party of Bangladesh (CPB) 53, 88r, 124, 128, 129, 131, 145, 183, 189
   Conventionist Muslim League (CML) 49, 99
   Freedom Party 183, 185, 211r
   Gono Forum (GF) 124
   Gonotantri Party 189
   Islamic Democratic League (IDL) 124, 125
   Jamaat-e-Islami Bangladesh (JI) 23, 67, 69, 71, 89r, 130, 131, 134, 154, 155, 159, 160, 161, 165, 166, 170, 175r, 182, 183, 188, 189, 195, 197, 199, 200, 201, 204, 205-07, 210, 212r-215r
   Jamiat-e-Ulema Pakistan (JUP) 102
   Jamiat-i-Ahl-i-Hadees 109
   Janadal 63
   Japanese Liberal Democratic Party 21
   Jatiya Gonomukti Union (JAGMU) 124
   Jatiya League (JL) 88r, 139r, 145
   Jatiya Party (JP) 23, 64, 67, 69, 71, 73, 128, 130-32, 135, 154, 155, 160-62, 182, 183, 185, 188, 189, 196, 197, 199, 200, 204, 206, 209

Jatiya Samajtantrik Dal (JSD) 52.
  53, 76, 124-26, 139r, 144-47,
  162, 165, 166
Jatiya Samajtantrik Dal (JSD-Inu)
  183
Jatiya Samajtantrik Dal (JSD-Rab)
  72, 131, 183, 201
Jatiya Samajtantrik Dal (JSD-Siraj)
  131, 189
Jatiyotabadi Gonotantrik Dal
  (JAGODAL) 121, 124
Krishak Sramik Party 88r, 95, 139r
Muslim League (ML) 26, 44, 49,
  86r, 95-97, 119
National *Awami* Party (Achakzai)
  109
National *Awami* Party –Bhasani
  (NAP – B) 86r, 145
National *Awami* Party-Muzaffar
  (NAP-M) 53, 86r-88r, 124, 131,
  145, 189
National *Awami* Party-Naser (NAP-
  N) 124, 139r
National *Awami* Party-Nurur-Zahed
  (NAP-NZ) 124, 139r
National Democratic Front (NDF)
  101, 102, 139r
National Democratic Party (NDP)
  71, 165, 189
Nizam-e-Islam 95, 109
Pakistan Muslim League (PML) 96,
  101-103, 105
Pakistan People's Party (PPP) 106,
  107
People's League – Razee 124, 139r
pro-Chinese National *Awami* Party
  (NAP-C) 52
pro-Moscow National *Awami* Party
  (NAP-B) 52, 139r
Sammyobadi Dal 53, 88r
Sarbohara Party 53
Sindh Karachi Punjabi Pathan
  Muttahida Mahaz 109
United People's Party (UPP) 124,
  139r
Zaker Party 182, 183, 215r
Political Parties Regulation Order (PPR)
  123
political patronage 6, 143
political polarisation 50, 107, 228

political power 59, 229
political prisoners 124, 133
political socialisation 4, 77
political stability 4, 46, 60, 73, 228, 229
political standoff 69, 172, 193
political vacuum 118
politician 121
politics
  confrontational 73
  democratic 2, 227
  electoral 94, 118,143, 178
  hartal 76
  hereditary 225
  land 28
  palace 58, 122
  pork-barrel 155
  provincial 46
  village 28, 147, 219
  village-based 137, 218
polling agents 100, 127, 149
polling booths 20, 138
polling officers 161, 164, 206
  kidnapping of 165
polling stations 167, 195
pourasavas (municipalities) 146, 181
poverty 1
  chronic 2, 5, 221
power
  abuse of 8
  media 21
  ministerial 21
  money 21, 29
  muscle 21, 29
pre-election survey 188
presidential election(s) 28, 121, 122,
  123, 132, 218, 220
  1965 103, 104, 105
  1988 121, 123
  1981 59, 143, 147, 168, 170
  1986 132
presiding officer(s) 100, 130, 163, 167,
  205
  partisan role of 202
process
  civilianisation 137
  electoral 6, 25, 134, 137, 157, 164,
    207, 221, 226-28
  legitimisation 61
  nomination 21
  political 178

pro-election activists 164
professional groups 67, 129, 134, 151, 163
   Combind Action Committee of Professionals 151
   The Fedaration of Bangladesh Chambers of Commarce and Industries (FBCCI) 72
   Sramik Karmachari Oikkya Parisad (SKOP) 64, 88r
   Supreme Court Bar Association 151
programme(s)
   17-point 148
   18-point 128
   anti-election 166
   anti-government 191
   six-day action 163
   six-point 50, 106, 111
   social 125
   television 200, 201
   training 119, 195
   voter education 196, 196
propaganda 161
propaganda literature 104
provincial autonomy 95, 96
provincial election(s) 95, 102
provisional Bangladesh government 51
public awareness 18, 30
public rallies/meetings 99, 106, 219
Public Service Commission (PSC) 51
Punjab 95
puppet government 52

Quran 107, 197

Rab, A. S. M. A. 82r, 145, 149
racialism 125
racketeering 11
Rahim, A. 147
Rahman, M. H. 173, 179, 193
Rahman, S. F. 133
Rahman, S. M. (Mujib) 50, 52, 53, 55-58, 61, 82r-85r, 89r, 106, 115r, 126, 130, 132, 138r, 143, 144, 148, 150, 168, 171, 174r, 182, 183, 221, 225
   Mujibism 150
   Mujib government 146, 170
   Mujib regime 51, 143
   Mujib's nepotism 55
   Mujib's one-party government 148
   Mujib's second revolution
   Mujib's one party system 57
   Mujib's personal rule 55
Rahman, Z. (Zia) 56, 58, 61, 66, 87r, 90r, 118-21, 123, 126, 137, 144, 148, 150, 168, 170, 182, 184, 191, 221, 225, 226
   19-point programme of 57, 119, 120, 122, 147
   assassination of 60, 147
   canal digging programme of 57
   gram sarkar 57
   honesty of 126
   personal image of 126
   popularity of 126
   soldier-turned politician 125
   Zia regime 137
Railroad Legislation 11
Rajshahi 152, 157
Raphel, R. 69
rebellion 121
Red Shirts 46
Referendum 61, 97, 101, 109, 112, 119, 120, 128, 151-53, 165,
   1959 216
   1960 100, 121
   1977 119, 123
   1985 128
   1997 57
   1991 143, 151, 168, 170, 171, 217
   first national 119
   national 25, 119
Registration of under-aged people 19
reign of terror 161
regime(s)
   AL 52
   Authoritarian 178
   Civilian 2, 27, 151, 178, 227
   first military 119
   illegal 133
   military 57, 60, 118, 127, 131, 132, 135, 178, 179, 185, 203, 216
   second military 27
   totalitarian 4
regime transition 24
regionalism 46
Relief materials 54
religion 65, 137, 170, 184, 198
   use of 108, 136, 209, 226
Representation of Public Order 1962 195

Republic 10
Republic Officers' Coordination Council 191
returning officer(s) 131, 167
revolution 96
  second 125
revolutionary activities 53
revolutionary groups 53
revolutionary movement 56
rigging 19, 26, 97, 112, 127, 131, 137, 146, 147, 152, 166, 167, 168, 205, 209, 217-218, 224
  allegations of 26, 126, 161
  degree of 137, 147, 168
  election 29
  massive 131, 150, 205
  poll 149, 205
  post-election 224
  vote 135, 163, 202, 205, 218, 219, 226
rigging resistance bodies 149
rigging statement 131
right-wing parties 119
robberies 53
Round Table Conference 106
rule(s)
  authoritarian 55, 226
  chronic military 112
  civilian 30, 94, 112, 143, 168
  civilianised military 216
  electoral 118
  emergency 57
  first military 94, 144
  military 1, 3, 29, 30, 78, 111, 118, 120, 138, 216, 217, 222, 226, 227
  Mughal 44
  NCG 30
  one party 122
  quasi-military 29

Satpathi, N. 20
Sattar, A. 59, 121, 143, 147-51, 171
Sattar interregnum 59, 147
Sayem, A. S. M. 56, 119
Scott, J. C. 8, 11, 16, 22, 32r, 34r, 39r
seat sharing agreement 129
secret balloting 6
  killings 55
  political 53
secularism 57, 122, 183, 190

sentiment(s)
  anti-Indian 138, 184
  anti-JP 191
  anti-military 49
  Islamic 58
  religious 224
Sepoy Mutiny 56
Sessan, T. N. 21
seven-point charter of demands 131
Shalikha 163
shanty bahini (peace force) 74
shito fumekin (unexplained expending) 11
shuttle diplomacy 66
Siddiqui, A. B. 204
Siddiqui, K. 167
Sikder, S. 53, 55
Sindh 95
Singapore 20
six point demand 192
six-point formula 47
sixth parliament 27
slogan(s) 23
  Bangladesh *Jindabad* (long live Bangladesh) 183, 184
  Islam is our faith; Democracy is our polity; Socialism is our economy; All power to the people 107
  Joy Bangla (victory of Bengal) 116r, 184
  La Ilaha Illallah Dhaner Shishay Bismillah (Allah is only the master, vote for sheaf of paddy [the electoral symbol of the BNP]) 211r
  Vote Diley Pallai Khushi Hobay Allai (voting for scale [the electoral symbol of the JI] will make Allah glad) 198, 199
smuggling 46, 53, 54, 55, 78
smuggling operations 54
snatching of identity cards 19
social cleavage 1
social fragmentation 2
social justice 125
social tension 126
Socialist Party 21
South Asia 43, 118, 220
South Asian Association for Regional Cooperation (SARRAC) 184

South Asian states 3
South Korea 3,
Southeast Asia 3,
sovereign parliament 125, 151
speaker 71, 72, 157
Special Powers Act (SPA) 55, 73, 144, 244
state language 45, 96
state of emergency 55, 66, 144
state-controlled television 73
state principles 122
state religion 65
Stephen, Sir. N. 69
student killings 64
student organisations
    All Parties Student Unity (APSU) 66
    Chattra League 148
    Dhaka University Central Student's Union (DUCSU) 190
    Jatiyatabadi Chattra Dal 129, 190, 206
student-police clashes 64
student politics 57,
    violent 77
sub-divisional officer (SDO) 49, 102
Suhrawardy, H. S. 95
Sukarno 12
Superintendent of Police (SP) 63, 193, 194
Supreme Court 51, 66, 68, 70, 106, 153, 179, 199
Syed Group 46
system(s)
    BD 26, 97, 98, 103
    British parliamentary 94
    British political 111
    civilian authoritarian 182
    democratic 145
    electoral 18, 25, 227
    multi-party 57, 78
    multi-party parliamentary 148
    one-party 130
    one-party presidential 94, 144
    parliamentary 48, 95, 104, 151, 152, 182
    presidential 94, 122, 144, 151, 184
    secret ballot 5, 15
    upazila, 197
    western electoral 5

Taher, A. 56
Tangail 167
territorial identity 57
terrorism 67, 155, 156, 160, 164, 196
Thailand 3,
Thai bureaucracy 12
Thakur, T. 56
The Arms Law 181
The Constitution (8th Amendment) Act (1988) 65
The Election Officials (Special Act) Ordinance 1990 179
The Union Parisad and Paurasava (Special Responsibilities) Ordinance, 1991 181
threatening voters 17
thugs 228
Tim, R. W. 176r, 177r, 180, 186, 210r, 211r, 214
Toha, M. 53, 147
tolerance 4
touts 228
Transparency International 13
trouble makers 156
Tuglak Sultanate 44
turnout 203
two-nation theory 45
tyranny of the majority 55

unholy alliance 69, 130
union council 97
union *parisad* 119, 146, 155, 181, 188, 207
Union Parisad and Pourashava (Special Responsibility) Ordinance 1991 188
union *parisad* leaders 120
Unionists 46
United Nations 24, 52
United States 18, 24
    US ambassador 72, 167
    US Assistant Secretary of State for
    US Embassy 163
    US government 54
    US State Department 73, 165
universal adult suffrage 5
upazila 62
upazila administration 62
Urdu 45

vassal state 198
vice president 121
village *matbar* (headmen) 220
village leaders 119
violence 5, 17, 29, 73, 108, 112, 127,
    130, 134, 138, 147, 156, 160, 161,
    164, 165, 167, 170, 171, 172, 181,
    185, 188, 202, 205, 209, 216-19,
    222, 226, 227
   allegation of
   anti-election 164
   electoral 29, 131, 134, 188
   political 1, 55, 73
   post-poll 159
   pre-election 148
Voice of America 159, 190
vote bandits 165
vote centre(s) 163
   capturing 224
vote counting 224
   manipulation in 224
vote dacoity 161
vote piracy 131
vote-buying 12, 17, 18, 222
vote-selling 20
voter education 15
voter registration 15
voter identity card system 15
voters 146, 182,
   absentee 157
   bribing poor 224
   female 198, 207, 221
   Hindu 149
   intimidating 224
   intimidating minority 222
   politically educated 6
   recounting of 131
   religious-minded 206, 224
   rural 147
   selling of 15
   swinging 207
voters' list 100, 154
vote(s) 120, 130

affirmative 100
false 146, 157
Invalid 153
ladies' 100
no 153
selling and purchasing of 20
valid 153
venal 20
yes 120, 128, 153
voting 5, 98, 162, 188
   bogus 100, 112, 127, 218, 224
   bribed 19
   coerced 19
   dummy 15
   false 17, 100, 205
   ghost 19, 100
   indirect 216
   multiple 15, 19
   open 18
   postponment of 207
   proxy 17
   secret 18
   surrogate 19

Wadiril, L. 69
watergate 9, 10
West Bengal 21
West Pakistan 95, 101, 104, 107
western democracies 5

yang-lien 12
Younus, M. 204, 214r

Zia, K (Khaleda) 65, 66, 68, 71, 89r, 92r,
    128, 130, 143, 150, 172, 174r, 178,
    184, 193, 200, 201, 202, 225, 229
   Khaleda government 162, 209
   Khaleda regime 67, 76, 160
   non-compromising attitude of 130
zila parisad 63, 74, 197
Zila Parisad Bill 75
Zimbabwe 13